directory of

management consultants

Compiled and published by *Consultants News,* the confidential newsletter of the consulting profession, Templeton Road, Fitzwilliam N.H. 03447.

Table of Contents

Preface

This is the most comprehensive compilation of information about management consulting firms ever published in the United States.

While other listings (notably *Consultants and Consulting Organizations*) include some management consulting firms along with a wide range of other business services (engineering, advertising, public relations, etc.), this work is the first significant effort devoted exclusively to management consultants since American Management Association published a directory of its consultant members (from 1956 to 1970).

Years in preparation, this directory is a natural outgrowth of the extensive data on management consulting amassed by *Consulants News*, monthly newsletter reporting on the profession. This second edition lists some 575 firms, 30% more than the first edition, now obsolete.

Questionnaires completed by listed firms provided much — but not all — of the information in raw form. Every effort has been made to assure accuracy, but it cannot be guaranteed. User cooperation is earnestly solicited to correct any errors that may have crept in: please send them to the publisher.

Not *all* consulting firms are included. Some are omitted by design because of poor reputation. Information on others was incomplete at press time. Still others — some of whom call themselves management consultants and some who do not — do not fall within our definition of management consulting because of the way they sell, charge for their services, or otherwise operate. Names of management consulting firms that should be considered for listing in future editions, should be sent to the editor.

Because this work is designed primarily for users of management consulting services (not as a service to the profession itself), *there were no charges for listing, and no advertising has been accepted.*

The sense of accomplishment accompanying publication of this work is tempered by the knowledge of its deficiencies (other firms that should be included, absence of a quality rating, etc.). This leads us to ask the indulgence of users and is backed by our determination to make each succeeding editon even better.

James H. Kennedy,
Editor

Fall, 1979

What You'll Find in This Directory

First there's a bit of text: PLEASE READ IT. Just as reading the instruction manual for a new car or a new appliance can save lots of headaches later, so too some time spent on understanding how this directory is put together can save you considerable time and improve the publication's usefulness to you.

The main section lists some 575 management consulting firms alphabetically. While this is a directory of *firms*, solo practitioners are also included (they are, in effect, the smallest of firms). Individual consultants employed by another entity, however, are not listed (but the firm they work for should be).

After the alphabetical listings come the various cross-indexes:
Services Offered (first the generalists, then the specialists)
Industries Served (first the generalists, then the specialists)
Geographic (alphabetically, by state and city)

How to Use This Directory

Think first about what *type* of management consulting firm might best serve your needs:

Generalist . . . . or Specialist?

"Generalist", by our definition, is a firm that claims expertise in most of the functional areas or most of the industries listed. Firms in these two categories are listed under "Firms Offering Most Services", and "Firms Serving Most Industries".

"Specialist" is a firm offering a relatively limited range of services. Names of firms offering specific services follow after the generalists in the same sequence as the Principal Areas of Competence. Similarly, names of firms specializing in specific industries follow after the generalists under Industries Served.

NOTE 1: There may be some overlap. A truly giant firm can be expected to be expert (specialist) in literally dozens of functional areas and industries . . . yet you'll find them (because of the ultimate compromises necessary in any cross-referenced directory) under Generalists. On the other hand, a small firm may have stretched its credibility by claiming even a half dozen specialties . . . yet you'll find them under Specialists.

Ideally, whoever is responsible for buying consulting services in your organization should spend a few hours studying this directory.

—Check off firms that sound compatible for one reason or another, and send for their brochures. (Be sure to specify "For Future Reference" to avoid unwanted solicitation in the form of telephone or personal follow-up.)

—Mark the directory sections that you think you'll be referring to most. . . so you can find them easily next time.

—Send for the appropriate books and pamphlets on consulting, so you'll be able to make a more intelligent decision regarding which firms to invite to serve you.

Importance of Professional Affiliation

If this directory has any bias, it is toward firms that have indicated some commitment to professionalism in the management consulting field — through membership in one or more of the organizations listed and explained below.

ACME — Association of Consulting Management Engineers (230 Park Ave., New York, NY 10017). "Grandfather" of all the U.S. management consulting organizations, ACME was founded in 1929 and has about 50 member firms. Originally limited to larger organizations, it has since broadened its scope . . . but admission is still only after stringent review and reference checking. This is particularly applicable and current pertaining to newer members, and it will have greater timeliness for all members when an ongoing reaccreditation process catches up with some of the older member firms. On balance, membership in ACME is the most meaningful in the business.

AMC — Association of Management Consultants (331 Madison Ave., New York, NY 10017). Founded in 1959 and focussed on the smaller firm, AMC has some 100 members, of which half are solo practitioners, a third with up to five professionals, and the remainder with more.

IMC — Institute of Management Consultants (19 W. 44th St., New York, NY 10036). An accrediting organization for individual consultants (not firms, as are ACME and AMC), IMC was founded in 1970 and has over 800 members. About a third are with ACME firms, a third with public accounting firms, and a third either solo practitioners or with smaller firms. Members earn the appellation CMC: Certified Management Consultant.

SPMC — Society of Professional Management Consultants (205 W. 89th St., New York, NY 10024). Founded in 1959 as an individual accrediting body, SPMC has about 125 members.

Membership in any of the above professional groups is indicated first under "Professional Affiliations" in the basic listing of each management consulting firm. Listees were invited to name additional affiliations that they considered to be significant, and these are given after the slash mark (/). . . i.e.

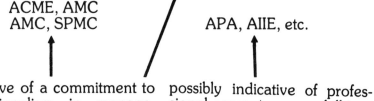

ACME, AMC
AMC, SPMC

APA, AIIE, etc.

indicative of a commitment to professionalism in management consulting

possibly indicative of professional competence or skill in a specific field

Note that some listees have included "professional" affiliations that are relatively meaningless. (Some, for example, proudly mentioned membership in American Management Association, but such references have been mercifully deleted: to our knowledge AMA's admission requirements do not equate with professional recognition in any accrediting sense.)

Because we don't know enough about other professional bodies, however, we've allowed most of the claimed memberships to stand. Users of this directory familiar with specific industries or areas of technical/functional expertise can get added insight into each consulting firm by judging the "Other Professional Affiliations" it has claimed.

Remember that many "experts" don't make good consultants. Thus a firm of PhD's who have been accredited by APA (American Psychological Association) might make good researchers, teachers, executives. . . and might also make good consultants. But only by showing affiliation with a management consulting association does a firm (or the individuals in it) indicate a commitment to certain consulting ethics and skills.

Management Consulting Groups Not Listed

Every year or so, it seems, a new management consulting group is formed for one reason or another (usually ranging from disaffection with one of the established groups to crass commercialism). Sometimes the names are clever enough to sound authentic. . . and thereby mislead unsuspecting outsiders.

As reported in *Consultants News* since 1970, the following combinations of words appearing to represent legitimate accreditation of management consultants have so far failed to achieve significant membership or recognition within the profession:

Institute of American Business Consultants
International Association of Management Consultants
International Association of Consultants to Business
American Academy of Consultants
Consultants Committee of One Hundred
American Society of Business & Management Consultants
American Institute of Professional Consultants
Independent Consultants of America

Key to "Other" Professional Affiliations

AAA	American Academy of Actuaries
AAA	American Arbitration Association
AAAE	American Association of Airport Executives
AAAS	American Association for the Advancement of Science
AACE	American Association of Cost Engineers
AAHC	American Association of Hospital Consultants
AAHP	American Association for Hospital Planning
AAPOR	American Association for Public Opinion Research
ABA	American Bar Association
ABCA	American Business Communications Association
ACA	American Compensation Association
ACCCE	Association of Consulting Chemists & Chemical Engineers
ACF	Association of Consulting Foresters
ACG	Association for Corporate Growth
ACHA	American College of Hospital Administrators
ACM	Association for Computing Machinery
ACS	American Chemical Society
ACTSU	Association of Time-Sharing Users
AEA	American Economic Association
AERC	Association of Executive Recruiting Consultants
AES	Audio Engineering Society
AGA	American Gas Association
AGAC	Association of Graphic Arts Consultants
AGC	Associated General Contractors of America
AHA	American Hospital Association
AHS	American Helicopter Society
AICPA	American Institute of Certified Public Accountants
AIIE	American Institute of Industrial Engineers
AIMC	American Institute of Medical Climatology
AIME	American Institute of Mining, Metallurgical & Petroleum Engineers
AIP	American Institute of Planners
AIPE	American Institute of Plant Engineers
AIPLU	American Institute of Property & Liability Underwriters
ALDA	American Land Development Association
AMA	American Marketing Association
AMS	Administrative Management Society
ANA	American Nurses Association
APA	American Psychological Association
APGA	American Personnel & Guidance Association
APHA	American Public Health Association
APMHC	Association of Professional Material Handling Consultants
AREA	Association of Records Executives & Administrators
ARIA	American Risk & Insurance Association
ARMA	American Records Management Association
ASA	American Scientific Association
ASA	American Statistical Association
ASAC	Association of Ski Area Consultants
ASAE	American Society of Association Executives
ASCE	American Society of Civil Engineers
ASIS	American Society of Industrial Security
ASM	Association for Systems Management
ASME	American Society of Mechanical Engineers
ASPA	American Society of Personnel Administration
ASQC	American Society for Quality Control
ASSE	American Society of Safety Engineers
ASTD	American Society for Training & Development
AWS	American Welding Society
CAMC	Canadian Association of Management Consultants
CAPP	Conference on Actuaries in Public Practice

C&CS	Classification & Compensation Society
CHA	Catholic Hospital Association
CIA	Canadian Institute of Actuaries
CMMA	Club Management Association of America
CMRA	Chemical Market Research Association
CPCU	Chartered Property & Casualty Underwriter
CSI	Construction Surveys Institute
CSA	Cryogenic Society of America
DPMA	Data Processing Management Association
ECMRA	European Chemical Market Research Association
EDA	Executive Development Association
EMPC	Educational Media Producers Council
ERGIP	European Research Group for Industrial Psychology
ES	Econometrics Society
FEI	Financial Executives Institute
FSEA	Food Service Executives Association
GHHA	Group Health Association of America
HFMA	Hospital Financial Management Association
HFS	Human Factors Society
IABC	International Association of Business Communicators
IAMC	Institute of Association Management Companies
ICF	International Consultants Foundation
ICS	Insurance Consultants Society
IFSEA	International Food Service Executives Association
IMMS	International Material Management Society
IPMS	International Personnel Management Society
IRMC	Institute of Risk Management Consultants
IRRA	Industrial Relations Research Association
IWPA	International Word Processing Association
LES	Licensing Executive Society
MANA	Manufacturers Agents National Association
MCEI	Marketing Communications Executives International
MFOA	Municipal Finance Officers Association
MSI	Marketing Science Institute
MHA	Massachusetts Hospital Association
MTM	Methods-Time Measurement Association
NAA	National Association of Accountants
NABE	National Association of Business Economists
NACM	National Association of Credit Management
NACUBO	National Association of College & University Business Officers
NAMAC	National Association of Merger & Acquisitions Consultants
NASCP	North American Society for Corporate Planning
NATA	National Air Transportation Association
NBAA	National Business Aircraft Association
NCARB	National Council of Architectural Registration Boards
NCPDM	National Council of Physical Distribution Management
NEA	National Education Association
NEHA	New England Hospital Assembly
NLN	National League for Nursing
NPCM	National Psychological Consultants to Management
NRMA	National Retail Merchants Association
NSPE	National Society of Professional Engineers
NVGA	National Vocational Guidance Association
NYSSA	New York Society of Security Analysts

ORSA   Opérations Research Society of America

PATCA   Professional & Technical Consultants Association
PE   Professional Engineer
PEI   Planning Executives Institute
PEPP   Professional Engineers in Private Practice
PMI   Project Management Institute
PRSA   Public Relations Society of America

SA   Society of Actuaries
SAEI   Society of Automotive Engineers Inc.
SAF   Society of American Foresters
SAVE   Society of American Value Engineers
SNAME   Society of Naval Architects and Marine Engineers
SNAP   Society of National Association Publications
SOCAP   Society of Consumer Affairs Professionals
SPI   Society of the Plastics Industry
SPIE   Society of Photographic Instrumentation Engineers
STC   Society for Technical Communication
SLRCM   Society of Labor Relations Consultants to Management
SLRP   The Society for Long Range Planning
SME   Society of Manufacturing Engineers
SMIS   Society for Management Information Systems
SOLE   Society of Logistics Engineers
SPBC   Society of Professional Business Consultants
SPE   Society of Plastics Engineers
SPHE   Society of Packaging & Handling Engineers
SPMHE   Society of Professional Material Handling Consultants
STC   Society for Technical Communication

TAPPI   Technical Association of Pulp & Paper Industry
TIMS   The Institute of Management Sciences
TRB   Transportation Research Board

ULI   Urban Land Institute

USGA   United States Golf Association
USTA   United States Tennis Association

WAD   World Association of Detectives

Other Sources of Information

Each consulting association has its own literature, which may be helpful, but the one best publication is a 56-page booklet from ACME. . . and it's free:

How To Get the Best Results from Management Consultants (Association of Consulting Management Engineers, 230 Park Ave., New York City 10017)

The management consulting business is beginning to spawn good books, and several are of interest to users of these services:

Management and Consulting:
An Introduction to James O. McKinsey
First & only book about this consulting pioneer. Includes 30-page management audit said to be firm's "bible" even today. Fascinating. (NY State School of Industrial & Labor Relations) . . .by William B. Wolf/112 p/paperback/$7.95.

The Marketing of Professional Accounting Services
Primarily for CPAs but of interest to inquisitive management consultants as well. Details a McKinsey-like approach & stresses building confidence at all levels including social & community. (John Wiley)
. . .by James J. Mahon/189 p/hardbound/$15.95

Managing Your Accouting & Consulting Practice
2-inch handbook covering administrative, nuts & bolts aspects from timekeeping & bookkeeping to partnership agreements & compensation . . . also fee-setting, art of billing, filing systems, liability insurance, etc. (Matthew Bender)
. . . by Mary Ann Altman & Robert I Weil/640 pp/post-bound/$50

How to Become a Successful Consultant in Your Own Field
Highly personalized account of how one solo made it, full of practical advice for beginners. First of this genre we can recommend. Very easy reading. (Bermont Books)
. . . by Herbert Bermont/157 pp/ringbound/$20

The Professional Services Enterprise: Theory & Practice
A mind-stretcher for consultants who have time to think. Good sections categorizing professional employees & describing client buying psychology. (Los Angeles Pub. Co: out of print)
. . . by Don Lebell/211 pp/hardbound/$10.50 (while supply lasts)

The Consulting Process in Action
Forces consultants to analyze their work, yet is rarely theoretical. Good for self-development & broader training sessions. (University Associates)
. . . by Gordon & Ronald Lippitt/130 pp/paperbook/$9.50

The Marketing of Professional Services
Classic reference that's unduplicated. Full of conceptual guides
& practical ideas. Gets into all aspects. (McGraw-Hill)
. . . by Aubrey Wilson/193 pp/hardbound/$22.50

Making the Most of Management Consulting Services
Aimed at users and full of basic stuff, including necessary client
homework & cooperation. Appendix describes 106 consulting
services in detail (American Management Association)
. . . by Jerome H. Fuchs/214 pp/hardbound/$12.95

*Other People's Business — A Primer on Management Con-
sultants*
Written by a businessman for other businessmen and the best
justification for consulting we've seen. The only popular book on
the subject that isn't an expose. Beautiful. (Mason/Charter
. . . by Howard M. Klein/200 pp/hardbound/$8.95

Management Consulting — A Guide to the Profession
First & only basic text on this business. Essential for every
consulting & business library. Helpful information for practitioners as well as users. (International Labor Office)
. . . by M. Kubr/368 pp/hardbound/$22.50

Management Consultants and Clients
Bibliography with summaries of "everything" written about
consulting in 60s & early 70s. Over 1200 entries. Published '72
& treasure trove of info even today (Michigan State University
Press)
. . . by Stanley C. Hollander/541 pp/hardbound/$12

The Marketing of Management Consulting Services
Flip chart/book/sales meeting in itself. Tells how big firms get
bigger.
. . . by Brian A. Smith/8½ x 11 spiral-bound/includes
cassette/$45

HOW TO ORDER: all of the above books are available through
your local bookseller, or for same day shipment, from Consultants Bookstore, Templeton Road, Fitzwilliam, NH 03447.

+ + + + + + + + + + + + +

Consultants News, monthly newsletter covering the
management consulting and executive recruiting world, is read
by practitioners and users alike as a source of continuing information, trends as well as news. (Sample copy: $2 / Con-
sultants News / Templeton Road / Fitzwilliam, N.H. 03447)

Management

Consulting

Firms

A-Z

Abbott, Langer & Associates

Box 275
Park Forest, Illinois 60466
(312)748-2200

Rather than attempt to be all things to all men, we place limits on the types of assignments which we will accept. In line with the particular specialties of our staff, we provide comprehensive consulting services in all phases of human resources management (but specifically excluding the area of labor relations).

Contact: Steven Langer, mng. con.
Areas Served: U.S.
Founded: 1967 *Staff:* 1-3 *Revenues:* $100-$500,000
Services: 3.1 3.2 3.4 3.6 3.7 3.8 3.10 3.11 4.9 4.15
Industries: Most

Advanced Management Institute, Inc.

109 Yessler Way
Hillsdale, New Jersey 07642
(201)666-8064

Computer-oriented general management consulting with emphasis on management information systems and use of quantitative techniques to assist management decision making.

Contact: William A. Bocchino, pres.
Areas Served: Worldwide
Founded: 1967 *Staff:* 3-10 *Revenues:* $500,000-1 million
Services: 1.3 1.9 1.13 2.5 3.11 4.8 5.3 9.8 11.0
Industries: Most

Aiken, Madden & Associates

2566 Mission St.
San Marino, California 91108
(213)682-3871

Advise management in matters of personnel, industrial and labor relations; direct anti-union campaigns; represent clients before NLRB; handle elections; negotiate labor agreements; administer labor agreements; represent clients before all government agencies involving employee relations.

Contact: J. Allen Madden, ptnr.
Areas Served: CA
Founded: 1962 *Staff:* 1-3 *Revenues:* $100-$500,000
Professional Affiliations: /SLRC
Services: 3.3 3.6
Industries: Most

Louis A. Allen Associates, Inc.
3600 W. Bayshore Rd.
Palo Alto, California 94303
(415)493-1222

We continue to offer our clients the best of current management practices. Based upon proven concepts, principles and techniques which are basic to management as a recognized profession, our philosophy is to emphasize that which is logical, durable and realistic.

Contact: G. L. Green, mktg. dir.
Affiliates/branches: New York; Chicago; Houston; Sydney; S. Africa; Manila
Founded: 1958 *Staff:* 10-25 *Revenues:* $500,000-1 million
Services: 1.0 1.1 1.3 3.1 3.8 3.10
Industries: Most

Rufus Allen & Associates
1001 Navaho Dr.
Raleigh, North Carolina 27609
(919)762-4478

Specializing in client relationships conducive to intermittent or short-term use of consultants, with maximum feasible involvement of client personnel.

Contact: Rufus Allen, owner
Areas Served: Southeast U.S.
Founded: 1961 *Staff:* 1-3 *Revenues:* under $100,000
Professional Affiliations: IMC
Services: 1.0 2.0 3.0 5.0 6.4
Industries: Most

Altenburg & Co., Inc.
587 Spring St.
Westbrook, Maine 04092
(207)856-6348

Specialists in all phases of manufacturing except labor relations and personnel. Most assignments are in Northeast U.S. Special skills in oil-spill control take us to West Coast, Gulf of Mexico, and Canada. Technical and economic studies for federal, state and municipal governments.

Contact: William M. Altenburg, pres.
Areas Served: U.S. & Canada
Founded: 1962 *Staff:* 3-10 *Revenues:* under $100,000
Professional Affiliations: IMC
Services: 1.0 2.0 4.0 5.0 7.0
Industries: D.00 D.29 E.45 E.46

Altman & Weil, Inc.
326 W. Lancaster Ave.
Ardmore, Pennsylvania 19003
(215)649-4646

Full range of management consulting services, with emphasis on the legal & accounting professions. Word processing, data processing & office systems for private law firms, corporate law and patent departments, government legal agencies, and bar organizations. Also expert witness services with respect to law practice.

Contact: Robert I. Weil, CMC
Affiliates/branches: 111 Sutter St., San Francisco, California 94104; 140 W. Myrtle St.,

Duluth, Minnesota 55811
Areas Served: U.S. & Canada
Founded: 1970 *Staff:* 3-10 *Revenues:* $500,000-1 million
Professional Affiliations: AMC, SPMC, IMC
Services: 1.0   3.0   5.3   5.4   5.8   5.9   9.0
Industries: I.73   I.81   J.91   J.92

American Executive Management, Inc.
30 Church St.
Salem, Massachusetts 01970
(617)744-5926
Top management and specialized assistance in planning, organization, human
resources, marketing, operational and profitability issues; emphasis on
improving operations and useable results of value to management.
Contact: Sherman K. Okun, CMC
Areas Served: North America
Founded: 1977 *Staff:* 3-10 *Revenues:* $100-$500,000
Professional Affiliations: IMC
Services: 1.0   2.1   2.9   3.1   4.1   4.2   7.3   9.5   10.4   11.1
Industries: C.15   C.16   C.17   D.28   D.29   D.30   D.34   D.35   D.36   D.38

American Management Systems
(Management Consulting Division)
1515 Wilson Blvd.
Arlington, Virginia 22209
(703)841-6000
Management & administration of computer and systems activities, largely for
federal government clients: also distribution management and data processing
for business clients.
Contact: Charles X. Rossotti
Affiliates/branches: New York; Chicago; San Francisco
Areas Served: U.S.
Founded: 1970 *Staff:* 50-100 *Revenues:* $5-$10 million
Services: 1.8   1.9   9.3
Industries: J.00

Anacapa Sciences, Inc.
PO Drawer Q
Santa Barbara, California 93102
(805)966-6157
Serving government agencies and industrial companies by improving human
performance. We conduct research and development projects, consult, provide
technical assistance, and develop and conduct training programs. Services
emphasize the behavioral sciences, but are strongly influenced by system and
operational considerations.
Contact: Dr. Douglas H. Harris, pres.
Areas Served: worldwide
Founded: 1969 *Staff:* 10-25 *Revenues:* $500,000-1 million
Professional Affiliations: /APA
Services: 1.1   1.8   2.7   3.1   3.4   3.5   3.10   3.11   3.21   9.5
Industries: D.36   D.37   E.41   E.48   I.82   I.83   J.91   J.92   J.94   J.97

Arthur Andersen & Co.
(Administrative Services Division)
69 W. Washington St.
Chicago, Illinois 60602
(312)346-6262

> Systems and consulting services involving 1) planning, design and installation of information systems for management planning and control; and 2) analytical studies to support management decision-making.

Contact: Victor E. Millar, ptnr.

Affiliates/branches: 25 Park Place, NE, Atlanta, Georgia 30303; 221 W. 6th St., Austin, Texas 78701; 201 N. Charles St., Baltimore, Maryland 21201; 417 N. 20th St., Birmingham, Alabama 35203; 999 Main St., Boise, Idaho 83702; 100 Federal St., Boston, Massachusetts 02110; 300 S. College St., Charlotte, North Carolina 28282; 734 Market St., Chattanooga, Tennessee 37402; 69 W. Washington St., Chicago, Illinois 60602; 105 E. Fourth St., Cincinnati, Ohio 45202; 1717 E. Ninth St., Cleveland, Ohio 44114; 1301 Gervais St., Columbia, South Carolina 29201; 100 E. Broad St., Columbus, Ohio 43215; 1201 Elm St., Dallas, Texas 75270; Court House Plaza SW, Dayton, Ohio 45402; 400 Renaissance Ctr., Detroit, Michigan 48243; 2929 E. Commercial Blvd., Ft. Lauderdale, Florida 33308; 1300 1st Nat'l. Bldg., Fort Worth, Texas 76102; 300 Ottawa Ave. NW, Grand Rapids, Michigan 49503; 201 N. Elm St., Greensboro, North Carolina 27401; 1 Financial Plaza, Hartford, Connecticut 06103; 711 Louisiana, Houston, Texas 77002; 1 Indiana Sq., Indianapolis, Indiana 46204; 200 E. Capitol St., Jackson, Mississippi 39201; 911 Main St., Kansas City, Missouri 64105; 1 Huntington Quad., Huntington, L.I., New York 11746; 1320 W. 3rd St., Los Angeles, California 90017; 165 Madison Ave., Memphis, Tennessee 38103; 1 Biscayne Tower, Miami, Florida 33131; 777 E. Wisconsin Ave., Milwaukee, Wisconsin 53201; 801 Nicollet Mall, Minneapolis, Minnesota 55402; 300 Union St., Nashville, Tennessee 37238; 1010 Common St., New Orleans, Louisiana 70112; 1345 Ave. of the Americas, New York, New York 10019; 33 Washington St., Newark, New Jersey 07102; 1 Kaiser Plaza, Oakland, California 94612; 100 Broadway, Oklahoma City, Oklahoma 73102; 1700 Farnham St., Omaha, Nebraska 68102; 255 S. Orange Ave., Orlando, Florida 32801; 10 Forest Ave., Paramus, New Jersey 07652; 5 Penn Ctr. Plaza, Philadelphia, Pennsylvania 19103; 101 N. 1st Ave., Phoenix, Arizona 85003; 2200 Grant Bldg., Pittsburgh, Pennsylvania 15219; 500 Morgan Bldg., Portland, Oregon 97205; 2 Main St. E., Rochester, New York 14614; 1 Memorial Dr., St. Louis, Missouri 63102; 386 N. Wabasha, St. Paul, Minnesota 55102; 36 S. State, Salt Lake City, Utah 84111; 110 W. A St., San Diego, California 92101; 1 Market Plaza, San Francisco, California 94105; 100 Park Ctr. Plaza, San Jose, California 95113; 1666 N. Main St., Santa Ana, California 92701; 501 Norton Bldg., Seattle, Washington 98104; 1 Landmark Sq., Stamford, Connecticut 06901; 111 Madison St., Tampa, Florida 33602; 300 Madison Ave., Toledo, Ohio 43604; 1 Williams Ctr., Tulsa, Oklahoma 74103; 1666 K St., NW, Washington, D.C. 20006; Pan Am Bldg., Hato Rey, Puerto Rico 00936; 700 335-8th Ave., SW Calgary, Alberta, T2P 1C9 Canada; 800 Dorchester Blvd. W. Montreal, Quebec H3B 1X9 Canada; 99 Bank St. Ottawa, Ontario K1P 6B9 Canada; Toronto Dom. Ctr. Toronto, Ontario M5K 1B9 Canada; 1055 W. Hastings St Vancouver, B.C. V6E 2J2 Canada; 1400-444 St. Mary Ave. Winnipeg, Manitoba R3C 3T1 Canada; Paseo de la Reforma Mexico City 6 Mexico; Argentina; Australia; Bahrain; Belgium; Bermuda; Brazil; Columbia; Denmark; Ecaudor; France; West Germany; Greece; Hong Kong; Iran; Ireland; Italy; Ivory Coast; Japan; Netherlands; Nicaragua; Nigeria; Norway; Panama; Peru; Portugal; Sengal; Singapore; South Africa; Spain; Sweden; Switzerland; Turkey; UK; USSR; Venezuela

Areas Served: worldwide

Founded: 1913 *Staff:* over 100 *Revenues:* over $10 million
Services: 1.0   2.0   3.7   3.8   4.0   5.0   6.0   7.0   9.0
Industries: Most

Anderson/Roethle & Associates, Inc.
811 E. Wisconsin Ave.
Milwaukee, Wisconsin 53202
(414)276-0070

Results-oriented firm specializing in long-range strategic planning for corporations, educational institutions, and government. Divisions directed toward each of these markets. Also operations audits, market research and market strategy projects, primarily for manufacturing firms from $2 million to $40 million in sales.

Contact: John D. Roethle, pres.
Areas Served: U.S. & Canada
Founded: 1963 *Staff:* 10-25 *Revenues:* $500,000-1 million
Professional Affiliations: AMC, IMC
Services: 1.1   1.3   1.6   4.1   4.2   4.3   4.5   4.11
Industries: C.15   D.00   F.50   F.51   G.52   G.56   H.60   H.65   I.82

Anson, Lee, Rector & Associates
23 S. Walton Ave.
Tarpon Springs, Florida 33589
(813)937-6294

Though relatively new, we have combined experience well over half a century. Services include financial planning and evaluation, public accounting, management and operational audits, organizational planning, business forecasting, marketing evaluation and research. Seminar training, and computer system design evaluation.

Contact: Robert L. Rector, princ.
Areas Served: U.S.
Founded: 1975 *Staff:* 3-10 *Revenues:* $100-$500,000
Professional Affiliations: /IMS
Services: 1.0   2.0   4.1   4.2   5.0   6.3   6.4   9.5
Industries: Most

Applied Leadership Technologies, Inc.
554 Bloomfield Ave.
Bloomfield, New Jersey 07003
(201)429-9499

We are committed to the principle that caring, responsible leadership is an essential element in the workplace. We supply knowledge and support to help clients implement such leadership and thus gain their institutional objectives —while recognizing that every organization has unique attributes, needs and goals. We bring to each client engagement integrity, objectivity, and professionalism.

Contact: Al Webster, pres.
Affiliates/branches: 1026 Connecticut Ave., NW, Washington, D.C. 10036
Areas Served: U.S.
Founded: 1976 *Staff:* 3-10 *Revenues:* $100-$500,000
Professional Affiliations: IMC, SPMC
Services: 1.1   1.14   1.15   2.3   3.0   4.1   4.9   4.15   9.1   9.5
Industries: Most

Aquatec International, Inc.
311 Chaffinch Island Rd.
Guilford, Connecticut 06437
(203)453-4803

A multi-disciplined, world-wide aquaculture and fisheries development consulting company, providing experts in aquaculture feasibility studies, economics, marketing, engineering, biology and management, as well as fisheries development personnel with expertise in fisheries resources evaluation, vessel design, gear selection and design, fishing techniques and fishery processing, by-products utilization, wholesaling and retailing.

Contact: Barry B. White, chmn.

Areas Served: worldwide

Founded: 1973 *Staff:* 3-10 *Revenues:* under $100,000

Services: 1.5   3.5   4.2   7.1   7.3   10.4   11.0

Industries: A.02   A.09

Arneson & Co.

12715 High Dr.

Leawood, Kansas 66209

(913)341-7722

Advisory services to presidents, boards and owners of small to medium-sized companies, particularly those closely-held, in areas of business continuity, turnaround and distress situations, special financing, and merger/acquisitions. Provide professional, working or advisory directorships. Expert witness on due-diligence, business valuation for tax and estate purposes—particularly closely-held and minority situations.

Contact: George S. Arneson

Founded: 1973 *Staff:* 1-3 *Revenues:* under $100,000

Professional Affiliations: IMC/NAMAC

Services: 1.1   1.3   1.4   1.5   1.6   1.10   1.11   5.3   5.10

Industries: Most

William B. Arnold Associates, Inc.

1776 S. Jackson St.

Denver, Colorado 80210

(303)759-9941

Specializing in solving management-level human resource problems—all industries and functional areas. Services include organizational planning and development, management development, executive evaluation, internal career planning, management separation services and executive retirement planning.

Contact: William B. Arnold, pres.

Areas Served: U.S.

Founded: 1964 *Staff:* 3-10 *Revenues:* $100-$500,000

Services: 1.1   3.1   3.2

Industries: Most

Arthur Aschauer & Co., Inc.

4841 N. Scottsdale Rd.

Scottsdale, Arizona 85251

(602)941-1242

Management counseling services for senior level management by former line executives. Three principal areas; (1) organization design and planning, (2) all phases of marketing and sales, and (3) information systems management. Thirteen years experience serving large corporations and medium sized firms in manufacturing, banking, services industries, as well as state and local government. Committed to senior level counseling with bottom-line orientation.

Clients served nationally, particularly in East and Mid West. Some European experience.

Contact: Arthur Aschauer, pres.
Areas Served: U.S. & some European
Founded: 1966 *Staff:* 3-10 *Revenues:* $100-$500,000
Professional Affiliations: SPMC/SMIS
Services: 1.0 3.0 4.0 9.3
Industries: D.34 D.35 D.36 E.48 H.60 J.91

Assessment Designs, Inc.

1 Purlieu Place
Winter Park, Florida 32792
(305)671-0665

Human resource management consultants; leading firm specializing in tailoring assessment center technology to organization's needs; performance appraisal systems and training consultation; personnel selection, training, and career development consultation.

Contact: Dr. Cabot L. Jaffee
Areas Served: worldwide
Founded: 1974 *Staff:* 10-25 *Revenues:* $500,000-1 million
Professional Affiliations: /ASTD, APA
Services: 3.0 3.1 3.4 3.5 3.8 3.9 3.11
Industries: Most

Associated Consultants in Education

1018 Thomasville Rd.
Tallahassee, Florida 32303
(904)224-4821

Professional services to educational institutions of all levels. Associates are nationally known educators and members of related professions. Non-members are freely used whenever their services are needed by any client. Serve schools, community colleges, colleges and the states.

Contact: Hazen A. Curtis, exec. dir.
Areas Served: U.S.
Founded: 1954 *Staff:* 3-10 *Revenues:* under $100,000
Industries: I.82

ASYST-Administrative Systems Consultants

162 Lenox Ave.
Green Brook, New Jersey 08812
(201)968-7527

Specialization in the management of information resources and transition to the office of the future.

Contact: Charles Lehmann, mng. ptnr.
Areas Served: U.S. & Canada
Founded: 1976 *Staff:* 3-10 *Revenues:* $100-$500,000
Professional Affiliations: IMC
Services: 1.5 1.8 1.9 3.5 9.1 9.2 9.3 9.5 9.6 9.7
Industries: Most

Joseph Auerbach
33-74 Utopia Pkwy.
Flushing, New York 11358
(212)463-0466

> An independent consultant serving small and medium-sized organizations.
> Assist management to define problem areas. When required, assemble and
> coordinate project teams with engineering, marketing and personnel consult-
> ants. Deeply involve client personnel in developing and implementing
> recommendations in order to increase effectiveness and minimize resistance to
> change.

Contact: Joseph Auerbach
Areas Served: NY,NJ,CT,MA & PA
Founded: 1956 *Staff:* 1-3 *Revenues:* under $100,000
Professional Affiliations: IMC, SPMC
Services: 1.1   1.8   1.9   2.15   5.2   6.4   9.3   9.5   9.6
Industries: D.23   D.27   D.39   F.50   F.51   G.53   G.57   H.64   I.89

Peter August & Associates, Inc.
10801 National Blvd.
Los Angeles, California 90064
(213)474-0561

> Our services are designed to assist clients in achieving profit improvement
> through increased labor productivity and reduced labor costs. We provide the
> most advanced techniques of work methods, work measurement production
> standards, wage incentives and labor controls. Projects are fully developed and
> implemented and client personnel thoroughly trained.

Contact: Richard S. Foster, pres.
Areas Served: North & South America, Europe, Far East
Founded: 1963 *Staff:* 3-10 *Revenues:* $100-$500,000
Services: 1.10   2.1   2.3   2.4   2.6   2.10   2.13   2.14   3.8   9.5
Industries: Most

The Austin Co.
(Management Consulting Division)
820 Davis St.
Evanston, Illinois 60201
(312)869-3130

> Formerly Management Research & Planning, Inc., we complement Austin's
> facility planning, design and construction services with broad-based manage-
> ment consultation, using a systems analysis approach.

Contact: A. John Ward, vp/gen mgr.
Areas Served: U.S.
Founded: 1964 *Staff:* 3-10 *Revenues:* $100-$500,000
Services: 1.0   2.0   4.0   6.0   9.0
Industries: D.00   E.00   F.00

Austin & Lindberg, Ltd.
Box 6019
Salt Lake City, Utah 84106
(801)364-5022

> Our corporate goal is to prosper from providing cost-effective management
> consultation services performed with fidelity to each client's interests and to the
> aims of each assignment accepted.

Contact: Sudhir Amembal, gen. mgr.
Areas Served: U.S.
Founded: 1978 *Staff:* 3-10 *Revenues:* $100-$500,000
Services: 1.0   5.0   10.0
Industries: Most

Don Aux Associates, Inc.

1 Lincoln Plaza
New York, New York 10023
(212)877-2115

Specialize in serving the owners of privately held companies by helping them increase the effectiveness of their organization and people. We further assist them to attain their goals. Clients in all manufacturing, wholesale, retail and service industries, primarily throughout the Northeast.

Contact: Michael Karp, pres.
Areas Served: Primarily Northeast
Founded: 1964 *Staff:* 25-50 *Revenues:* $1-$5 million
Services: Most   1.0   2.0   3.0   4.0   5.0   6.0   9.0
Industries: Most

Aviation Consultants, Inc.

Box 45
Findlay, Ohio 45840
(419)424-0248

Corporate aircraft fleets: needs analysis, equipment specification and acquisition, operations, controls.

Contact: C. Sam Benson, pres.
Areas Served: U.S.
Founded: 1976 *Staff:* 1-3 *Revenues:* $100-$500,000
Professional Affiliations: /NBAA
Services: 2.17
Industries: Most

Aviation Consulting Enterprises, Inc.

Box 1312
Fort Dodge, Iowa 50501
(515)576-7444

Feasibility planning and pre-acquisition studies for organizations contemplating aircraft ownership. Also establishment and maintenance of flight operations departments, plus efficiency audits.

Contact: Mark H. Goodrich, pres.
Areas Served: U.S.
Founded: 1971 *Staff:* 1-3 *Revenues:* under $100,000
Services: 2.17
Industries: Most

Emory Ayers Associates

950 Third Ave.
New York, New York 10022
(212)752-3606

General consulting practice with four broad areas of service: general management, marketing, operations management and computer systems devepment. Clients include companies in more than 50 industries (both domestic and international), not-for-profit institutions and government agencies. To help clients achieve marked improvement in performance, we work closely with clients in all project phases, including implementation.

Contact: Emory D. Ayers, pres.

Areas Served: worldwide

Founded: 1974 *Staff:* 10-25 *Revenues:* $1-$5 million

Professional Affiliations: ACME

Services: 1.0   2.0   3.10   4.0   5.0   6.0   9.0   10.0

Industries: A.00   B.00   C.00   D.00   E.48   G.58   H.60   H.65   I.00

Bain Management Consulting, Inc.
4410 West Vickery Blvd.
Fort Worth, Texas 76107
(817)738-0201

Our primary objective is to provide quality, reasonably priced consulting to management of small to medium sized firms in the Fort Worth-Dallas area. The specific capabilities of the firm are related to data processing and range from feasibility studies to management reviews of existing installations.

Contact: H.E. Bain, pres.

Areas Served: Fort Worth/Dallas

Founded: 1979 *Staff:* 1-3 *Revenues:* under $100,000

Services: 1.5   1.8   9.3   9.5   9.7

Industries: Most   C.15   C.16   D.25   D.34   D.37   E.42   F.51   G.55   I.00   J.00

Bain & Co., Inc.
3 Faneuil Hall Marketplace
Boston, Massachusetts 02109
(617)367-3700

Formulation and implementation of corporate strategy for large, multidivisional, multinational corporations.

Contact: William X. Bain, Jr.

Areas Served: U.S.

Founded: 1973 *Staff:* over 100 *Revenues:* over $10 million

Services: 1.3

Industries: Most

James S. Baker Management Consultants, Inc.
10204 Garden Way
Potomac, Maryland 20854
(301)299-2150

Domestic and international consulting services to meet specific client needs in two principal areas: research studies in public management, and appraisals of capital development projects. The principal officer of the firm plays a key role in assignment planning and supervision and in and in many instances personally performs a significant portion of the work.

Contact: James S. Baker, pres.

Areas Served: worldwide

Founded: 1974 *Staff:* 1-3 *Revenues:* under $100,000

Professional Affiliations: IMC/NSPE

Services: 1.1   1.3   1.5   1.7   4.2   5.3   10.2   10.5

Industries: A.07   D.20   E.49   H.60   H.67   I.86   J.91   J.95

Ballew, Reinhardt & Associates, Inc.
2670 Union Ave. Extended
Memphis, Tennessee 38112
(901)454-0393

Ballew, Reinhardt & Associates, Inc. is a results-oriented management firm consulting with clients throughout the U.S. We specialize in solving and preventing people problems. Each professional has a sound knowledge of theory, a high ability to perform, and a proven record of achieving positive objectives through practical application.

Contact: C. W. Ballew, pres.
Areas Served: U.S.
Founded: 1967 *Staff:* 1-3 *Revenues:* $100-$500,000
Professional Affiliations: AMC, IMC
Services: 1.1   1.2   1.14   3.0
Industries: Most

Ballinger-Meserole
841 Chestnut St.
Philadelphia, Pennsylvania 19107
(215)629-0920

Consulting industrial engineers specializing in warehousing, materials handling, physical distribution, and related areas for the industrial and hospital/health care fields. Emphasis on practical, economical solutions to operating problems and facilities design.

Contact: David L. Schaefer, pres.
Areas Served: U.S.
Founded: 1945 *Staff:* 3-10 *Revenues:* $100-$500,000
Professional Affiliations: /AIIE, NCPD, IMMS
Services: 2.2   2.3   2.4   2.5   2.8   2.11   2.12   2.13   2.16   2.17
Industries: Most

Barbrisons Management Systems, Inc.
(BMS, Inc.)
2957 Annwood St.
Cincinnati, Ohio 45206
(513)861-8505

Management consulting, education and research. Participative consultants assisting clients in diagnosing problems and implementing solutions. Specializing in executive effectiveness, human resources, operations management, and organization. Traditional quality at state-of-the-art levels with a results orientation tailored to the needs of our clients.

Contact: Brian R. Durbrow, pres.
Affiliates/branches: Tampa, Florida
Areas Served: U.S.-mostly Midwest & Southeast
Founded: 1969 *Staff:* 3-10 *Revenues:* $100-$500,000
Services: 1.0   2.0   3.0   4.0   5.0   7.0   9.0   11.1
Industries: B.00   C.00   D.00   E.00   G.00   H.00   J.00   K.00

Barnett & Engel
9 Marion Rd.
Westport, Connecticut 06880
(203)226-0118

Economic and industrial development planning and research services to government and government grantees. Program evaluations and management audits for government. Feasibility studies, market research and management/organization studies for business.

Contact: Stanley A. Barnett, ptnr.
Affiliates/branches: 421 Links Dr., E., Oceanside, New York 11572
Areas Served: Worldwide
Founded: 1976 *Staff:* 3-10 *Revenues:* $100-$500,000
Professional Affiliations: IMC/AICPA
Services: 1.4   1.5   1.7   4.1   4.2   4.3   4.10   10.1
Industries: E.47   J.91   J.96

Barron-Clayton, Inc.
Box 276
Andover, Massachusetts 01845
(617)687-3322

Specialize in organizational studies, development and training; work measurement and indirect cost reduction; EDP systems; and manufacturing planning Y controls, i.e., purchasing, production & inventory control, materials management, quality and the manufacturing/engineering interface. We are also generalists with much of our business under retainer agreements. Clients primarily manufacturing corporations.

Contact: William B. Gerraughty, CMC, pres.
Areas Served: U.S. & Canada
Founded: 1965 *Staff:* 3-10 *Revenues:* $100-$500,000
Professional Affiliations: IMC
Services: 1.1   1.12   2.2   2.7   3.1   3.7   9.3   9.4   9.5   11.1
Industries: D.30   D.31   D.32   D.33   D.34   D.35   D.36   D.37   D.38   D.39

David T. Barry Associates
572 Washington St.
Wellesley, Massachusetts 02181
(617)235-1520

General management consulting, with emphasis on marketing, systems, acquisitions and mergers, management development. Much of the work we do involves counseling the chief executive or other top management people on a continuing basis.

Contact: David T. Barry, princ.
Areas Served: worldwide
Founded: 1961 *Staff:* 3-10 *Revenues:* $100-$500,000
Professional Affiliations: IMC
Services: Most
Industries: Most

Theodore Barry & Associates
1520 Wilshire Blvd.
Los Angeles, California 90017
(213)413-6080

We provide a full range of management consulting services. In addition to the standard disciplines we have added A & E capabilities, as well as construction services, facilities planning, and project management. We stress innovation and implementation, and have served many of the finest firms in the world. We have performed more management audits of utilities than any other consulting firm.

Contact: Dennis Callaghan, pres.

Affiliates/branches: 229 Peachtree St. NE, Atlanta, Georgia 30303; 934 Old Taos Hwy.,
Santa Fe, New Mexico 87501; 245 Park Ave., New York, New York 10017; 1618 SW
1st Ave., Portland, Oregon 97201; 208 S LaSalle St., Chicago, Illinois 60604; Brazil;
France; Germany; Japan; Kuwait; Venezuela
Areas Served: worldwide
Founded: 1954 *Staff:* over 100 *Revenues:* over $10 million
Professional Affiliations: ACME, IMC
Services: Most
Industries: Most

Barry & Co.
900 Wilshire Blvd.
Los Angeles, California 90017
(213)620-1590
> Founded by Robert J. Barry in 1945, we provide effective, ethical, highly-
> competent and valuable professional consulting service to clients throughout
> the world. We employ senior consultants who have a minimum of twenty years
> of varied non-consulting experience.

Contact: William P. Barry, sr. vp.
Areas Served: worldwide
Founded: 1945 *Staff:* 25-50 *Revenues:* $500,000-1 million
Services: 1.0 1.1 2.0 2.1 2.4 2.13 3.0 3.3 4.0 5.0
Industries: D.20 D.25 D.27 D.30 D.34 D.35 D.36 D.37 D.38 G.53

Bartow Associates
335 Dartmouth Ave.
Swarthmore, Pennsylvania 19081
(215)544-8335
> Organizations have life cycles which require changes in management styles. We
> offer the implementation of creative processes useful in the early stages of
> product and program planning, result-oriented techniques for obtaining
> planned-for objectives on schedule, and the interpersonal and experimental
> exchanges useful in realigning an organization either before and/or after
> periods of transition.

Contact: Philip E. Bartow, pres.
Affiliates/branches: 205 S.W. Gibson Lane, Issaquah, Washington 98027
Areas Served: U.S.
Founded: 1972 *Staff:* 3-10 *Revenues:* $100-$500,000
Services: 1.1 1.12 1.15 2.1 3.1 4.1 5.4 6.4 7.2 9.4
Industries: D.38 D.39 E.40 I.79 I.80 I.82 I.83 J.94

Batten, Batten, Hudson & Swab, Inc.
820 Keosauqua Way
Des Moines, Iowa 50309
(515)244-3176
> Our basic philosophy can be found in our book "Tough-Minded Management"
> by Joe Batten, our president. General management consulting with particular
> emphasis on management research and education, both in-house and public
> programs. Organization studies, employee attitude studies, compensation
> system installation, training and installation of MBO programs; contract film
> production and educational films and cassettes.

Contact: Leonard C. Hudson, vp. cons. svcs.
Affiliates/branches: 2711 E. Coast Hwy., Corona del Mar, California 92625; 2131 Lone

Rock Rd., Kingwood, Texas 77339
Areas Served: U.S. Canada, Mexico
Founded: 1957 *Staff:* 25-50 *Revenues:* $1-$5 million
Services: 1.0   1.1   1.2   1.3   1.7   3.0   4.0
Industries: Most

Bavier, Bulger & Goodyear, Inc.
270 Amity Rd.
New Haven, Connecticut 06525
(203)389-1534
General management consulting firm specializing in industrial-type industries. Major strengths in manufacturing areas including support functions such as financial control, data processing, organization, and industrial marketing. Some activity with service organizations such as banks & insurance, in the area of clerical work management.
Contact: Arthur C. Bulger
Areas Served: U.S. & Canada
Founded: 1952 *Staff:* 10-25 *Revenues:* $500,000-1 million
Professional Affiliations: ACME, IMC
Services: 1.0   2.0   3.0   4.0   5.0   6.0   9.0
Industries: D.00   F.50   F.51   H.60   H.63

BCMA Associates
485 Fifth Ave.
New York, New York 10017
(212)867-6341
Supplying high-level consulting services in all areas of the publishing, communications and learning media - print and nonprint, "software" and "hardware". Advising specifically in all aspects of the publishing process: research and development, planning, editorial, production, marketing, distribution, finance, administration.
Contact: Cameron S. Moseley, pres.
Affiliates/branches: Washington, D.C.; Chicago, Illinois; San Francisco, California
Areas Served: U.S., Europe & Latin America
Founded: 1971 *Staff:* 10-25 *Revenues:* $100-$500,000
Services: 1.1   1.4   1.6   3.2   4.1   4.2   4.15   5.9   7.1   10.4
Industries: D.27   G.59   I.82

David N. Beach Associates, Inc.
753 Janice Ct.
Wyckoff, New Jersey 07481
(201)891-9587
Business & executive continuity: business and organizational planning; executive selection, development and continuity; management processes, including planning, implementation and controls and their impact on behavior; change and training processes to support these activities.
Contact: David N. Beach, pres.
Areas Served: Continental North America
Founded: 1969 *Staff:* 1-3 *Revenues:* $100-$500,000
Professional Affiliations: IMC
Services: 1.1   1.2   1.3   1.7   1.9   3.1   3.4   3.10   3.11   4.0
Industries: D.00   E.48   E.49   H.60   H.63   I.70   I.82   I.86

Ernest Beachley & Associates Inc.
218 La Rue Dr.
Corapolis, Pennsylvania 15108
(412)264-3431

Maintenance improvement programs, installation and "debugging" new equipment, management of construction projects, organiztional analysis, manufacturing efficiency, and turnaround of loss plants and loss companies.

Contact: Ernest Beachley, pres.
Areas Served: worldwide
Founded: 1970 *Staff:* 3-10 *Revenues:* $100-$500,000
Professional Affiliations: IMC
Services: 1.10 1.11 2.3 2.6 2.8 2.9 2.10 2.11 3.7 3.8
Industries: B.12 D.00 D.20 D.24 D.28 D.29 D.32 D.33 D.34 D.35

Bedford-Post Associates, Inc.
3450 Wilshire Blvd.
Los Angeles, California 90010
(213)389-1279

General line consulting firm with industrial engineering emphasis. Staff are mature individuals who have served in management functions for a minimum of ten years as well as five years in a consulting specialty. Human relations and results-oriented having served firms from five million to one billion sales volume.

Contact: Robert T. Flynn, pres.
Areas Served: U.S., Canada & Europe
Founded: 1969 *Staff:* 3-10 *Revenues:* $100-$500,000
Professional Affiliations: AMC
Services: 1.0 2.0 3.0 4.1 5.0 6.0 9.0 11.1
Industries: C.00 D.00 G.00 H.60 H.64 I.00 J.00

N.C. Berkowitz & Co.
1 Sutter St.
San Francisco, California 94104
(415)788-4120

General management & financial consulting to organizations with difficult problems. We provide unique solutions.

Contact: Nathaniel Berkowitz
Areas Served: worldwide
Founded: 1958 *Staff:* 1-3 *Revenues:* $100-$500,000
Services: Most 1.0 2.0 4.1 5.3 5.4 5.7 5.10 7.3 10.2 10.3
Industries: D.34 D.36 D.38 E.40 H.67

Brooks Bernhardt & Associates
230 S. Bemiston Ave.
Clayton, Missouri 63105
(314)862-0190

Serving business, industry, hospitals, governmental and social service agencies and school systems. Also offer three salary workshops (beginning, intermediate and advanced) in St. Louis each spring and fall.

Contact: Brooks Bernhardt, pres.
Areas Served: U.S.
Founded: 1968 *Staff:* 1-3 *Revenues:* $100-$500,000
Professional Affiliations: AMC

Services: 1.1 1.3 1.7 3.1 3.2 3.7 3.8
Industries: Most I.73

The Berwick Group, Inc.
1 Walnut St.
Boston, Massachusetts 02108
(617)367-8100

  Our work is primarily with the executives of large industrial firms throughout the U.S. and U.K., helping them apply strategic concepts to a broad range of business problems. Productivity improvement and the quality of work life in organizations are two other areas of interest.
Contact: Anthony R. Biancaniello, vp.
Areas Served: worldwide
Founded: 1976 *Staff:* 10-25 *Revenues:* $1-$5 million
Services: 1.0 2.0 3.1 3.2 4.1 4.2 4.3

Bess Management Services, Inc.
35 E. Wacker Dr.
Chicago, Illinois 60601
(312)263-5465

  Specialize in the foodservice industry: marketing of food and equipment, executive recruitment. Also serve trade ass'ns and professional societies.
Contact: Norman E. Bess, pres.
Areas Served: U.S.
Founded: 1965 *Staff:* 3-10 *Revenues:* $100-$500,000
Services: 3.4 4.0
Industries: D.20 D.34 I.86

Betterley Consulting Group
200 Clarendon St.
Boston, Massachusetts 02116
(617)267-4300

  Risk and insurance management consultants to organizations large and small. Strategic planning to control financial consequences of accidental loss. Analysis of risks, loss prevention and loss funding procedures. Evaluation and design of insurance, self-insurance programs (no insurance sold). Risk management audits include corporate policy, organizational structure, personnel, administrative systems.
Contact: George M. Betterley, mng. dir.
Areas Served: worldwide
Founded: 1932 *Staff:* 10-25 *Revenues:* $500,000-1 million
Professional Affiliations: /IRMC, ARIA, ASSE
Services: 1.7 3.6 3.21 5.9 5.10 11.0 11.8
Industries: Most

D. A. Betterley Risk Consultants, Inc.
446 Main St.
Worcester, Massachusetts 01608
(617)754-1704

  Expert assistance to management in the identification, control, and evaluation of funding for property and liability risks. Services include evaluation of risk management systems and funding strategies, design of loss control and reporting programs, and implementation assistance.

Contact: Richard S. Betterley, treas.
Areas Served: worldwide
Founded: 1932 *Staff:* 3-10 *Revenues:* $100-$500,000
Professional Affiliations: IMC/IRMC, ARIA
Services: 1.1   1.7   3.6   3.21   5.8   5.9   5.10   11.0   11.8
Industries: Most

Bickert, Browne, Coddington & Associates

100 S Madison
Denver, Colorado 80205
(303)321-2547

Assistance provided in a variety of applied business or economic situations. Financial institution services, marketing or feasibility are emphasized.

Contact: T. D. Browne, pres.
Areas Served: Rocky Mountains
Founded: 1970 *Staff:* 10-25 *Revenues:* $100-$500,000
Services: 1.1   1.6   4.1   4.2   5.6   5.11   7.1   10.4
Industries: B.12   C.17   E.41   G.00   H.60   H.61   H.67

The Billings Group

1 Main St.
Concord, Massachusetts 01720
(617)369-2790

Market development projects since 1960. The companies for whom we work are industrial firms interested in diversification of expansion into new areas. Our clients initiate these projects because of: their interest in market development under their control; or because of interest in a growth business outside their normal working area.

Contact: Curtis Billings, princ.
Areas Served: North America
Founded: 1960 *Staff:* 3-10 *Revenues:* $100-$500,000
Professional Affiliations: ACME
Services: 1.0   4.0   10.4
Industries: A.00   D.00   E.00   I.73

Birch & Davis Associates, Inc.

1112 Spring St.
Silver Spring, Maryland 20910
(301)589-6760

General management consulting services to public and private sector organizations with particular emphasis on services to government and voluntary agencies. Strong focus on financial management information systems, program planning and evaluation, and technical assistance. Also, extensive experience with health care delivery programs, pat + rticularly through HMOs and innovative ambulatory care modalities.

Contact: Willie H. Davis, pres.
Affiliates/branches: 60 Sturbridge Hill Rd., New Canaan, Connecticut 06840
Areas Served: U.S.
Founded: 1976 *Staff:* 10-25 *Revenues:* $500,000-1 million
Professional Affiliations: IMC

Services: 1.0   2.3   2.9   4.5   4.7   4.11   5.0   9.0
Industries: B.14   D.00   I.80   J.91   J.94   J.97

Serge A. Birn Co.
1049 Bardstown Rd.
Louisville, Kentucky 40204
(502)451-6640

We strictly adhere to the ACME code of ethics in all dealings with industrial, financial, and government clients. Our philosophy is to actively assist clients by having our consultant work with client personnel to tailor the results of all assignments to meet the client's needs.

Contact: H. W. Nance, pres.
Affiliates/branches: Fort Lauderdale, Florida; Ireland; England; W. Germany
Areas Served: U.S., Canada & Europe
Founded: 1944 *Staff:* 10-25 *Revenues:* $500,000-1 million
Professional Affiliations: IMC
Services: 1.0   2.0   3.2   3.5   3.7   3.8   6.0   9.2   9.4   9.5
Industries: D.24   D.25   D.30   D.34   D.35   D.36   D.39   H.60   H.63

Birnberg & Associates
405 N. Wabash Ave.
Chicago, Illinois 60611
(312)329-0233

Full service management consultants specializing in assisting design and related firms, with services in computer applications, marketing of professional services, personnel and motivation programs, surance counseling, and general financial and management. As fellow design professionals we are very aware of the problems and operations of design and related firms.

Contact: Howard G. Birnberg, pres.
Affiliates/branches: Boston, Massachusetts; San Francisco, California
Areas Served: U.S. & Canada
Founded: 1976 *Staff:* 3-10 *Revenues:* $100-$500,000
Services: 1.0   3.0   4.0   5.0   7.4   9.0
Industries: H.63   H.64   H.65   I.73

Bjorkman Associates
Calle Madrid ♯ 1
Santurce, Puerto Rico 00907
(809)724-5726

Subscribe to the Code of Ethics of the Institute of Management Consultants. Practice covers: financial and administrative management, computers and systems design, long range business planning and feasibility studies.

Contact: George A. Bjorkman
Areas Served: Southeast U.S. & Caribbean
Founded: 1971 *Staff:* 1-3 *Revenues:* under $100,000
Professional Affiliations: IMC
Services: 1.2   1.3   1.5   1.8   1.9   5.3   5.4   5.8   9.3   9.5
Industries: D.28   D.39   E.40   E.42   E.45   F.51   G.53   G.54   G.59   K.00

Blades & Macaulay
2444 Morris Ave.
Union, New Jersey 07083
(201)687-3735

Property and casualty insurance and risk management consulting services to corporate, private and public entities in all fields. Our primary objective is to help a client structure a program which provides the best possible balance between risk retention and risk transfer through insurance on a sound economic basis.

Contact: Arthur Macaulay, Jr., ptnr.
Areas Served: U.S., Canada & Bermuda
Founded: 1926 *Staff:* 1-3 *Revenues:* $100-$500,000
Professional Affiliations: /IRMC
Services: 11.8
Industries: Most

Blessing/White Inc.

900 State Rd.
Princeton, New Jersey 08540
(609)924-2080

Employee training in areas of: career planning, self-development, performance appraisal, improving supervisor-subordinate communications about these issues.

Contact: Tod White, pres.
Affiliates/branches: Washington, D.C.; Chicago, Illinois
Areas Served: U.S. & Canada
Founded: 1973 *Staff:* 3-10 *Revenues:* $1-$5 million
Professional Affiliations: /ASTD
Services: 3.1 3.5
Industries: Most

Boeing Computer Services, Inc.

(Consulting Division)
(subsidiary of the Boeing Co.)
505 Baker Blvd.
Seattle, Washington 98188
(206)773-9726

Assist companies, institutions, and governmental agencies, specializing in operations research, systems analysis, economic analysis, and management consulting services. Nearly 100 experienced professional scientists, engineers, managers, and planners who possess an average of 12 years experience in their working careers.

Contact: Tom Stewart
Founded: 1971 *Staff:* 50-100 *Revenues:* $1-$5 million
Services: Most 1.0 2.0 3.0 4.0 5.0 6.4 7.0 9.0 10.0

Wallace A. Boesch Associates

110 N. High St.
Gahanna, Ohio 42340
(614)476-0100

Specialists in serving financial institutions; services available include preparation of branch applications, relocation applications, evaluating potential site locations for branches, feasibility studies, branch protests, new charters, preparation of merger applications, personnel organizational studies, assistance with holding company and service corporation structures and activities, arranging mergers and acquisitions.

Contact: Wallace A. Boesch

Areas Served: North Central U.S.
Founded: 1974 *Staff:* 3-10 *Revenues:* $100-$500,000
Services: 1.1   1.5   1.6   4.10

Booz-Allen & Hamilton, Inc.

245 Park Ave.
New York, New York 10017
(212)697-1900

We are the largest worldwide professional organization of career consultants in management, technology and market research, skilled in resolving clients' problems with multidisciplinary teams. We have thus made possible what our clients need: effective task forces that combine skills to do the analytic and action tasks that are most difficult to accomplish in a complex and volatile world. In short, we provide professional counsel for managerial action.

Contact: Stephen X. Oresman, sr.vp.
Affiliates/branches: New York; San Francisco; Washington; Boston; Cleveland; Cincinnati; Philadelphia; Algiers; Bangkok; Brussels; Caracas; Dusseldorf; London; Paris; Sao Paulo; Tokyo
Areas Served: worldwide
Founded: 1914 *Staff:* over 100 *Revenues:* over $10 million
Services: Most
Industries: Most

Donald R. Booz & Associates, Inc.

20 N. Wacker Dr.
Chicago, Illinois 60606
(312)372-8487

We emphasize a style of consulting in which we counsel and advise client general management and lead, persuade and guide client personnel in the solution of corporate problems, rather than presenting our own solutions for installation. Wherever possible we utilize client personnel in the planning and conduct of assignments, under the guidance of the senior company executive concerned.

Contact: Donald R. Booz
Areas Served: U.S.
Founded: 1961 *Staff:* 3-10 *Revenues:* $100-$500,000
Professional Affiliations: ACME, IMC
Services: 1.0   2.0   3.0   10.0
Industries: D.00   F.00   G.00   I.00

The Boston Consulting Group, Inc.

1 Boston Place
Boston, Massachusetts 02106
(617)722-7800

We are primarily concerned with competitive strategy and the management of the firm as a whole.

Contact: Bruce Henderson, pres.
Affiliates/branches: 200 W. Monroe St., Chicago, Illinois 60606; 2180 Sand Hill Rd., Menlo Park, California 94025; London; Paris; Tokyo Tokyo
Areas Served: U.S., Europe & Japan
Founded: 1963 *Staff:* over 100 *Revenues:* over $10 million
Services: 1.0   1.2   1.3
Industries: Most

Bostrom Management Corporation

435 N Michigan Ave.
Chicago, Illinois 60611
(312)644-0828

Specialize in all phases of trade association, professional society, and foundation management. This includes formation and structure; development of mission, goals and objectives, and strategies for achieving; cost control systems; personnel selection and development; complete management of operations with fiduciary responsibility.

Contact: Glenn W. Bostrom, pres.
Affiliates/branches: 2600 Garden Rd., Monterey, California 93940; 1629 "K" St. NW, Washington, D.C. 20002
Areas Served: U.S.
Founded: 1975 *Staff:* 10-25 *Revenues:* $500,000-1 million
Professional Affiliations: /IAMC, ASAE
Services: 1.0 3.0 4.0 5.0 9.0 11.1

Boyle/Kirkman Associates, Inc.

230 Park Ave.
New York, New York 10017
(212)986-0405

Specializing in helping corporations solve people problems in the most productive way. We help clients develop and implement programs to improve recruitment, reduce turnover, and increase employee performance while retaining managerial prerogatives. The result is higher morale and increased profit potential.

Contact: Sharon Kirkman Donegan, vp.
Founded: 1972 *Staff:* 10-25 *Revenues:* $1-$5 million
Services: 1.1 1.4 1.15 3.1 3.4 3.5 3.6 3.9 3.10 3.11
Industries: Most

A. Val Bradley Associates, Inc.

2950 Metro Dr.
Minneapolis, Minnesota 55420
(612)854-6661

Concentrating on all phases of management bottom-line effectiveness, with emphasis on management, employee and union relations. NLRB proceedings and elections are a specialty; and executive, middle management and first-line supervisory training are featured. Recognition of client's right to sensitive, unobtrusive, professional counsel is the firm's basic philosophy.

Contact: William M. Siegel, exec. vp.
Affiliates/branches: 757 Third Ave., New York, New York 10017; 104 E. Market St., West Chester, New York 19380; 6520 Powers Ferry Rd., Atlanta, Georgia 30339
Areas Served: worldwide
Founded: 1964 *Staff:* 3-10 *Revenues:* $500,000-1 million
Professional Affiliations: AMC, IMC
Services: 1.1 1.3 1.7 1.10 2.6 2.9 3.0 9.1
Industries: Most D.00 I.00 J.94

Brecker & Merryman, Inc.

575 Madison Ave.
New York, New York 10022
(212)751-7510

As consultants in human resource management and communications, the firm offers a wide range of services to personnel professionals in fields such as college relations and recruiting, career planning and development, affirmative action, employee communications, work analysis and management development. Clients include over 80 Fortune 500 companies from coast to coast.

Contact: Richard L. Brecker, pres.

Areas Served: U.S.

Founded: 1974 *Staff:* 10-25 *Revenues:* $500,000-1 million

Services: 1.0 3.0 3.1 3.4 3.5 3.6 3.8 3.9 3.10

W. E. Brennan & Co., Inc.

2101 Central Park Ave.
Evanston, Illinois 60201
(312)864-0088

We are a general management consulting/industrial management firm with experience dating from 1961. We adhere to the principles and practices of ACME and IMC.Sub-specialties in pricing, industrial marketing, task force leadership in strategic and tactical planning functions. Testimony for regulated companies.

Contact: William E. Brennan, pres.

Areas Served: U.S. & Europe

Founded: 1974 *Staff:* 1-3 *Revenues:* $100-$500,000

Professional Affiliations: IMC/AMA, NCPDM

Services: Most

George W. Bricker

216 Forest Beach Rd.
South Chatham, Massachusetts 02659
(617)432-4595

Assist companies in the planning and execution of strategies for organization development and development of individual executives, including recommendations of appropriate campus programs for that purpose, based on personal knowledge of the programs reported in Bricker's International Directory of University-Sponsored Executive Development Programs, now in its tenth annual edition.

Contact: George W. Bricker, princ.

Areas Served: U.S. & Canada

Founded: 1958 *Staff:* 1-3 *Revenues:* under $100,000

Professional Affiliations: /ABA

Services: 1.1 3.1

Industries: Most

A.E. Brim & Associates, Ltd.

177 N.E. 102nd Ave.
Portland, Oregon 97220
(503)256-2070

Complete consulting services to the health care industry including fiscal/business office services/systems/planning/development/management training and accreditation review. Special emphasis to turnaroud situations and creative growth requirements.

Contact: A.E. Brim, pres.

Areas Served: Western U.S.

Founded: 1971 *Staff:* 50-100 *Revenues:* $100-$500,000
Services: 1.0   3.1   3.5   5.0   5.1   5.2   5.8   9.1   9.5   9.6

Earl D. Brodie & Associates
111 Sutter St.
San Francisco, California 94104
(415)986-4834
> I help independent business owners make more money.

Contact: Earl D. Brodie, princ.
Areas Served: worldwide
Founded: 1963 *Staff:* 1-3 *Revenues:* under $100,000
Professional Affiliations: IMC
Services: Most
Industries: Most

Charles Brooks Associates, Inc.
1207 W. Bessemer Ave.
Greensboro, North Carolina 27408
(919)274-6969
> Programs implemented for maximizing and safeguarding profits through
> productivity improvements and corporate strategy development. A participative
> approach with emphasis on the training and development of client's staffs.
> Particular expertise in the analytical method of training (operators, mechanics
> and supervisors) and controlled maintenance.

Contact: Charles E. Brooks, pres.
Affiliates/branches: Box 88524, Atlanta, Georgia 30338; Box 221122, Charlotte, North
Carolina 28222
Areas Served: U.S.
Founded: 1971 *Staff:* 3-10 *Revenues:* $100-$500,000
Services: 1.0   2.0   3.0   4.0   10.0
Industries: Most

Brooks/Gay & Associates, Inc.
50 Park Ave.
New York, New York 10016
(212)686-8917
> Professional security consulting; physical security surveys and vulnerability
> analysis of public & private facilities. Design and implementation of total assets
> protection programs for business & government. Evaluation of electronic
> security systems and physical safeguards. Computer and data security surveys
> and programs.

Contact: Earle B. Gay, pres.
Areas Served: worldwide
Founded: 1969 *Staff:* 3-10 *Revenues:* $100-$500,000
Professional Affiliations: /ASIS
Services: 11.0   11.1   11.4
Industries: Most

Jack Brown & Associates, Inc.
300 N State St.
Chicago, Illinois 60610
(312)565-0006

Management objectives can be achieved when adequate effort is made and the proper management tools are available. We assist management in defining objectives, providing adequate effort and training proper management technique. Results are attained with participation that strengthens client personnel and prepares them for the future.

Contact: Jack Brown, pres.

Areas Served: U.S.

Founded: 1977 *Staff:* 3-10 *Revenues:* $100-$500,000

Professional Affiliations: IMC

Services: 1.0 2.0 2.3 2.9 2.10 3.5 6.0 9.0 11.0

Industries: B.10 B.12 B.14 D.26 D.29 E.40 E.42 I.80 I.82 J.94

Frank C. Brown & Co., Inc.

342 Madison Ave.
New York, New York 10017
(212)697-4575

General and specialized management consulting for a wide variety of businesses, including consumer products, heavy industry, chemical, electronics, aerospace, oceanography, as well as governments and institutions.

Contact: Frank C. Brown, pres.

Areas Served: worldwide

Founded: 1947 *Staff:* 10-25 *Revenues:* $100-$500,000

Professional Affiliations: ACME, IMC

Services: Most

Industries: Most

Buckley & Co.

36 Washington St.
Wellesley Hills, Massachusetts 02181
(617)235-4592

General management, marketing & financial assignments. Emphasis on small to medium manufacturing firms.

Contact: John M. Buckley

Areas Served: worldwide - primarily NE US

Founded: 1970 *Staff:* 1-3 *Revenues:* $100-$500,000

Professional Affiliations: IMC

Services: Most

Industries: Most

Burgess Management Associates

111 Cooper Ave.
Upper Montclair, New Jersey 07043
(201)744-2668

Specializes in numerical analysis of business problems, design and implementation of programs to improve profitability. Handles project feasibility studies for international ventures and new business developments. Modernization of accounting systems and management reporting. Planning and management of turn-around situations.

Contact: T. Peter Burgess, princ.

Areas Served: U.S., U.K., Africa, Middle East

Founded: 1978 *Staff:* 1-3 *Revenues:* under $100,000

Services: 1.0 2.0 3.1 4.0 5.0 6.0 7.0 9.0 10.0

Industries: A.08 A.09 C.15 D.00 E.00 G.59 I.73 I.75 J.96

Burns International Security Services, Inc.
(Burns International Consulting Service Div.)
320 Old Briarcliff Rd.
Briarcliff Manor, New York 10510
(914)762-1000

Physical security audits and plans, executive protection plans, security administration, computer security, communications security, contingency emergency preparedness and disaster plans, nuclear plant security, loss prevention programs, construction planning, applied research and evaluation of protective systems and devices.

Contact: Joseph A. Malley, mgr. MAS
Areas Served: US, Canada, Great Britian, South America & Spain
Founded: 1963 *Staff:* 10-25 *Revenues:* $500,000-1 million
Professional Affiliations: /ASIS
Services: 11.4
Industries: Most

Business Psychology International
890/2 National Press Bldg.
Washington, D.C. 20045
(202)638-3951

Management consultation for 1) participative management systems, as a means to improve earnings and morale, to eliminate pilfering and avoid bankruptcy...2) advanced R & D innovation systems, as a means for greater flexibility to scientific enquiry with improved findings.

Contact: Hillyer Senning, chmn.
Areas Served: North America & Europe
Founded: 1971 *Staff:* 1-3 *Revenues:* under $100,000
Professional Affiliations: /AIMC
Services: 1.0   4.1   7.0
Industries: J.97

Michael Busler Group
22 Cypress La.
Berwyn, Pennsylvania 19312
(215)644-0106

Business strategy consulting, economic forecasting, feasibility studies, investment counseling.

Contact: Michael Busler, pres.
Areas Served: Philadelphia
Founded: 1976 *Staff:* 1-3 *Revenues:* under $100,000
Services: 1.3   1.5   1.10   5.3   7.5
Industries: C.15   D.24   G.53   H.65

Cambridge Research Institute
15 Mt. Auburn St.
Cambridge, Massachusetts 02138
(617)492-3800

Helping executives understand the future, plan for it, and manage change are services provided through research, consulting, and education. This includes creative business and economic assessments of the impacts of changes in governmental regulation. Clients are corporations, financial institutions, trade associations, health care institutions, and government.

Contact: Gerald A. Simon, mng. dir.
Areas Served: North America
Founded: 1959 *Staff:* 25-50 *Revenues:* $1-$5 million
Professional Affiliations: ACME, IMC
Services: 1.1   1.2   1.3   1.4   1.5   1.6   1.7   4.1   5.0   11.9
Industries: B.00   C.00   D.00   E.00   F.00   G.00   H.00   I.80   I.81   I.86

Daniel J. Cantor & Co., Inc.

Suburban Station Bldg.
Philadelphia, Pennsylvania 19103
(215)563-9646

> Consultation and surveys in business economics and management practices, specializing in work for the legal profession, including studies of planning, income and costs, organization, personnel and salary administration, systems, layout and office automation.

Contact: Daniel J. Cantor, pres.
Affiliates/branches: Merchants Exchange Bldg., San Francisco, California 94104
Areas Served: North America
Founded: 1975 *Staff:* 3-10 *Revenues:* $100-$500,000
Professional Affiliations: IMC
Services: 1.0   3.0   5.0   9.0   11.1
Industries: I.81

Caribbean Consulting Services, Inc.

46-47 Company St.
Christiansted, St. Croix, Virgin Islands 00820
(809)773-4555

> We adhere to the AMC Code of Professional Practice and provide services to the private and public sectors. Our philosophy is to actively assist clients by having our consulting firm help them accomplish their desired goals and needs Our experienced staff enables us to provide quality services that are results-oriented.

Contact: Hortence M. Rowe, pres.
Areas Served: Eastern Caribbean & US
Founded: 1975 *Staff:* 3-10 *Revenues:* $100-$500,000
Professional Affiliations: /IAFP
Services: Most
Industries: Most

C. L. Carter Jr. & Associates, Inc.

Box 5001
Richardson, Texas 75080
(214)234-3296

> Management training & development seminars; workbooks; technical publi-cations-books-slides-films relating to quality, reliability, safety, purchasing, materials management, organization & people development. Philosophy is based on professional programs and people working to prevent, control, assure & audit to benefit management and increase effectiveness/profitability.

Contact: G. M. Carter, pres.
Areas Served: worldwide
Founded: 1964 *Staff:* 1-3 *Revenues:* under $100,000
Professional Affiliations: SPMC/ASTD, SME, ASSE, ASQC, AMS

Services: 1.1   1.2   1.4   1.7   1.8   1.9   2.7   3.1   3.5   3.21
Industries: C.15   D.34   D.35   D.36   D.38   D.39   E.48   G.59   I.82   J.91

Caruthers Consulting Inc.

150 E. 58th St.
New York, New York 10022
(212)755-0323

Assist clients in: new product design & development, acquisitions planning & implementation, reorganizing in general management & marketing areas development & implementation of business & marketing plans.

Contact: H. D. Caruthers
Areas Served: U.S. & Western Europe
Founded: 1974 *Staff:* 1-3 *Revenues:* $100-$500,000
Services: 1.0   4.0

Case & Co., Inc.

90 Park Ave.
New York, New York 10016
(212)687-9010

Specialized consulting services - from cost reduction and sales improvement to corporate reorganization and strategic planning - to both domestic and foreign organizations, private, public and nonprofit. Our professionals have served most of the Fortune 500 largest industrials and thousands of smaller organizatios in virtually all the major industry groups.

Contact: Robert G. Frick, pres.
Affiliates/branches: 1111 Summer St., Stamford, Connecticut 06905; 100 Exec. Ctr. Dr., Greenville, South Carolina 29615; 2109 Prudential Plaza, Chicago, Illinois 60601; 235 Montgomery St., San Francisco, California 94104; 4314 Marina City Dr., Marina Del Rey, California 90291; Munich
Areas Served: worldwide
Founded: 1962 *Staff:* 25-50 *Revenues:* $1-$5 million
Professional Affiliations: ACME, IMC
Services: Most
Industries: Most

David Caulkins Associates

28 West Way
Old Greenwich, Connecticut 06870
(203)637-0832

Professional practice in management/executive compensation organiztion development, human resources management. Serve industrial and professional clients in medium-sized to large categories. I personally perform the professional services.

Contact: David Caulkins, princ.
Areas Served: Northeast
Founded: 1976 *Staff:* 1-3 *Revenues:* $100-$500,000
Services: 3.0   3.1   3.2   3.8   3.9
Industries: Most

J. P. Cavanaugh & Associates

202 West Berry
Fort Wayne, Indiana 46802
(219)423-2506

Our areas of competence: operations cost reductions, management controls, information systems, data processing, industrial engineering, production and inventory control, training and development, employee relations, coaching in the management process, catalytic agents in the management of change.
Contact: James P. Cavanaugh, pres.
Areas Served: U.S.
Founded: 1969 *Staff:* 3-10 *Revenues:* $100-$500,000
Professional Affiliations: AMC
Services: Most 1.0 2.0 3.0 4.0 5.0 6.0 8.0 9.0
Industries: Most D.00 F.00 G.00 H.00 I.00 J.00 K.00

Centaur Associates, Inc.
1120 Connecticut Ave., NW
Washington, D.C. 20036
(202)296-4100
Our aim is to serve client needs for research, management and technical expertise...in both the public and private sectors.
Contact: John G. Birdsong, pres.
Areas Served: U.S.-primarily Mid-Atlantic
Founded: 1968 *Staff:* 25-50 *Revenues:* $1-$5 million
Services: 1.1 1.5 1.7 1.8 1.12 7.3 9.5 11.0
Industries: A.09 B.12 I.80 J.91 J.96

The Center for Applied Management, Inc.
4918 S Imperial Cir.
Greenfield, Wisconsin 53220
(414)281-0251
Management education services in fields of manufacturing and materials management.
Contact: C. Lee Toms, exec. dir.
Areas Served: U.S. & Canada
Founded: 1964 *Staff:* 1-3 *Revenues:* $100-$500,000
Professional Affiliations: IMC/AIIE, APICS
Services: 1.8 1.13 2.0 3.0 4.8 4.14 5.2 6.4 6.5
Industries: D.00 F.50

Cexec, Inc.
1911 N. Fort Meyer Dr.
Arlington, Virginia 22209
(703)243-1700
An employee-owned management consulting and system development firm. Develop automated information systems, computer applications and a line of software products. Expert consulting services in energy, regulation analysis, policy planning and small computer selection.
Contact: Mark T. Veith, vp. bus. dev.
Affiliates/branches: 1341 W. Mockingbird La., Dallas, Texas 75247
Areas Served: US-primarily VA & TX
Founded: 1976 *Staff:* 25-50 *Revenues:* $500,000-1 million
Services: 1.0 2.15 2.17 4.2 4.14 5.4 5.8 7.1 9.0
Industries: B.00 D.00 H.60 I.00 J.00

Joseph Shaw Chalfant
Box 375
New Albany, Indiana 47150
(812)944-6751

General consulting practice including financial management, capital formation for small business, advising the small and medium-sized company president and board of directors. Services also include capital formation and management assistance for the entrepeneur. In addition, licensed to value and appraise commercial real estate, plant and equipment.

Contact: J. S. Chalfant, pres.
Areas Served: U.S.
Founded: 1972 *Staff:* 1-3 *Revenues:* $100-$500,000
Professional Affiliations: AMC/NAR, PI
Services: 1.0   1.1   1.2   1.3   1.6   1.11   2.10   5.10   8.1
Industries: D.20   D.26   D.36   G.58   H.65

Joseph Chanko Associates
1901 N. Atlantic Blvd.
Fort Lauderdale, Florida 33305
(305)566-5444

Specialize in management consultation to executives in printing and publishing fields. Offer complete counsel for every phase of printing operation and management, based on broad, extensive first-hand practical experience. Because of intimate knowledge of these fields and their special needs, can readily recommend streamlined procedures and effective improvements in organization and profit.

Contact: Joseph Chanko, pres.
Areas Served: FL, TX & East Coast
Founded: 1964 *Staff:* 1-3 *Revenues:* $100-$500,000
Professional Affiliations: SPMC
Services: 1.0   2.0   6.4   9.5   9.6   9.7
Industries: D.27

Sonia Charif Associates
30 Fifth Ave.
New York, New York 10011
(212)982-0820

Application of human relations expertise in consultation and direct services. Special emphasis on employment of minorities and women, cultural influences, corporate social and community activities, quality of working life, health and mental health, human resources development, career planning and review systems, management and organizational development, retirement counseling, etc.

Contact: Sonia Charif, princ.
Areas Served: U.S.
Founded: 1964 *Staff:* 1-3 *Revenues:* under $100,000
Professional Affiliations: SPMC
Services: 1.0   1.6   1.14   1.15   3.0   4.2   4.9   4.12
Industries: Most

Charles River Associates Inc.
200 Clarendon St.
Boston, Massachusetts 02116
(617)266-0500

Innovative economics research and consulting services to private and public decision makers and policy makers. Work combines thorough topical knowledge with advanced analytical techniques. Staff includes engineers, psychologists, programmers, statisticians, planners, and mathematicians as well as economists. Principal research areas are transportation, energy, urban and regional development, commodity markets, environment, industrial organization and regulation.

Contact: Gerald Kraft, pres.
Areas Served: worldwide
Founded: 1965 *Staff:* over 100 *Revenues:* $5-$10 million
Professional Affiliations: /TRB, NABE, TIMS, ORSA, AEA, NASCP
Services: 1.2   1.6   2.10   2.17   3.10   5.10   7.0   10.1
Industries: A.09   B.10   B.11   B.12   B.13   D.29   D.33   D.34   D.37   E.00

Cicco & Associates, Inc.
Box A
Murrysville, Pennsylvania 15668
(412)325-4600

A network of on-call specialists ready with practical problem-solving abilities for small and medium-sized organizations.

Contact: John A. Cicco, Jr., pres.
Areas Served: U.S.
Founded: 1976 *Staff:* 1-3 *Revenues:* under $100,000
Services: Most
Industries: Most

Cleveland Consulting Associates
25550 Chagrin Blvd.
Beachwood, Ohio 44122
(216)831-0430

A results-oriented firm. Services cover the interface between a company and its customers - marketing and physical distribution. Action orientation requires a tempered mix of objectivity and mutual involvement. Problems never approached with preconceived solutions. Client personnel always involved in consulting assignments.

Contact: James C. Spira, dir.
Affiliates/branches: Lansing, Michigan
Founded: 1974 *Staff:* 10-25 *Revenues:* $1-$5 million
Services: 1.0   2.0   4.0   6.4

CMI Investment Corp.
700 Bishop St.
Honolulu, Hawaii 96813
(808)531-4189

Despite name, generalists ... plus legal staff and real estate department. Diversified staff has aided hundreds of companies.

Contact: Ronald R. Rewald, pres.
Areas Served: Hawaii, Mid-West, West Coast, Far East
Founded: 1965 *Staff:* 10-25 *Revenues:* $100-$500,000

Professional Affiliations: AMC/AIC
Services: 1.4 1.11 2.10 3.3 3.8 3.11 4.2 5.6
Industries: I.73 I.97

Coffay, Marshall Associates, Inc.
5313 St. Albans Way
Baltimore, Maryland 21212
(301)752-0783
> Dedicated to: 1) assist management in developing up-dated points of view about its future plans and objectives, 2) extend the capabilities of managers, 3) help in motivating organizations to achieve planned goals, 4) select and apply technical expertise. Capable. Objective. Unbiased.

Contact: Clyde T. Marshall, CMC, chmn.
Areas Served: U.S.
Founded: 1959 *Staff:* 1-3 *Revenues:* under $100,000
Professional Affiliations: AMC, IMC
Services: Most 1.0 3.0 4.0 5.0 9.0 9.6
Industries: Most D.27 D.28 E.42 E.48

Colarelli Associates, Inc.
7751 Carondelet Ave.
St. Louis, Missouri 63105
(314)721-1860
> Organizational psychologists providing a wide range of management and organizational devepment services. The firm emphasizes: a systems approach; assisting in analysis and implementation; and "shirtsleeve" involvement with the client. Clients include business, industrial, professional, governmental, religious, and educational organizations.

Contact: Nick J. Colarelli, pres.
Areas Served: U.S.
Founded: 1975 *Staff:* 1-3 *Revenues:* $100-$500,000
Services: 1.1 1.2 1.3 1.6 1.7 1.9 1.10 1.15 3.0
Industries: Most

Cole, Warren & Long Inc.
2 Penn Ctr Plaza
Philadelphia, Pennsylvania 19102
(215)563-0701
> Nationwide general management and executive search consulting studies for all size companies. We specialize in dealing with presidential and board of directors concerns involving general business directions.

Contact: Richard B. Warren, pres.
Areas Served: U.S.
Founded: 1971 *Staff:* 10-25 *Revenues:* $500,000-1 million
Professional Affiliations: IMC/ACA
Services: 1.1 1.3 1.6 1.7 3.2 3.7 4.9 4.11 9.4 11.1
Industries: Most

Cole & Associates
(subsidiary of The Wyatt Co.)
100 Summer St.
Boston, Massachusetts 02110
(617)542-7191

General management consulting firm serving clients (industrial, financial, and governmental) throughout the U.S. Specialize in organization planning, executive compensation, salary administration, personnel consulting, and bank financial consulting. Also (through Cole Surveys, Inc.) comprehensive annual compensation studies and quarterly financial studies, primarily for financial institutions.

Contact: Don Sagolla, exec. vp.

Areas Served: U.S.

Founded: 1956 *Staff:* 25-50 *Revenues:* $1-$5 million

Professional Affiliations: IMC

Services: 1.0   3.0   5.9   9.1

Industries: D.39   E.49   H.60   H.63   H.67   J.94   J.95

Coleman Consulting Inc.

6301 Castle Dr.

Oakland, California 94611

(415)482-4669

Organization structuring-financial planning- security funds- inventory control- product prospect analysis & potentials- sales distribution planning & control- evaluating research programs- arranging sales & mergers.

Contact: Ira J. Coleman, pres.

Areas Served: CA

Founded: 1948 *Staff:* 1-3 *Revenues:* $100-$500,000

Professional Affiliations: AMC, IMC

Services: 1.1   1.6   3.2   4.1   5.3   5.4   6.4   7.1   10.3

Industries: A.01   D.23   F.50   F.51   G.53   G.56   H.65

Thomas Collier & Associates

10889 Wilshire Blvd.

Los Angeles, California 90024

(213)477-5515

International consulting services for companies seeking to market their products, technology, and know how by establishing overseas sales and distribution channels, or manufacturing under patent licenses, joint ventures or subsidiary operations. Mr. Collier is a former founder, president and chief executive officer of Motorola Int'l. Corp. Company has served 150 clients.

Contact: Thomas P. Collier, pres.

Areas Served: worldwide

Founded: 1964 *Staff:* 3-10 *Revenues:* $500,000-1 million

Services: 1.3   1.6   1.7   2.10   4.1   4.2   10.0   10.3

Industries: D.36   D.37

Communication Innovation, Inc.

2919 Sydney St.

Jacksonville, Florida 32205

(904)388-9927

Offering small-firm flexibility, we provide specialized and technical research; market research; analysis; short-term hands-on management of projects, assets, and companies; and a fundamental approach to management consulting in formulating and implementing realistic and practical results-oriented problem-solving alternatives for new, developing, and established organizations.

Contact: William S. Batchelder, pres.

Areas Served: Primarily east of Mississippi & Intermountain
Founded: 1970 *Staff:* 1-3 *Revenues:* $100-$500,000
Services: Most
Industries: Most

Compass Management Group, Inc.
1200-112th Ave., NE
Bellevue, Washington 98004
(206)454-8328

Consulting services to federal, state and local governments and health insurance organizations. Areas of speciality: law and justice, data processing, health claims processing, Medicare, Medicaid, welfare systems, higher education, public schools.

Contact: Roger J. Collier, pres.
Areas Served: U.S.
Founded: 1973 *Staff:* 10-25 *Revenues:* $500,000-1 million
Services: 1.1   1.5   1.7   1.8   1.9   1.12   1.15   7.3   9.3   9.5
Industries: H.63   I.82   I.83   J.00   J.91   J.92   J.94   J.95

Computer-Based Business Systems, Inc.
1105 Main St.
Menomonie, Wisconsin 54751
(715)235-9116

Fully automated production & inventory control systems: forecasting, planning, production and purchase ordering, capacity planning, machine loading & scheduling, inventory control.Automated systems for generating process routings and time standards. Management information systems. Results-oriented, but sensitive to the organization, communication, and people-participation aspects of successful systems.

Contact: William Hoffman, pres.
Areas Served: worldwide
Founded: 1969 *Staff:* 1-3 *Revenues:* under $100,000
Professional Affiliations: AMC
Services: 1.0   2.0   6.0   9.0
Industries: A.07   D.25   D.26   D.27   D.35   D.36   D.38   D.39

Concepts & Systems, Inc.
Box 9616
Greensboro, North Carolina 27408
(919)379-1596

We are consultants who help decision-makers and their teams to do a better job in the areas of managing accountability and responding to change. Our work is dedicated to surveying, identifying, and solving problems to increase productivity and improve quality of working life.

Contact: Samuel W. Earle, pres.
Areas Served: U.S. & Canada
Founded: 1970 *Staff:* 3-10 *Revenues:* $100-$500,000
Services: 1.0   2.0   3.0   4.14   5.0   6.0   7.0   9.0
Industries: Most

The Concord Consulting Group
191 Sudbury Rd.
Concord, Massachusetts 01742
(617)369-8744

Staffed only by senior management consultants with extensive background in high technology areas. Assignments with Fortune 500, small and new venture clients throughout the US. Typical projects: growth & strategic planning; organization development; merger & acquisition analyses; executive search; customer image studies; marketing research; incentive programs; new venture analyses; marketing audits.

Contact: Michael J. Lydon, prin.
Areas Served: U.S.
Founded: 1976 *Staff:* 3-10 *Revenues:* $100-$500,000
Services: 1.0   2.6   3.0   4.0   11.1
Industries: Most

Consultants International Ltd.
1139 E. Knapp St.
Milwaukee, Wisconsin 53202
(414)271-6555

All assignments are directed by consultants with firsthand experience of day-to-day business pressures, who have been responsible for profit for their previous employers or companies, and can differentiate between academic theory and practical application. No juniors or trainees are employed. Foreign offices are staffed by nationals of those countries.

Contact: Leslie M. Anderson, pres.
Affiliates/branches: Columbia; Venezuela; Brazil; England; France; Hong Kong; Canada; Switzerland; Italy; Greece; Lebanon; Africa; Australia; Mexico
Areas Served: worldwide
Founded: 1970 *Staff:* 3-10 *Revenues:* $100-$500,000
Professional Affiliations: AMC, IMC
Services: Most
Industries: Most

Frederic W. Cook & Co., Inc.
90 Park Ave.
New York, New York 10016
(212)986-6330

Our primary objective is to assist our clients in the design and operation of their employee compensation programs so that they better enhance and complement management's strategic goals and style. Our assignments often result in the implementation of new or revised plans, particularly plans designed to effectively motivate and reward senior executives.

Contact: Frederic W. Cook, pres.
Areas Served: U.S., Canada, Europe & Japan
Founded: 1973 *Staff:* 3-10 *Revenues:* $500,000-1 million
Services: 3.2   3.7   3.8
Industries: Most

Coopers & Lybrand
(Management Consulting Services)
1900 Three Girard Plaza
Philadelphia, Pennsylvania 19102
(215)569-2000

Coopers & Lybrand's Consulting Group operates as a single, national unit. Ours is a broad-based practice, active in multiple facets of consulting and not confined to any one. Our service philosophy is to assist clients in the implementation of recommendations and not merely in the provision of those recommendations.

Contact: Gary Mozenter, grp. mng. ptnr. MAS

Affiliates/branches: 100 Equitable Bldg., Atlanta, Georgia 30303; 100 Federal St., Boston, Massachusetts 02110; 222 S. Riverside Plaza, Chicago, Illinois 60606; 100 East Broad St., Columbus, Ohio 43215; 5000 First Int'l Bldg., Dallas, Texas 75270; 2500 Anaconda Twr., Denver, Colorado 80202; 400 Renaissance Ctr., Detroit, Michigan 48243; 1010 Jefferson, Houston, Texas 77002; 1000 W. 6th St., Los Angeles, California 90017; 101 S. 5th St., Louisville, Kentucky 40202; 2900 First Federal Bldg., Miami, Florida 33131; 1251 Ave. of the Americas, New York, New York 10020; 1 Busch St., San Francisco, California 94104; 4700 First Nat'l Bank Bldg., Seattle, Washington 98154; 1800 M St., NW, Washington, D.C. 20036; Apartado Postal 24-348 Mexico 7, D.F. Mexico; 500 Chancery Hall Edmonton, Alberta T5J 2C3 Canada; 630 Dorchester Blvd. W. Montreal, Quebec H3B 1W6 Canada; 99 Bank St. Ottawa, Ontario K1P 6B9 Canada; PO Box 1029 Quebec, Quebec G1R 4V3 Canada; 145 King St. W Toronto, Ontario M5H 1V8 Canada; 2 Shepphard Ave. E. Willowdale, Ontario M2N 5Y7 Canada; PO Box 11128 Royal Ctr. Vancouver, B.C. V6E 3R2 Canada; Argentina; Australia; Austria; Bahamas; Bangladesh; Barbados; Belgium; Belize; Bermuda; Botswana; Brazil; Brunei; Channel Islands; Chile; Columbia; Costa Rica; Cyprus; Denmark; Dominica; Dominican Republic; Ecuador; Egypt; El Salvador; Fiji; Finland; France; Germany; Ghana; Grand Cayman; Greece; Grenada; Guatemala; Hong Kong; Iceland; India; Indonesia; Iran; Italy; Ivory Coast Republic; Jamaica; Japan; Kenya; Korea; Kuwait; Lebanon; Liberia; Luxemborg; Malawi; Malyasia; Malta G.C.; Mauritus; Netherlands; New Caledonia; New Hebrides; New Zealand; Nicaragua; Nigeria; Northern Ireland; Norway; Oman; Pakistan; Panama; Papua New Guinea; Paraguay; Peru; The Philippines; Portugal; Puerto Rico; Republic of Ireland; Republic of Korea; Republic of South Africa; Rhodesia; St. Lucia; St. Vincent; Saudi Arabia; Singapore; Spain; Sudan; Sultanate of Oman; Swaiziland; Sweden; Switzerland; Taiwan; Tanzania; Trinidad & Tobago; Turks & Caicos Islands; Uganda; United Arab Emirates; United Kingdom

Areas Served: worldwide

Founded: 1898 *Staff:* over 100 *Revenues:* over $10 million

Professional Affiliations: IMC

Services: Most

Industries: most

Guy Cornman
610 Hilltop Dr.
Lexington, North Carolina 27292
(704)246-4902

Our prime purpose is to increase the long term profitability of our clients. This must necessarily include operations beneficial to client employees on a long term basis. Operation of our firm adheres strictly to the letter and spirit of rules and regulations issued by the Institute of Management Consultants.

Contact: Guy L. Cornman, Jr., CMC

Areas Served: East Coast

Founded: 1974 *Staff:* 1-3 *Revenues:* under $100,000

Professional Affiliations: IMC/AAA

Services: Most

Industries: Most

The Corporate Director Inc.
222 E. 39th St.
New York, New York 10016
(212)682-4889

Counselors to boards of directors on role and organization of the board.
Conduct board audits and director search. Conduct board and management
seminars emphasizing "What Management Is" and the unit president concept.

Contact: J. Keith Louden, pres.
Areas Served: worldwide
Founded: 1970 *Staff:* 1-3 *Revenues:* $100-$500,000
Services: 1.0   1.1   1.2   1.3   1.7   1.11   3.1   3.2   3.5   5.3   5.4
Industries: A.00   D.00   E.45   F.00   G.00   I.00   J.00

Cotman Consultants Inc.
4365 Hamilton Rd.
Medina, Ohio 44256
(216)723-1730

Consultants to manufacturing management. Senior staff experienced in all
phases of operating management and control. Heavily implementation-
oriented, with many years of operating experience.

Contact: C. Roger Cotman, pres.
Areas Served: U.S.
Founded: 1976 *Staff:* 3-10 *Revenues:* $100-$500,000
Services: 1.0   2.0   3.0   5.0   6.0   9.5
Industries: D.23   D.25   D.26   D.30   D.33   D.34   D.35   D.37   D.38   D.39

Coughlin, Elkes & Senensieb, Inc.
1801 Century Park E.
Los Angeles, California 90067
(213)277-2600

To counsel top and middle management on: 1.) effective management of
information systems and data processing organizations and resources (including
planning of computer applications and equipment, project management, and
computer security): 2.) general management effectiveness (including organization structure analysis, operational audits, systems and procedures, and office
automation); 3.) systems training for managerial personnel.

Contact: N. Louis Senensieb, pres.
Areas Served: CA & other western states
Founded: 1979 *Staff:* 3-10 *Revenues:* $100-$500,000
Professional Affiliations: IMC/ASM, DPMA
Services: 1.0   2.5   3.1   3.5   5.8   9.0
Industries: Most

Coxe Associates, Inc.
1900 Chesnut Bldg.
Philadelphia, Pennsylvania 19103
(215)561-2020

Counseling design professionals on matters of practice management, we operate
as a collaboration of professionals with education and background in
behavioral science, organization management, financial management, marketing, architecture and computer applications. We have served more than 275
clients in architecture, engineering, planning, construction, and real estate
development located in 40 of the United States and Europe.

Contact: Weld Coxe, pres.
Areas Served: U.S. & Europe
Founded: 1967 *Staff:* 3-10 *Revenues:* $100-$500,000
Services: 1.1   1.6   3.1   4.11   5.9
Industries: I.73

CPS Management Co.
4007 Old Poste Rd.
Columbus, Ohio 43220
(614)876-2151

We are an operating management company that also offers certain related consulting services on as-needed basis to small businesses, primarily in connection with general management, personnel, and marketing problems. We recognize small business's frequent need for pragmatic, financially-feasible, and workable solutions right now, recommending others when in-depth longer term consultation appears advisable.

Contact: Paul B. Nelson, Jr., mng. ptnr.
Areas Served: OH & adjoining states
Founded: 1978 *Staff:* 1-3 *Revenues:* under $100,000
Services: 1.0   3.0   4.0
Industries: D.00   G.00   I.00

Craig/Cutten & Wollman, Inc.
414 Pendleton Way
Oakland, California 94621
(415)632-9313

An individualized appraoch is basic. Although there are similarities in all enterprises, there is no predetermined program for universal solution to fit all situations. Each assignment presents a fresh set of conditions which is analyzed, evaluated, and formulated into programs for improved performance.

Contact: Homer T. Craig, pres.
Areas Served: CA & NV
Founded: 1953 *Staff:* 1-3 *Revenues:* $100-$500,000
Professional Affiliations: IMC
Services: 1.0   3.0   5.0   9.5

Cresap, McCormick & Paget, Inc.
245 Park Ave.
New York, New York 10017
(212)958-7000

General management consulting firm specializing in strategy, human resources, and management processes. Serve top management of public and private institutions worldwide. Specific functional skills include long-range planning, marketing, diversification, executive compensation, facilities planning, management audits, cost reduction, productivity and operations improvement, and management of data processing.

Contact: George M. Whitmore, mng. dir.
Affiliates/branches: 1776 K St., NW, Washington, D.C. 20006; 100 W. Monroe St., Chicago, Illinois 60603; 650 California St., San Francisco, California 94108; London; Sao Paulo; Melbourne
Areas Served: worldwide
Founded: 1946 *Staff:* over 100 *Revenues:* $5-$10 million
Professional Affiliations: ACME, IMC

Services: Most
Industries: Most

Cresheim Co., Inc.

1408 E. Mermaid La.
Philadelphia, Pennsylvania 19118
(215)836-1400

An independent, private corporation controlled by the members of its professional staff, the company's main objective is to help client organizations improve their effectiveness.

Contact: James E. Barrett, pres.
Areas Served: North America, Europe & Latin America
Founded: 1968 *Staff:* 10-25 *Revenues:* $500,000-1 million
Professional Affiliations: IMC
Services: 1.1   1.3   3.1   4.0   6.3   7.2   9.5   10.2   11.0   11.1
Industries: D.26   D.28   D.29   D.34   D.36   E.47   E.48   F.50   H.63   J.96

Crickenberger Associates

Box 8082
Roanoke, Virginia 24014
(703)989-9526

Union-avoidance consulting. Se]vices to management of non-union companies include: counteracting union organization attempts; winning NLRB elections (last loss in 1966); preventive employee relations; periodic employee relations audits; plant-site searches for non-union operations; writing of employee handbooks; and executive searches for plant managers, employee relations managers, union avoidance managers, and employee communicators.

Contact: Harold P. Crickenberger, pres.
Areas Served: South, East & Midwest US
Founded: 1973 *Staff:* 1-3 *Revenues:* under $100,000
Services: 3.0   11.2
Industries: D.25   D.34   D.35   D.36   D.37   D.38   E.00   E.48   G.53   H.00

The Croner Company

700 Larkspur Landing
Larkspur, California 94939
(415)461-6655

Counsel to top management on business tactics; organization planning; compensation design; human resources consulting.

Contact: Mel Croner, pres.
Areas Served: CA
Founded: 1978 *Staff:* 3-10 *Revenues:* $100-$500,000
Professional Affiliations: IMC
Services: 1.1   1.3   1.4   1.6   1.7   3.2   3.7   3.8
Industries: C.15   D.24   D.36   D.38   E.42   G.54   H.60   H.65   H.67

Dailey Consultants & Co.

10140 Louise Ave.
Northridge, California 91325
(213)886-2873

A general management consulting firm providing services to both industrial and governmental clients. Major areas of emphasis are data processing, manage-

ment information systems, management planning and control, finance and accounting, organizational development and operational effectiveness.
Contact: Leonard Dailey, pres.
Areas Served: CA & Western U.S.
Founded: 1973 *Staff:* 1-3 *Revenues:* under $100,000
Professional Affiliations: IMC
Services: 1.1   1.7   1.8   1.9   1.10   2.1   2.2   5.4   9.3   9.5
Industries: D.20   D.26   D.34   D.36   E.43   E.45   F.50   H.60   I.78   J.92

Dallmeyer & Co., Inc.
20 N. Wacker Dr.
Chicago, Illinois 60606
(312)782-0773
General management consultants to business entities. Emphasize marketing & sales management, corporate & division strategy, organization planning, and management information systems, as well as interrelationships of these functions. Staff all gained extensive experience in consulting prior to association here. Clientele includes companies of all sizes.
Contact: Rudolph Dallmeyer, pres.
Areas Served: worldwide
Founded: 1977 *Staff:* 3-10 *Revenues:* $100-$500,000
Professional Affiliations: IMC
Services: Most   1.0   4.0
Industries: Most

R. Danner, Inc.
1660 S. Albion
Denver, Colorado 80222
(303)758-2566
Dealing at board level with top management in areas of strategic planning, organization, and financial planning.
Contact: Robert E. Danner, pres.
Areas Served: West/Southwest U.S. & Canada
Founded: 1961 *Staff:* 3-10 *Revenues:* $100-$500,000
Professional Affiliations: IMC
Services: 1.0   1.1   5.0
Industries: Most

Data Sciences, Inc.
1600 One Indiana Sq.
Indianapolis, Indiana 46204
(317)632-3916
An independent information-processing consulting firm providing technical assistance to senior management for improving the effectiveness and efficiency of information-processing efforts. Serve several state and local governments and a diverse group of provate sector corporations.
Contact: Alan C. Stanford, pres.
Areas Served: U.S.-primarily Midwest
Founded: 1973 *Staff:* 3-10 *Revenues:* $500,000-1 million
Professional Affiliations: /ACM, SMIS
Services: 1.3   1.8   2.5   5.8   9.3   9.7   9.8
Industries: D.00   D.26   D.34   E.48   F.50   H.63   I.80   I.86   J.91   J.92

Data Systems Consultants
S 820 McClellan St.
Spokane, Washington 99204
(509)747-0020

> Data-processing operation audits (controls, security, backup, etc.); feasibility studies, equipment selection, procedure analysis, systems design, programming supervision, documentation, control; project supervision/implementation; related areas.

Contact: Earl H. Martinson, owner
Areas Served: worldwide
Founded: 1967 *Staff:* 1-3 *Revenues:* under $100,000
Professional Affiliations: IMC
Services: 1.9   2.2   9.1   9.2   9.3   9.4   9.5   9.6   9.7
Industries: A.01   D.39   E.49

Datamatics Management Services, Inc.
140 Route 9W
Englewood Cliffs, New Jersey 07632
(201)947-6100

> Dedicated to ensuring that client organizations realize optimum returns from computer technology. Continuing with Fortune 500 clients and smaller growth businesses from data processing audits thru implementation of mini-computers. Representative projects include systems planning, systems design, facilities management, and staff appraisal and development. Successes achieved in a cross-section of industries.

Contact: Norman C. Heinle, Jr., pres.
Affiliates/branches: Washington, D.C.
Areas Served: worldwide
Founded: 1966 *Staff:* 10-25 *Revenues:* $500,000-1 million
Professional Affiliations: AMC/DPMA, AAA
Services: 1.7   1.8   1.13   2.15   3.1   3.4   9.3   9.4   9.5   9.8
Industries: Most

Jack R. Dauner & Associates
Box 1828
Pinehurst, North Carolina 28374
(919)295-3208

> Marketing and management consultants with specific emphasis on organization development, sales training, customer and employee attitude surveys, marketing research programs and manpower planning, recruitment and selection.
> Frequent planners, developers and participants on 1-3 seminars programmed specifically for client needs.

Contact: Jack R. Dauner, pres.
Areas Served: U.S.
Founded: 1964 *Staff:* 1-3 *Revenues:* under $100,000
Professional Affiliations: /AMA
Services: 1.1   3.1   3.10   4.3   4.4   4.7   4.9   4.10   4.15
Industries: Most

James W. Davidson Co., Inc.
415 Madison Ave.
New York, New York 10017
(212)752-1470

Experienced, senior-level management consultants. Strategy testing and development; organization and management improvement; profit improvement/turnarounds; management controls and business planning requirements, systems, implementation. Executive search to recruit top-notch talent. Over 80% of assignments are with existing clients.

Contact: James W. Davidson, pres.

Areas Served: worldwide

Founded: 1973 *Staff:* 1-3 *Revenues:* $100-$500,000

Services: 1.0   1.1   1.2   1.3   1.9   1.10   1.11   3.4   5.4   7.2

Industries: B.00   D.00   D.20   D.33   D.34   D.35   D.36   I.00   I.73   I.79

Herbert W. Davis & Co.
120 Charlotte Place
Englewood Cliffs, New Jersey 07632
(201)871-1760

Specialized services in marketing, physical distribution and the application of modern computer and operations research techniques to business problems. Our principals have completed over 300 client engagements.

Contact: Herbert W. Davis, pres.

Areas Served: U.S. & Canada

Founded: 1974 *Staff:* 3-10 *Revenues:* $100-$500,000

Professional Affiliations: ACME

Services: 2.2   2.10   2.11   2.12   2.13   2.16   2.17   4.12   4.14   9.0

Industries: Most

Dawcon
310 Tara Trail NW
Atlanta, Georgia 30327
(404)255-6212

Management advisory services in the field of assurance technologies (quality assurance from the initial design concepts, design assurance, production quality assurance, and after delivery support). Also services in program management for a total quality program including the identification of records to be established and then their retention schedule.

Contact: David A. Webster, owner

Areas Served: U.S.

Founded: 1976 *Staff:* 1-3 *Revenues:* under $100,000

Services: 2.7

Industries: Most   D.37

Day & Zimmermann, Inc.
(Consulting Services Div.)
1818 Market St.
Philadelphia, Pennsylvania 19103
(215)299-8461

A broad gauge professional consulting firm with staff capability extending from highly personalized executive counsel to large multi-discipline projects. Especially strong in services for industrials, railroads, mass transit, utilities and public administration. Adhere to ACME code of ethics. Experience throughout US and in essentially all international areas.

Contact: Frederick D. Brown, pres. cons. div.

Affiliates/branches: 60 E. 42nd St., New York, New York 10017; 230 N. Michigan Ave., Chicago, Illinois 60601; 1701 K St., NW, Washington, D.C. 20006; 15 Court St.,

Buffalo, New York 14202
Areas Served: worldwide
Founded: 1901 *Staff:* over 100 *Revenues:* over $10 million
Professional Affiliations: ACME
Services: 1.0   2.0   3.2   3.7   4.0   5.3   5.10   6.1   9.0
Industries: D.00   E.40   E.41   G.00   H.60   H.63   I.80   I.86   J.91   J.96

Decision Sciences Corporation

528 Fox Pavillion
Jenkintown, Pennsylvania 19046
(215)887-1970

We provide senior level skilled professional teams with extensive practical experience & training in the management and decision sciences to work with top level company & divisional executives to identify, analyse, solve—and most important, successfully implement—solutions to complex strategic & tactical problems. We deal with the entire decision process & leave our client with a full understanding of the process as well as the solution.

Contact: Donald F. Blumberg, pres.
Areas Served: U.S., Canada, Europe & Asia
Founded: 1969 *Staff:* 25-50 *Revenues:* $1-$5 million
Services: 1.0   2.0   4.0   5.0   6.0   9.0   10.0
Industries: D.00   E.00   J.00

Decision Studies Group

(division of Science Management Corp.)
1120 Conn. Ave., NW
Washington, D.C. 20036
(202)293-5700

Washington-based firm with nationwide staff of professionals providing services to private industry and Federal, state, and local governments in human resources management (including occupational alcohol/drug abuse prevention programs), organizational and management systems analysis, workload audits, productivity measurement and improvement, econometric forecasting, sample survey data collection and analysis, marketing research, and employee utilization programs.

Contact: Billy K. Farris
Affiliates/branches: Moorestown, New Jersey
Areas Served: U.S.
Founded: 1963 *Staff:* 10-25 *Revenues:* $1-$5 million
Professional Affiliations: IMC
Services: 1.0   3.0   4.0   7.2   9.0
Industries: J.91   J.94

Frederick C. Decker Co., Inc.

Counsel House
Brookfield, Connecticut 06805
(203)775-2508

Magazine publishing specialists. Profit building through advertising sales development, marketing planning, circulation strategy, cost control, internal management. New publication feasibility analysis, personnel recruiting, acquisition evaluation.

Contact: Frederick C. Decker, pres.
Areas Served: worldwide

Founded: 1972 *Staff:* 1-3 *Revenues:* $100-$500,000
Services: Most

Curt Deckert Associates, Inc.
18061 Darmel Place
Santa Ana, California 92705
(714)639-0746

Our work is usually related to R & D, ranging from strategic decision-making to tactical problem-solving and of a technological bent.

Contact: Curt X. Deckert
Areas Served: Western U.S.
Founded: 1976 *Staff:* 1-3 *Revenues:* under $100,000
Professional Affiliations: /ASA, SPIE
Services: 1.1   1.3   1.5   1.8   1.12   4.1   4.2   4.10   7.0
Industries: D.00

John deElorza Associates
1640 Vauxhall Rd.
Union, New Jersey 07083
(201)686-5511

Management and financial consulting firm specializing in corporate development, venture capital guidance and financial public relations. Among services provided are general management, feasibility studies, mergers and acquisitions, organization and business planning.

Contact: John deElorza
Founded: 1965 *Staff:* 3-10 *Revenues:* $100-$500,000
Professional Affiliations: IMC
Services: 1.0   2.0   3.0   4.0   5.0   6.0   7.4   9.0   11.1
Industries: D.22   D.34   F.00   G.00   H.60   H.65   I.00   J.00

Irving A. Delloff
5-18 Essex Place
Fair Lawn, New Jersey 07410
(201)796-1534

Our staff has had extensive experience with productivity improvement programs, work measurement and incentive programs, industrial relations, supervisory and management training and development programs. Our clients, in the public as well as the private sector, include hospitals, public utilities, manufacturing, pharmacueticals, newspapers, employers and professional associations.

Areas Served: NY & NJ
Founded: 1957 *Staff:* 3-10 *Revenues:* under $100,000
Professional Affiliations: IMC
Services: 1.0   1.10   2.0   2.3   2.6   2.9   2.14   3.0
Industries: D.31   D.33   D.34   E.43   I.81   I.82

Deloitte Haskins & Sells
(Management Advisory Services)
1114 Ave. of the Americas
New York, New York 10036
(212)790-0500

Our management advisory service is offered along with auditing, tax and other

separate identified parts of our practice to assist organizations to develop more
effective and viable operations through improved controls and other management techniques. Our concern normally is with the organization, planning,
performance measuring, accounting and reporting aspects of the various
management functions.

Contact: Leonard Pace, nat'l. mas coord.

Affiliates/branches: 35 Broad St., NW, Atlanta, Georgia 30303; 28 State St., Boston,
Massachusetts 02109; 2100 S. Nat'l. Ctr., Charlotte, North Carolina 28202; 200 E.
Randolph Dr., Chicago, Illinois 60601; 1 E. Fourth St., Cincinnati, Ohio 45202; 155
E. Broad St., Columbus, Ohio 43215; 1 Main Place, Dallas, Texas 75250; 633 17th
St., Denver, Colorado 80202; 100 Renaissance Ctr., Detroit, Michigan 48243; 745
Fort St., Honolulu, Hawaii 96813; 1200 Travis, Houston, Texas 77002; Box 60205,
Los Angeles, California 60250; 1 SE Third Ave., Miami, Florida 33131; 1950 IDS
Twr., Minneapolis, Minnesota 55402; 550 Broad St., Newark, New Jersey 07102;
2500 Three Girard Plaza, Philadephia, Pennsylvania 19102; 1010 Standard Plaza,
Portland, Oregon 97204; 10 Broadway, St. Louis, Missouri 63102; Kearns Bldg., Salt
Lake City, Utah 84101; 44 Montgomery St., San Francisco, California 94104; GPO
Box 4748, San Juan, Puerto Rico 00936; 1001 Fourth Ave., Seattle, Washington
98154; 1101 Fifteenth St., NW, Washington, D.C. 20005

Areas Served: worldwide

Founded: 1895 *Staff:* over 100 *Revenues:* over $10 million

Professional Affiliations: /AICPA

Services: Most

Industries: Most

Delta Group, Inc.

369 San Miguel Dr.
Newport Beach, California 92660
(714)640-5430

Specialized services for small and large corporations and public and private
institutions or a retained hourly fee basis: corporate and business planning;
executive search and selection; executive financial planning; compensation
management; employee communication; merger, acquisition and divestiture.

Contact: Frederick M. Linton

Areas Served: Southern CA

Founded: 1974 *Staff:* 3-10 *Revenues:* $100-$500,000

Services: 1.0   3.0   4.0   5.3   5.9

Industries: Most   D.29   D.39   F.50   H.63   H.64   H.66   I.72   I.73   I.82

Denmark Donovan & Oppel Inc.

45 Rockefeller Plaza
New York, New York 10020
(212)586-6757

Evaluation and recommendation of communities and sites for manufacturing,
distribution, office & R&D facilities. Determine relative merits of existing
locations compared with advantages of establishing satellite units or trans-
ferring facilities to new sites. Detailed studies of economic, social, political and
quality of life factors relating to locations. Consultants to communities for
design of area economic development programs.

Contact: Bernhardt Denmark, chmn.

Areas Served: U.S.

Founded: 1978 *Staff:* 3-10 *Revenues:* $100-$500,000

Services: 2.10   2.12   2.13   11.0

Industries: D.00   F.00   H.63   H.67   J.96

Alfred B. DePasse & Associates
10 E. 39th St.
New York, New York 10016
(212)725-2186

We serve industrial firms, financial institutions and service organizations. The primary focus of our business is marketing and strategic planning. We provide a broad range of marketing services and assist our clients on organization planning and executive search.

Contact: Alfred B. DePasse, pres.
Areas Served: U.S.
Founded: 1970 *Staff:* 1-3 *Revenues:* $100-$500,000
Professional Affiliations: IMC
Services: 1.0 3.1 3.4 3.10 4.0
Industries: Most

Derrick & Associates, Inc.
2815 E. Skelly Dr.
Tulsa, Oklahoma 74105
(918)749-6471

Full time senior level staff members, all have prior executive experience in business and industry. Capabilities include executive and middle management search and all areas of manufacturing, finance, marketing and employee relations. Strong dedication to the improvement of client's profitability in all assignments.

Contact: Michael J. Derrick, vp.
Areas Served: U.S.
Founded: 1971 *Staff:* 10-25 *Revenues:* $1-$5 million
Services: 1.0 2.0 3.0 4.0 5.0 6.0 9.3 9.5 9.6 11.1
Industries: B.13 D.00 G.00 H.60 I.70 J.93 J.94

Dexter-Kranick & Associates
Box 480
Milwaukee, Wisconsin 53201
(414)671-3636

International and domestic consulting service; economic analysis and long range planning; market and product surveys and analysis, mergers and acquisitions; manufacturing methods and systems; organization structure and development programs; interim management service.

Contact: Lewis G. Kranick, princ. owner
Areas Served: worldwide
Founded: 1966 *Staff:* 1-3 *Revenues:* under $100,000
Professional Affiliations: AMC
Services: 1.0 2.0 7.0 10.0
Industries: D.24 D.27 D.30 D.35 D.36

Dickson Associates
Box 1005
Neenah, Wisconsin 54956
(414)725-8237

General management consulting for small to medium sized employers in business, industry, education and local government. Emphasis on positive, simple solutions to achieve desired results.

Contact: James B. Dickson, pres.

Areas Served: Midwest
Founded: 1965 *Staff:* 1-3 *Revenues:* under $100,000
Professional Affiliations: AMC, IMC
Services: 1.0   3.0   4.1   4.15   11.1
Industries: D.00   H.00   I.00   J.91

Dielman Consultants, Inc.
Box 525
Palos Heights, Illinois 60463
(312)448-0162
> Management advisors to the health care industry; technical advisors in medical imaging and bio assay.

Contact: Ray Dielman, CMC, pres.
Areas Served: U.S.
Founded: 1967 *Staff:* 1-3 *Revenues:* $100-$500,000
Professional Affiliations: IMC, AMC
Services: 1.0   2.0   4.0   5.0   6.0   7.0   9.0
Industries: D.00   D.28   D.36   D.38   I.00   I.80

D. Dietrich Associates, Inc.
Box 511
Phoenixville, Pennsylvania 19460
(215)935-1563
> Personnel management consulting to the consulting engineering, architectural and design-construct professions. Publish numerous compensation and benefit surveys of engineering and scientific personnel. Surveys cover design engineering firms, industrials, utilities, management consultants and research & development firms. Emphasis on design and implementation of salary administration programs.

Contact: J. Douglas Dietrich, pres.
Areas Served: U.S. & Canada
Founded: 1973 *Staff:* 3-10 *Revenues:* $100-$500,000
Services: 1.1   1.4   3.1   3.2   3.4   3.6   3.7   3.8   3.10   11.0
Industries: K.00

Distribution Projects, Inc.
2 N. Riverside Plaza
Chicago, Illinois 60606
(312)454-0331
> As former operations managers and executives and as management consultants we are experts in the day to day operations requirements and priorities of our specialized recruiting, planning and program implementation activities.

Contact: R.F. Lehner, exec. vp.
Areas Served: U.S.
Founded: 1976 *Staff:* 3-10 *Revenues:* $100-$500,000
Professional Affiliations: /NCPDM
Services: 1.8   2.16   2.17   4.14   9.3
Industries: Most

Donovan, Zappala & Associates, Inc.
Box 629
Andover, Massachusetts 01810
(617)475-2882

We assist manufacturing clients in planning and implementing programs necessary to achieve objectives for growth, turnaround, profit improvement, service improvement, and inventory reduction. Employing only career consultants with manufacturing management experience, we work at all levels of client management to improve resources—organizational, human, systems, computers, facilities and methods.

Contact: Fred S. Zappala, pres.
Areas Served: U.S., Canada & Europe
Founded: 1973 *Staff:* 3-10 *Revenues:* $100-$500,000
Services: 1.0 2.0 3.0 4.0 5.0 6.0 7.2 8.1 9.0 10.0
Industries: C.15 D.00 E.00 F.50 H.65 H.66 I.73 I.76 I.80

Donworth, Taylor & Co.

1004 Norton Bldg.
Seattle, Washington 98104
(206)622-9840

Our services are focused on the entire personnel management process. We are a well-balanced team of results-oriented professionals with expertise in organization development, labor relations, affirmative action, training, compensation, recruiting, and employee communications.

Contact: William H. Taylor
Areas Served: Pacific Northwest & Alaska
Founded: 1955 *Staff:* 10-25 *Revenues:* $500,000-1 million
Services: 3.0 3.1 3.2 3.3 3.4 3.5 3.7 3.8 3.9 3.10

Thomas Dowdell/Associates

7349 Via Lorado
Rancho Palos Verdes, California 90274
(213)377-2339

Engineering & marketing consultants in the fields of cryogenic equipment and industrial gases; liquefied natural gas projects; nuclear power plant gaseous emissions; and alternate energy sources. Help clients sell their products, find new products and services, evaluate markets, develop competitive information.

Contact: T. Dowdell, pres.
Areas Served: worldwide
Founded: 1976 *Staff:* 1-3 *Revenues:* under $100,000
Professional Affiliations: /SNAME, MANA, CSA, AGA, AWS
Services: 4.0 4.1 4.2 4.4 4.5 4.7 4.8 4.9 4.12 4.16
Industries: D.00 D.29 D.33 D.34 I.76

Drake Sheahan/Stewart Dougall Inc.

330 Madison Ave.
New York, New York 10017
(212)697-0294

Consulting services in integrated logistics (materials management, manufacturing services, customer service, physical distribution) and marketing, together with implementation of recommendations.

Contact: Joel C. Wolff, pres.
Affiliates/branches: 5725 E. River Rd., Chicago, Illinois 60631
Areas Served: worldwide
Founded: 1945 *Staff:* 25-50 *Revenues:* $1-$5 million
Professional Affiliations: ACME, IMC
Services: 1.0 2.0 3.5 4.0 6.0 8.1 9.4 9.5
Industries: Most

Drake-Beam & Associates Inc.
277 Park Ave.
New York, New York 10017
(212)888-2800

A broad-based human resource management consulting firm which specializes in the application of behavioral sciences to the solution of "people challenges" in business. We assist over 600 corporations, and are proud to list 17 out of the top 25 Fortune 500 Corporations as clients. They have first had knowledge of our ability to maximize the use of human resources to impact profits.

Contact: William S. Swan, vp. mktg.

Affiliates/branches: 1011 E. Touhy Ave., Des Plaines, Illinois 60018; 16630 Imperial Valley Dr., Houston, Texas 77060; 3420 Bristol St., Costa Mesa, California 92626; Washington, D.C.; Paris

Areas Served: U.S. & Europe

Founded: 1967 *Staff:* 25-50 *Revenues:* $1-$5 million

Professional Affiliations: /ASTD, APGA, APA

Services: 3.0   3.1   3.2   3.5   3.9   3.10   3.11

Industries: A.00   B.00   D.00   E.00   F.00   G.00   H.00   I.00   J.00

Murray Dropkin & Co.
390 George St.
New Brunswick, New Jersey 08901
(201)828-3211

Basically involved in working with non-profit and governmental agencies, performing a variety of services ranging from auditing to comprehensive training in accounting and management. Our clients are carefully evaluated to determine the "real" problem, then a custom-designed solution is delivered and implemented. We believe implementation is key to a successful engagement in this area.

Contact: Murray Dropkin, ptnr.

Areas Served: Northeast & Midwest

Founded: 1974 *Staff:* 3-10 *Revenues:* $100-$500,000

Professional Affiliations: /AICPA, MFOA

Services: 1.0   3.9   4.0   5.0   6.4   7.2   9.0

Industries: I.72   I.73   I.80   I.81   I.82   I.83   I.86   J.91   J.93   J.94

Dickey Dyer Management Consultants
107 Carter Rd.
Princeton, New Jersey 08540
(609)896-1745

Counsel on the whole range of ways and means for increasing return on assets employed and capital invested, with particular emphasis on marketing and marketing support activities. Clients are principally distributors (and Wholesalers) to industry furnishing merchandise characterized as "hard goods" (75%)—and their merchandise supplying firms (10%)—and their services supplying firms such as computer hardware manufacturers and software purveyors (10%)—and their trade associations (5%).

Contact: Dickey Dyer, princ.

Areas Served: U.S., Canada, British Isles, Australia and New Zealand

Founded: 1957 *Staff:* 1-3 *Revenues:* $100-$500,000

Services: 1.6   1.10   2.3   2.6   3.2   4.1   6.3   6.4   9.1   9.3

Industries: D.26   D.34   D.35   D.36   D.38   F.50   I.80   I.83   J.94   J.95

Economics Research Associates

(A Planning Research Co.)
10960 Wilshire Blvd.
Los Angeles, California 90024
(213)477-9585

Wide range of service in economics, finance, marketing, palnning, organization, design implementation and operations. Principal areas of expertise are: recreation, real estate and services to government agencies. Serve corporate, government and institutional clients in both the public and private sector.

Contact: Christopher Lee, dir. corp. dev.

Affiliates/branches: 680 Beach St., San Francisco, California 94109; 7616 LBJ Freeway, Chicago, Illinois 75240; 1100 Jorie Blvd., Chicago, Illinois 60521; 255 S. Orange Ave., Orlando, Florida 32801; 334 Boylston St., Boston, Massachusetts 02116; 7798 Old Springhouse Rd., Washington, D.C. 22101

Areas Served: worldwide

Founded: 1958 *Staff:* over 100 *Revenues:* $5-$10 million

Services: 1.0   2.0   3.0   4.0   5.0   6.0   7.0   9.0   10.0

Industries: A.00   D.00   E.00   G.00   H.00   I.00   J.00

Edgar, Dunn & Conover Inc.

100 California St.
San Francisco, California 94111
(415)433-2236

General management consulting services to senior management in both the private and public sector. Our primary job is to help our clients improve their performance. Thus, each assignment is tailor-made to meet a specific client need. We take a stand on what actions should be taken and emphasize the implementation of our recommendations.

Contact: James M. Edgar, ptnr.

Areas Served: U.S. & Int'l.

Founded: 1978 *Staff:* 10-25 *Revenues:* $500,000-1 million

Professional Affiliations: IMC/AICPA, FEI, ACG

Services: 1.1   1.3   1.6   1.8   1.10   1.11   2.1   4.1   5.9   6.4

Industries: D.20   D.34   E.44   E.45   G.53   H.60   H.61   H.63   I.70   J.91

George D. Edwards & Co., Inc.

20 Exchange Place
New York, New York 10005
(212)344-7450

Specializing in matters of concern to the top management of commercial banks and other financial institutions and to the financial management function of corporations. Work with client personnel to develop recommendations for solving major problems and to implement these recommendations effectively.

Contact: George D. Edwards, princ.

Areas Served: worldwide

Founded: 1971 *Staff:* 1-3 *Revenues:* $100-$500,000

Professional Affiliations: IMC

Services: Most

Industries: H.60

The Emerson Consultants, Inc.

30 Rockefeller Plaza
New York, New York 10020
(212)245-5738

A general management consulting firm whose clients are industrial, transportation and public utility corporations, and some government agencies. Projects focus on increasing client profits through better utilization of assets: personnel, management skills, materials, facilities and capitol. Commited to achieving tangible, measurable results for clients by assisting them to implement and prove out recommendations.

Contact: Dana Devereux, pres.
Affiliates/branches: 44 Montgomery St., San Francisco, California 94111
Areas Served: North & South America, Europe & Middle East
Founded: 1899 *Staff:* 25-50 *Revenues:* $1-$5 million
Professional Affiliations: ACME, IMC
Services: 1.0 2.0 6.3 6.4 6.5

Employee Relations Consultants, Inc.

6800 France Ave. S.
Minneapolis, Minnesota 55435
(612)927-9795

Specializing in advising and assisting the management of client firms in the areas of general management, administration, organizational development, personnel management, labor relations, and employee relations—with a broad range of experience and skills in meeting specific needs of clients in business, industry, service organizations, educational institutions, and government.

Contact: Dean V. Dannewitz, pres.
Areas Served: U.S.
Founded: 1972 *Staff:* 1-3 *Revenues:* $100-$500,000
Professional Affiliations: AMC/ASPA, APA, ACA
Services: 1.0 3.0 4.7 4.9 4.15 7.2 9.1 9.5 9.6
Industries: A.00 C.00 D.00 E.00 G.00 H.00 I.00 J.00

Equity Services Corporation

300 W. Wiecua Rd. 100
Atlanta, Georgia 30342
(404)255-4178

Broad range of consulting services to equity participants in the hospitality industry: hotels, clubs, restaurants, resorts, and food service operations; as well as to investors in the recreational aspects of planned unit development projects (PUD). We are a small group of senior consultants each with extensive operating experience.

Contact: Donald D. Woodworth, pres.
Areas Served: U.S. & Caribbean
Founded: 1968 *Staff:* 1-3 *Revenues:* $100-$500,000
Professional Affiliations: /IFSEA
Industries: G.58 H.65 I.70 I.79 I.86

Ernst & Whinney

(Management Advisory Services)
1300 Union Commerce Bldg.
Cleveland, Ohio 44115
(216)861-5000

International public accounting and management consulting firm. Management consultants since 1908. Provide wide range of consulting services in corporate planning and development; decision-oriented management information systems; organization, staffing and compensation; data systems; financial and management planning and control; operational systems; productivity improvement; cost control; management sciences; and marketing. Consulting staff numbers over 1000 specialists experienced in almost every industry: manufacturing; retailing; health care; banking; insurance; utilities, etc.

Contact: Thomas R. Testman, nat'l dir. MAS

Affiliates/branches: Akron; Albany; Albuquerque; Allentown; Anchorage; Atlanta; Austin; Baltimore; Baton Rouge; Birmingham; Boise; Boston; Buffalo; Canton; Century City; Charleston, SC; Charleston, WV; Charlotte; Chattanooga; Chicago; Cincinnati; Cleveland; Columbia; Columbus, GA; Columbus, OH; Corpus Christi; Dallas; Dayton; Denver; Des Moines; Detroit; El Paso; Erie; Ft. Lauderdale; Fort Wayne; Fort Worth; Fresno; Grand Rapids; Hackensack; Hamilton; Harrisburg; Hartford; Honolulu; Houston; Huntsville; Indianapolis; Jackson, MI; Jackson, MS; Jacksonville; Kalamazoo; Kansas City; Knoxville; Lansing; Laredo; Lexington; Little Rock; London; Long Island; Los Angeles; Louisville; Manchester; Marquette; Memphis; Miami; Milwaukee; Minneapolis; Mobile; Nashville; Newark; New Haven; New Orleans; New York; Norfolk; Oakland; Oklahoma City; Omaha; Orlando; Philadelphia; Phoenix; Pittsburgh; Port Huron; Newport Beach; Portland, ME; Portland, OR; Providence; Raleigh; Reading; Richmond; Roanoke; Rochester; Sacramento; Saginaw; St. Louis; St. Paul; Salt Lake City; San Antonio; San Diego; San Francisco; San Jose; San Juan; Santa Ana; Santo Domingo; Seattle; South Bend; Spokane; Springfield; Syracuse; Tacoma; Tampa; Terre Haute; Toledo; Trenton; Tucson; Washington; White Plains; Wichita; Winston-Salem; Youngstown; Greenville; Spartanburg

Areas Served: worldwide

Founded: 1903 *Staff:* over 100 *Revenues:* over $10 million

Professional Affiliations: IMC

Services: most

Industries: most

E & T Associates

Box 2763
Rolling Hills Estates, California 90274
(213)378-2562

One-man firm working with, rather than for clients. Absolutely no written reports—just tangible results.

Contact: Eric Teltscher, pres.

Areas Served: worldwide

Founded: 1961 *Staff:* 1-3 *Revenues:* under $100,000

Services: 2.1 2.3 2.4 2.6 2.8 2.9 2.10 2.11 2.13 2.14

Industries: D.22 D.23 D.25 D.26 D.30 D.31 D.34 D.39

Euramco Associates, Inc.

52 Exchange St.
Binghamton, New York 13901
(607)724-1900

Euramco provides professional consulting services in three different but related areas- management, architecture, and engineering. Parts of our managemen consulting services are often readily blended with our A/E services to provide an unusually comprehensive and effective solution for clients wanting to expand or relocate business operations.

Contact: Frank C. Petrulis, princ.

Areas Served: U.S., Canada, Europe & Mid-East

Founded: 1977 *Staff:* 3-10 *Revenues:* $100-$500,000

Professional Affiliations: IMC

Services: 1.0   2.4   2.10   4.0   9.2   9.3   9.8
Industries: C.00   D.00   F.50   F.51   G.00   H.00   I.00

Eurequip Consulting Group
4801 Woodway Dr.
Houston, Texas 77056
(713)871-9336
> Development of human and managerial effectiveness in technology transfers: preliminary survey, planning, control recruitment, training, organization, team-building, phasing-out of expatriates—mainly in oil, gas, nuclear, mines, agribusiness—also definition of technology transfer strategies.

Contact: Georges F. Hostache, pres.
Areas Served: worldwide
Founded: 1978 *Staff:* 3-10 *Revenues:* $100-$500,000
Services: 10.2   11.0   11.1
Industries: Most   A.00   B.00   D.00   D.28   D.29   E.00   I.00   J.00

William Exton, Jr. & Associates
40 Central Park S.
New York, New York 10019
(212)755-4486
> "We can only help you if you deal with people". Over thirty years helping managements achieve improved performance/behavior (productivity, quality, accuracy, effectiveness, coordination, etc.) of production/clerical employees, supervisors, staff/sales/professional personnel, executives, customers, etc.- through superior programs of error-reduction, motivation, communication, training/development, organizational up-grading, etc.

Contact: William Exton, Jr., princ.
Affiliates/branches: RFD, Dover Plains, New York 12522; London
Areas Served: Primarily northern hemisphere
Founded: 1948 *Staff:* 1-3 *Revenues:* under $100,000
Professional Affiliations: IMC, SPMC
Services: 1.0   2.0   3.0   4.0   5.8   6.4   9.0   11.0
Industries: Most

Fairbanks Associates, Inc.
509 Madison Ave.
New York, New York 10022
(212)755-5616
> Specializing in the organization, promotion, administrative, personnel, and data processing requirements of: direct marketing firms; trade, professional & fraternal associations; periodical & book publishers; book & record clubs.

Contact: Gerald S. Murphy, vp.
Areas Served: U.S.
Founded: 1953 *Staff:* 3-10 *Revenues:* $100-$500,000
Professional Affiliations: IMC
Services: Most   1.1   1.5   1.8   2.12   3.8   4.4   5.2   9.1   9.2   9.3
Industries: I.86

Thomas A. Faulhaber
146 Mt. Vernon St.
Boston, Massachusetts 02108
(617)723-2030

Counsel to corporations in North America and Western Europe seeking acquisition of companies manufacturing industrial products; representation for divestitures; design and work with management in execution of corporate strategies for growth and change.

Contact: Thomas A. Faulhaber, CMC
Areas Served: worldwide
Founded: 1977 *Staff:* 1-3 *Revenues:* $100-$500,000
Professional Affiliations: IMC/NASCG, AIIE, NSPE
Services: 1.0 2.0 5.0
Industries: C.15 C.16 C.17 D.20 D.33 D.34 D.35 D.36 D.38 H.67

Mitchell Fein, Inc.

202 Saddlewood Dr.
Hillsdale, New Jersey 07642
(201)664-2055

Concentrate on developing ways of increasing productivity; primarily concerned with people problems that arise between employees and management to retard productivity. During past 35 years have developed various approaches to motivate employees to raise producticity. Have served over 400 companies in borad range of industries.

Contact: Mitchell Fein, CMC
Areas Served: worldwide
Founded: 1942 *Staff:* 1-3 *Revenues:* $100-$500,000
Professional Affiliations: IMC
Services: 1.10 2.0 3.7 3.8
Industries: Most

Fensterstock & Co.

625 N. Michigan Ave.
Chicago, Illinois 60611
(312)266-6456

Our basic objective is to assist clients identify, evaluate and implement business opportunities which result in additional profitable growth. We also assist clients analyze, select and execute optimum supporting financial strategies. Our activities thus integrate the business strategy developent expected from a management consultant with the financial implementation sought from an investment banker.

Contact: Lyle S. Fensterstock, pres.
Areas Served: U.S., Canada & Europe
Founded: 1978 *Staff:* 1-3 *Revenues:* $100-$500,000
Professional Affiliations: /ACG
Services: 1.2 1.3 1.4 1.5 1.6 5.3 5.8 5.9 5.10
Industries: A.07 D.20 D.21 D.27 D.28 E.48 G.53 G.54 G.58

Fenvessy Associates, Inc.

745 Fifth Ave.
New York, New York 10022
(212)751-3707

Broad range of services in the general area of administrative operations and mass paperwork handling. Work oriented :owards three principal objectives: cost reduction, service improvement and system simplification. Particular expertise in mail order, publishing, membership, fund raising, & literature, fulfillment. (Affiliate specializes in direct marketing counsel.)

Contact: Stanley J. Fenvessy, CMC, pres.

Affiliates/branches: 221 N. LaSalle St., Chicago, Illinois 60601
Areas Served: U.S.
Founded: 1966 *Staff:* 10-25 *Revenues:* $500,000-1 million
Professional Affiliations: ACME, IMC/DMMA
Services: 1.8   2.12   4.4   9.1   9.2   9.3   9.5   9.6   9.7
Industries: Most

Financial Concepts Inc.

9 Mercer Rd.
Natick, Massachusetts 01760
(617)655-6944

Specialists for financial-services industry (banks, s/l assns., credit unions). Turn-key construction of premises; project management; interior space planning/design; provide architectural; construction; or consultation.

Contact: Robert C. Rier, pres.
Areas Served: New England & Florida
Founded: 1972 *Staff:* 10-25 *Revenues:* $1-$5 million
Services: 1.3   1.4   1.5   4.1   4.11   6.1   6.3   9.2
Industries: C.15   H.60

First Risk Management Co.

835 Glenside Ave.
Wyncote, Pennsylvania 19095
(215)927-3404

Specialize solely in matters of risk and insurance management (working with insurance-buying firms; selling no insurance).

Contact: Leonard J. Silver, pres.
Affiliates/branches: San Juan, Puerto Rico
Areas Served: worldwide
Founded: 1962 *Staff:* 3-10 *Revenues:* $500,000-1 million
Professional Affiliations: /ICS
Services: 11.0
Industries: Most

Fogel & Associates, Inc.

130 E. 40th St.
New York, New York 10016
(212)686-6500

Consultants to the construction industry and related industries including owners, engineers, contractors, suppliers, and surety companies.

Contact: Irving M. Fogel, dir.
Affiliates/branches: 25 Mt. Auburn St., Cambridge, Massachusetts 10016; 1420 Walnut St., Philadelphia, Pennsylvania 19102; New Terminal Bldg./Airport, Detroit, Michigan 48213; 1400 N. Bristol St., Newport Beach, California 92660
Areas Served: worldwide
Founded: 1969 *Staff:* 25-50 *Revenues:* $1-$5 million
Professional Affiliations: /NSPE, PMI, AACE, ASCE
Services: 1.1   1.8   1.9   1.10   1.12   5.2   9.7
Industries: C.15   C.16   C.17   I.73

Folger & Co., Inc.
214 Lewis Wharf
Boston, Massachusetts 02110
(617)227-5900

General management consulting firm providing counsel and assistance to senior executives in planning, organizing and directing management of human, financial and physical resources in achieving corporate goals. Wide range of services to manufacturing, distribution and service organizations. Only experienced staff used under direct supervision of principals.

Contact: J. H. Folger
Areas Served: worldwide
Founded: 1970 *Staff:* 3-10 *Revenues:* $1-$5 million
Professional Affiliations: IMC
Services: 1.0   2.6   2.9   3.0   4.0   5.0   7.4
Industries: B.00   C.00   D.00

Foussard Associates
Box 6569
St. Paul, Minnesota 55106
12)772-2511

Hospital laundry/linen services only, including feasibility studies, design, construction, on-going management.

Contact: S. J. Carr, dir. cons. svcs.
Areas Served: U.S.
Founded: 1951 *Staff:* 10-25 *Revenues:* $500,000-1 million
Professional Affiliations: AMC/AHA
Services: 1.5
Industries: I.80

Fowler, Anthony & Company
20 Walnut St.
Wellesley Hills, Massachusetts 02181
(617)237-4201

Focus upon marketing, financial & general management consulting for small businesses. Specialty in mergers & acquisitions & high technology industries.

Contact: John A. Quagliaroli
Areas Served: U.S.-Mostly Northeast & CA.
Founded: 1976 *Staff:* 1-3 *Revenues:* under $100,000
Services: 1.6   1.8   4.0   5.6   5.10   9.3   11.1
Industries: Most

Elmer Fox, Westheimer & Co.
1660 Lincoln St.
Denver, Colorado 80264
(303)861-5555

As the 11th largest CPA firm is in the U.S., we strictly adhere to the AICPA and IMC cpdes of ethics. Our philosophy is to provide strategically oriented services in our industries and areas of expertise. All of our consulting personnel deal with management consulting on a full-time basis. Our policy is to offer a new service only after we have the expertise on board for at least one year.

Contact: Jack E. Blumenthal, nat. dir. cons. svcs.
Affiliates/branches: 101 N. 1st. Ave., Phoenix, Arizona 85003; 808 Home Fed. Twr., Tuscon, Arizona 85702; 5225 Business Ctr. Dr., Bakersfield, California 93309; 2455

West Shaw, Fresno, California 93711; 100 Oceangate, Long Beach, California
90802; 1880 Century Park E., Los Angeles, California 90067; 1698 Crocker Bank Pl.,
Los Angeles, California 90017; 1746 Broadway, Oakland, California 94612; 507
Union Bank Pl., Pasadena, California 91101; 6 El Dorado S., Stockton, California
95201; 15 S 7th St., Colorado Springs, Colorado 80901; 1660 Lincoln St., Denver,
Colorado 80264; 535 Grand Ave., Grand Junction, Colorado 81501; 1220 19th St.,
NW, Washington, D.C. 20036; 1666 Kennedy Causeway, Miami, Florida 33141;
3340 Peachtree Rd., NE, Atlanta, Georgia 30326; 707 Bank of Idaho Bldg., Boise,
Idaho 83702; 180 N. LaSalle St., Chicago, Illinois 60601; 35 Fountain Sq. Pl., Elgin,
Illinois 60120; 617 Second Ave., Dodge City, Kansas 67801; 228 W. Central, El
Dorado, Kansas 67042; 117 E. 13th St., Hays, Kansas 67601; 316 Main St., Russell,
Kansas 67665; 1500 1st Natl Bank Twr., Topeka, Kansas 66603; 800 4th Fin. Pl.,
Wichita, Kansas 67202; 140 Federal St., Boston, Massachusetts 02110; 300 Town
Ctr., Southfield, Michigan 48075; 1800 NW Fin. Ctr., Minneapolis, Minnesota
55101; 918 Commerce Twr., Kansas City, Missouri 64199; 720 Olive St., St. Louis,
Missouri 63101; 150 Landmark Bldg., Springfield, Missouri 65806; 115 N 10th St.,
Nebraska City, Nebraska 68401; 250 Plaza of the Americas, Omaha, Nebraska
68106; 810 Livestock Exch. Bldg., Omaha, Nebraska 68107; 300 S 4th St., Las Vegas,
Nevada 89101; 241 Ridge, Reno, Nevada 89505; 100 Hamilton Plaza, Paterson,
New Jersey 07505; 600 Plaza del Sol, Albuquerque, New Mexico 87125; 306 1st
Nat'l Bank Bldg., Artesia, New Mexico 88210; 300 W Arrington, Farmington, New
Mexico 87401; 600 N. Richardson, Roswell, New Mexico 88201; 1 North St.,
Hastings-on-Hudson, New York 10706; 91 N Franklin, Hempstead, New York
11550; 1211 Ave of the Americas, New York, New York 10036; 1300 E 9th St.,
Cleveland, Ohio 44114; 1 Williams Ctr., Tulsa, Oklahoma 74172; 1110 SE Alder St.,
Portland, Oregon 97214; 2200 LTV Tower, Dallas, Texas 75201; 1100 State Natl Pl.,
El Paso, Texas 79901; 1213 Hermann Dr., Houston, Texas 77004; 1 Marienfield
Place, Midland, Texas 79701; 3755 Washington Blvd., Ogden, Utah 84403; 1675 N.
200 W., Provo, Utah 84601; Beneficial Life Twr., Salt Lake City, Utah 84147; 133 E.
Midwest, Casper, Wyoming 82601
Areas Served: U.S., Canada, Mexico & Europe
Founded: 1918 *Staff:* 25-50 *Revenues:* $1-$5 million
Professional Affiliations: IMC/AICPA
Services: 1.5   1.7   1.8   1.10   5.1   5.2   5.3   5.8   6.4   9.5
Industries: B.13   C.15   D.34   D.35   E.47   H.60   H.63   I.80   I.81   J.93

Bertrand Frank Associates, Inc.

475 Fifth Ave.
New York, New York 10017
(212)685-4460

Marketing strategies; sales forecasting; organization structure development;
merchandising planning and implementation; multi-season planning; merchandising responsibility for manufacturing response; manufacturing plant
layout; work simplification; incentives; equipment feasibility studies; operator
and management training; systems; pre-production and production analysis
fashion-flo scheduling. Corporate turnarounds.

Contact: Bertrand Frank, pres.
Areas Served: U.S., Canada, Carribean & Europe
Founded: 1946 *Staff:* 10-25 *Revenues:* $500,000-1 million
Professional Affiliations: ACME, IMC
Services: 1.10   1.11   2.1   2.3   2.6   4.1   4.6   4.14   9.4   10.4
Industries: D.22   D.23   D.30   D.36   D.39

George E. Frankel & Associates
75 E. Wacker Dr.
Chicago, Illinois 60601
(312)332-7797

Financial, control, and general management counsel for the smaller company, generally on a continuing basis. Principal enrolled to practice before the I.R.S. and has had 40 years experience - 15 on medium C.P.A. staff, 10 as chief financial officer of mfg. corporation and 15 as independent management consultant.

Contact: George E. Frankel
Areas Served: Chicago metropolitan
Founded: 1962 *Staff:* 1-3 *Revenues:* under $100,000
Professional Affiliations: AMC
Services: 1.1 1.2 1.6 1.9 5.0 9.1 9.5

Freeman Associates
211 E. Carrillo St.
Santa Barbara, California 93101
(805)963-3853

We help clients—develop new business, market and product strategies; devise implementation plans to execute them successfully; recruit key individuals required by the new plans; segment markets and differentiate products; assess acquisition/investment candidates from a market point of view; and establish or upgrade their corporate identity.

Contact: Raymond C. Freeman, Jr., owner
Areas Served: U.S., Europe & Japan
Founded: 1977 *Staff:* 1-3 *Revenues:* under $100,000
Services: 1.2 1.3 1.5 4.1 4.2 4.5 4.16 10.4 11.1
Industries: D.35 D.36 D.38 D.39

Freeman, Penrose & Kajinura, Ltd.
745 Fort St.
Honolulu, Hawaii 96813
(808)524-5490

A professional firm providing financial planning and investment counseling services combined with realistic implementation planning provided by a group of individuals with professional training and applied business and investing experience. Services include financial planning reports, investment analysis, economic feasibility studies and tax impact analysis. Clients include individual professionals and executives as well as corporations.

Contact: R. Carter Freeman, Jr.
Areas Served: Hawaii & U.S. mainland
Founded: 1975 *Staff:* 3-10 *Revenues:* $500,000-1 million
Professional Affiliations: IMC/AICPA
Services: 1.1 1.3 1.5 1.7 1.11 5.1 5.3 5.6 5.9 5.11
Industries: I.70

R. L. French & Company, Inc.
1240 E. Irvington
South Bend, Indiana 46614
(219)234-3203

Specialist in productivity improvement for volume manufacturers of semi-durable consumer goods. Heavy emphasis on the development of manufacturing control systems, training line management for installation of the system and follow up to insure improved control, upgraded customer service, increased inventory turnover and lower operating costs.

Contact: Robert L. French, pres.
Areas Served: IN,OH,MI,IL
Founded: 1974 *Staff:* 1-3 *Revenues:* under $100,000
Professional Affiliations: SPMC
Services: 1.8 1.9 1.10 2.0 6.4 9.4
Industries: D.23 D.24 D.25 D.30 D.31 D.34 D.38 D.39

Walter Frederick Friedman & Co., Inc.

111 Northfield Ave.
West Orange, New Jersey 07052
(201)325-3700

Specialized in physical distribution management geared to helping managements prepare for long-range growth, decide on capital investments of distribution facilities and equipment, uncover profitable opportunities in the distribution function, and implement short- and long-range distribution plans. Services include diagnostic, planning and implementation programs.

Contact: Walter F. Friedman, pres.
Areas Served: U.S.
Founded: 1969 *Staff:* 10-25 *Revenues:* $100-$500,000
Professional Affiliations: ACME, IMC
Services: 1.0 2.0 3.1 3.5 4.12 4.14 6.4 8.1 8.4 9.5
Industries: D.00 E.42 E.47 F.50 F.51 G.00 I.80

Jack Frost & Associates

7 Springwood Dr.
Lawrenceville, New Jersey 08648
(609)896-0606

Experienced, professional consultants with in-depth background in industries served and services offered. Extensive background in conceiving, planning and implementing movement into new businesses through diversification programs and starting new companies. Practice covers small, medium and large companies in U.S., developed and developing countries outside U.S.

Contact: H. C. Frost, princ.
Areas Served: worldwide
Founded: 1971 *Staff:* 3-10 *Revenues:* $100-$500,000
Services: 1.0 2.0 3.4 4.0 6.0 7.0 9.0
Industries: A.07 D.20 D.28 D.38 G.54 G.58

Fry Consultants

(owned by Day & Zimmerman, Inc.)
60 East 42nd St.
New York, New York 10017
(212)986-1166

One of the oldest general management consulting firms in continuous services to management. As a member of Day & Zimmermann's Consulting Group, Fry's affiliation further broadens its scope of consulting services. The total professional staff of the parent firm is in excess of 500, with offices located throughout the United States.

Contact: John Rich
Areas Served: worldwide

Founded: 1942 *Staff:* 25-50 *Revenues:* $1-$5 million
Services: most
Industries: most

Fuchs Associates
30 Cabot Rd. W.
Massapequa, New York 11758
(516)799-0928
> Warehouse distribution, materials management, production planning and control, profit improvement programs, corporate turnarounds, financial controls, clerical work measurement, office systems and computerized data processing applications.

Contact: Jerome H. Fuchs, sr. ptnr.
Areas Served: Worldwide
Founded: 1960 *Staff:* 1-3 *Revenues:* $100-$500,000
Professional Affiliations: IMC, SPMC
Services: 1.0   2.0   5.0   6.0   9.0
Industries: B.00   C.00   D.00   F.00   H.00   I.00   I.80

Fuel & Energy Consultants, Inc.
(A Reliance Group Company)
1450 Broadway
New York, New York 10018
(212)730-1288
> Energy audits and energy management programs: development of corporate energy policies.

Contact: Harvey Morris, pres.
Areas Served: worldwide
Founded: 1966 *Staff:* 3-10 *Revenues:* $100-$500,000
Services: 11.12
Industries: Most

Gagnon & Associates
1006 City View Dr.
Minnetonka, Minnesota 55343
(612)544-4611
> Specialists ln productivity improvement, cost reduction programs and facilities planning, utilizing recognized industrial engineering techniques. Services equally distributed among warehousing, distribution, retail, manufacturing, health services and clerical. Excellent reputation as attested by former client referrals who have enjoyed benefits from systems installed which maximize existing manpower, materials, and equipment.

Contact: Gene Gagnon, pres.
Areas Served: U.S., Canada & Mexico
Founded: 1960 *Staff:* 3-10 *Revenues:* $100-$500,000
Professional Affiliations: AMC
Services: 1.0   1.5   1.10   2.0   6.0   6.4   9.0
Industries: Most

The Galaxy Organization
11 W. Jefferson St.
Phoenix, Arizona 85003
(602)254-5246

Independent management practitioner with diversified stable of associates. Perform overviews; create strategic plans, only in specific industries. Provide executive counsel where capable. Twenty years domiciled in the Pacific Southwest with a broad range of product service capabilities; plus real estate development and investment orientation.

Contact: James W. Soudriette
Areas Served: U.S., Europe & Asia
Founded: 1959 *Staff:* 1-3 *Revenues:* $100-$500,000
Professional Affiliations: AMC
Services: 1.0 3.0 3.1 4.0 5.0 6.4 7.2 7.3 7.4
Industries: D.00 F.00 G.00 H.65 H.67 I.72 J.94

The Galles Resource
7373 W. 147th St.
Apple Valley, Minnesota 55124
(612)432-4443

Evaluation, design and implementation of personnel systems and programs in both private and public sector organizations. Major emphasis on effectiveness of personnel techniques and practices as tools for cost reduction and employee productivity. Extensive experience as corporate executive, office holder, and consultant in industry, government and community organizations.

Contact: Glen F. Galles, pres.
Areas Served: U.S.
Founded: 1972 *Staff:* 1-3 *Revenues:* under $100,000
Professional Affiliations: AMC, IMC
Services: 1.1 1.7 3.1 3.2 3.4 3.5 3.6 3.7 3.8 3.9
Industries: Most

W. L. Ganong Co.
Box 2727
Chapel Hill, North Carolina 27514
(919)929-0421

We help healthcare and other human-service clients improve performance results in clinical, operational, and human resources management...hospital and nursing surveys...implementatio assistance...cost containment...staff development...labor relations...authors and publishers of HELP series of management guides (16 titles)...blending human/technical modes in management functions, techniques, skills.

Contact: Warren L. Ganong, pres.
Affiliates/branches: San Francisco
Areas Served: U.S. & Canada
Founded: 1956 *Staff:* 3-10 *Revenues:* $100-$500,000
Professional Affiliations: AMC, IMC/AHA, ASTD, NLN, ANA, CHA
Services: 1.0 3.0 9.0
Industries: I.80 I.82 J.94

Newell Garfield & Co., Inc.
310 Madison Ave.
New York, New York 10017
(212)697-2676

We specialize in development and implementation of programs and strategies designed to produce constructive change in the future of an enterprise, providing effective, non-captive staff to complement management during transitional periods. Client personnel are involved as much as possible to obtain optimal commitment to recommendations resulting from joint effort.

Contact: Newell Garfield
Areas Served: U.S.
Founded: 1978 *Staff:* 3-10 *Revenues:* $100-$500,000
Professional Affiliations: AMC, IMC
Services: 1.0 4.0
Industries: Most

Garr Associates, Inc.

2812 New Spring Rd.
Atlanta, Georgia 30339
(404)434-6494

Garr Associates, Inc., is an industrial engineering consulting firm offering technical knowledge, skills and experience in the design of physical distribution networks. In addition, the firm conducts work measurement programs and ancillary services for the retailing, manufacturing and wholesaling industries. The Garr Corporation is a management consulting firm offering a number of profit improvement programs which have been successfully applied to client operations throughout the U.S.

Contact: M. A. Garr, Jr., pres.
Areas Served: U.S. & Canada
Founded: 1961 *Staff:* 10-25 *Revenues:* $1-$5 million
Professional Affiliations: /MMT, NRMA
Services: 1.0 2.0 3.0 4.0 6.0 6.4 7.0 9.0 10.4
Industries: D.00 F.00 G.00

Gelb Consulting Group, Inc.

3701 Kirby Dr.
Houston, Texas 77098
(713)526-5711

Marketing and management consultants, specializing in the use of marketing research techniques to develop marketing and advertising strategy, to analyze the sales force and distribution channels, and to create more effective personnel and industrial relations.

Contact: Gabriel M. Gelb, pres.
Areas Served: U.S.
Founded: 1965 *Staff:* 3-10 *Revenues:* $100-$500,000
Professional Affiliations: IMC
Services: 1.5 3.9 3.10 4.1 4.2 4.5 4.7 4.11 4.12 4.13
Industries: B.12 B.13 D.28 D.29 E.41 E.49 G.55 H.60 H.61 I.80

Gemar Associates

74 Greenwich Ave.
Greenwich, Connecticut 06830
(203)869-6765

A deliberately small operations-oriented consulting group whose principals work on client projects. We help clients: correctly identify and solve problems; make decisions that improve profitability; develop short-term and long-range action plans and successfully implement them. We stress the joint (client/Gemar) effort approach.

Contact: R. J. Andersen, Jr., pres.
Areas Served: North America
Founded: 1945 *Staff:* 3-10 *Revenues:* $100-$500,000
Professional Affiliations: IMC
Services: 1.5   1.7   1.10   2.0   4.14   6.4   6.5   8.1
Industries: Most   D.00

Frank N. Giampietro Associates, Inc.
425 Broad Hollow Rd.
Melville, New York 11747
(561)293-4595

Food service industry only: master planning- feasibility studies- surveys-facilities design- interior layout planning- working drawings-specifications-coordination- construction supervision-equipment selection- operational supervision-contract food service analysis- site selection- lease evaluation & negotiation. GSA- 254 form on request. Projects: World Trade Center, Newark Int'l. Airport, hotels, hospitals, corporate facilities.

Contact: Frank N. Giampietro, pres.
Areas Served: worldwide
Founded: 1970 *Staff:* 3-10 *Revenues:* $100-$500,000
Professional Affiliations: SPMC/ISFSC
Services: 1.5   3.6   9.2   10.1
Industries: D.20   D.34   G.54   G.58   I.70   I.79

Gilbert Commonwealth
Box 1498
Reading, Pennsylvania 19603
(215)775-2600

Assist client management with a variety of diversified services. The technically oriented services produce results measured by increased profitability, successful project financing, and satisfactory solutions of government regulatory requirements.

Contact: Alexander Smith, pres.
Areas Served: worldwide
Founded: 1906 *Staff:* 50-100 *Revenues:* $1-$5 million
Services: 1.0   3.0   5.0   9.0
Industries: E.00   H.00   J.00

Michael R. Gingold Associates, Inc.
2096 St. Georges Ave.
Rahway, New Jersey 07065
(201)382-2244

Primarily engaged in real-estate related fields; site acquisition, planning, architecture, engineering, construction management, investment. Also provide general management for turnaround operations and acquisitions and mergers.

Contact: Michael R. Gingold, pres.
Affiliates/branches: San Diego, California
Areas Served: U.S., Central & South America
Founded: 1962 *Staff:* 3-10 *Revenues:* $500,000-1 million
Professional Affiliations: AMC/NAREB
Services: 1.0   1.5   1.6   5.0   5.6   10.0   10.1   10.2   10.3
Industries: C.00   C.15   H.00   H.65   H.67   I.00   I.73

Gladstone Associates
2030 M St., NW
Washington, D.C. 20036
(202)293-9000

Specializing in land use and real estate development analysis, urban and regional economics, and public policy evaluation. Work involves market and financial analysis for private companies, program design and management strategies for achieving objectives, and evaluation of government programs and management policies in housing, urban redevelopment, land use planning, and other related issues.

Contact: Gordon Kennedy, pres.
Affiliates/branches: 1401 Brickell Ave., Miami, Florida 33131; 438 Main Rd. E., Newport, Rhode Island 02840
Areas Served: worldwide
Founded: 1963 *Staff:* 50-100 *Revenues:* $1-$5 million
Services: 1.5 2.10 5.9 5.10 7.3
Industries: E.40 E.41 G.00 H.65 H.66 H.67 I.70 I.80 J.00

Glendinning Associates
1 Glendinning Place
Westport, Connecticut 06880
(203)226-4711

Generally recognized as the largest, most sophisticated marketing and sales consulting organization in the world. Best known for consulting projects with over 80 of "top 100" advertisers. We believe our business has prospered because we consistently define our objective as helping clients produce measurable and profitable results in the marketplace.

Contact: Stephen T. Heymann, pres.
Affiliates/branches: London; Paris
Areas Served: worldwide
Founded: 1960 *Staff:* 25-50 *Revenues:* over $10 million
Services: 1.3 1.6 4.0 4.1 4.2 4.3 4.5 4.9 4.10 7.0
Industries: D.00 E.00 F.00 G.00 G.53 G.54 G.58 H.00 H.60 I.00

GlennCo Services Inc.
1860 NW 42nd Terrace
Ft. Lauderdale, Florida 33313
(305)739-3927

Operations, general management, management of human resources, manufacturing, physical distribution, administration, Industrial engineering, information and control systems, feasibility studies, work measurement, compensation, organization, productivity, incentives.

Contact: Donald T. Glenn, Jr., pres.
Areas Served: worldwide
Founded: 1972 *Staff:* 1-3 *Revenues:* $100-$500,000
Professional Affiliations: IMC/AIIE
Services: Most
Industries: Most

Global Management Services, Inc.
Box 203
Lake Hamilton, Arkansas 71951
(501)525-8372

Established in 1974 to aid manufacturers develop -- and profit from -- the many stabilizing and growth elements of export. Before forming GMS the founder devoted 40 years to world trade and is recognized as a specialist in that area by competent arbitration groups here and abroad.

Contact: G. J. Pateneaux, chmn. & ceo

Areas Served: worldwide

Founded: 1974 *Staff:* 3-10 *Revenues:* $100-$500,000

Services: 1.0   3.0   4.0   5.0   6.0   6.4   9.0   10.0

Industries: D.00   D.20   D.22   D.28   D.30   D.34   D.35   D.36   D.37   F.00

Goggi Associates, Inc.
505 Thornall St.
Edison, New Jersey 08817
(201)494-3222

The true test of a consultant is not only how well he defines problems but how effectively he motivates clients to implement remedies. We have a proven record of over 35 years experience in responding to a client's needs and an unmatched reputation in the highly specialized and sensitive area of labor relations.

Contact: P. Paul Goggi, pres.

Founded: 1959 *Staff:* 3-10 *Revenues:* $100-$500,000

Professional Affiliations: IMC/AAA

Services: 1.0   2.0   3.0   11.1

Industries: Most   B.00   D.00   E.00   F.00   G.00   I.00   J.00

Golightly & Co. International, Inc.
(a division of Harbridge House)
1 Rockefeller Plaza
New York, New York 10020
(212)245-0900

General management consultants working on problems of concern to top management, including: organization planning, corporate planning; management information systems; executive recruitment; development, appraisal and compensation; marketing; growth planning; and many others. We provide each chief executive with plans to meet his special needs and assist in installing our recommendations.

Contact: Kenneth A. Meyers, pres.

Affiliates/branches: 2242 Sul Ross Ave., Houston, Texas 77098; London

Areas Served: worldwide

Founded: 1960 *Staff:* 10-25 *Revenues:* $1-$5 million

Professional Affiliations: ACME, IMC

Services: most

Industries: most

Gottfried Consultants Inc.
3435 Wilshire Blvd.
Los Angeles, California 90010
(213)387-2271

Assist successful companies and associations to more effectively utilize management and data processing resources. Major emphasis on consumer-oriented service industries including financial, healthcare, entertainment, retailing, and utilities. Employ only former industry executives with significant reputations in area of consulting specialities.

Contact: Ira S. Gottfried, pres.
Affiliates/branches: 44 Montgomery St., San Francisco, California 94104
Areas Served: Western U.S. & Canada
Founded: 1964 *Staff:* 10-25 *Revenues:* $1-$5 million
Professional Affiliations: ACME, IMC
Services: 1.1 1.3 1.7 1.8 2.5 3.1 9.3 9.5 9.8 11.0
Industries: Most D.33 E.42 E.48 E.49 G.53 H.69 I.78 I.80 I.86 J.91

Government Sales Consultants, Inc.
7023 Little Rover Tnpk.
Annadale, Virginia 22003
(703)354-4050
   Emphasis on procurement in the federal government. Also conduct seminars for
   government contracting officers and vendors.
Contact: Terry D. Miller, pres.
Affiliates/branches: Denver, Colorado
Areas Served: U.S.
Founded: 1973 *Staff:* 3-10 *Revenues:* $100-$500,000
Services: 6.0
Industries: J.00

Frank K. Griesinger & Associates, Inc.
815 Superior Ave.
Cleveland, Ohio 44114
(216)241-3228
   Specialize in teaching cost control and service improvement in the use of
   domestic and international telecommunications facilities. Author of two
   McGraw-Hill books, How To Cut Costs & Improve Service of Your Telephone,
   Telex, TWX and Other Telecommunications and Sales-Leasebacks and Leasing
   in Real Estate & Equipment Transactions. He wrote the entries of Telecom-
   munications and Leasing for the new McGraw-Hill Encyclopedia of Man-
   agement and for their Handbook of Modern Office Management Adminis-
   trative Services. He is currently writing a new book on equipment leasing for
   McGraw-Hill.
Contact: Frank Griesinger, pres.
Areas Served: worldwide
Founded: 1960 *Staff:* 1-3 *Revenues:* $100-$500,000
Services: 9.1 9.5 9.8 11.0
Industries: E.48

J. George Gross & Associates
608 Linden Ave.
Woodbridge, New Jersey 07095
(201)636-2666
   Consultants in distribution, material handling and warehousing. Specialists in
   the total design and implementation of new warehouses and plants and the
   redesign of old ones into integrated and improved operations: layout,
   equipment, methods and systems, inventory control, protective packaging,
   paper work procedures, organization, controls, and training.
Contact: J. George Gross, pres.
Areas Served: U.S., Canada & Europe
Founded: 1962 *Staff:* 3-10 *Revenues:* $100-$500,000
Professional Affiliations: SPMC/APMHC, NCPDM, SPHE, AIIE, IMMS

Services: 2.2   2.3   2.4   2.8   2.10   2.11   2.12   2.16   6.5   8.0
Industries: D.00   D.20   D.26   D.28   D.33   D.35   D.36   D.38   F.50   F.51

Group Arcon

800 Wilshire Blvd.
Los Angeles, California 90017
(213)680-4550

A professional consulting and architectural design firm, we merge three separate but closely related disciplines: operations consulting, industrial engineering and architecture.

Contact: Joseph W. Verwiel, exec. vp.
Areas Served: worldwide
Founded: 1976 *Staff:* 10-25 *Revenues:* $1-$5 million
Services: 1.5   2.3   2.4   2.8   2.11   2.13

Guenther Associates

52 Wildwood Ave.
Rumford, Rhode Island 02916
(401)434-4559

Serve small and medium-size companies with services essentially through the principal, augmented when required by qualified sophisticates in other disciplines. Long client associations attest to the success of this formula. Many years in corporate management, plus fifteen in consulting, provide mature capability in the areas defined.

Contact: Louis J. Guenther, pres.
Areas Served: worldwide
Founded: 1959 *Staff:* 1-3 *Revenues:* under $100,000
Professional Affiliations: AMC/AIIE, NSPE, IMMS
Services: 1.0   2.0   3.8   6.3   6.4   6.5   7.3   9.2   9.4
Industries: C.00   D.00   F.50   F.51   G.00   I.00   J.91   J.97

Alvin R. Haerr & Co.

6919 N. Knoxville Ave.
Peoria, Illinois 61614
(309)692-5520

Specialist in consulting with medium and smaller sized firms on a wide basis and in all areas. Major market studies of in-depth nature all size companies. Special expertise in training seminars for business owners and managers, which have been attended by over 25,000 businessmen. Also seminars on developing transition plans for the privately-held firm.

Contact: Alvin R. Haerr, pres.
Areas Served: U.S., Canada & Mexico
Founded: 1965 *Staff:* 1-3 *Revenues:* $100-$500,000
Services: 1.0   3.1   4.0   4.1   4.2   4.11   11.1
Industries: Most

Hales & Associates, Inc.

20 N. Wacker Dr.
Chicago, Illinois 60606
(312)782-7915

We specialize in corporate development activities emphasizing the financial, administrative and personnel aspects of insurance agencies, brokerages and

companies. Specifically, our concentration is on internal ownership perpetuation, mergers & acquisitions, appraisals of fair market value, compensation
studies, executive recruitment, product design and systems.

Contact: David Hales, pres.

Affiliates/branches: Cleveland

Areas Served: worldwide

Founded: 1972 *Staff:* 3-10 *Revenues:* $100-$500,000

Services: 1.0   3.1   3.2   4.0   5.0   9.3   9.4   9.5   10.0   11.1

Industries: H.63   H.64   I.73

S. E. Hall & Co.

1647 S. Hill Blvd.
Bloomfield Hills, Michigan 48013
(313)852-7234

Our management consultants assist and supplement management in the
effective use of resources lo clearly define problems, recognize opportunities,
and accomplish useful results. We value each client relationship and expect to
provide high quality professional services to each one on a long term basis.

Contact: Stephan E. Hall, pres.

Areas Served: U.S.

Founded: 1976 *Staff:* 1-3 *Revenues:* $100-$500,000

Professional Affiliations: IMC

Services: 1.1   1.3   1.4   1.8   1.10   1.12   5.1   9.3   9.5   9.7

Industries: D.26   D.37   D.39   G.53   H.60   H.61   I.73   I.80   I.89   J.92

Hans & Associates, Inc.

4229 N. 16th St.
Phoenix, Arizona 85016
(602)265-4200

Independent hospitality management consultants-specialists-total range of
services: 1) research and development, layout, design. Construction manage-
ment-coordination, property management, food and beverage troubleshooting,
marketing, financial reporting, feasibilities. 2) executive search, and 3) real
estate brokerage.

Contact: Hans R. Schacke, pres.

Areas Served: worldwide

Founded: 1969 *Staff:* 10-25 *Revenues:* $100-$500,000

Professional Affiliations: /AHMA

Services: Most   1.0   2.0   3.0   4.0   5.0   6.0   7.0   8.0   9.0   10.0

Industries: D.20   G.58   H.64   H.65   I.00   I.70   I.72   I.73   I.79

H. J. Hansen Co.

1550 Northwest Hwy.
Park Ridge, Illinois 60068
(312)824-6601

Organized to provide broad range of services to commerce, industry,
institutions and government: policy formation to implementation of recommendations. Skills of permanent staff combined with those of recognized
specialists to focus upon and respond to client needs with greater intensity.

Contact: H. Jack Hansen, CMC, pres.

Areas Served: U.S., Europe & South America

Founded: 1971 *Staff:* 3-10 *Revenues:* $100-$500,000

Professional Affiliations: IMC

Services: 1.0   2.0   3.0   4.14   5.0   6.0   7.0   9.0   10.0
Industries: D.00   E.00   F.50   G.53   H.60   I.73

A. S. Hansen, Inc.
1080 Green Bay Rd.
Lake Bluff, Illinois 60044
(312)234-3400

> A professional firm offering broad, but related, actuarial and consulting services in employee benefits and incentives, insurance company management, communications, and computer applications. We provide a source of continuous objective counsel, research and assistance to those with decision-making responsibility in these areas.

Contact: Larry M. Fisher, pres.
Affiliates/branches: 400 Colony Sq., Atlanta, Georgia 30361; 600 Atlantic Ave., Boston, Massachusetts 02210; 150 N. Wacker Dr., Chicago, Illinois 60606; Box 1995, Columbus, Georgia 31902; 200 First Int'l. Bldg., Dallas, Texas 75270; 717 Seventeenth St., Denver, Colorado 80202; 410 W. Seventh St., Fort Worth, Texas 76102; 711 Louisiana St., Houston, Texas 77002; 626 Wilshire Blvd., Los Angeles, California 90017; 165 Madison Ave., Memphis, Tennessee 38103; 700 N. Water St., Milwaukee, Wisconsin 53202; 2520 Fairlane Dr., Montgomery, Alabama 36116; 1 Shell Sq., New Orleans, Louisiana 70139; 529 Fifth Ave., New York, New York 10017; 555 California St., San Francisco, California 94104; 5401 W. Kennedy Blvd., Tampa, Florida 33609; 1 Williams Ctr., Tulsa, Oklahoma 74172; 2101 L. St., NW, Washington, D.C. 20037; 710 Fourth Financial Ctr., Wichita, Kansas 67202; 255 Ponce de Leon Ave., Hato Rey, Puerto Rico 00917; 304 The East Mall Islington, Ontario M9B 6E2 Canada; Melbourne; Brussels; London; Frankfurt; Hong Kong; Dublin; Johannesburg
Founded: 1930 *Staff:* over 100 *Revenues:* over $10 million
Professional Affiliations: ACME, IMC
Services: 1.1   3.2   3.6   3.7   3.8   3.9   4.15   10.0   11.0
Industries: Most

Harbridge House Inc.
11 Arlington St.
Boston, Massachusetts 02116
(617)267-6410

> A large international professional firm providing a range of services including socioeconomic research and analysis, management development, and systems training. Have served a variety of government agencies and clients in virtually every major industry in the United States, Europe, and Latin America. The range of functions in which services are provided include energy/environment/land use; human services/social systems; organization: planning and control; juridical services; marketing; materials management; executive/manpower development; project management; systems and data processing; and transportation.

Contact: Charles D. Baker, chmn.
Affiliates/branches: 222 S. Riverside Plaza, Chicago, Illinois 60606; 2875 Milwaukee Ave., Northbrook, Illinois 60062; 1515 Arapahoe St., Denver, Colorado 80202; 3949 Ann Arbor Dr., Houston, Texas 77063; 2101 L St., NW, Washington, D.C. 20037; London; Paris; Frankfurt
Areas Served: worldwide
Founded: 1950 *Staff:* over 100 *Revenues:* over $10 million
Services: Most
Industries: Most

Harley, Little Associates Inc.

920 Yonge St.
Toronto, Ontario M4W 3C7, Canada
(416)967-6900

Specialists in consulting to top management and planners of hotels, restaurants, recreation facilities, corporate feeding, camp and plant feeding, health care, education, military, corrections and transportation. We prepare market and feasibility studies for sites and concepts, financial studies, design and operate programs, layouts and contract documents, site supervision and operating advice.

Contact: James H. Little, pres.
Affiliates/branches: 3337 118th St. Edmonton, Alberta T6J 3J5 Canada
Areas Served: North America,Venezuala, Mid-East, Australia
Founded: 1957 *Staff:* 10-25 *Revenues:* $500,000-1 million
Professional Affiliations: /ISFSC, FFCS
Services: 1.0   3.0   4.0
Industries: I.70   I.79   I.80   I.82

E. G. Harper & Company, Inc.

222 Wisconsin Ave.
Lake Forest, Illinois 60045
(312)295-3191

Merger aquisitions and industrial marketing for industrial manufacturing clients. This includes related distributors and field service operations. Industry specializations: electronic/electrical, mechanical machinery and components, chemical, metallurgical and hydraulic/fluidic.

Contact: Ernest B. Harper, Jr., pres.
Areas Served: U.S.
Founded: 1971 *Staff:* 1-3 *Revenues:* under $100,000
Professional Affiliations: AMC/ACG, AMA
Services: 4.0
Industries: D.00   F.00   I.76

Harris, Kerr, Forster & Co.

(Management Advisory Services)
420 Lexington Ave.
New York, New York 10017
(212)867-8000

Our role can be short-term or long-term, depending on the client's requirements. A specific assignment is usually completed in four to six weeks ... but the client may want help in implementation. Often we are a continuing resource to management, throughout the lifetime of his entire business venture: from original concept through development and profitable operation and sometimes to eventual sale.

Contact: Eric Green, ptnr.
Founded: 1900 *Staff:* 25-50 *Revenues:* $1-$5 million
Professional Affiliations: /AICPA
Services: 1.0   4.0   5.0   9.0
Industries: I.70

Paul Harthorne Associates
23 Hedgerow
Falmouth, Maine 04105
(207)781-3724

Counsel to top management of United States and Latin American corporations, banks and government institutions on Latin America, on organization, costs and budgets, policy and objectives, labor relations, computer systems and procedures, planning, finance, investment budgets and profit improvement. Clients in banking, mining, petroleum, steel, metallurgy, aviation and construction and government. Active throughout Latin America.

Contact: Paul D. Harthorne, pres.
Affiliates/branches: Buenos Aires; Bogota; Caracas
Areas Served: Latin America
Founded: 1960 *Staff:* 10-25 *Revenues:* $100-$500,000
Services: 1.1   1.2   1.3   1.8   1.9   2.1   3.0   5.4   5.9   10.2
Industries: B.00   D.29   D.33   D.34   D.39   E.44   H.60

J. W. Haslett & Associates
12 McLaren Rd. S.
Darien, Connecticut 06820
(203)655-2204

General management services at all levels of small, medium and large companies. One major focus is on developing within a company its own inhouse capability for organizational and systems analysis and management training. Within a particular company's needs we: plan the establishment or extension of these functions; determine how and when plan should be put into effect; develop innovative programs and projects to be undertaken; train company employees to staff the functions; conduct appraisals of performance of the functions.

Contact: J. W. Haslett
Areas Served: U.S.
Founded: 1967 *Staff:* 1-3 *Revenues:* under $100,000
Professional Affiliations: SPMC/ASM
Services: 1.1   1.7   1.8   1.9   1.14   3.1   3.5   9.1   9.5
Industries: B.13   D.29   E.40   J.91   J.93

William M. Hawkins
6949 Fairway Rd.
La Jolla, California 92037
(714)459-7550

William M. Hawkins provides management consulting in sales and marketing of sophisticated electronic products and systems. His background is particularly well suited to provide assistance to the managers of growing, high technology companies in the San Diego area.

Contact: William M. Hawkins, princ.
Areas Served: CA
Founded: 1976 *Staff:* 1-3 *Revenues:* under $100,000
Services: 4.0   4.1   4.2   4.4   4.5   4.7   4.9   4.10   4.12
Industries: D.36   D.38

Hay Associates
229 S. 18th St.
Philadelphia, Pennsylvania 19103
(215)875-2300

International consulting to assist top management in all areas of human resource utilization including planning, business strategy and policy; organization design and development; selection, development and assessment of managers; motivation, compensation, incentives and total reward programs; pension planning through Hay-Huggins Division; actuarial services through Huggins & Co., affiliate.

Contact: Milton L. Rock, mng. ptnr.

Affiliates/branches: 1 E. Wacker Dr., Chicago, Illinois 60601; 2480 Pershing Rd., Kansas City, Missouri 64108; 4842 IDS Tower, Minneapolis, Minnesota 55402; 1100 17th St., NW, Washington, D.C. 20036; 1 Boston Place, Boston, Massachusetts 02108; 1 Dag Hammarskjold Plaza, New York, New York 10017; 3 Gateway Ctr., Pittsburgh, Pennsylvania 15222; 57 Executive Park S., NE, Atlanta, Georgia 30329; 12700 Park Ctr., Dallas, Texas 75251; 3435 Wilshire Blvd., Los Angeles, California 90010; 1 Maritime Plaza, San Francisco, California 94111; 1621 114th Ave., SE, Bellevue, Washington 98004; 55 University Ave. Toronto, Ontario M5J 2H7 Canada; 1 Place Ville Marie Montreal, Quebec, H3B 3M4 Canada; 700 Second St., SW Calgary, Alberta T2P 2W2 Canada; Box 49173/Bentall Ctr. Vancouver, B.C. V7X 1K8 Canada; Insurgentes Sur 1216-7 piso Mexico 12, DF Mexico; Avenida Pina Suzrez N. Monterrey, N.L. Mexico; Manchester; Edinburgh; Dublin; Helsinki; Paris; Lyon; Frankfurt; Dusseldorf; Milan; Utrecht; Madrid; Barcelona; Caracas

Founded: 1943 *Staff:* over 100 *Revenues:* over $10 million

Professional Affiliations: ACME, IMC

Services: 1.0 3.0 4.0 10.0 10.2 11.1

Industries: Most A.00 B.00 C.00 D.00 E.00 F.00 G.00 H.00 I.00 J.00

Robert H. Hayes & Associates, Inc.

(part of Hayes/Hill Consulting Group)
20 N. Wacker Dr.
Chicago, Illinois 60606
(312)984-5250

An international management consulting firm specializing in business strategy, marketing, acquisition evaluation, compensation, and organization for industrial and institutional clients. Emphasis on intensive fact-finding and analysis leading to pragmatic, action-oriente implementable solutions. High repeat client ratio. Experienced staff.

Contact: Robert H. Hayes, pres.

Affiliates/branches: Dallas; London; Belgium; Germany; France; Brazil

Areas Served: U.S., Europe, Far East & South America

Founded: 1963 *Staff:* 25-50 *Revenues:* $1-$5 million

Professional Affiliations: ACME, IMC

Services: Most 1.1 1.3 1.6 1.10 3.2 3.7 4.1 4.2 4.5 4.15

Industries: Most

Health-Care Management Services

111 Westport Plaza
St. Louis, Missouri 63141
(314)878-2590

Extensive experience at all levels of the health-care industry. MIS and HIS requirements development; financial and operational efficiency studies & EDP technical planning and implementation. Most consultants have advanced degrees in hospital administration, computer science, engineering or business with ten years' field experience.

Contact: Lawrence V. Covington, ptnr.

Areas Served: U.S.

Founded: 1973 *Staff:* 3-10 *Revenues:* $100-$500,000
Services: 1.1   1.3   1.5   1.8   5.3   5.8   5.9   9.7   9.8
Industries: D.36   I.73   I.80   I.83   J.91   J.93

Hendrick & Co., Inc.

395 Totten Pond Rd.
Waltham, Massachusetts 02154
(617)890-3310

> Organization structure: ratios of managers to workers; cost of managing each
> dollar of worker payroll; spans of control; levels of management; combinations
> of homogeneous activities; backstopping; performance; compensation differ-
> entials between managers. Productivity: functional costs, misplaced work, work
> of marginal value, fragmentation of payroll dollars.

Contact: Charles K. Rourke, pres.
Areas Served: worldwide
Founded: 1965 *Staff:* 3-10 *Revenues:* $1-$5 million
Services: 1.1   1.7   1.10
Industries: Most

Henning Associates, Inc.

Box 11300
Pittsburgh, Pennsylvania 15238
(412)784-1121

> We function as an integral part of your organization, although working for you
> on a temporary basis. While we work with your management team as peers, we
> maintain independence which provides an objective evaluation of performance
> against plans. Our approach is to work with you on specific programs that result
> in i?proved profits, improvement of cash flow, creased return on equity and
> increased net worth.

Contact: Edward I. Henning, pres.
Areas Served: U.S.-primarily PA, OH, NY
Founded: 1979 *Staff:* 1-3 *Revenues:* $100-$500,000
Services: Most   1.0   2.0   3.0   4.0   5.0   6.0   7.0   8.0   9.0   10.0
Industries: Most   D.00   E.47   F.50   G.53   H.60   I.72   I.73   J.91   J.94   J.95

Porter Henry & Co., Inc.

103 Park Ave
New York, New York 10017
(212)679-8835

> Perform whatever is required to make sales and marketing personnel more
> effective on the job: sales and sales management training, organization and
> management development; sales and sales training aids; sales control and sales
> management systems.

Contact: Warren Kurzrock, pres.
Areas Served: U.S.
Founded: 1945 *Staff:* 10-25 *Revenues:* $500,000-1 million
Services: 1.0   3.1   3.2   4.0   4.7   4.9   4.15
Industries: Most

Hickling-Johnston Ltd.

415 Yonge St.
Toronto, Ontario M5B 2E7, Canada
(416)964-9336

An independent employee-owned firm with over 500 public and private sector clients from coast to coast in Canada, as well as in the US, Europe and the Middle and Far East. Expertise spans and integrates the behavioral and management sciences.

Contact: D.V. Fowke, chmn.
Affiliates/branches: Montreal; Ottawa
Areas Served: Canada
Founded: 1965 *Staff:* 25-50 *Revenues:* $1-$5 million
Professional Affiliations: /CAMC
Services: Most
Industries: B.00 D.00 E.00 F.00 G.00 H.00 I.00 J.00

W. H. Higginbotham
7733 Forsyth Blvd.
St. Louis, Missouri 63105
(314)727-7184

General management consultant specializing in: management development training; employee opinion surveys; organization studies, personnel policies and procedures; performance appraisals; management employee communications; creative problem-solving seminars; compensation analysis; labor relations; educational training resources. Diversified clientele: large and small including general manufacturing and service industries, education, and banking.

Contact: W. H. Higginbotham, owner
Areas Served: worldwide
Founded: 1963 *Staff:* 1-3 *Revenues:* under $100,000
Professional Affiliations: AMC, IMC
Services: 1.1 1.2 1.7 3.0 9.1
Industries: Most

Duane L. Hile & Associates
14077 Cedar Rd.
Cleveland, Ohio 44118
(216)371-0353

Our primary objective is to provide management with the service necessary to extend its range of managability and achieve desired results. In support of this aim, we endeavor to: conduct thorough evaluations; develop practical, workable solutions; and provide implementation assistance, as required.

Contact: Duane L. Hile, dir.
Founded: 1978 *Staff:* 1-3 *Revenues:* under $100,000
Services: 1.6 2.2 2.16 4.0
Industries: D.00 E.49 F.50 F.51 G.52 G.55 I.75

William H. Hill Associates, Inc.
3100 University Blvd. S.
Jacksonville, Florida 32216
(904)721-8956

Financial management consulting, strategic planning, mergers & acquisitions. Executive search done in conjunction with assignments.

Contact: William H. Hill, pres.
Areas Served: Southeast
Founded: 1977 *Staff:* 1-3 *Revenues:* under $100,000
Services: 1.1 1.2 1.3 1.6 1.7 5.3 5.9 5.10
Industries: D.00 H.00 I.00

Nathaniel Hill & Associates, Inc.
4513 Creedmoore Rd.
Raleigh, North Carolina 27612
(919)787-6919

> Our staff is selected for high achievement and strong results in significant managerial skills—oriented to improving the productiveness of the total enterprise and/or its resources, with primary emphasis on human resources. Our hallmark is excellence of "transfer of ownership" of our work to middle management.

Contact: Nathaniel M. Hill, pres.
Affiliates/branches: 500 E. Morehead St., Charlotte, North Carolina 28202
Areas Served: Primarily South Atlantic
Founded: 1960 *Staff:* 10-25 *Revenues:* $500,000-1 million
Professional Affiliations: AMC, IMC
Services: 1.0   1.10   1.11   2.0   3.0   3.10   3.10   5.0   9.0   11.1
Industries: Most

William E. Hill & Co., Inc.
(part of Hayes/Hill Consulting Group)
640 Fifth Ave.
New York, New York 10019
(212)582-5959

> A general management consulting firm which assists senior management in making and carrying out decisions critical to corporate profitability and growth. Major service areas include: corporate planning and development; marketing; acquisitions, mergers & divestures; organization and compensation; and technology planning. Serve a wide variety of clients: industrial and consumer products companies, financial institutions, distribution and service organizations, utilities, government bodies and associations.

Contact: Gordon Canning, dir.
Affiliates/branches: 475 L'Enfant Plaza, Washington, D.C. 20024; Munich; London; Utrecht
Areas Served: North America, Europe & Latin America
Founded: 1953 *Staff:* 25-50 *Revenues:* $1-$5 million
Professional Affiliations: ACME/MSI, NASCP, ACG
Services: 1.0   3.0   4.0   5.3   7.0   7.2   7.3   10.0
Industries: Most

Charles L. Hoffman, Inc.
Box 11
Weatogue, Connecticut 06089
(203)658-0903

> Our philosophy is to remain very small in order to provide a broad-gauge, entrepreneurial focus. Our speciality is industrial/technical market research and assessment as well as optimizing marketing strategy and selling operations to industrial markets.

Contact: Charles L. Hoffman, princ.
Areas Served: U.S.
Founded: 1967 *Staff:* 1-3 *Revenues:* under $100,000
Professional Affiliations: /AMA
Services: 1.3   1.4   1.5   4.1   4.2   4.5   4.7   4.8   4.9   4.16
Industries: Most   D.30   D.33   D.34   D.35   D.36   D.38

William H. Hoffmann

900 Valley Rd.
Melrose Park, Pennsylvania 19126
(215)635-3385
> Particular strength in industrial product studies, including machinery, instrumentation, electronics, chemicals and raw materials. This is augmented by a considerable background in evaluating market opportunities for consumer appliances and other hard goods.

Contact: William H. Hoffmann, CMC
Areas Served: worldwide
Founded: 1970 *Staff:* 1-3 *Revenues:* under $100,000
Professional Affiliations: IMC
Services: 1.5 1.6 4.2 4.5 10.3 10.4
Industries: Most

Daniel D. Howard Associates, Inc.

307 N. Michigan Ave.
Chicago, Illinois 60601
(312)372-7041
> Consultants to management in the behavioral sciences.

Contact: Daniel D. Howard, pres.
Areas Served: U.S. & Europe
Founded: 1946 *Staff:* 10-25 *Revenues:* $500,000-1 million
Professional Affiliations: ACME
Services: 3.0 4.2 4.9
Industries: Most

Louis H. Howe & Associates, Inc.

Box 3051
Industry, California 91744
(714)492-3651
> We are business & financial management counselors—operations oriented —helping all levels of management: to more effectively manage & control; to raise levels of performance & communications via improved planning, organization development, determining financial requirements & resources by establishing master information & management control systems (with or without computers).

Contact: Louis H. Howe, pres.
Affiliates/branches: Box 1601, Annapolis, Maryland 21404
Areas Served: S. CA, DC & MD
Founded: 1968 *Staff:* 3-10 *Revenues:* $100-$500,000
Professional Affiliations: AMC
Services: Most
Industries: Most

Hoyles Associates Ltd.

975 Sherwood Lane
West Vancouver, B.C. V7V 3Y1, Canada
(604)922-2121
> Management consultants to the design professions: exclusively serving consulting engineers, planners, and architects in Canada, US and overseas. All members of our staff have senior operating experience in a private professional design practice with post graduate degrees in either business or law. General

management services provided to clients.
Contact: Herbert A. Hoyles
Areas Served: Canada & U.S.
Founded: 1976 *Staff:* 3-10 *Revenues:* $100-$500,000
Services: 1.0   3.0   4.0   5.0   9.0   10.0
Industries: I.89

Louis A. Hradesky
4920 NW 47th Terrace
Fort Lauderdale, Florida 33319
(305)731-1561
Specializing in industrial engineering services to large and small industries. Short or long term contracts considered. Areas of proficiency embrace; management organization, plant layout, production control, manufacturing methods, material handling, motion & time study, wage incentives and allied functions.
Contact: Louis A. Hradesky, owner
Areas Served: Southeastern U.S.
Founded: 1947 *Staff:* 1-3 *Revenues:* under $100,000
Services: 1.1   1.12   2.0   3.1   6.4   6.5   7.2
Industries: D.33   D.34   D.35   D.36   D.37   D.39

Human Resource & Profit Associates, Inc.
2430 Pagehurst Dr.
Midlothian, Virginia 23113
(804)794-4914
Personnel, industrial & labor relations consulting for private & public sector domestically and internationally. 99% win rate in counter-organizing, labor negotiations results. Arbitration, EEOC, OPCCP, NLRB, federal wage hour, affirmative action, attitude surveys, team building, profit programs, management & non-management training, recruiting, compensation, policies, vulnerability audits, organization evaluation.
Contact: Herbert W. Larrabee, pres.
Areas Served: U.S.
Founded: 1970 *Staff:* 3-10 *Revenues:* $100-$500,000
Professional Affiliations: /ASPA
Services: 3.0   3.1   3.3   3.4   3.5   3.6   3.7   3.8   3.9   3.10
Industries: Most

Humber, Mundie & McClary
2021 Marine Plaza
Milwaukee, Wisconsin 53202
(414)271-6220
Licensed consulting psychologists whose purpose is to serve business and industry by providing the expert knowdge and special techniques of the behavioral sciences to the end that their enterprises may become better managed and their organizations more effective in achieving their business objectives. Services include executive development, psychological descriptions of key people and applicants, leadership training and organization development, career appraisal and planning, and personal counseling.
Contact: Susan Keminsky, off. mgr.
Affiliates/branches: 1628 IDS Ctr., Minneapolis, Minnesota 55402; 1580 Sherman Ave., Evanston, Illinois 60201

Areas Served: Primarily Mid-west
Founded: 1952 *Staff:* 10-25 *Revenues:* $500,000-1 million
Professional Affiliations: /APA, NPCM
Services: 1.7   3.0   3.1   3.4   3.5   3.8   3.9   3.10   3.11
Industries: Most

Hurdman & Cranstoun

140 Broadway
New York, New York 10005
(212)269-5800

An international public accounting firm providing a variety of management advisory services. Clients range from small, embryonic operations requiring basic counseling in professional maangement techniques to multi-national corporations who supplement their own consulting staffs with technical expertise available from our firm.

Contact: Albert Kushner, dir. MAS
Affiliates/branches: New York, New York; Chicago, Illinois; Los Angeles, California; San Francisco, California; Sacremento, California
Areas Served: worldwide
Founded: 1917 *Staff:* 25-50 *Revenues:* $1-$5 million
Professional Affiliations: IMC/AICPA
Services: 1.6   1.8   1.9   1.10   1.11   2.0   5.0   6.4   9.3   9.5
Industries: Most

IMS Systems Corp.

1 Penn Plaza
New York, New York 10001
(212)736-5210

We provide assistance in the design and programming of computerized management information systems. We work on COBOL, BAL & PL/I. We also provide OS systems programming support and computer operations technical support. Our motto is "excellent performance in everything we do."

Contact: Ira B. Brown, pres.
Areas Served: NY metropolitan
Founded: 1968 *Staff:* 25-50 *Revenues:* $1-$5 million
Professional Affiliations: /ACM, ASM
Services: 1.8   5.8   9.3   9.5   9.6   9.8
Industries: D.00   E.00   H.00   I.00   J.00

Industrial Technological Associates, Inc.

2108 Payne Ave.
Cleveland, Ohio 44114
(216)771-4151

The greatest measurement of management efficiency is profit. Profit improvement can be made through productivity. Productivity demands efficient management of capital assets, labor, energy and materials. For improving productivity, we emphasize providing manufacturing services related to machines, methods, materials, management, but we realize all profit improvement is made through people.

Contact: Jack M. Stewart, pres.
Affiliates/branches: 912 Thayer Rd., Silver Spring, Maryland 20910
Areas Served: U.S.-East & Midwest
Founded: 1957 *Staff:* 25-50 *Revenues:* $500,000-1 million

Services: Most
Industries: Most

Infotek Corporation
16535 West Bluemound Rd.
Brookfield, Wisconsin 53005
(414)784-3500
> Specializing in information management for a broad range of clients. Results-oriented, we work with the client through implementation. We provide counseling and professional services—customized to client requirements—in the planing, implementation and management of information systems. EDP operational audits are also provided.

Contact: Kenneth C. Muehlbauer, vp.
Affiliates/branches: 1920 American Court, Neenah, Wisconsin 54956
Areas Served: Midwest
Founded: 1973 *Staff:* 10-25 *Revenues:* $100-$500,000
Services: 1.5   1.8   2.15   5.8   6.4   9.3   9.5   9.6   9.7   9.8
Industries: D.23   D.24   D.32   D.33   D.34   D.35   D.36   D.38   F.50   F.51

Ingersoll Engineers Inc.
707 Fulton Ave.
Rockford, Illinois 61101
(815)987-6110
> Exclusively serving the manufacturing function of the metalworking industry...Principal projects involve developing state-of-the-art manufacturing systems (machines, equipment, tools, fixtures, etc.) for plant modernizations, expansions, and technology transfers to other countries...Other projects include productivity improvement, design of large complex machines and products, and product manufacturability studies.

Contact: Robert L. Callahan, pres.
Affiliates/branches: Belgium; England
Areas Served: worldwide
Founded: 1963 *Staff:* 50-100 *Revenues:* $1-$5 million
Services: 2.4   2.5   2.8   2.11   2.13   2.15
Industries: D.34   D.35   D.37

The Innovative Group
Box 1433
LaJolla, California 92038
(714)459-3871
> Corporate business consulting firm of problem-solvers. Entrepreneurial group specializing in increasing human effectiveness and resource-development. Customized learning systems based on client needs.

Contact: Jack Hayes, pres.
Areas Served: worldwide
Founded: 1969 *Staff:* 10-25 *Revenues:* $500,000-1 million
Professional Affiliations: /ICF, ASTD
Services: 1.0   3.0   4.0   7.0   10.0   11.0
Industries: Most

Insight Development Services
5 Ridgeview Ave.
West Orange, New Jersey 07052
(201)731-6688

> Primary emphasis upon the improvement of internal relationships by eliciting
> new insights into roles and functions and establishing structure and practises to
> produce maximum effectiveness in decision-making and performance; suppor-
> ted by internal audit of attitudes and relationships; evaluation of management
> methods; training; team-building; and individual and group development.

Contact: Manheim S. Shapiro, princ.
Areas Served: U.S. & Europe
Founded: 1966 *Staff:* 1-3 *Revenues:* under $100,000
Professional Affiliations: SPMC/ASTD, ASA
Services: 1.0   3.0   4.9   4.12   7.0   7.2
Industries: Most

Institutional Strategy Associates, Inc.
51 Brattle St.
Cambridge, Massachusetts 02138
(617)492-7812

> Assistance to universities, foundations, and health service providers in
> addressing major non-recurring problems involving the future direction of their
> institutions. Work concentrated in the health field. Major areas of interest
> include strategic planning, finance, management of ambulatory health services,
> and medical school/teaching hospital relationships.

Contact: Martin S. Klein, pres.
Areas Served: U.S. & Canada
Founded: 1973 *Staff:* 3-10 *Revenues:* $100-$500,000
Services: 1.2   1.3   1.5   5.3
Industries: I.80   I.82   I.83   I.84   I.86

Insurance Management Group, Inc.
1 Landmark Sq.
Stamford, Connecticut 06901
(203)357-7169

> Complete range of consulting service to the life and property and casualty
> insurance industry except for personnel search. When a project has been
> completed, our staff remains available to help the client's staff implement
> recommendations and to audit the effectiveness of the implementation.

Contact: George Goldbeck, princ.
Areas Served: North America
Founded: 1954 *Staff:* 3-10 *Revenues:* $100-$500,000
Services: 1.0   3.0   4.0   5.0   9.0
Industries: H.63   H.64

International Commercial Services
Box 4082
Irvine, California 92716
(714)552-8494

> Performance-oriented, practical counsel and active impelementary assistance
> here and abroad, in all areas of international business. Also, US/Canadian
> market developments. International corporate seminars and training programs.

Contact: David A. Harquail, vp.

Affiliates/branches: New York, New York; Toronto; Osaka; Sydney; London;
Dusseldorf; Bern; Sao Paulo; Milan
Areas Served: worldwide
Founded: 1946 *Staff:* 1-3 *Revenues:* under $100,000
Services: 1.3   1.7   4.1   4.2   10.1   10.2   10.3   10.4   10.5
Industries: Most

International Management
711 Green, NW
Gainesville, Georgia 30501
(404)532-4262

Management and marketing consulting including cost calculation and control;
sales forecasting, production and inventory control, physical distribution,
business analysis and planning, and related activities.
Contact: Frank C. Wilson, pres.
Areas Served: worldwide
Founded: 1963 *Staff:* 1-3 *Revenues:* under $100,000
Professional Affiliations: IMC/PE
Services: 1.0   2.0   3.1   4.0   5.0   6.4   9.5   10.0
Industries: D.22   D.23   D.25   D.28   D.34   D.39   G.57

International Resource Development, Inc.
Box 1131
New Canaan, Connecticut 06840
(203)966-5615

We maintain an extensive data base (both computerized and manual)
containing market, financial, company and product information in the
computer, telecommunications, office products and financial services markets.
This is used as the starting point for many client studies, including product
planning, market planning and competitive assessment.
Contact: K. G. Bosomworth, pres.
Areas Served: U.S., Canada, Japan & Europe
Founded: 1971 *Staff:* 10-25 *Revenues:* $1-$5 million
Services: 1.3   4.0   4.1   4.2   4.5   4.11   4.12   9.3   9.8   10.4
Industries: D.26   D.27   D.36   D.38   E.43   E.48   H.60   I.73

International Resources & Applications
13773 N. Central Expwy.
Dallas, Texas 75243
(214)231-9817

Employee relations with emphasis on employee opinion surveys, climate
building activities between employees and management, and international
compensation.
Contact: Charles W. Eisemann, pres.
Areas Served: U.S., Central America, Canada, Europe & Far East
Founded: 1974 *Staff:* 3-10 *Revenues:* $100-$500,000
Services: 3.0   3.1   3.3   3.5   3.9   3.10   10.2
Industries: Most   I.73

Interplex Management Associates, Ltd.
625 N. Michigan Ave.
Chicago, Illinois 60611
(312)440-1007

The philosophy of Interplex is to provide peer-level or one-to-one consulting to management. The firm is staffed with mature, well-experienced people who have varied business and consulting backgrounds. David M. Goldsmith, CMC, is the founder and president. Practice areas are broad in both discipline and industry.

Contact: David M. Goldsmith, pres.
Areas Served: U.S., Canada
Founded: 1970 *Staff:* 3-10 *Revenues:* $100-$500,000
Professional Affiliations: IMC
Services: 1.0   2.0   3.1   4.0   5.0   6.0   7.0   9.0   10.0
Industries: A.0   B.14   D.00   E.00   F.50   H.00   I.00   J.00

Isaacs Associates
625 N. Michigan Ave.
Chicago, Illinois 60611
(312)787-8661

A resource to managements who wish to design and install their own information systems. Guide and instruct their staffs to perform the tasks required. Trouble-shoot problems with clerical or computer-based systems. Improve productivity of client's data processing staffs.

Contact: George Isaacs, pres.
Areas Served: U.S.
Founded: 1975 *Staff:* 1-3 *Revenues:* under $100,000
Professional Affiliations: AMC, IMC
Services: 1.4   1.5   1.8   1.9   1.12   2.1   2.2   6.4   9.3   9.5
Industries: Most

Isaacs & Associates
2070 Sheridan Dr.
Buffalo, New York 14223
(716)875-2550

Materials handling management, including facilities planning and design, layout, methods, equipment application, cost reduction, productivity improvement, automation, control systems, warehousing, and distribution for plants, offices, warehouses, and institutions. Our philosophy is: "Minimum costs for maximum results."

Contact: Samuel H. Isaacs, pres.
Affiliates/branches: London
Areas Served: U.S. & Europe
Founded: 1948 *Staff:* 3-10 *Revenues:* $100-$500,000
Professional Affiliations: IMC/SME, APMHC, AIIE
Services: Most   1.0   2.0   8.0   9.0
Industries: Most   D.00   E.00   F.00   G.00

Jagerson Associates, Inc.
501 Madison Ave.
New York, New York 10022
(212)725-0154

Provides private and public sector employers with professional tools and assistance to address the Equal Employment Opportunities issues. Clients include over 300 of the Fortune 500 companies.

Contact: G. Todd Jagerson
Affiliates/branches: Los Angeles, California

Areas Served: U.S.
Founded: 1970 *Staff:* 3-10 *Revenues:* $500,000-1 million
Services: 1.15   3.4   3.5   3.8   3.9

JDA Management Services
157 Lindell Ave.
Leominster, Massachusetts 01453
(617)537-2938
> Small highly trained and motivated group serving institutional, governmental and industrial clients nationally in all areas of organization and operational efficiency and effectiveness.

Contact: James E. Driscoll
Areas Served: U.S.
Founded: 1963 *Staff:* 1-3 *Revenues:* under $100,000
Professional Affiliations: IMC/AIIE
Services: 1.0   2.0   3.7   3.8   6.1   6.4   7.1   9.4   9.5
Industries: Most

Robert S. Jeffries, Jr.
72 Park St.
New Canaan, Connecticut 06840
(203)972-0226
> An individual consultant in industrial operations management-manufacturing, physical distribution, and logistics. Supporting experience and understanding of marketing, finance, and general management. Particularly interested in operations problems that have important marketing, financial or strategic impact, or that involves suppliers and customers.

Contact: Robert S. Jeffries, Jr.
Areas Served: U.S.
Founded: 1971 *Staff:* 1-3 *Revenues:* under $100,000
Professional Affiliations: IMC
Services: 1.0   2.0   4.0   6.0   7.0
Industries: Most   D.00   E.42   E.45   G.00   G.53   G.54   I.73

JMG Associates Ltd.
750 Birch St.
Bristol, Connecticut 06070
(203)583-8410
> Serving the plastics industry exclusively with a broad range of services.

Contact: John M. Grigor, pres.
Areas Served: North America, Europe, Latin America
Founded: 1977 *Staff:* 1-3 *Revenues:* under $100,000
Professional Affiliations: /SPE, SPI
Services: Most   1.0   2.13   3.0   4.0   5.0   8.2   10.2   10.3   10.4
Industries: D.30   D.35

J. Lloyd Johnson Associates
778 Frontage Rd.
Northfield, Illinois 60093
(312)441-7060
> Specializing in the problems of change inherent in high technology, medical products industries, we bring a proven approach and unique experience to each

client assignment. All of our consultants possess graduate degrees in business administration or economics and have been chosen for their intelligence, analytical abilities, and maturity. Previous experiences are deliberately varied: some are technical and medical; others are business generalists. The variety has insured fresh and multidisciplined approaches to problem solving.

Contact: Jerry L. Johnson, mng. dir.
Areas Served: U.S.
Founded: 1966 *Staff:* 3-10 *Revenues:* $100-$500,000
Professional Affiliations: ACME
Services: 1.1   1.3   1.5   1.6   1.8   4.2   4.16
Industries: I.80

Johnson, Pratt & Stewart

22 E. First S.
Salt Lake City, Utah 84111
(801)531-6430

Combine a strong academic background with extensive business experience to provide economic and financial consulting and expert testimony to the corporate, legal, governmental, banking and investment communities. Reputation for thorough, objective and independent analysis.

Contact: John A. Scowcroft, gen. mgr.
Areas Served: worldwide
Founded: 1975 *Staff:* 3-10 *Revenues:* $100-$500,000
Services: 1.3   1.5   1.6   5.3   5.6   5.9   5.10   10.5
Industries: H.60   H.61

Henry Jordan & Associates

941 Carlisle Rd.
Stone Mountain, Georgia 30083
(404)296-6020

Specialize in inventory management, production planning and control, materials management and purchasing. Expertise in production forecasting, master scheduling, material requirements planning and capacity requirements planning.

Contact: Henry H. Jordan, chmn.
Areas Served: U.S., Canada & Europe
Founded: 1970 *Staff:* 1-3 *Revenues:* $100-$500,000
Professional Affiliations: IMC/APICS, IMMS, AIIE
Services: 1.12   2.1   2.2   2.16   4.8   6.0   6.1   6.2   6.3   6.4   6.5
Industries: Most

The Joynt Group, Inc.

10 Park Ave.
New York, New York 10016
(212)689-7970

Several years ago we made a vital decision which stamps us from most of the larger consulting firms. We deliberately decided to keep ourselves small and highly professional --- the Tiffany approach.

Contact: Jack Joynt, pres.
Areas Served: worldwide
Founded: 1961 *Staff:* 1-3 *Revenues:* under $100,000
Services: 1.0   2.0   3.0   4.0   9.0
Industries: D.28   D.33   D.34   E.00   G.53   G.54   H.60   H.63   I.00   J.00

Juarez & Associates, Inc.
1100 Glendon Ave.
Los Angeles, California 90024
(213)478-0826

Full range of services to business and government in the areas of general management; survey and socioeconomic research; general marketing; employment, training and development services; and program review and evaluation services. Complete bilingual (Spanish and English) capabilities. References and resumes available upon request.

Contact: Nicandro F. Juarez, pres.
Areas Served: U.S. & Latin America
Founded: 1971 *Staff:* 10-25 *Revenues:* $100-$500,000
Professional Affiliations: AMC, IMC/AMA, AAPOR, ASTD
Services: 1.0 3.0 5.0 7.0 10.0
Industries: Most

Jean Judge Associates, Inc.
125 Prospect Ave.
Hackensack, New Jersey 07601
(201)342-2643

Specialize in corporate consumer affairs; clients are in consumer product/service industries. Our philosophy is that a preventive/anticipatory, corporate consumer stance is mroe cost-effective than a reactive, curative one. Full range of services, including designing/evaluating corporation consumer affairs functions and programs; improving complaint-handling systems, dealing with consumerism, managing consumer panels.

Contact: Jean F. Judge, pres.
Areas Served: U.S.
Founded: 1974 *Staff:* 3-10 *Revenues:* $100-$500,000
Services: 1.1 1.2 1.3 1.7 3.1 3.5 4.3 4.12 9.00 11.5
Industries: D.20 D.23 D.37 D.39 E.48 G.00 H.60 H.63

Robert Kahn & Associates
Box 343
Lafayette, California 94549
(415)254-4434

Consultant to principals and major executives of retail organizations, including plans for operation, expansion, financing, merger, organization, branch locations. Active in areas outside retailing in the field of finance, acquisition and merger. Clients obtained primarily through referral. Publisher of "Retailing Today," an independent newsletter reaching major executives in retail firms doing over $120 billion annually.

Contact: Robert Kahn, princ.
Areas Served: Primarily CA
Founded: 1956 *Staff:* 1-3 *Revenues:* under $100,000
Professional Affiliations: AMC, IMC/NRMA
Services: 1.1 1.2 1.3 1.6 1.11 4.1 4.3 5.9 5.10 5.11
Industries: D.36 G.52 G.53 G.54 G.56 G.57 G.59

The Kampmeier Group
1631 NW Professional Plaza
Columbus, Ohio 43220
(614)451-1738

Concentrate on small businesses in the services sector, with special emphasis on individual and organizational effectiveness, strategic planning, and marketing. Currently operate as sole practitioner with "tribe" of professional associates. About 85% of billing is collaborative.

Contact: Curt Kampmeier, pres.
Founded: 1973 *Staff:* 3-10 *Revenues:* $100-$500,000
Services: 1.0 1.1 1.2 1.3 1.10 3.1 3.4 4.1 4.7
Industries: F.50 G.53 G.57 G.59 H.63 H.66 I.72 I.73 I.81 I.89

The Kappa Group
3300 University Dr.
Coral Springs, Florida 33065
(305)752-3870

Specialize in assisting companies in the computer and data communications industries to develop and implement strategic, marketing, product and sales plans. Prepare and conduct customized in-house training programs covering management development, planning, marketing and sales. These courses involve extensive case studies to build experience and confidence.

Contact: C. J. Kurtz, pres.
Affiliates/branches: New York, New York; Toronto
Areas Served: U.S. & Canada
Founded: 1974 *Staff:* 3-10 *Revenues:* $100-$500,000
Services: 1.0 3.1 3.5 4.0 10.4
Industries: D.36 E.48 I.73 I.82 I.89

William Karp Consulting Co., Inc.
900 N. Michigan Ave.
Chicago, Illinois 60611
(312)642-3452

A human resources organization specializing in personnel management, EEO/AA, organization development (training), labor relations and manpower planning. Apply problem-solving know-how and techniques of the social and behavioral sciences to problems encountered in industry, government, educational institutions, labor and community agencies.

Contact: Belle Allen, vp.
Areas Served: U.S.
Founded: 1952 *Staff:* 10-25 *Revenues:* $500,000-1 million
Professional Affiliations: /APA, ASPA, APGA, IRRA
Services: 1.0 3.0 3.1 3.3 3.4 3.6 3.7 3.8 3.10 3.11
Industries: Most

William Kather Associates, Inc.
664 N. Michigan Ave.
Chicago, Illinois 60611
(312)944-3460

Specialized resource performing marketing, commercial development and acquisitions studies in chemical, plastics, and related industries. Results-oriented. Our strategy studies have strongly changed and upgraded the performance of client businesses. 83% of business is from repeat clients. Literature, reprints and reference letters on request.

Contact: W. S. Kather, pres.
Areas Served: U.S.
Founded: 1970 *Staff:* 3-10 *Revenues:* $100-$500,000

Professional Affiliations: /ACS, CMRA
Services: 1.3   1.5   1.6   1.7   4.1   4.2   4.5   4.11   4.16   7.3
Industries: D.28   D.30

A. T. Kearney, Inc.
100 S. Wacker Dr.
Chicago, Illinois 60606
(312)782-2868

An international firm with a wide range of specialized and sophisticated consulting services. Devoted to pragmatic, results-oriented efforts on behalf of our clients delivered in a highly professional manner. Client satisfaction is indicated by our unusually high rate of repeat business and referrals.

Contact: Kenneth L. Block
Affiliates/branches: 437 Madison Ave., New York, New York 10022; 1725 K St., NW, Washington, D.C. 20006; 100 California St., San Francisco, California 94111; 1 Wilshire Bldg., Los Angeles, California 90017; Investment Plaza, Cleveland, Ohio 44114; Brussels; Tokyo; Dusseldorf; Milan; Paris; London
Founded: 1926 *Staff:* over 100 *Revenues:* over $10 million
Professional Affiliations: ACME, IMC
Services: Most
Industries: Most

Keenan, Wheeler & Bowman
3131 South Dixie
Dayton, Ohio 45439
(513)294-3803

Our approach takes into consideration that each client has unique circumstances, goals and objectives. Because of this, we offer no "packaged" solutions to managerial problems; however, we do employ basic principles and techniques which may aid the client's purposes.

Contact: Vernon Keenan, ptnr.
Areas Served: Midwest, Southeast & East
Founded: 1975 *Staff:* 1-3 *Revenues:* $100-$500,000
Professional Affiliations: AMC, IMC
Services: 1.1   1.3   1.8   1.9   2.14   3.2   3.7   5.2   5.7   9.5
Industries: D.25   D.26   D.27   D.33   D.34   H.60   H.61

Kendrick & Co.
1030 Woodward Bldg.
Washington, D.C. 20005
(202)638-7627

Services to governments and service organizations. Basic competencies in general management, communications, social and business research, and training/education. These skills are applied to the specific goals, needs, and problems of the client organization. We require the participation of the client's top management.

Contact: James E. Kendrick, pres.
Areas Served: worldwide
Founded: 1970 *Staff:* 3-10 *Revenues:* $100-$500,000
Professional Affiliations: SPMC
Services: 1.0   3.9   3.10   3.21   4.2   4.4   4.10   7.1   7.3
Industries: I.80   I.81   I.82   I.83   I.86   J.91   J.92   J.94   J.96

Kennedy & Kennedy, Inc.
2 Templeville Rd.
Fitzwilliam, New Hampshire 03447
(603)585-2200

Serving other management consultants and executive recruiters only...confidential counsel on organization, strategy, compensation, marketing, public relations...valuations for purchase & insurance purposes...referral of partners & principals...mergers & acquisition.

Contact: James H. Kennedy, pres.
Areas Served: U.S.
Founded: 1970 *Staff:* 1-3 *Revenues:* under $100,000
Services: 1.0 3.0 4.0 11.1
Industries: I.73

Kenneth Associates
2014 Judah St.
San Francisco, California 94122
(415)665-6500

Specializing in financial aspects of hospital and health services management--from business-office audit and evaluation to Medicaid appeals to facilities management.

Contact: Robert J. Kenneth, pres.
Affiliates/branches: Box 13247, El Paso, Texas 79912
Areas Served: Bay area-CA
Founded: 1970 *Staff:* 1-3 *Revenues:* under $100,000
Professional Affiliations: /GHAM
Services: 1.0 5.0 9.0
Industries: I.80

Kensington Management Consultants, Inc.
25 Third St.
Stamford, Connecticut 06905
(203)327-9860

Assist management in all areas of general management: improving profitability, return on equity and long-range stability; expanding into new business areas (internal product development and merger or acquisition); obtaining financing to support expansion; executive search. Work with financial institutions and help companies to whom loans have been made.

Contact: Earnest G. Campbell, pres.
Affiliates/branches: 860 Charleston Rd., Palo Alto, California 94303
Areas Served: U.S.
Founded: 1972 *Staff:* 10-25 *Revenues:* $100-$500,000
Professional Affiliations: ACME
Services: Most
Industries: Most

Warren King & Associates, Inc.
20 N. Wacker Dr.
Chicago, Illinois 60606
(312)726-0481

General management consulting organization offering a broad range of specialized services to state and local governments as well as educational units. Staffed withsenior management specialists capable of bringing highly developed, proven skills to clients' assignments. Proven record of producing optimum results in the shortest possible time. High degree of implementation of resulting recommendations. Special expertise in managing task force programs for public and private sector clients.

Contact: Warren J. King, pres.
Areas Served: U.S.
Founded: 1964 *Staff:* 10-25 *Revenues:* $500,000-1 million
Professional Affiliations: IMC
Services: 1.0   3.0   3.9   5.0   6.0   9.0
Industries: E.41   I.80   I.82   I.83   J.91   J.92   J.93   J.94   J.95   J.96

Klein Behavioral Science Consultants, Inc.
205 E. 42nd St.
New York, New York 10017
(212)687-3200

Manpower development and organization development with almost 40 years experience serving leading companies throughout the U.S. and Canada. Counsel on personnel selection techniques including psychological testing services for sales and middle management; compensation & sales incentive plans and behavioral studies. (Formerly the Klein Institute).

Contact: Mitchell Levitt, pres.
Affiliates/branches: Los Angeles
Areas Served: U.S. & Canada
Founded: 1940 *Staff:* 3-10 *Revenues:* $500,000-1 million
Professional Affiliations: IMC/APA
Services: 1.1   3.1   3.2   3.4   3.7   3.8   3.10   3.11   4.15
Industries: Most

C. H. Kline & Co., Inc.
330 Passaic Ave.
Fairfield, New Jersey 07006
(201)227-6262

Provide facts, forecasts, and recommendations to help management solve practical problems in marketing, business strategy, and applied technology. Services include confidential surveys, acquisition analyses, industrial multiclient surveys, and syndicated consumer industry analysis. Coverage is worldwide, with field experience in 46 countries and over 600 clients in 22 countries.

Contact: Edward J. Kliff, exec. vp.
Affiliates/branches: Brussels; Tokyo
Areas Served: worldwide
Founded: 1959 *Staff:* 25-50 *Revenues:* $1-$5 million
Services: 1.3   1.4   1.5   1.6   1.8   1.10   2.10   4.0   10.0
Industries: B.00   D.00   G.55

Virginia Knauer & Associates, Inc.
2033 M St., NW
Washington, D.C. 20036
(202)293-3370

We offer full service within our specialty, consumer affairs: a variety of programs dealing with customer satisfaction/repeat sales, government intervention, new marketing tools, opportunities for R & D, improved product assurance, fulfilling social-corporate responsibility programs, and lessening of legal conflicts. Command broad range of managerial, scientific and technical capabilities.

Contact: Martin R. Petersen, vp
Areas Served: worldwide
Founded: 1977 *Staff:* 3-10 *Revenues:* $100-$500,000
Professional Affiliations: /SOCAP
Services: 1.0 2.7 3.0 4.0 7.0 8.3 9.0 10.0 11.1
Industries: Most

Lester B. Knight & Associates, Inc.
549 W. Randolph St.
Chicago, Illinois 60606
(312)346-2100

The Knight organization, which offers a complete range of management consulting services to business and government, has completed more than 28,000 assignments in 53 countries. The firm believes in establishing a client/consultant project team to take advantage of their client's depth of experience and the consultant's breadth of experience.

Contact: Norman F. Atkinson, vp.
Affiliates/branches: 2550 M St., NW, Washington, D.C. 20037; 560 Mission St., San Francisco, California 94105; Dusseldorf; Frankfurt; London; Stockport; Vienna; Ah-Vught; Kolvgatan; Zurich; Paris
Areas Served: worldwide
Founded: 1945 *Staff:* over 100 *Revenues:* over $10 million
Professional Affiliations: ACME, IMC
Services: Most
Industries: Most

Kirk Knight & Co., Inc.
(arm of Menlo Financial Corp)
3000 Sand Hill Rd.
Menlo Park, California 94025
(415)854-1455

For small & medium-sized emerging growth companies: a positive impact on sales, profit-margins, company direction and strategy (rather than small improvements in production or work-flow efficiencies.) Many clients in high technology.

Contact: Kirk L. Knight, chmn.
Areas Served: West Coast
Founded: 1969 *Staff:* 3-10 *Revenues:* $100-$500,000
Services: 1.0 1.3 1.6 1.10 1.11 4.0 4.1 4.2 5.0 5.3
Industries: Most

Knox Consulting Services
3 Poplar Lane-North Oaks
St. Paul, Minnesota 55110
(612)484-4879

Studies of engineering, manufacturing & computer systems: unique computer systems, economical lot size formulas, standard part-number systems, assembly-line loading, etc.

Contact: Charlie Knox, princ.
Areas Served: U.S.
Founded: 1976 *Staff:* 1-3 *Revenues:* under $100,000

Services: 1.0 2.0 6.0 9.0
Industries: D.00 D.23 D.25 D.33 D.34 D.35 D.36 D.38 D.39

James B. Kobak, Inc.

774 Hollow Tree Ridge Rd.
Darien, Connecticut 06820
(203)655-8764

High level personal consulting. Particular knowledge of magazine, book, newsletter and allied fields.

Contact: James B. Kobak, pres.
Areas Served: worldwide
Founded: 1971 *Staff:* 1-3 *Revenues:* $100-$500,000
Professional Affiliations: /AICPA
Services: 1.1 1.2 1.3 1.4 1.6 4.4. 5.3 5.8 5.10

Robert E. Koogler

Box 141
Princeton Junction, New Jersey 08550
(609)448-8154

Management, industrial engineering, health services. Serve as advisors to other consulting firms.

Contact: Robert E. Koogler
Areas Served: U.S.
Founded: 1971 *Staff:* 1-3 *Revenues:* under $100,000
Services: 1.0 2.0 3.0 4.0 9.0
Industries: C.15 D.00 E.00 H.00 I.00 J.00

Sidney W. Koran Associates

33 Ridge Rd.
Port Washington, New York 11050
(516)883-5580

Consultants in personnel management to industry, business and government, with emphasis on the application of industrial psychological techniques to the prevention and solution of problems involving human resources: Psychological assessment of applicants. Assessment, counseling and development of executives and other key employees. Evaluation and installation of testing programs and other elements of personnel programs. Training interviewers at all levels.

Contact: Sidney W. Koran, pres.
Areas Served: U.S., Mexico & U.K.
Founded: 1956 *Staff:* 1-3 *Revenues:* under $100,000
Professional Affiliations: /APA
Services: 1.1 3.0 3.1 3.4 3.9 3.10 3.11 11.0 11.1
Industries: Most

Krall Management Inc.

2 Radnor Corporate Ctr.
Radnor, Pennsylvania 19087
(215)687-8410

Performs general management, organization and feasibility studies. The firm emphasizes information management—planning, organizing, developing and implementing. Services include information requirements and planning, resource and technology integration, systems design, advanced office systems, data processing and word processing. Industries include financial, leisure, manufacturing, transportation and wholesale/retail.

Contact: George F. Krall, Jr., pres.
Areas Served: worldwide
Founded: 1969 *Staff:* 25-50 *Revenues:* $500,000-1 million
Professional Affiliations: ACME
Services: 1.0 2.0 3.0 4.0 5.0 6.0 7.0 9.0
Industries: Most C.00 D.00 E.00 F.00 G.00 H.00 I.00 J.00 K.00

Robert Kruhm
2212 Drury Rd.
Silver Spring, Maryland 20906
(301)924-4473

Association publication consultant: areas covered include publication management, advertising sales development, market research, surveys, circulation promotion and advertising. Write for list of publications served and sample promotions. Specializing in newsletters, magazine, directories and annual reports.

Contact: Robert H. Kruhm, pres.
Areas Served: U.S.
Founded: 1977 *Staff:* 1-3 *Revenues:* $100-$500,000
Professional Affiliations: /PRSA, ASAE, IABC, SNAP
Services: 1.4 1.7 1.14 3.9 3.10 4.2 4.4 4.10 4.11 7.3
Industries: Most

Michael E. Kurtz Associates
Box 1185
Sunset Beach, California 90742
(213)592-2422

Organization psychologists primarily providing consultant services in organization development, training, management and supervisory development using an applied behavioral science model. Specialists in health-care organization and manpower development with an emphasis on team-building. All programs designed individually to meet client needs.

Contact: Michael E. Kurtz, princ.
Areas Served: worldwide
Founded: 1973 *Staff:* 1-3 *Revenues:* under $100,000
Professional Affiliations: /ASTD
Services: 3.1 3.5 3.9 3.11 7.2
Industries: I.80 I.82 J.91 J.94

Peter Lambros & Associates
1635 N.E. Loop 410
San Antonio, Texas 78209
(512)826-7006

A small, independent consulting firm specializing exclusively in assisting company presidents to improve their bottom-line profit performance and cash flow using highly sophisticated and technical propriety techniques not available from any other financial, accounting or consulting firm. Serve select profit-motivated companies representing divisions of major corporations including 1000 coporations on NYSE and AMEX.

Contact: S. Peter Lambros, pres.

Affiliates/branches: 1625 N. Michigan Ave., Chicago, Illinois 60611; 230 Peachtree St., Atlanta, Georgia 30303
Founded: 1963 *Staff:* 1-3 *Revenues:* $100-$500,000
Professional Affiliations: AMC, IMC
Services: 1.0   2.0   3.0   4.0   5.0   6.0   7.0   9.0   9.4
Industries: D.24   D.25   D.33   D.34   D.35   D.36   D.37   D.38   D.39

Rex Land & Associates, Inc.
800 W. 6th St.
Los Angeles, California 90017
(213)629-4400

> We provide consulting services in areas of direct interest to senior executives, primarily of large and medium sized industrial corporations and utilities. Much of our practice involves dealing with issues that affect a business as a whole, this includes developing overall business strategies, diversification, and acquisition programs, new products planning, organizational evaluations, executive compensation, management reporting systems, project management, and examinations of companies for investors.

Contact: Rex Land
Affiliates/branches: San Francisco
Areas Served: U.S., Europe & Middle East
Founded: 1968 *Staff:* 10-25 *Revenues:* $500,000-1 million
Services: Most
Industries: Most

Laughlin Associates
56 N. Salt Creek Rd.
Roselle, Illinois 60172
(312)893-3257

> We specialize in two areas: 1) direct marketing- sales/sales management: sales meetings, training systems, recruitment, etc. 2) pay roll taxes- reduction of FICA, state unemployment insurance, and workman's compensation costs.

Contact: T.X. Laughlin, pres.
Areas Served: worldwide
Founded: 1967 *Staff:* 3-10 *Revenues:* under $100,000
Services: 3.1   3.4   3.6   4.3   4.4   4.7   4.9   4.15   5.11   10.4
Industries: G.55   G.59   H.63   H.64   H.65   H.66   I.73   I.82   I.86   K.00

Laventhol & Horwath
1845 Walnut St.
Philadelphia, Pennsylvania 19103
(215)491-1600

> Provide management advisory services to clients in accordance with the Code of Ethics of the AICPA and comparable international regulatory bodies. Clients range from publicly-held companies to individual entrepreneurs covering a variety of industries, particularly leisure time, health care, real estate and retail.

Contact: Rudolph L. Leone, natl. ptnr. MAS
Affiliates/branches: 310 K St., Anchorage, Alaska 99501; 5151 E. Broadway, Tucson, Arizona 85711; 3700 Wilshire Blvd., Los Angeles, California 90010; 660 Newport Ctr. Dr., Newport Beach, California 92660; 1200 Third Ave., San Diego, California 92101; 50 California St., San Francisco, California 94111; 8630 Fenton St., Silver Spring, Maryland 20910; 201 Alhambra Circle, Coral Gables, Florida 33134; 1st Florida Twr., Tampa, Florida 33602; 777 W. Peachtree St., Atlanta, Georgia 30308;

1116 W. Main St., Carbondale, Illinois 62901; 111 E. Wacker Dr., Chicago, Illinois 60601; 2 Ctr. Plaza, Boston, Massachusetts 02108; 26400 Lasher Rd., Southfield, Michigan 48034; 801 Nicollet Mall, Minneapolis, Minnesota 55402; 450 Ten Main Ctr., Kansas City, Missouri 64105; 10 Broadway, St. Louis, Missouri 63102; 714 S. 4th St., Las Vegas, Nevada 89101; 197 Hwy 18, E. Brunswick, New Jersey 08816; 425 Broadhollow Rd., Melville, New York 11746; 919 Third Ave., New York, New York 10022; 1 NCNB Pl., Charlotte, North Carolina 28280; E. 9th & Superior, Cleveland, Ohio 44114; 1500 Georgia Pac. Bldg., Portland, Oregon 97204; 2101 N Front St., Harrisburg, Pennsylvania 17110; 2 Chestnut St., Lewistown, Pennsylvania 17044; 1845 Walnut St., Philadelphia, Pennsylvania 19103; 15 S Franklin St., Wilkes-Barre, Pennsylvania 18703; 1701 Banco Popular Ctr., Hato Rey, Puerto Rico 00918; 40 Westminster St., Providence, Rhode Island 02903; 2001 Bryan Twr., Dallas, Texas 75201; 601 Jefferson St., Houston, Texas 77002; Plaza 600, Seattle, Washington 98101; 777 E. Wisconsin Ave., Milwaukee, Wisconsin 53202; Argentina; Australia; Austria; Bahamas; Belgium; Brazil; Chile; Columbia; Denmark; Dominican Republic; Ecuador; Egypt; England; Ethiopia; Finland; France; Germany; Greece; Guatemala; Hong Kong; India; Iran; Ireland; Israel; Italy; Jamaica; Japan; Korea; Lebanon; Malysia; Mexico; Netherlands; New Zealand; Nicaragua; Nigeria; Norway; Panama; Peru; Philippines; Singapore; South Africa; Spain; Sweden; Switzerland; Taiwam; Tunisia; Venezuela
Areas Served: worldwide
Founded: 1915 *Staff:* over 100 *Revenues:* over $10 million
Professional Affiliations: /AICPA
Services: 1.0 2.0 3.0 4.0 5.0 6.0 7.0 9.0 10.0
Industries: Most A.00 C.00 D.00 E.41 E.42 G.00 H.00 I.00 J.95 J.96

Lawrence-Leiter & Co.
427 W. 12th St.
Kansas City, Missouri 64105
(816)474-8340

A general consulting firm providing services in general management, marketing, management development, executive recruiting, human resources management, industrial relations, administrative services, data processing services, and feasibility studies. Clients include associations, banks, governments, merchandisers, hospitals, insurance companies, manufacturers, non-profit organizations, professional societies, retailers, savings and loan associations and utilities.

Contact: David R. Bywaters, pres.
Areas Served: worldwide
Founded: 1950 *Staff:* 25-50 *Revenues:* $1-$5 million
Professional Affiliations: ACME, IMC
Services: Most
Industries: Most

Learned & Mahn
360 Sonna Bldg.
Boise, Idaho 83702
(208)336-2281

We are a financial consulting firm. We limit our services to financial planning and information systems.

Contact: Kevin E. Learned, ptnr.
Areas Served: ID
Founded: 1973 *Staff:* 3-10 *Revenues:* $100-$500,000

Services: 5.1   5.2   5.3   5.4   5.6   5.8   5.9
Industries: Most

A.M. Lederer & Co., Inc.

515 Madison Ave.
New York, New York 10022
(212)751-0515

> General management and manufacturing services with heavy emphasis on international operations and United Nations agencies.

Contact: A.M. Lederer, pres.
Founded: 1951 *Staff:* 1-3 *Revenues:* under $100,000
Professional Affiliations: IMC/PE
Services: 1.0   2.0   5.6   10.0
Industries: D.20   D.26   D.27   D.38   D.39   H.62   I.82   K.00

Lee-Hecht & Associates

200 Park Ave.
New York, New York 10017
(212)557-0009

> Behavioral science consultants specializing in outplacement counseling, management training, organization planning and development.

Contact: Robert Lee, pres.
Areas Served: U.S.
Founded: 1974 *Staff:* 3-10 *Revenues:* $500,000-1 million
Services: 3.1   3.4   3.8   3.9   3.10   3.11   4.9
Industries: Most

Legge Associates, Inc.

110 Allen's Creek Rd.
Rochester, New York 14618
(716)461-3550

> Specialists in general management, manufacturing management, and facilities planning. Innovative programs tailored to client's specific needs. Clients include diverse divsions of large multi-national corporations, small locally-owned corporations, not-for-profit institutions, and government agencies.

Contact: Richard C. Legge, CMC
Areas Served: US- primarily Rochester area
Founded: 1962 *Staff:* 3-10 *Revenues:* $100-$500,000
Professional Affiliations: IMC
Services: 1.0   2.0   3.8   5.2   5.3   5.9   6.4   6.5   9.2
Industries: D.00   F.00   F.50   I.75   I.80   I.82   J.91   J.92   J.94   J.96

Samuel F. Leigh Associates, Inc.

322 Noroton Ave.
Darien, Connecticut 06820
(203)655-7276

> Consulting services for users and manufacturers of paperbound packaging, in areas of graphic and structural design, purchasing, converting equipment, including packaging machinery, specifications, quality control and cost evaluation. Counseling packaging manufacturers in management, marketing, sales, service, personnel search and recruitment, mergers and acquisitions.

Contact: Samuel F. Leigh, pres.

Areas Served: U.S.
Founded: 1972 *Staff:* 1-3 *Revenues:* under $100,000
Professional Affiliations: SPMC
Services: 2.0   3.4   4.0   4.7   5.0   5.2   6.0   6.3   8.0
Industries: D.26   D.27

Allen Levis Organization, Inc.

466 Central Ave.
Northfield, Illinois 60093
(312)441-9400

A marketing services firm that works with general merchandise manufacturers and retailers to improve their marketing efficiency, sales effectiveness and profitability in supermarkets and other mass retail outlets. Service include industry and consumer research and analysis, and the development and implementation of marketing, sales and communication strategies.

Contact: Allen Levis, pres.
Areas Served: worldwide
Founded: 1967 *Staff:* 10-25 *Revenues:* $500,000-1 million
Services: 4.0   4.1   4.2   4.3   4.6   4.9   4.11

Walter K. Levy Associates Inc.

415 Madison Ave.
New York, New York 10017
(212)688-6852

Retail marketing and management consultants providing services in such areas as corporate planning and strategy development, market and location research and analysis, market merchandising research and program, organization audits and design, expense reduction programs, operations audits, systems review and concept design and executive search.

Contact: Walter K. Levy
Areas Served: U.S., Europe & Japan
Founded: 1971 *Staff:* 3-10 *Revenues:* $100-$500,000
Services: 1.1   1.3   1.4   1.5   1.7   1.10   3.4   4.1   4.3   4.4
Industries: F.50   F.51   G.52   G.53   G.56   G.57   G.58   G.59

Rensis Likert Associates, Inc.

630 City Center Bldg.
Ann Arbor, Michigan 48104
(313)769-1980

Founded by Dr. Rensis Likert and colleagues to translate the most current findings in behavioral science into practical application. Professional services in organizational diagnosis and human resource development to many kinds of organizations, the results of which have been widely published.

Contact: Dr. David
Founded: 1971 *Staff:* 10-25 *Revenues:* $500,000-1 million
Services: 1.0   2.0   3.0   4.0   5.0   6.0   9.0
Industries: Most

Kwasha Lipton

429 Sylvan Ave.
Englewood Cliffs, New Jersey 07632
(201)567-0001

Consulting actuaries, employee benefit and compensation services--domestic and international. Plan design, implementation, actuarial valuation, cost studies and projections; insurance retention and dividend analyses; employee communication programs--benefit statements, brochures, handbooks, audio-visuals, etc.; trust investment objective and performance studies, money manager selection; defined contribution plan computerized recordkeeping; executive compensation, salary administration and performance appraisal programs.

Contact: Harry F. Bremer, ptnr.
Areas Served: worldwide
Founded: 1944 *Staff:* over 100 *Revenues:* over $10 million
Professional Affiliations: /SA, CIA, AAA, CAPP
Services: 3.2   3.3   3.6   3.7   3.8   3.9   3.10   5.3   5.8   5.9
Industries: Most

Arthur D. Little, Inc.

25 Acorn Park
Cambridge, Massachusetts 02140
(617)864-5770

An international research, engineering, and menagement consulting organization. Our business is to help industry, governmental agencies and institutions solve the problems and exploit the opportunities inherent in change. Our 1000-member professional staff includes specialists in virtually all of the management, technical, and scientific disciplines.

Contact: Karl H. Klaussen, pres.
Affiliates/branches: 1735 Eye St., NW, Washington, D.C. 20006; 1 Maritime Plaza, San Francisco, California 94111; 17 New England Exec. Park, Burlington, Massachusetts 01803; 120 Eglinton Ave. E. Toronto, Ontario Canada; London; Brussels; Paris; Wiesbaden; Madrid; Athens; Rio de Janeiro; Sao Paulo; Tokyo
Areas Served: worldwide
Founded: 1886 *Staff:* over 100 *Revenues:* over $10 million
Services: Most
Industries: Most

Loer & Bradford Consultants, Inc.

2201 E. 46th St.
Indianapolis, Indiana 46205
(317)259-1379

Personnel & labor relations--personnel policies and systems, union avoidance, attitude measurement, affirmative action plans, contract negotiations, grievance administration. General management--organization planning, manpower development, management by objective. Plant site location--manpower availability, (present and future), prevailing pay rates, benefits and practices, union climate, other environmental factors. Business brokerage--merger, sale, acquisition.

Contact: Earl F. Bradford, pres.
Areas Served: Indiana, neighboring Mid-West and Mid-Southern states
Founded: 1953 *Staff:* 1-3 *Revenues:* $100-$500,000
Professional Affiliations: AMC/NAMAC, ASPA
Services: 1.1   1.2   1.6   1.15   2.9   2.10   3.0   11.2
Industries: Most

William T. Lorenz & Co.
31 Fairfield St.
Boston, Massachusetts 02116
(617)266-1784

Services restricted to marketing. We "get in" & "get out", earning respect on a 1-1 basis throughout the organization.

Contact: William T. Lorenz, pres.
Areas Served: U.S.
Founded: 1976 *Staff:* 3-10 *Revenues:* $100-$500,000
Professional Affiliations: /AMA
Services: 1.3 1.4 1.6 1.14 3.9 4.2 4.5 4.9 4.11 4.16
Industries: C.16 C.17 D.26 D.29 D.35 D.38 H.62 I.70 I.73 J.95

Lovejoy Management Consultants
90 Corona
Denver, Colorado 80218
(303)777-7252

Resourceful and innovative approaches to management level people decisions. Smaller corporations. Parallel planning relationships to develop client self-sufficiency.

Contact: Alan K. Lovejoy, mng. ptnr.
Areas Served: U.S.
Founded: 1976 *Staff:* 1-3 *Revenues:* under $100,000
Services: 1.1 1.7 3.1 3.4 11.0 11.1
Industries: Most

Lund Management & Marketing Services, Inc.
15315 SW Bull Mountain Rd.
Tigard, Oregon 97223
(503)620-0500

Corporate effectiveness studies and programs, manager development, marketing programs for industry and consulting firms. Strategic planning. Generalist services in management and marketing.

Contact: R.G. Lund, CMC, pres.
Areas Served: U.S.
Founded: 1959 *Staff:* 1-3 *Revenues:* $100-$500,000
Professional Affiliations: AMC, IMC
Services: Most
Industries: Most

Carl F. Lutz
305 Palos Verdes Dr.
Austin, Texas 78734
(512)261-6010

Specialist in job evaluation, wage and salary administration, performance appraisal systems and career development programs. Clients have included US local, state and federal governments; foreign national governments and government corporations; oil industry; airlines; private industry and quasi-public organizations. Principal has had over 25 years experience in US, Middle East, and Latin America consulting work.

Contact: Carl F. Lutz, princ.
Areas Served: U.S., Middle East, Central & South America
Founded: 1972 *Staff:* 3-10 *Revenues:* under $100,000

Professional Affiliations: AMC/ACA, CCS
Services: 1.1   3.1   3.2   3.6   3.7   3.8
Industries: D.29   E.45   I.80   I.82   J.91   J.94

LWFW, Inc.
12700 Park Central Place
Dallas, Texas 75251
(214)233-5561

Multidisciplinary professional management consulting services varying from those dealing with problems of individual effectiveness and productivity to projects dealing with the larger scope of organizational functioning. Present clients include private businesses, financial institutions, governmental organizations and not-for-profit associations.

Contact: Charles R. Ferguson, chmn.
Affiliates/branches: Houston; Austin
Areas Served: U.S.- primarily Southwest
Founded: 1954 *Staff:* 25-50 *Revenues:* $1-$5 million
Professional Affiliations: ACME, IMC
Services: 1.0   2.0   3.0   4.0   5.0   6.0   9.0
Industries: C.00   D.00   E.00   F.00   G.00   H.00   I.00   J.00

MacFarlane & Co., Inc.
1 Park Place
Atlanta, Georgia 30318
(404)352-2290

General management and marketing consulting firm specializing in serving industrial product and service clients in such product areas as market studies, acquisition reviews, general management audits, competitive situation analyses, industrial marketing planning, organization, long-range and diversification planning, executive and sales compensation, feasibility, and related areas.

Contact: Ian MacFarlane, pres.
Affiliates/branches: Toronto; Mexico City; Frankfurt
Areas Served: U.S., especially Southeast
Founded: 1972 *Staff:* 3-10 *Revenues:* $100-$500,000
Professional Affiliations: SPMC/AMA
Services: 1.0   1.3   1.7   3.0   4.0   4.3   4.5   4.11   9.0   10.3
Industries: A.00   C.00   D.00   D.24   D.28   E.00   F.00   G.00   H.00   I.00

Macphie-James, Inc.
20 Birch St.
Boston, Massachusetts 02131
(617)325-1800

Nine senior consultants with complementary specialities ranging from organization & planning to merketing, employee opinion & attitude surveys, security, industrial relations & management development.

Contact: Rodney P. Macphie, pres.
Areas Served: Eastern U.S.
Founded: 1973 *Staff:* 3-10 *Revenues:* $100-$500,000
Professional Affiliations: IMC
Services: 1.0   2.0   3.0   4.0   7.0   8.0
Industries: D.00   D.26   D.30   D.33   D.34   D.35   D.38   E.42

Macro Systems, Inc.
8630 Fenton St.
Silver Spring, Maryland 20910
(301)588-5484

Founded by individuals who consider responsiveness to client needs, in specific functional areas, a top priority. Concentration in only four areas: 1) general management, 2) finance and accounting, 3) information systems, and 4) R & D management and evaluation. Our client base is a selective group of larger scale projects in the public and private sector.

Contact: Frank J. Quirk, vp.
Areas Served: U.S. & Caribbean
Founded: 1969 *Staff:* 50-100 *Revenues:* $1-$5 million
Services: 1.1   1.5   1.6   1.8   1.9   5.1   5.2   5.8   7.1   9.0
Industries: I.80   I.82   I.83   I.86   J.91   J.92   J.94   J.96

William J. Mager & Associates
6400 Goldsboro Rd.
Washington, D.C. 20034
(301)229-0661

Professional-service and technical-firm oriented. General management consultants to professional engineers, architects, development and research laboratories, management and business consultants. Functional areas: organization, long-range planning, MBO, business development and client relations, performance evaluation and incentive compensation plans, equity buy-sell agreements, financial management, international operations, acquisitions-mergers.

Contact: William J. Mager, CMC, princ.
Areas Served: U.S., Canada, Europe & Far East
Founded: 1963 *Staff:* 1-3 *Revenues:* $100-$500,000
Professional Affiliations: IMC
Services: 1.0   3.0   4.0   5.O   7.2   10.0   11.0
Industries: A.07   A.08   D.28   D.38   E.44   I.73

Mahler Associates, Inc.
10-B Midland Park Ctr.
Midland Park, New Jersey 07432
(201)447-1130

A small group of experienced consultants. We concentrate on making a design contribution, on a collaborative basis, for very large companies. This contribution would be made in areas of executive continuity, planning organization structure, management education, and revitalizing the human resource function. Conduct an eight-week Advanced Management Skills program for general managers. Attendence is one week a quarter.

Contact: Walter R. Mahler, pres.
Areas Served: U.S. & Europe
Founded: 1954 *Staff:* 3-10 *Revenues:* $100-$500,000
Professional Affiliations: AMC
Services: 1.1   1.2   1.3   1.4   1.6   1.7   3.1   3.10
Industries: Most

Thomas P. Mahoney Associates

4961 Brookview Rd.
Rockford, Illinois 61125
(815)398-2005

Specializing in management appraisals, marketing, production and technology for magazine, book and newspaper publishers; commercial printers; in-plant printing departments; corporate communications organizations; suppliers of equipment and materials to these fields. Acquisitions and mergers: confidential searches and negotiations.

Contact: Thomas P. Mahoney, pres.
Affiliates/branches: La Habra, California; New York, New York
Areas Served: North America
Founded: 1965 *Staff:* 1-3 *Revenues:* $100-$500,000
Professional Affiliations: /AGAC
Services: 1.0   2.0   4.0   5.10   9.0   10.3   11.1
Industries: D.26   D.27

Main,Jackson & Garfield

535 Fifth Ave.
New York, New York 10017
(212)867-7948

General management consulting services to small-to-medium size as well as large organizations. Senior staff directly involved in client studies. Reflecting staff interests and backgrounds, firm's strongest competences are in the fields of organization; business planning, including acquisitions and divestments; all facets of marketing; and overhead cost reduction.

Contact: John G. Main, mng. dir.
Areas Served: U.S. & Canada
Founded: 1968 *Staff:* 1-3 *Revenues:* $100-$500,000
Professional Affiliations: AMC
Services: Most   1.1   1.3   1.4   1.6   1.10   2.1   3.2   4.1   4.5   4.15
Industries: Most   D.20   D.26   D.27   D.28   D.34   D.36   D.38   F.50   F.51   G.54

Management Analysis Center, Inc.

1100 Massachusetts Ave.
Cambridge, Massachusetts 02138
(617)661-7600

Concentrate on formulating and implementing strategic change. This includes methods to determine strategy (environmental scanning, industry study, internal analysis) and change management behavior (organization structure, management processes, control systems, reward systems). This work is done through the firm's extensive full-time professional staff and affiliated business and economic faculty members.

Contact: James N. Kelly, pres.
Affiliates/branches: Washington, D.C.; Chicago, Illinois; San Francisco, California; Barcelona
Areas Served: U.S., Canada, Mexico, South America & Europe
Founded: 1964 *Staff:* 50-100 *Revenues:* over $10 million
Services: 1.0   3.1   4.1   4.2   4.11   5.3
Industries: Most

Management Campus, Inc.

2000 Clearview Ave.,NE
Atlanta, Georgia 30340
(404)458-9021

Management Campus, Inc. is a process-oriented management consulting firm with a depth of experience and design of business education programs, as well as the development and consulting related to the facilities appropriate to support a learning center environment.

Contact: John P. Sullivan, pres.
Areas Served: North America
Founded: 1972 *Staff:* 10-25 *Revenues:* $500,000-1 million
Services: 1.0 3.0 4.0 5.0
Industries: Most

Management Decision Systems, Inc.

300 Third Ave.
Waltham, Massachusetts 02154
(617)890-1100

Marketing, finance and planning. Faster, more responsive, more thorough problem solving through consultants leveraged by propriety computer tools. Developers of the Express language for business analysis and planning. Developers of Assessor system for laboratory test marketing of new consumer products. Specialists in consumer market models, sales forecasting, and marketing analysis. Software tools available for use by our staff.

Contact: Walter E. Lankau, Jr., vp
Affiliates/branches: San Francisco; Paris
Areas Served: U.S. & Europe
Founded: 1967 *Staff:* over 100 *Revenues:* $5-$10 million
Services: 1.5 1.10 1.13 4.14
Industries: Most D.20 D.21 D.27 D.29 G.54 G.56 H.60 H.62

Management Horizons, Inc.

450 W. Wilson Bridge Rd.
Columbus, Ohio 43085
(614)846-9555

A distribution-focused professional consulting firm serving North American and European retailers, wholesalers, manufacturers and trade associations.

Contact: Cyrus Wilson, exec. vp.
Affiliates/branches: 50 California St., San Francisco, California 94111; Richmond,Surrey
Areas Served: North America & Western Europe
Founded: 1968 *Staff:* 25-50 *Revenues:* $1-$5 million
Services: 1.0 1.6 1.8 2.12 4.1 4.2 4.3 4.6 4.11 4.14
Industries: D.22 D.23 D.25 D.31 G.00 G.52 G.53 G.56 G.57 I.82

Management & Marketing

176 Second Ave.
Waltham, Massachusetts 02154
(617)890-7788

General management and marketing consulting. Interim management of smaller companies or marketing departments. Marketing studies. Search.

Contact: William M. Rand, Jr.
Areas Served: New England
Founded: 1966 *Staff:* 1-3 *Revenues:* under $100,000

Professional Affiliations: IMC
Services: 1.0   1.1   1.10   4.0   5.0   7.0   8.0   9.0   9.5
Industries: C.17   D.20   D.23   D.28   D.34   D.35   D.38   D.39   I.80

Management/Marketing Associates,Inc.
Bank of California Tower
Portland, Washington 97205
(503)228-9327
> Marketing-oriented consultants to management with depth experience in marketing and organization research, strategic and marketing planning, and organization development relating to MBO and marketing. Services include customized training, product evaluation and positioning, polling, forecasting, industrial and consumer analyses. Depth experience in all Pacific Northwest markets and numerous national industries.

Contact: Donald T. Jacobson, CMC, pres.
Areas Served: Pacific Northwest & CA
Founded: 1974 *Staff:* 3-10 *Revenues:* $100-$500,000
Professional Affiliations: IMC/AAA, PEI, AEA, NABE, AMA
Services: 1.3   1.5   1.6   1.7   4.1   4.2   4.3   4.5   4.8   4.11

Manley Management & Marketing Services Corp.
283 Greenwich Ave.
Greenwich, Connecticut 06830
(203)869-2601
> Strategic business planning, feasibility and diversification studies, profit improvement programs, corporate turn-arounds, market and product research, sales management and compensation, R & D and international evaluations, sales forecasts. Blue chip clients in over 100 areas: manufacturing (electronic printing, chemicals, ceramic, machinery and instruments, electronics including military), petrochemicals, medical, agriculture, mining, banking, etc.

Contact: Robert R. Manley, pres.
Areas Served: worldwide
Founded: 1959 *Staff:* 3-10 *Revenues:* $500,000-1 million
Professional Affiliations: IMC, , SPMC/ACG, ACCCE
Services: 1.0   1.6   4.1   4.2   4.5   4.8   4.15   7.0   10.0   11.1
Industries: A.00   B.00   C.00   D.00   D.28   D.36   D.38   E.00   F.00   I.00

Frank B. Manley & Co.
(Division of Alexander & Alexander)
1 Pickwick Plaza
Greenwich, Connecticut 06830
(203)661-6606
> Consultants in the management of human resources. Services typically include executive compensation and financial counseling, organization planning, management development, and personnel administration. Clients are served in a wide range of industry and size of organization.

Contact: Frank B. Manley, pres.
Areas Served: U.S.
Founded: 1972 *Staff:* 10-25 *Revenues:* $1-$5 million
Professional Affiliations: ACME, IMC/ASPA
Services: 1.1   1.7   1.15   2.6   3.0   4.9   4.15
Industries: Most

Arthur Manning Associates
31 Windsor Place
Upper Montclair, New Jersey 07043
(201)744-5324

We specialize in assisting owners of smaller manufacturing companies with problems of organization and managerial control of operations. In the past two years we have assisted with administration of human resources programs of local governments.

Contact: Arthur Manning, pres.
Areas Served: Northeastern U.S.
Founded: 1964 *Staff:* 1-3 *Revenues:* under $100,000
Professional Affiliations: SPMC
Services: 1.10 2.1 2.7 2.9 3.8 5.4 9.5 9.6
Industries: D.20 D.22 D.30 J.94

F.L. Mannix & Co., Inc.
65 William St.
Wellesley Hills, Massachusetts 02181
(617)237-1921

Founded to provide services to management that will enable them to operate more efficiently by having stronger communications with their employees, a better understanding of their functions and working relationships, and the assurance that they are adequately compensated and staffed with the best possible talent.

Contact: F.L. Mannix, pres.
Areas Served: U.S.
Founded: 1959 *Staff:* 1-3 *Revenues:* under $100,000
Professional Affiliations: AMC, IMC
Services: 1.1 1.6 3.1 3.2 3.4 3.7 3.8 3.10 4.2 4.11
Industries: D.20 D.27 D.28 D.30 D.33 D.34 D.35 D.36 D.38 D.39

Manplan Consultants
20 N. Wacker Dr.
Chicago, Illinois 60606
(312)726-3538

As organization and human resources consultants, we utilize creative and client-centered approaches in establishing the proper structure and climate for management motivation and productivity. Both corporate and individual needs are analyzed, goals set, and time parameters determined.

Contact: W.L. Davidson, ptnr.
Areas Served: Mid-West & East
Founded: 1962 *Staff:* 3-10 *Revenues:* $100-$500,000
Professional Affiliations: IMC
Services: 1.1 1.7 3.1 3.2 3.4 3.5 3.7 3.8 3.10 3.11
Industries: D.00 H.60 I.80

Manresa Management Consultants, Inc.
1612 Summit Ave.
Fort Worth, Texas 76102
(817)336-2244

We depend on our staff's professional understanding of management objectives and industrial systems to identify and correct problems for manufacturers and other businesses. Dedicated to increasing profits, the staff is experienced in

improving productivity of industries as varied as plastics, potato chips, shoes, kitchen cabinets, aluminum foundries, engines and candy.
Contact: Emiliano Manresa, pres.
Areas Served: U.S., Europe & South America
Founded: 1966 *Staff:* 1-3 *Revenues:* $100-$500,000
Professional Affiliations: AMC
Services: 1.1   1.7   1.11   2.1   2.3   2.4   2.6   2.9   2.14   3.8
Industries: D.20   D.24   D.25   D.30   D.31   D.34   D.35   D.37   D.39

Manuals Corporation of America

Box 247
Setauket, New York 11733
(516)751-2626

Specialize in developing, designing, preparing, writing, and maintaining internally required manuals, guidebooks, handbooks. Conduct seminars and workshops (including in-house programs) on how to develop effective and efficient manuals programs. Clients include industrial organizations, banks and related financial institutions, insurance companies, governments, hospitals, businesses.
Contact: Karl Schricker, pres.
Areas Served: worldwide
Founded: 1964 *Staff:* 3-10 *Revenues:* $100-$500,000
Professional Affiliations: /ASM, IABC, NAGC, ARMA, ABCA, IWPA
Services: 3.9   9.0   11.0
Industries: Most

Marcept Consulting & Research

Box 7871
Boise, Idaho 83707
(208)343-4607

We provide our clients with professional marketing assistance through expertly designed and implemented research and analysis- for organizations concerned about improving their effectiveness among the markets and publics they serve.
Contact: Thomas R. Brown, pres.
Areas Served: Western U.S.
Founded: 1973 *Staff:* 1-3 *Revenues:* $100-$500,000
Services: 3.10   4.0   4.1   4.2   4.3   4.4   4.5   4.8   4.10   4.11
Industries: D.20   D.24   D.25   D.39   G.00   H.60   I.73   I.80

Bill Marcus & Associates, Inc.

515 Travelers Tower
Southfield, Michigan 48076
(313)354-1124

Consultant to the automotive companies and to individual car dealers, concentrating on parts department operations and controls. Also design of factory programs and systems to implement the above and enhance profitability by reducing obsolescence, increasing cash flow and improving marketing techniques.
Contact: W.E. Marcus, pres.
Areas Served: U.S.
Founded: 1979 *Staff:* 1-3 *Revenues:* $100-$500,000
Professional Affiliations: /AIC

Services: 1.1   1.2   1.7   1.9   1.10   3.9   5.8   6.3   6.4   9.5
Industries: G.55   I.75

Marketing & Systems Development Corporation
1200 Wall St. W.
Lyndhurst, New Jersey 07071
(201)935-9200
>   Specializing in telecommunications. Optimization and cost control for large,
>   multi-location corporations. Our objectives are carried out for our clients by our
>   staff of over seventy communication professionals and they basically are: 1)
>   maintain or improve the level of service for telephone users and 2) effect
>   substantial cost reductions.

Contact: Joseph J. Cacopardo
Affiliates/branches: Chicago; Dallas; Hartford; Los Angeles; New York; Pittsburgh
Areas Served: U.S.
Founded: 1974 *Staff:* 50-100 *Revenues:* $1-$5 million
Services: 11.3
Industries: Most

Marpet Consultants, Inc.
2 Bell Ave.
Somerville, New Jersey 08876
(201)526-1700
>   General consultant and advisor to small business. Specialist in small business
>   management and financial accounting.

Contact: Peter A. Schkeeper, CMC, pres.
Areas Served: Metro NY
Founded: 1961 *Staff:* 1-3 *Revenues:* under $100,000
Professional Affiliations: IMC
Services: 1.0   5.0
Industries: C.17   D.34   D.36   D.38   D.39   G.55   G.59   I.00

Marshall Institute
529 S. Clinton Ave.
Trenton, New Jersey 08611
(609)394-7153
>   Concentrate on maintenance- housekeeping management maintenance systems
>   and procedures- maintenance supervisory development and maintenance craft
>   skills training programs. Plant operations & facilities feasibility studies-
>   problem definition studies.

Contact: George F. Smith, sr. vp.
Areas Served: U.S. & South America
Founded: 1976 *Staff:* 3-10 *Revenues:* $500,000-1 million
Professional Affiliations: IMC
Services: 1.4   1.5   1.7   1.10   2.3   2.4   2.9   2.13   2.15   3.5
Industries: Most

Martech Inc.
592 Preble St.
Cape Elizabeth-Portland, Maine 04107
(207)799-6489
>   We are a small firm and our principle market is small and medium-sized

business (although we have a couple of Fortune 500 firms as clients). Our areas of expertise are marketing, business start-ups, capital location, industrial product marketing and research, and small business trouble shooting. As a small firm we offer a very personal service, usually undertaking no more than 3 projects at any one time.

Contact: J.B. Maxwell, dir.
Areas Served: ME, NH, Eastern MA, RI & Maritime Canada
Founded: 1968 *Staff:* 3-10 *Revenues:* $100-$500,000
Services: 1.0   3.1   3.5   3.10   4.0   5.6   5.9   5.10   7.0   10.4
Industries: C.15   C.17   D.00   F.00   G.52   G.53   I.73   I.80   I.82   I.86

MAS International, Ltd.

Box 199
Sterling, Virginia 22170
(703)450-5310

Management advisory services to CPA firms and the general business community on specific engagements as well as on-going retainer basis in the areas of financial, administrative, marketing and operational management.

Contact: Louis H. Milotte, Jr., GMC, pres.
Affiliates/branches: Box 300, Frankford, Delaware 19945; 108 Lancer Dr., Summerville, South Carolina 29483
Areas Served: VA,MD,DC,DE & SC
Founded: 1973 *Staff:* 3-10 *Revenues:* $100-$500,000
Professional Affiliations: IMC
Services: Most   1.2   1.8   3.2   3.7   4.16   5.2   5.5   5.9   5.11   9.5
Industries: Most   B.14   C.15   C.17   D.34   E.45   G.54   H.65   I.79   I.80   I.86

E. Gilbert Mathews, Inc.

Box 429
Guilford, Connecticut 06473
(203)453-3963

The firm is small, personal, responsible with high performance rating & meticulous ethics- our services are technical but we also function in sales-marketing, production & management to the packaging converter as well as the user (large & small) & also the graphic arts. Most clients are "long time" accounts plus a number of long term retainers- we also publish two newsletters.

Contact: E. Gilbert Mathews,pres.
Areas Served: U.S-primarily East & Midwest, England, Europe & South America
Founded: 1966 *Staff:* 3-10 *Revenues:* $100-$500,000
Professional Affiliations: SPMC/AIIE
Services: 1.0   2.0   3.0   4.0   5.10   6.3   7.0   8.0   9.0   10.3
Industries: D.26   D.27   D.35   I.7.

Lawrence M. Matthews

958 N. Fifth St.
Philadelphia, Pennsylvania 19123
(215)627-2031

In addition to general management consulting, mainly in operations, conduct series of 2-day management seminars at over 50 US universities, for manufacturers associations, and for management centre Europe.

Contact: Lawrence M. Matthews, CMC
Areas Served: U.S., England, Holland, Canada, Germany, Switzerland & Venezuela
Founded: 1972 *Staff:* 1-3 *Revenues:* under $100,000

Professional Affiliations: IMC
Services: 1.0   2.0   3.0   4.0   5.0   6.0   7.0
Industries: D.00   F.50

George S. May International Co.
111 S. Washington St.
Park Ridge, Illinois 60068
(312)825-8806

We are the largest firm of management consultants devoted to solving the problems of the small and medium size business; manufacturers, wholesalers, retailers. We operate throughout the U.S., Canada, and most of Western Europe. Established in 1925. More than 250,000 firms have used our service.

Contact: J.J. Coffey, Jr., dir. pr
Affiliates/branches: 291 Geary St., San Francisco, California 94102; 620 Cathcart St. Montreal, Quebec Canada; Amsterdam; Brussels; Dusseldorf; London; Mexico City; Milan; Paris
Areas Served: U.S., Canada & Western Europe
Founded: 1925 *Staff:* over 100 *Revenues:* over $10 million
Services: 1.1   1.9   2.1   2.6   3.8   4.7   5.1   5.2   6.4   9.5
Industries: C.15   D.21   D.24   D.31   D.39   E.42   G.52   G.55   G.58

H.B. Maynard & Co.
2040 Ardmore Blvd.
Pittsburgh, Pennsylvania 15221
(412)351-4100

Production and maintenance consultants specializing in productivity improvement, facilities planning, and wage plans for business, industry and all levels of government.

Contact: W.M. Aiken, pres.
Affiliates/branches: 212 S. Tryon St., Charlotte, North Carolina 28281; 1100 Jorie Blvd., Oak Brook, Illinois 60521; 100 Constitution Plaza, Hartford, Connecticut 06103; 10960 Wilshire Blvd., Los Angeles, California 90024; 60 E. 42nd St., New York, New York 10017; London; Paris; Madrid; Zurich; Gothenburg; Helsinki; Copenhagen; Milan; The Hague; Dusseldorf
Areas Served: North America, Western Europe
Founded: 1934 *Staff:* 50-100 *Revenues:* $5-$10 million
Professional Affiliations: ACME
Services: 1.0   2.0   3.0   4.7   4.15   5.0   6.0   9.0
Industries: B.12   C.16   D.00   E.00   H.60   J.94   J.96

McBer & Co.
137 Newbury St.
Boston, Massachusetts 02116
(617)261-5570

A research-oriented behavioral science consulting firm founded by David C. McLelland, specializing in competency assessment and applications of competency assessment via training, selection, performance appraisal, career development etc., as well as providing special management and organizational development programs based on human motivation and competency concepts and research.

Contact: Richard E. Boyatzis, pres.
Areas Served: U.S.
Founded: 1963 *Staff:* 25-50 *Revenues:* $1-$5 million

Services: 1.1 3.1 3.4 3.8 3.10 3.11 4.7 7.1
Industries: Most

McClenahan Associates
20 E. 46th St.
New York, New York 10017
(212)490-3336

We provide general management consulting services to senior business
management, adhering to the ACME code of professional standards and ethics.
We serve both private and publicly-held businesses from major diversified
concerns to smaller companies. We specialize in marketing, planning,
management organization, and business growth and development.

Contact: Don M. Guthrie, princ.
Areas Served: U.S.- primarily East & Midwest
Founded: 1977 *Staff:* 3-10 *Revenues:* $100-$500,000
Services: 1.0 2.0 3.0 4.0 5.0 10.0
Industries: B.00 D.00 E.00

McCormack & Associates
5022 Park Rd.
Charlotte, North Carolina 28209
(704)527-0646

General management consultants dedicated to improving client profitability.
We undertake no projects without a prior conference and defined program to
achieve the desired results.

Contact: James S. McCormack
Areas Served: U.S.
Founded: 1973 *Staff:* 1-3 *Revenues:* $100-$500,000
Services: 1.0 2.0 3.0
Industries: C.00 D.00 I.00

C.H. McCormack & Associates, Inc.
800 W. Belt S.
Houston, Texas 77042
(713)780-1323

We specialize in the financial area and assist our clientele in financial planning,
execution programming (how plans are implemented), and control. We also
provide many clients with a unique computerized bond portfolio as a whole and
generates detailed accounting information.

Contact: C.H. McCormack, CMC, pres.
Areas Served: South & Midwest
Founded: 1968 *Staff:* 1-3 *Revenues:* $100-$500,000
Professional Affiliations: IMC
Services: 1.0 5.0 9.3 9.5
Industries: H.60 H.62 H.63

McCormick & Co.
2 Overhill Rd.
Scarsdale, New York 10583
(914)723-5200

Established international management-engineering firm with key focus on
control, profitability, and planning. Highly specialized and implementation-

oriented, featuring unique marginal income techniques and utilizing a working liaison with in-house staff. The result is immediately operational controls, quickly established targets, improved profitability and planning analysis, with client personnel implementation continuing smoothly and effectively.

Contact: R.L. Staehle, pres.
Affiliates/branches: 6900 E. Camelback Rd., Scottsdale, Arizona 85251
Areas Served: U.S.
Founded: 1946 *Staff:* 25-50 *Revenues:* $1-$5 million
Professional Affiliations: ACME, IMC/AICPA
Services: 1.0 2.0 5.0 6.0 7.4 9.0
Industries: Most

McCutcheon Associates NW

10700 S.W. Beaverton Hwy.
Beaverton, Oregon 97005
(503)644-1104

Operating philosophy is that of providing client firms totally tailored programs in areas of organizational development, supervisory and middle management training, employee attitude surveys and training to maximize return on the most critical investment of any business firm: its people.

Contact: Don M. McCutcheon, CMC
Areas Served: U.S., Canada, Mexico & Far East
Founded: 1977 *Staff:* 1-3 *Revenues:* under $100,000
Professional Affiliations: IMC/ASTD
Services: 1.0 3.0 4.0 9.1 9.2 9.5 9.6
Industries: G.58 I.70 I.73 J.80 J.86

McElrath & Associates

6700 France Ave. S.
Minneapolis, Minnesota 55435
(612)920-5761

Profit improvement through identification and solution of major cost, quality, and scheduling problems. Strategies are developed for organization of management resources, and technical skills for problem solution and implementation. The program is fully integrated into the company and trains company personnel to be self-sustaining. We are results-committed.

Contact: Gayle W. McElrath, pres.
Areas Served: Worldwide
Founded: 1978 *Staff:* 3-10 *Revenues:* $100-$500,000
Services: 1.0 2.0 3.1 3.5 4.12 6.3 9.5 11.0
Industries: D.20 D.26 D.28 D.32 D.33 D.34 D.35 D.36 D.39 I.82

McGinnis Associates

25 W. 45th St.
Brant Beach, New Jersey 08008
(609)494-0785

Assistance to public and private sector clients in: personnel administration, management training, collective bargaining negotiations, management audits, institutional and corporate reorganization, business purchases and acquisitions, real property management, selected accounting services, policy drafting and employee relations programs implementation

Contact: William J. McGinnis, Jr., pres.
Affiliates/branches: Long Island Beach, New Jersey; Philadelphia, Pennsylvania; Cocoa

Beach, Florida
Areas Served: U.S., Europe, Asia & Africa
Founded: 1965 *Staff:* 3-10 *Revenues:* $100-$500,000
Professional Affiliations: SPMC
Services: Most   1.0   2.9   3.0   4.10   7.2   9.1   11.4
Industries: Most   B.00   C.00   D.00   E.00   F.00   G.00   H.65   I.00   J.00

McKinsey & Co., Inc.
245 Park Ave.
New York, New York 10017
(212)692-6000

Specializing in top management problem-solving and program implementation on priority issues from the perspective of the key decision maker. Seeking to serve a diverse international clientele as an instrument of constructive change, improvement, and adaptation by working in the forefront of advanced management thinking and technique. Dedicated to the highest professional standards for quality of work and people: self-ownership to insure rigorous objectivity and continuous evolution of practice elements.

Contact: R. Donald Daniel, mng. dir.
Affiliates/branches: 1800 Peachtree Ctr., Atlanta, Georgia 30303; 2 First National Plaza, Chicago, Illinois 60603; 100 Erieview Plaza, Cleveland, Ohio 44114; 5944 Luther Lane, Dallas, Texas 75225; 1095 South Twr-Penzoil Pl., Houston, Texas 77002; 611 W Sixth St., Los Angeles, California 90017; 245 Park Ave., New York, New York 10017; 555 California St., San Francisco, California 94104; 3 Landmark Sq., Stamford, Connecticut 06901; 1700 Pennsylvania Ave., Washington, D.C. 20006; Manuel Avila Camacho #1 Piso 13, Mexico 10 Mexico; 80 Bloor St. W Toronto, Ontario Canada M5S 2V1; Amsterdam; Copenhagen; Dusseldorf; Frankfurt; London; Hamburg; Melbourne; Milan; Munich; Paris; Sydney; Tokyo; Zurich
Areas Served: worldwide
Founded: 1924 *Staff:* over 100 *Revenues:* over $10 million
Services: Most
Industries: Most

McLean Associates
Box 695
Simsbury, Connecticut 06070
(203)527-3816

Network Approach: general management principal, client knowledgeable in own field and, if needed, third-party specialists collaborate. Scope: needs assessment, development (see "Services"), problems or opportunities, governmental or community relations. Evaluation: progress and post-project. Settings: business, life insurance, associations, industry, government, community. Philosophy: ethical, independent, politically neutral, people-productivity-profit oriented.

Contact: Franklin J. McLean, pres.
Areas Served: U.S. & Canada
Founded: 1975 *Staff:* 1-3 *Revenues:* under $100,000
Professional Affiliations: /NASCP
Services: 1.1   1.2   1.3   1.7   1.9   1.12   3.1   4.1   5.4   7.2
Industries: Most

McManis Associates, Inc.
1201 Connecticut Ave.,NW
Washington, D.C. 20036
(202)466-7680

Staff of predominantly senior consultants has executive experience in types of organizations we serve: educational institutions, industry, federal/state/local government, and associations. Our philosophy stresses through problem-diagnosis; joint development of pragmatic, tailored solutions; and implementation planning and assistance. Doubling of volume in five years is indicator of achievement.

Contact: Gerald L. McMannis, pres.
Areas Served: worldwide
Founded: 1964 *Staff:* 25-50 *Revenues:* $1-$5 million
Professional Affiliations: AMC
Services: 1.0   2.10   3.0   4.1   4.11   5.0   7.2   9.5   11.1
Industries: I.82   I.86   J.91   J.92   J.93   J.94   J.95   J.96

MDC Systems Corp.
(owned by MDC Corp.)
1818 Market St.
Philadelphia, Pennsylvania 19103
(215)299-8213

Professional services in the planning and implementation of capital investments to clients involved in airports, health, education, recreation, mass transit, environmental, industrial, chemical, and petrochemical facilities. Services include taking complete responsibility for the total project as agent of owner or for specific services such as financial feasibility studies, identification and arrangement of required funding studies, design management, budget and cost control, value engineering, field supervision and inspection, CPM scheduling and project management information systems.

Contact: Thomas J. Driscoll
Areas Served: Eastern U.S., Iran, Costa Rica, Venezuela
Founded: 1965 *Staff:* 1-3 *Revenues:* under $100,000
Professional Affiliations: SPMC
Services: 1.0   2.0   5.0   6.0   9.0
Industries: C.15   C.16   D.28   D.29   D.32   E.40   E.41   E.43   E.45   I.80

Medical Management Associates
1530 Budfield St.
Johnstown, Pennsylvania 15904
(814)736-9604

A professional organization dedicated to improvement and change in ambulatory health care systems. Organizational personnel each have over ten years experience in medical office/clinic management. Experience includes grants management and third-party billing. The firm is directed by a physician.

Contact: Richard E. Kirkpatrick, vp.
Areas Served: U.S.
Founded: 1978 *Staff:* 1-3 *Revenues:* under $100,000
Professional Affiliations: /AHA, NAA, APHA, AGPA, MGMA
Services: 1.1   1.3   3.2   3.9   5.5   5.8   7.2   9.1   9.2   9.5
Industries: I.80

Medicus Systems Corporation
990 Grove St.
Evanston, Illinois 60611
(312)866-1500

With more than 250 full-time employees, provide a full range of systems services exclusively for health care organizations. Utilizing principles of computer science management engineering, operations research and related disciplines, to provide practical consultation to health care institutions in three major areas: computer and information systems, management systems, and planning.

Contact: Dr. John R. Freeman, exec. vp.
Areas Served: U.S. & Canada
Founded: 1969 *Staff:* over 100 *Revenues:* $5-$10 million
Services: 1.0   3.0   5.0   7.0   9.0
Industries: I.80

Edward M. Melton Associates
15 Eton Rd.
Scarsdale, New York 10583
(914)723-5567

Major emphasis on international operations. Reciprocal working arrangements with consulting firms in Europe, UK, Japan, Australia, India & Canada.

Contact: Edward M. Melton, pres.
Areas Served: U.S., Canada, Europe, Latin America, Japan, Australia
Founded: 1953 *Staff:* 1-3 *Revenues:* under $100,000
Services: 1.0   2.10   2.13   3.4   4.0   5.0   8.1   8.3   9.5   10.0
Industries: Most

Belden Menkus
Box 85
Middleville, New Jersey 07855
(201)383-3928

General services to management in design and improvement of information-handling systems. Specialized competence in security matters.

Contact: Belden Menkus
Areas Served: worldwide
Founded: 1970 *Staff:* 1-3 *Revenues:* under $100,000
Professional Affiliations: SPMC/ASIS, ACM, ASM
Services: 1.7   9.0   11.4
Industries: Most

William H. Meyer & Associates, Inc.
666 Fifth Ave.
New York, New York 10019
(212)581-1223

A general management consulting firm which places special emphasis on the area of facilities strategy: the determination of the location, size and type of physical facility required to serve or penetrate a selected market. Clients include financial, retail, municipal and development organizations.

Contact: Carl S. Meyer, CMC, pres.
Areas Served: Northeast & East Coast U.S.
Founded: 1968 *Staff:* 3-10 *Revenues:* $100-$500,000
Professional Affiliations: AMC, IMC
Services: 1.5   2.10   4.2   4.5   4.8   5.6   9.2
Industries: G.00   H.60   J.95

MHT Services, Inc.
510 Sylvan Ave.
Englewood Cliffs, New Jersey 07632
(201)567-1333
> We only accept engagements that we are confident of completing to the satisfaction of our client. We have a broad background in data processing in many environments, with emphasis on financial institutions and service bureaus. Our services include feasibility studies, operational audits, conversions, systems design, programming, and processing.

Contact: Martin Tillinger, pres.
Areas Served: NY-NJ metro
Founded: 1972 *Staff:* 3-10 *Revenues:* $100-$500,000
Services: 9.3 9.5 9.8
Industries: Most

Donald B. Miller
3600 Pruneridge Ave.
Santa Clara, California 95051
(408)244-9590
> Human resource management consultant with emphasis on improving the effectiveness and utilization as well as satisfactions and individual development, primarily although not exclusively with professional employees. Programs include design of continuing managerial, technical, and personal education, vitality enhancement strategies, career management and planning, and improved quality of work life.

Contact: Donald B. Miller, princ.
Areas Served: U.S.
Founded: 1978 *Staff:* 1-3 *Revenues:* under $100,000
Professional Affiliations: /
Services: 1.0 3.0 7.0
Industries: Most

Donald R. Miller
575 Madison Ave.
New York, New York 10022
(212)581-0944
> Services focus on counsel to chief executives, primarily on matters concernign the continued growth and development of the business, including: corporate strategy and plans, management organization arrangements and profit improvement programs. The emphasis is on analytical and disciplined approach with clear-cut, actionable decisions as the end result.

Contact: Donald R. Miller, mng. dir.
Areas Served: U.S., Canada & Europe
Founded: 1978 *Staff:* 1-3 *Revenues:* under $100,000
Professional Affiliations: IMC
Services: 1.1 1.3 1.4 1.6 1.7 1.10 4.6
Industries: G.00 G.53 G.54 I.86

Mitchell & Co.
146 Mt. Auburn St.
Cambridge, Massachusetts 02181
(617)965-4690
> We work with our clients to develop and implement business strategies.

Emphasis is placed onstrategies tailored to management's style and needs of the corporation. Proven analytical approaches are used to develop tactics necessary to pursue the strategy successfully. Empirical research is used to ensure that these strategies reflect the successful experiences of similar businesses.

Contact: Donald W. Mitchell, mng. dir.

Areas Served: U.S.

Founded: 1977 *Staff:* 3-10 *Revenues:* $500,000-1 million

Professional Affiliations: /AIMCO

Services: 1.1   1.2   1.3   1.4   1.5   3.1   4.1   4.11   5.4   10.2

Industries: Most

M & M Protection Consultants

(owned by Marsh & McLennan, Inc.)
1221 Ave. of the Americas
New York, New York 10020
(212)997-5874

An organization devoted to the protection of lives, the conservation of property, and the continuity of business. Over 250 people provide consultation concerning a total loss control concept in all areas of exposure, including property and earnings, public liability, environment and occupationaL health, products liability, crime and security, goods in transit, marine, vehicles, nuclear, property valuation and training programs.

Contact: A. C Rand, sr. vp.

Affiliates/branches: 222 S. Riverside Plaza, Chicago, Illinois 60606; 3 Embarcadero Ctr., San Francisco, California 94119; 7 King St. E. Toronto, Ontario Canada; Melbourne

Founded: 1871 *Staff:* over 100 *Revenues:* over $10 million

Services: 1.7   3.21   5.10   7.0

Industries: Most

Moeller Associates

Box 177
Towanda, Pennsylvania 18848
(717)265-6523

We concentrate on the organization, planning and direction of management staff and the internal ethical concerns and the external social responsibilities of organizations. Clients have included private business, public agencies and not for profit organizations. All work is tailored to the specific situation of the client organization.

Contact: Clark Moeller, pres.

Areas Served: U.S.

Founded: 1976 *Staff:* 1-3 *Revenues:* under $100,000

Professional Affiliations: /AIP

Services: 1.2   1.3   1.15   3.1   3.5   3.8   3.9   7.2   7.3

Industries: I.73   I.86   J.91   J.94

Montgomery & Associates, Inc.

67 Turtle Back Rd. W.
New Canaan, Connecticut 06840
(203)972-0302

Strategic planning, new product planning and development, marketing counsel and marketing research. Especially strong experience in banking, insurance, investments and other financial services industries.

Contact: Robert C. Montgomery, CMC, pres.
Areas Served: U.S. & Canada, Western Europe
Founded: 1971 *Staff:* 1-3 *Revenues:* $100-$500,000
Professional Affiliations: IMC
Services: 1.1 1.2 1.3 1.4 1.5 1.14 4.1 4.2 4.11 4.12
Industries: D.26 H.60 H.62 H.63 H.64 I.70 I.72 I.73 I.86 I.89

John O. Morris Associates
Box 230
West Hartford, Connecticut 06107
(203)523-7692

We help people in organizations improve their written communications--particularly complex, analytical materials. We design training programs to meet specific needs. Our focus is on clear thinking, orderly structure, and writing for your audience. We also prepare models of effective communications and rewrite manuals.

Contact: John O. Morris, pres.
Areas Served: U.S. & Canada
Founded: 1965 *Staff:* 1-3 *Revenues:* under $100,000
Professional Affiliations: /ASTD, ABA
Services: 3.1 3.5 11.0
Industries: Most H.60 H.63 I.81 J.91

Moshman Associates, Inc.
6400 Goldsboro Rd.
Washington, D.C. 20034
(301)229-3000

Using our extensive experience and analytical expertise, our staff assists businesses, trade associations and legal counsel in solving practical operating problems, identifying policy options and supporting the client positions in regulatory proceedings. Special divisions are responsible for planning and conducting meetings and conferences and for developing customized mini-computer systems.

Contact: Jack Moshman, pres.
Areas Served: worldwide
Founded: 1970 *Staff:* 25-50 *Revenues:* $1-$5 million
Services: 1.5 1.8 1.13 2.7 2.10 3.10 4.14 9.5 10.1 11.0
Industries: B.12 D.39 E.40 E.42 E.44 I.80 I.81 J.92 J.94 J.96

Clinton P. Mott & Associates
1210 Kennecott Bldg.
Salt Lake City, Utah 84133
(801)355-2851

Professional management consulting and industrial engineering services to operating and executive management in the larger firms in the U.S.A. Most clients are among Fortune 500. Emphasis on lower costs and high productivity through better management. Reputation built on the respect of top level management.

Contact: Clinton P. Mott, princ.
Areas Served: U.S. & Canada
Founded: 1961 *Staff:* 3-10 *Revenues:* $100-$500,000
Professional Affiliations: AMC
Services: 1.0 2.0 3.7 3.8 9.1
Industries: B.00 D.33 D.34 E.49 I.70 I.75 I.80 I.82

MRP Associates
1653 Melville Ave.
Fairfield, Connecticut 06430
(203)374-3898
> We serve all clients who have the need to coordinate and control the financial and operational functions of their business responsibilities: profit planning, reduction of costs, operations analysis, forecasting, interpretation and business evaluation, taxation and financial counseling.

Contact: Murray Portnoy, sr. ptnr.
Areas Served: NY, NJ, New England
Founded: 1967 *Staff:* 1-3 *Revenues:* under $100,000
Professional Affiliations: SPMC
Services: 1.3   1.6   1.7   1.9   1.10   1.11   5.0   9.5   9.6

Paul B. Mulligan & Co., Inc.
2 Overhill Rd.
Scarsdale, New York 10583
(914)472-0800
> Specialize in office productivity improvement through systems re-design, method improvement, work simplification and work measurement. Training of in-house staff provides capability for continuing cost reduction and control programs. Our unique Manual of Standard Time Data (the result of our continuing research) assures rapid, accurate, and consistent development of office work measurement standards. Company operations are international in scope.

Contact: William B. Hines, pres.
Affiliates/branches: Sydney
Areas Served: worldwide
Founded: 1947 *Staff:* 10-25 *Revenues:* $500,000-1 million
Professional Affiliations: ACME, IMC
Services: 1.0   2.6   2.7   3.0   9.0
Industries: Most

Multinational Perspectives, Inc.
Box 14- Lenox Hill Station
New York, New York 10021
(212)988-5458
> Advise corporations on the management of external (government, social, labor and cultural) relations, particularly with Europe and the developing countries. Aspects: relationships between corporate headquarters and subsidiaries abroad; impact of external environment on corporate activities analysis of effectiveness of public affairs policies and programs, and information systems. And more.

Contact: Vita Toros, pres.
Affiliates/branches: Nigeria
Areas Served: Europe & developing countries
Founded: 1975 *Staff:* 3-10 *Revenues:* $100-$500,000
Services: 1.0   2.0   3.0   3.9   5.4   5.8   5.9   10.0   11.1

Leo Murphy Inc.
270 Madison Ave.
New York, New York 10016
(212)685-6550
> Strategic reappraisal to turn around projected erosion of profits and

growth ... move on major expansion opportunities ... series of full-day group deliberations with consultant serving as moderator ... clients are major multinational manufacturing corporations with technilogical orientation ... volume and specialty products ... highest standards of professional integrity/independence/competence.

Contact: Leo Murphy
Areas Served: U.S. & Canada
Founded: 1959 *Staff:* 1-3 *Revenues:* $100-$500,000
Services: 1.0 1.1 1.2 1.3 1.4 1.11 10.0 10.2
Industries: D.24 D.28 D.30 D.32 D.34 D.35 D.36 D.37 D.38 D.39

Richard Muther & Associates, Inc.

6155 Oak St.
Kansas City, Missouri 64113
(816)444-3232

A small firm--the philosophy being to consult, advise, and coach clients--to help them help themselves. Aim is to provide clients with man-to-man professional assistance and thus guide them to an acceptable solution to their requirements. Techniques recognized worldwide.

Contact: Richard Muther, pres.
Affiliates/branches: Zurich; Sydney
Areas Served: North & South America, Asia & Europe
Founded: 1956 *Staff:* 3-10 *Revenues:* $100-$500,000
Professional Affiliations: AMC, IMC/APMHC, TIMS, IMMS
Services: 2.1 2.2 2.3 2.4 2.6 2.8 2.9 2.10 2.11 9.2
Industries: Most

MWS Consultants, Inc.

55 E. Monroe St.
Chicago, Illinois 60603
(312)726-8730

Planned concentration on certain services for especially utility, health care, and mining industries as related to marketing, information systems, industrial management, human resources, financial management and strategic planning ... which services are also applied to the other industries, institutions, and government by management engineering and general management divisions.

Contact: R.L. Johnson, pres.
Affiliates/branches: 12860 Hillcrest Rd., Dallas, Texas 75230; Atlanta, Georgia; Greenville, South Carolina; 1900 M St., NW, Washington, D.C. 20036; McLean, Virginia; Greenwood, Arkansas; London; Saudi Arabia
Areas Served: worldwide
Founded: 1912 *Staff:* over 100 *Revenues:* $5-$10 million
Professional Affiliations: ACME, IMC
Services: Most
Industries: Most

Naremco Services, Inc.

60 E. 42nd St.
New York, New York 10017
(212)697-0290

We are the first management consulting organization specializing exclusively in the design and control of administrative support facilities (including word processing) as well as paperwork and information management systems. Our accumulated experience (over 850 clients since 1948) and composite professional skills have developed pace-setting techniques and facilities.

Contact: Robert A. Shiff, pres.

Areas Served: worldwide

Founded: 1948 *Staff:* 10-25 *Revenues:* $500,000-1 million

Professional Affiliations: ACME/IMC, AMS, ARMA

Services: 1.8   9.1   9.2   9.3   9.4   9.5   9.6   9.7   9.8

Industries: Most

Alan Negus Associates, Inc.

Box 15226
Sarasota, Florida 33579
(813)955-5199

Records and information management systems, office systems and procedures, records retention and storage, microfilm, vital records protection.

Contact: Alan G. Negus, CMC, pres.

Areas Served: worldwide

Founded: 1976 *Staff:* 3-10 *Revenues:* $100-$500,000

Professional Affiliations: IMC

Services: 1.9   9.1   9.2   9.5   9.6   9.7

Industries: Most

Rich Nelson Associates

311 California St.
San Francisco, California 94104
(415)362-3275

A solo practioner with over 20 years experience in the design and implementation of personnel and manpower development programs including: recruiting, selection and psychological testing programs, salary grade and incentive programs, sales incentive programs, training and career path systems, manpower inventory & morale audit projects, and affirmative action compliance consultation.

Contact: Richard Nelson, CMC

Areas Served: U.S.

Founded: 1969 *Staff:* 1-3 *Revenues:* under $100,000

Professional Affiliations: AMC, IMC

Services: 1.1   1.7   3.0   3.1   3.2   3.4   3.7   3.10   3.11   4.15

Industries: C.16   D.00   E.42   E.45   F.50   G.52   H.63

Neville & Currie Associates Inc.

148 Linden St.
Wellesley, Massachusetts 02181
(617)237-5120

Management consulting and corporate training services primarily to manufacturers of capital goods which are sold through dealer/distributor organizations. Clients are all large national corporations. Firms is small by design, and principals are involved in all projects.

Contact: Richard O. Neville, pres.

Affiliates/branches: Silverton, Oregon

Areas Served: U.S. & Canada

Founded: 1971 *Staff:* 1-3 *Revenues:* $100-$500,000

Services: 1.0   2.9   3.0   4.0   5.0

Industries: D.26   D.34   D.35   D.37   G.52   G.55   H.61   I.75

Robert Newsom & Associates
901 Fairgreen Road
Greensboro, North Carolina 27410
(919)294-2128

Facilities planning: in general and especially for corporate headquarters; cost systems & standards; manufacturing management studies.

Contact: R.W. Newsom
Areas Served: U.S.
Founded: 1976 *Staff:* 1-3 *Revenues:* under $100,000
Services: 2.9   2.13   2.14
Industries: Most

The Nielson-Wurster Group, Inc.
260 Madison Ave.
New York, New York 10016
(212)686-9044

Technical management and consulting services to those who own, commission, administer, develop, finance, design or construct buildings, structures and facilities of all kinds. Offer many services which provide the technical and managerial tools to assure the delivery of a project on time, within budget and of the scope initially desired.

Contact: Richard L. Wurster, vp.
Areas Served: worldwide
Founded: 1976 *Staff:* 25-50 *Revenues:* $1-$5 million
Professional Affiliations: /ASCE, AAA, PMI, AACE
Services: 1.5   1.8   1.9   1.12   6.1   7.3   9.3   9.7
Industries: C.16

Robert E. Nolan Co., Inc.
90 Hopmeadow St.
Simsbury, Connecticut 06070
(203)658-1941

Specialists in office management, with emphasis on banks and insurance companies. Primarily involved in productivity improvement through work simplification, work measurement, systems improvement, and supervisory/management development.

Contact: Bob Nolan, pres.
Areas Served: U.S., Canada & U.K.
Founded: 1973 *Staff:* 10-25 *Revenues:* $1-$5 million
Professional Affiliations: IMC
Services: 1.0   3.0   9.0
Industries: H.00   H.60   H.63   I.00   I.80   I.82

Normandale Associates Inc.
4813 Hibiscus Ave.
Minneapolis, Minnesota 55435
(612)925-3101

Planning and development services to the health services industry.

Contact: James N. Verhey, pres.
Areas Served: worldwide
Founded: 1977 *Staff:* 1-3 *Revenues:* under $100,000
Professional Affiliations: /ACHA
Services: 1.1   1.2   1.3   1.5   1.9   2.13   3.21   5.3   9.2   11.0
Industries: H.65   I.80

Norris Consultants Inc.
Box 16
Calabasas, California 91302
(213)999-4878

Operations consultants: data processing, production and inventory control, manufacturing, systems and procedures, organization. Consulting to growth organizations, entrepeneurs: hands-on, pragmatic, doing-type organizations.

Contact: David B. Norris, pres.
Affiliates/branches: 2172 DuPont Dr., Irvine, California 92715
Areas Served: worldwide
Founded: 1974 *Staff:* 3-10 *Revenues:* $100-$500,000
Professional Affiliations: AMC
Services: 1.8   1.9   1.12   2.0   6.4   7.2   9.3   9.4   9.5   9.8
Industries: Most

Norris & Elliott, Inc.
85 E. Gay St.
Columbus, Ohio 43215
(614)221-1514

Our policy is to work with management in the analysis and identification of operating problems, programming improvements and implementing recommended plans.

Contact: Ernest E. Roberts, pres.
Affiliates/branches: Greenwich, Connecticut
Areas Served: North America
Founded: 1931 *Staff:* 10-25 *Revenues:* $100-$500,000
Professional Affiliations: ACME, IMC
Services: 2.0   3.8   9.4   9.5
Industries: D.00   I.83

Northern Consultants Inc.
1 Merchants Plaza
Bangor, Maine 04401
(207)942-6776

Specializing the plastics, petrochemical, motor freight transportation, and banking fields. Emphasis on productivity analysis, operational audits of the marketing, sales, engineering, and manufacturing functions, and related systems, policies, and procedures. Also executive search.

Contact: James D. Brown, pres.
Areas Served: U.S., England & Germany
Founded: 1975 *Staff:* 3-10 *Revenues:* $100-$500,000
Professional Affiliations: IMC/SPE
Services: 1.0   3.0   4.1   4.7   6.3   8.2   9.0
Industries: D.28   D.29   D.30   D.35   D.39   E.42   H.60

Oatman Associates, Inc.
311 California St.
San Francisco, California 94104
(415)398-4562

Multinational management, global logistics, acquisitions, divestitures, management strategy, executive compensation, faciliti-s planning, sales force effectiveness, clerical and administrative controls work measurement, methods analysis, maintenance management.

Contact: Floyd Oatman, pres.
Areas Served: U.S.-primarily West Coast
Founded: 1978 *Staff:* 3-10 *Revenues:* $500,000-1 million
Professional Affiliations: IMC
Services: 1.3   1.6   1.7   1.9   2.1   4.1   5.3   10.2   10.3
Industries: Most   B.10   D.20   D.24   D.26   D.28   D.36   D.37   E.40   E.42

OBEX Consulting
400 N. 4th St.
St. Louis, MO 63102
(314)621-6130

Dedicated to assist clients in expanding sales and profitability. We are active internationally as well as domestically in general management and marketing. Our approach is professional and ethical, and we use only seasoned executives.

Contact: Peter G. Van der Spek, pres.
Affiliates/branches: New York; West Germany; Iran; India; Taiwan
Areas Served: Worldwide
Founded: 1972 *Staff:* 3-10 *Revenues:* $100-$500,000
Professional Affiliations: /NABE
Services: 1.0   2.10   4.1   4.2   4.3   4.5   10.0   11.0
Industries: D.00   F.00   J.91   J.96   J.97

George Odiorne Associates, Inc.
711 W. Ann Arbor Trail
Plymouth, Michigan 48170
(313)455-2860

A small independent consulting organization which specializes in the installation of corporate planning systems and performance-based management systems. Since our practice is limited to this narrow field, we have accumulated a wealth of experience in implementation of these two highly compatible systems and offer ourselves as a leading authority on the subjects.

Contact: Jack Bologna
Areas Served: U.S. & Canada
Founded: 1968 *Staff:* 1-3 *Revenues:* under $100,000
Services: 1.1   1.3   1.4   3.1   3.9   3.10   4.2   4.9   11.1
Industries: Most

Thomas Oland & Associates, Inc.
4930 W. 77th St.
Minneapolis, Minnesota 55435
(612)835-3311

Our goal on any engagement is to assist the client in making constructive change occur. To achieve that goal, we function in various capacities ranging from technical expertise and project management to members of a client implementation team, depending on the requirements of the client and the specific engagement.

Contact: Thomas E. Oland, pres.
Areas Served: Upper Midwest
Founded: 1977 *Staff:* 3-10 *Revenues:* $100-$500,000
Professional Affiliations: IMC
Services: 1.8   1.9   2.2   2.14   4.13   5.1   5.2   5.8   6.4   9.5
Industries: A.02   A.07   C.16   D.20   D.24   D.30   D.34   D.36   F.51   H.66

Olney Associates

15 Broad St.
Boston, Massachusetts 02109
(617)227-1642

As general management consultants, we provide a broad range of consulting services to over 275 clients throughout the Northeast: industrial organizations, financial organizations, financial institutions, health care facilities, municipalities, trade associations, school systems and colleges. Most assignements involve organizational planning, position analysis and evaluation, compensation and benefit studies, supervisory training, manager development, and employee attitude surveys.

Contact: Peter B. Olney, Jr., pres.
Areas Served: Northeast
Founded: 1966 *Staff:* 3-10 *Revenues:* $100-$500,000
Services: 1.1   1.7   3.1   3.2   3.5   3.6   3.7   3.8   3.9   3.10
Industries: Most   H.60   I.80   I.82   I.83

Oppenheimer Associates

222 E. Orange St.
Lancaster, Pennsylvania 17604
(717)393-0331

The purpose of our business is to help clients improve effectiveness and reduce costs. We do design and implementation, training and development, and analysis and audits in the areas of industrial engineering, production and inventory control and management organization.

Contact: Rick Oppenheimer, CMC
Areas Served: Mid Atlantic
Founded: 1968 *Staff:* 3-10 *Revenues:* $100-$500,000
Professional Affiliations: AMC, IMC
Services: 1.0   2.0   2.1   2.1   2.3   3.8   4.7   4.8   6.4   9.0
Industries: D.00   D.20   D.24   D.25   D.27   D.32   D.33   D.34   D.36   I.80

Organization Consultants, Inc.

Box 6025
Charlotte, North Carolina 28207
(704)333-6262

Professional services directed toward increasing organizational performance and individual productivity and morale through more effective human resource utilization, management and growth.

Contact: H.H. Bradshaw
Areas Served: U.S. & Canada
Founded: 1971 *Staff:* 3-10 *Revenues:* $100-$500,000
Professional Affiliations: IMC/ASTD, APA
Services: 1.1   3.1   3.2   3.3   3.5   3.8   3.9   3.10   3.11   4.9
Industries: D.00   G.55   H.60

Organization Renewal, Inc.

(The Gordon Lippitt Consulting Group)
755 Lincoln Ave.
Winnetka, Illinois 60093
(312)446-4114

A consortium of professional consultants representing a broad variety of disciplines and activities related to human resource development and

management, organization effectiveness, and human systems.
Contact: B.J. Chakiris, exec. vp.
Areas Served: U.S., Europe & South America
Founded: 1969 *Staff:* 25-50 *Revenues:* $500,000-1 million
Professional Affiliations: /ICF, APA
Services: 1.0 2.6 3.0 4.0 6.1 7.0 9.1 9.8 10.2
Industries: A.08 C.00 D.00 E.00 G.00 H.00 I.00 J.00

Organization Resource Counselors, Inc.
1211 Ave of the Americas
New York, New York 10036
(212)575-7500
> Professional assistance to management in dealing with the human resources of organizations ... through consulting, meeting groups and subscription services. The purpose is to aid clients in developing organization structures, policies and practices that motivate employees to contribute more effectively to the success and/or profitability of the organization.

Contact: Richard A. Beaumont, CMC, pres.
Affiliates/branches: Santa Monica, California 90401; I St., NW, Washington, D.C. 20036
Founded: 1926 *Staff:* 25-50 *Revenues:* $1-$5 million
Professional Affiliations: IMC
Services: 1.0 2.6 2.9 2.10 3.0 7.2 10.2
Industries: Most A.00 B.00 C.00 D.00 E.00 F.00 G.00 H.00 I.00 J.00

Organization Resources Inc.
63 Atlantic Ave.
Boston, Massachusetts 02110
(617)742-8970
> Committed to helping clients improve managerial and operating effectiveness by providing highly individualized management consulting and executive recruiting services. We also have assumed interim operating responsibility to implement our recommendations.

Contact: John R. Kris, pres.
Areas Served: U.S.
Founded: 1967 *Staff:* 3-10 *Revenues:* $500,000-1 million
Professional Affiliations: /ASPA
Services: 1.1 1.2 1.3 1.7 1.11 2.6 3.0
Industries: Most

Organizational Consultants, Inc.
Box 3111
West LaFayette, Indiana 47906
(317)463-2793
> Professionals trained in the applied behavioral sciences offering consultation and training to a wide variety of client organizations. Most of our work is consultative in nature (in contrast to training) because our experience continues to teach us that consultation is more likely to make an enduring contribution.

Contact: John J. Sherwood, pres.
Areas Served: worldwide
Founded: 1972 *Staff:* 3-10 *Revenues:* under $100,000
Services: 1.0 1.1 1.7 1.11 1.15 3.1 3.3 3.9 3.10 3.11
Industries: Most J.94

Organizational Consulting Services
111 Old Pickard Rd.
Concord, Massachusetts 01742
(617)369-4300

> We use organizational diagnosis to help top management define present resources and future strategies and goals. We use organizational design to create the structures and processes necessary to get from here to there. We use organizational development to implement the design and actually achieve the desired goals.

Contact: Rodney B. Plimpton, pres.
Areas Served: U.S.
Founded: 1976 *Staff:* 1-3 *Revenues:* under $100,000
Services: 1.1   1.2   1.3   1.7   1.9   3.1   4.1   9.5
Industries: D.00   E.48   G.55   I.73   J.91   J.94

Organizational Directions, Inc.
3868 Carson St.
Torrance, California 90503
(213)540-3331

> We are a management consulting firm specializing in tailored management development programs for middle and upper level management. We normally conduct a "management training needs analysis" before entering the proposal stage. Our consulting services activities are usually designed to assist our clients in maximizing their return for their training dollars.

Contact: Barry T. Deutsch, pres.
Areas Served: U.S.
Founded: 1970 *Staff:* 3-10 *Revenues:* $500,000-1 million
Professional Affiliations: /ASTD, ASBMC
Services: 1.0   2.6   3.0   4.0   5.4   9.1
Industries: Most

ORU Group, Inc.
(A Reliance Group Company)
1450 Broadway
New York, New York 10018
(212)730-1286

> We work with clients to create and accomplish cost-justifiable programs, undertaken after mutual definition of the situation including approach, results expected, fee and time parameters. We improve: 1) current operations (forecasts, systems, schedules, flows, productivities, cycles, inventories, services); 2) capital projects (reduced time/cost exposure through event planning, material/manpower control).

Contact: Edward J. Rand, vp.
Areas Served: worldwide
Founded: 1961 *Staff:* 50-100 *Revenues:* $1-$5 million
Services: 1.8   1.9   1.10   2.0   3.8   3.9   3.10   3.11   6.4   9.4
Industries: C.00   D.00   E.00   G.00   H.60   I.70

Outlook Associates
2105 Rampart Drive
Alexandria, Virginia 22308
(703)360-9395

> The majority of our work is in the sales and sales training areas. We are well

known for our work with sales forces in trouble. We analyze sales problems, make recommendations and carry out training programs if needed. We prefer to work with small and medium-sized firms.

Contact: Jim Rapp, pres.
Areas Served: worldwide
Founded: 1975 *Staff:* 1-3 *Revenues:* under $100,000
Professional Affiliations: /ASTD, NSSTE
Services: 3.1   3.4   3.5   3.8   3.11   4.0
Industries: D.20   F.51   G.54   G.59   H.65   I.82   I.86

James H. Owens Associates, Inc.
800 Baker Bldg.
Minneapolis, Minnesota 55402
(612)338-3785

Marketing & sales consultants specializing in consumer goods.

Contact: Jim Owens, pres.
Areas Served: worldwide
Founded: 1975 *Staff:* 3-10 *Revenues:* $100-$500,000
Professional Affiliations: AMC
Services: 1.1   1.6   4.0
Industries: G.54   G.59   I.72   I.80

PA International Management Consultants, Inc.
200 Park Ave.
New York, New York 10001
(212)682-1330

Comprehensive range of services for owners, directors, managers and employees of all types of organizations. Over 1000 qualified professionals are employed in a total staff of about 1500 worldwide. Annual revenue exceeds $50 million. In the US our field of speciality are marketing, executive search, and manufacturing/production management. As the largest consultancy outside of the US, we are ideally qualified to assist with clients' overseas problems.

Contact: Edward H. Jube, pres.
Affiliates/branches: Amsterdam; Barcelona; Brussels; Copenhagen; Dusseldorf; Frankfurt; Gothernburg; Helsinki; Lille; Lyons; Madrid; Malmo; Milan; Munich; Paris; Rome; Stockholm; Stuttgart; Turin; Zurich; Caracas; Sao Paulo; Adelaide; Auckland; Brisbane; Djakrta; Hong Kong; Kuala Lumpur; Melbourne; Perth; Port Moresby; Singapore; Sydney; Tokyo; Wellington; Belfast; Birmingham; Bristol; Cambridge; Edinburgh; Glasgow; Harrogate; Leamington; Liverpool; London; Manchester; Nottingham; Newcastle; Sheffield; Winchester; Dublin
Areas Served: worldwide
Founded: 1943 *Staff:* 25-50 *Revenues:* $1-$5 million
Services: 2.1   2.2   3.1   3.5   4.1   4.2   4.5   4.9   10.2   10.4
Industries: B.00   D.00   E.00   F.00   H.00   J.00

The Pace Consulting Group, Inc.
2074 Park St.
Hartford, Connecticut 06106
(203)236-1951

Specializing in business turnarounds (improvement of sales and/or profit) for firms under $30 million in sales. Implementation of all aspects provided under our direction or by our staff of experienced business line managers. Capital restructuring and equity funding provided, and we will assume responsibility for complete operations.

Contact: Langdon G. Johnson, pres.
Areas Served: Northeastern U.S.
Founded: 1970 *Staff:* 10-25 *Revenues:* $500,000-1 million
Services: 1.3 1.10 1.11 2.2 2.9 3.4 4.1 4.7 5.3 5.8
Industries: D.24 D.27 D.30 D.34 D.36 E.47 F.50 G.52 H.60 I.82

D.L. Paden & Associates
1225 Pilgrim Lane
Berwyn, Pennsylvania 19312
(215)644-2345

We provide our clients with the specialized technical counsel and individual or team staff support needed to achieve soundly conceived, tightly planned, fully documented, and promptly completed action or information. All our field consultants are experienced senior-level professionals with advanced working, academic, and professional credentials.

Contact: David L. Paden, pres.
Areas Served: U.S. & Canada
Founded: 1976 *Staff:* 1-3 *Revenues:* $100-$500,000
Professional Affiliations: IMC
Services: 1.0 2.0 3.0 4.0 6.2 6.4 7.0 8.1 9.0 10.4
Industries: D.00 E.00 F.00 H.00 I.00 J.91

Parker, Eldridge, Sholl & Gordon
440 Totten Pond Rd.
Waltham, Massachusetts 02154
(617)890-0340

An established and reputable firm of trained and experienced professionals specializing in the recruiting, development, compensation and motivation of people in large and small organizations.

Contact: Calvin K. Sholl, pres.
Areas Served: U.S.
Founded: 1962 *Staff:* 3-10 *Revenues:* $100-$500,000
Professional Affiliations: AMC, IMC/AERC
Services: 1.0 3.0 4.0
Industries: Most

Paterson & Co.
1801 Ave. of the Stars
Los Angeles, California 90067
(213)277-3711

We specialize in a limited set of consulting services: human resources, business development, and acquisitions and divestments: all aimed at assisting clients in strategic management of their businesses. Our clients represent an important cross section of the national technology-centered industrial base: computer products and systems, electronic comppnents and equipment, instruments, military systems, and aerospace.

Contact: Cindy Ragognetti, vp.
Areas Served: U.S. & Europe
Founded: 1955 *Staff:* 3-10 *Revenues:* $500,000-1 million
Services: 1.3 1.6 2.1 3.2 11.1
Industries: Most

Patton Consultants, Inc.

2200 E. Devon Ave.
Des Plaines, Illinois 60018
(312)298-2660

We concentrate on services that bring about cost reduction through industrial engineering programs. For the past 30 years we have assumed responsibility for implementing our programs with and through management to assure successful results.

Contact: John A. Patton, pres.
Areas Served: U.S.
Founded: 1944 *Staff:* 10-25 *Revenues:* $1-$5 million
Professional Affiliations: IMC
Services: 1.0 2.0 3.0 6.0 9.0
Industries: D.00 E.00

Bruce Payne Consultants, Inc.

Time & Life Bldg.
New York, New York 10020
(212)581-5500

Our experienced professional consultants are available to organizations around the world requiring the new technologies and total systems management to meet their objectives of earnings, growth, productivity and cost effectiveness. We will be pleased to review those objectives and to point out where professional management counsel can be used profitably.

Contact: Bruce Payne, pres.
Areas Served: North & South America, Europe
Founded: 1946 *Staff:* 25-50 *Revenues:* $1-$5 million
Professional Affiliations: IMC
Services: Most
Industries: Most

Peat, Marwick, Mitchell & Co.

345 Park Ave.
New York, New York 10022
(212)758-9700

One of the largest management consulting practices in the world, whether measured against other public accounting firms or against organizations exclusively in the consulting field. Consultants provide a wealth of knowledge in such areas as information processing, management sciences, manufacturing techniques, accounting systems, marketing, and general management. Included among our consultants are some of the nation's outstanding experts in such specialized fields as government and and institutional management, acquisition advisoty services, actuarial studies, and environmental economics.

Contact: Stanley R. Klion, vice chmn.
Affiliates/branches: 225 Peachtree St., NE, Atlanta, Georgia 30303; 1 Boston Place, Boston, Massachusetts 02108; 222 S. Riverside Plaza, Chicago, Illinois 60606; 800 Superior Ave., Cleveland, Ohio 44114; 2001 Bryan Twr., Dallas, Texas 75201; 1600 Broadway, Denver, Colorado 80202; 1300 Ford Bldg., Detroit, Michigan 48226; 4300 One Shell Plaza, Houston, Texas 77002; Commerce Twr., Kansas City, Missouri 64199; 555 S. Flower St., Los Angeles, California 90071; 1000 Brickell Ave., Miami, Florida 33131; 777 E. Wisconsin Ave., Milwaukee, Wisconsin 53202; 80 S. 8th St., Minneapolis, Minnesota 55401; 225 Baronne St., New Orleans, Louisiana 70112; 1500 Walnut St., Philadelphia, Pennsylvania 19102
Areas Served: worldwide

Founded: 1897 *Staff:* over 100 *Revenues:* over $10 million
Professional Affiliations: /AICPA
Services: Most
Industries: Most

James S. Pepitone & Associates, Inc.

First Federal Bldg.
Greenville, South Carolina 29601
(803)233-7365

Comprehensive support to develop clients' sales and marketing effectiveness, including full-service research capability and implementation support. Conduct market analyses and new product evaluations, develop product strategies and promotional programs, and provide on-site marketing organiz ation management and training. All professionals are industry-seasoned and capable of concentrating on client problems and opportunities using proven marketing techniques and professional methods.

Contact: Jim Pepitone, ceo.
Affiliates/branches: 2305 Parklake Dr., NE, Atlanta, Georgia 30345; 1120 Connecticut Ave., Washington, D.C. 20036
Areas Served: U.S.
Founded: 1977 *Staff:* 3-10 *Revenues:* $100-$500,000
Services: 1.0   4.0   4.1   4.2   4.5   4.7   4.10   4.11   4.12   10.4
Industries: Most

Permark Management Consultants, Inc.

640 Nod Hill Rd.
Wilton, Connecticut 06897
(203)762-3682

Services equally divided between business and marketing consultation and merger/acquisition/divesture activities. Client include very large companies as well as smaller firms that are involved in the manufacture and distribution of consumer and industrial products.

Contact: Leonard L. DeCoster, pres.
Areas Served: Eastern & midwestern U.S.
Founded: 1969 *Staff:* 1-3 *Revenues:* $100-$500,000
Services: 1.0   1.3   1.6   4.0   4.1   4.3   4.5   4.14
Industries: D.00   F.50

The Personnel Laboratory, Inc.

733 Summer St.
Stamford, Connecticut 06901
(203)325-4348

Specialists in individual testing and assessment, serving a variety of clients in business, industry and municipal government. Also organizational studies, attitude surveys, management training and employee counseling.

Contact: King Whitney, Jr., pres.
Affiliates/branches: 211 E. 43rd St., New York, New York 10017
Areas Served: U.S.
Founded: 1944 *Staff:* 3-10 *Revenues:* $100-$500,000
Services: 3.1   3.4   3.9   3.10   3.11

Planaflex Co. Inc.
342 Madison Ave.
New York, New York 10017
(212)682-1885

For corporate growth, turnaround, venture start-up, and invention-commercialization: specializing in strategic planning, financing and development services. Learning-by-doing is used to achieve both the business result and an enhanced capability for managing future change more profitably. Includes assistance with acquisition, divestment, underwriting, information-planning-control-system.

Contact: John W. Jenkins, pres.
Areas Served: worldwide
Founded: 1965 *Staff:* 1-3 *Revenues:* under $100,000
Professional Affiliations: SPMC/ACG, NASCP
Services: 1.0   2.10   2.13   3.1   4.1   4.2   5.0   7.0   9.3   10.0
Industries: Most

Plante & Moran
Box 307
Southfield, Michigan 48037
(313)352-2500

Our management consulting services represent five broad areas of service: 1) systems and data processing, 2) organization planning, 3) operations management, 4) product and market research, and 5) strategic planning for capital formation. The practice extends to both the public and private sectors. The practice, which is conducted nationally, involves both inductive and deductive analytical problem solving.

Contact: Kenneth G. Myers, dir. mgmt. svcs.
Areas Served: U.S.
Founded: 1977 *Staff:* 10-25 *Revenues:* $500,000-1 million
Professional Affiliations: IMC/AICPA
Services: Most
Industries: Most

The Pofcher Co.
205 E. 42nd St.
New York, New York 10023
(212)661-1205

Consultants and advisors in the publishing, educational materials, communications and information fields, both in the U.S. and the U.K. Activities include arranging mergers and acquisitions, divestures, joint ventures, and financings; and consulting in corporate development, business planning, finance and marketing strategies.

Contact: Munroe F. Pofcher, pres.
Affiliates/branches: London
Areas Served: U.S. & Europe
Founded: 1972 *Staff:* 3-10 *Revenues:* $100-$500,000
Services: 1.2   1.3   1.6   5.9
Industries: D.27

Policy & Management Associates, Inc.
575 Boylston St.
Boston, Massachusetts 02116
(617)266-1600

In-depth research and analysis, quick-reaction policy review, or on-going analytic support to both government and private sector clients.

Contact: Robert Brandwein, pres.
Areas Served: U.S.
Founded: 1977 *Staff:* 3-10 *Revenues:* $100-$500,000
Services: Most
Industries: Most

Price Waterhouse & Co.
(Management Advisory Services)
1251 Ave. of the Americas
New York, New York 10020
(212)489-8900

The main objective, in our view, is to provide management with the means to obtain the financial and operational information needed to set the direction, shape the policies, and guide the operations of an enterprise. Our practice, accordingly, concentrates on assisting management to design and implement improved information structures and systems. But functional expertise is not the only capability required for the successful completion of projects. Equally important is a thorough understanding of the industry, particularly those of its characteristics that for the context of the individual problem and its solution. Accordingly we have specialists in more than 35 industries and government.

Contact: Henry Gunders, vice chmn.
Affiliates/branches: 606 S. Olive St., Los Angeles, California 90014; 555 California St., San Francisco, California 94104; 1601 1st Nat'l. Bank Bldg., Denver, Colorado 80202; 799 Main St., Hartford, Connecticut 06103; 1801 K St. NW, Washington, D.C. 20006; 330 Biscayne Blvd., Miami, Florida 33101; 3700 1st Nat'l Bk, Twr., Atlanta, Georgia 30303; 200 E. Randolph Dr., Chicago, Illinois 60601; 1 Indiana Sq., Indianapolis, Indiana 46204; 1010 Common St., New Orleans, Louisiana 70112; 20 St. Charles St., Baltimore, Maryland 21201; 2050 Marine Plaza, Milwaukee, Wisconsin 53202; 225 Franklin St., Boston, Massachusetts 02110; 211 W. Fort St., Detroit, Michigan 48226; 2015 1st. Nat'l. Bk. Bldg., Minneapolis, Minnesota 55402; 2900 Twr. Commerce Bldg., Kansas City, Missouri 64199; 2300 Jefferson 1st UN Plaza, Charlotte, North Carolina 28282; 2000 Dubois Twr., Cincinnati, Ohio 45202; 1900 Central Nat'l. Bank Bldg., Cleveland, Ohio 44114; Independence Mall W., Philadelphia, Pennsylvania 19106; 1 Commerce Sq., Memphis, Tennessee 38103; 1400 Republic Nat'l. Bk. Twr., Dallas, Texas 75201; 1200 Milam, Houston, Texas 77002; Financial Ctr., Seattle, Washington 98161
Areas Served: worldwide
Founded: 1890 *Staff:* over 100 *Revenues:* over $10 million
Professional Affiliations: IMC/AICPA
Services: 1.0   2.0   3.0   4.0   5.0   9.0   10.0   11.1
Industries: Most

Princeton Associates, Inc.
Box 820
Buckingham, Pennsylvania 18912
(215)794-5626

Assist organizations to analyze and resolve major problems, decisions, plans, etc. through the use of process consulting techniques such as: problem analysis, decision analysis, potential problem analysis, new product ideation, strategic objective setting, etc. These fundamental processes are applicable to any functional area and any type of organization.

Contact: William J. Altier, pres.
Areas Served: North America & Europe
Founded: 1976 *Staff:* 1-3 *Revenues:* under $100,000
Services: 11.10
Industries: Most

Harry J. Prior & Associates, Inc.
1305 IBM Bldg.
Seattle, Washington 98101
(206)623-2332

We work with business enterprises, government agencies and institutions. We assist in solving problems, planning for the future and improving operations to obtain the best possible results. Our future depends on satisfied clients who tell others about our work and who call us back as new problems arise.

Contact: Harry J. Prior, pres.
Areas Served: Pacific Northwest
Founded: 1961 *Staff:* 3-10 *Revenues:* $100-$500,000
Professional Affiliations: IMC
Services: Most
Industries: Most

Problem Solvers for Industry
345 Park Ave.
Chalfont, Pennsylvania 18914
(215)822-9695

Low profile, ahnds-on involvement in the analysis and colution of manufacturing and management problems. We furnish a wide variety of personalized services tailored to the specific needs, resources and personnel of small and medium size (1mm-25mm) clients.

Contact: Ben F. Gerding, CMC
Areas Served: Mid-Atlantic & New England
Founded: 1974 *Staff:* 1-3 *Revenues:* under $100,000
Professional Affiliations: IMC
Services: 1.0 2.0 3.8 5.4 6.1 6.4 7.4 9.5
Industries: D.34 D.36 D.38 D.39 J.94

The Product Integrity Co.
Box 255
Enfield, Connecticut 06082
(203)745-5225

Evaluation, design and installation of quality, reliability and product integrity systems; product liability prevention; statistical engineering and operations research; accelerating research and development programs.

Contact: C.W. Carter, pres.
Areas Served: Worldwide
Founded: 1976 *Staff:* 1-3 *Revenues:* under $100,000
Professional Affiliations: IMC
Services: 1.2 1.13 2.7 7.1
Industries: Most

Professional Practice Consultants, Inc.

Box 309
New London, New Hampshire 03257
(603)526-6832

We provide sercices to CPA firms and associations relating to: 1) quality control: documents and manuals, inspections and technical reviews; 2) professional development: Program development and presentation; 3) recruiting and practical development: brochures and program development; 4) management: administrative reviews, personnel manuals, general consultation. Principal is former national CPA firm partner and college professor.

Contact: Robert W. Colby, pres.
Areas Served: U.S. & Canada
Founded: 1977 *Staff:* 1-3 *Revenues:* $100-$500,000
Services: 1.7 3.4 3.5 4.1 4.10 9.5 9.6
Industries: I.73 I.86

Professional Services Int'l.

1100 Glendon Ave.
Los Angeles, California 90024
(213)477-1977

For professional services firms: problem-solving in finance, legal, management and operations problems from the former head of the nation's largest diversified professional services firm. Special emphasis on acquisitions.

Contact: Robert W. Krueger, pres.
Areas Served: U.S.
Founded: 1973 *Staff:* 1-3 *Revenues:* under $100,000
Services: 1.0
Industries: I.73

Profit Planning Associates

Box 1265
Montclair, New Jersey 07042
(201)746-9225

Highly focused help in profit and growth planning, analysis, and control. We are effective in helping business managers identify and focus on their profit opportunities. We believe key business decisions must be made by the responsible line managers, and effective consultants can be of substantial help.

Contact: George Seiler, princ.
Areas Served: U.S.
Founded: 1978 *Staff:* 1-3 *Revenues:* under $100,000
Services: 1.1 1.2 1.3 1.5 1.6 1.9 1.10 3.1 4.1 5.4
Industries: B.10 B.13 D.24 D.26 D.28 D.29 D.30 D.32 H.60 H.67

Profit-Improvement, Inc.

200 Park Ave.
New York, New York 10017
(212)697-6837

Helping organizations increase profitability in 3 areas-marketing, planning and internal operations. Work with top managements in identifying and implementing profit-improvement opportunities. Implementation carried out as studies progress and cash flows are generated during early stages of the work. The client is left with a built-in capability for extending the techniques to other areas of the business.

Contact: Joseph Eisenberg, CMC, pres.
Affiliates/branches: Los Angeles, California
Areas Served: U.S. & Canada
Founded: 1967 *Staff:* 3-10 *Revenues:* $100-$500,000
Professional Affiliations: IMC
Services: 1.0 2.0 3.0 4.0 5.0 6.0 7.4 9.0
Industries: D.00 G.53 H.60 H.63 H.64

Project Associates, Inc.
5605 Lamar Rd.
Washington, D.C. 20016
(301)320-4409

We provide for our clients the capabilities, creativity, and experience of a small group of behavioral sc1entists and management specialists. We are people-centered. We believe that many organizations achieve only partial effectiveness because of a preoccupation with the control of human energy rather than realizing its full potential by optimizing human energy.

Contact: Elinor Conversano, exec. dir.
Areas Served: U.S.
Founded: 1968 *Staff:* 10-25 *Revenues:* $100-$500,000
Professional Affiliations: /APA, ICF
Services: 1.0 3.0 7.0 9.1 10.2
Industries: C.00 D.00 E.00 G.00 H.00 I.00 J.00

Projections
47 Marlboro St.
Keene, New Hampshire 03431
(603)352-9500

Specialize in custom-designed marketing consulting and research. Develop marketing plans, and desigs, implement and analyze research. Conduct telephone, personal and mail surveys. Typical projects include concept and product tests, advertising research, new products development, public opinion research and new product development, public opinion research and marketing studies.

Contact: Michael Kenyon, pres.
Areas Served: U.S.
Founded: 1978 *Staff:* 1-3 *Revenues:* under $100,000
Services: 1.3 1.4 3.10 4.1 4.2 4.3 4.10 8.3 10.4
Industries: Most

Francis J. Przyluski
326 Ridge Rd.
Grosse Pointe Farms, Michigan 48236
(313)884-7158

General management consulting in international business. Principal interest: to provide counsel and assistance to clients operating or planning to operate in foreign countries.

Contact: F.J. Przyluski
Areas Served: Europe, Middle East & North Africa
Founded: 1970 *Staff:* 1-3 *Revenues:* under $100,000
Services: 1.1 1.4 1.5 2.13 4.2 5.3
Industries: D.35 D.37 D.39

Psychological Consultants, Inc.
6724 Patterson Ave.
Richmond, Virginia 23226
(804)288-4125

Broad range of services covering the assessment development and motivation of human resources. Clients include?public and private organizations worldwide concerned with effectiveness of personnel. Programs designed to identify talent and to improve productivity of available human resources.

Contact: Robert J. Filer
Affiliates/branches: London; Tokyo
Areas Served: worldwide
Founded: 1958 *Staff:* 3-10 *Revenues:* $1-$5 million
Professional Affiliations: AMC, IMC
Services: 1.0   3.0   3.1   3.4   3.5   3.8   3.10   3.11   11.0
Industries: Most

S. Pullano Associates
310 State Rd.
Gladwyne, Pennsylvania 19035
(215)649-4176

Our experience in testing product concepts in industrial and high technology markets allows marketers to evaluate new products with a high degree of assurance that those which are brought to market will have a high degree of acceptance, sales and profitability.

Contact: S. R. Pullano, pres.
Areas Served: U.S. & Canada
Founded: 1969 *Staff:* 3-10 *Revenues:* $100-$500,000
Services: 1.0   4.0   4.1   4.2   4.5   4.7   4.8   4.9   4.10   4.11
Industries: D.00   E.00   F.50

Purcell Consulting Associates, Inc.
510 First Nat'l Bank Bldg.
Decatur, Georgia 30030
(404)378-3657

Services to maximize profits and services of profit-motivated companies as well as non-profit public, private and governmental organizations and divisions. Interpretive analyses of both existing and proposed programs, with emphasis on being "long on practically" as well as "long on theory." Wide range and broad base of services.

Contact: Walter L. Purcell, pres.
Areas Served: U.S.
Founded: 1965 *Staff:* 1-3 *Revenues:* $500,000-1 million
Professional Affiliations: AMC, IMC
Services: 1.0   2.0   3.0   4.0   5.0   6.4   7.5   9.1   9.7
Industries: C.00   D.00   E.48   E.49   F.50   F.51   G.00   H.00   I.00   J.00

Quantum Consultants, Inc.
(subsidiary of the Quantum Science Corp.)
1114 Ave of the Americas
New York, New York 10036
(212)997-0070

Concentrating in high-technology industries, including data processing equipment, office products and systems, communications, information services, and electronics and related technologies. Specialized planning, forecasting and research techniques are utilized which have been designed specifically for these fast-evolving and high-business-risk fields.

Contact: William W. Cain, pres.
Affiliates/branches: London
Areas Served: U.S., Europe & Japan
Founded: 1975 *Staff:* 3-10 *Revenues:* $500,000-1 million
Professional Affiliations: ACME, IMC
Services: 1.1 1.2 1.3 1.6 4.1 4.2
Industries: Most

Quay Associates
Box 257
East Haddam, Connecticut 06423
(203)873-8398

Organization & personnel services including: general management surveys, management training, executive evaluation, compensation, management by objectives, succession planning, retirement planning

Contact: John Quay
Areas Served: U.S.
Founded: 1976 *Staff:* 1-3 *Revenues:* $100-$500,000
Professional Affiliations: IMC
Services: 1.1 1.2 1.4 1.7 3.0 3.1 3.2 3.10 4.15 11.0
Industries: D.33 D.34 E.48 H.62 H.67 I.84

Questor Associates
115 Sansome St.
San Francisco, California 94104
(415)433-0300

A financial consulting firm with particular experience in the real estate sector, serving individual, corporate, institutional and public sector clients on a non-contigency basis. The central service is applied economic analysis. Specific areas of specialization include valuation, legal economics, feasibility studies, investment analysis and strategy, and a comprehensive range of real estate consulting and management services.

Contact: William L. Ramseyer, exec. vp.
Areas Served: U.S.
Founded: 1976 *Staff:* 10-25 *Revenues:* $500,000-1 million
Services: 1.0 3.1 3.2 4.1 5.0 7.1
Industries: H.60 H.65 I.79 J.93

Quorum, Ltd.
3800 W. 61st Terrace
Fairway, Kansas 66205
(913)384-6622

The growth potential of any organization can be measured in the potential of the men and women who collectively make up its management. Helping these individuals push the limits outward on their understanding, confidence, and ability is our basic objective. Our practice is limited to professional presentations and specialized consulting where the assignment calls for high impact to cause the necessary follow through for success. Moving away from one-time presentations to gain higher effectiveness.

Contact: Allan J. Hurst, pres.

Areas Served: U.S.
Founded: 1977 *Staff:* 1-3 *Revenues:* $100-$500,000
Professional Affiliations: IMC
Services: Most
Industries: Most

Stan Radler Associates, Inc.
78 Pine Hill Rd.
Framingham, Massachusetts 01701
(617)875-1007

Specialize in marketing, sales management, promotions and product development areas for companies of all sizes/industries. Services include development of programs, schedules and budgets, sales force development and control, systems and procedures, performance analysis and upgrading, rep acquisition and maintenance programs. Venture capitol, mergers and acquisitions and other general management areas as well.

Contact: Stan Radler, pres.
Areas Served: U.S.
Founded: 1979 *Staff:* 1-3 *Revenues:* $100-$500,000
Professional Affiliations: IMC
Services: 1.0   4.0   8.3   10.3   10.4
Industries: Most

Albert Ramond & Assoc., Inc.
1615 Tribune Twr.
Chicago, Illinois 60606
(312)943-2323

While we are one of the oldest existing management consulting firms in the country, our principles and techniques in consulting are the most modern in design and application. We provide a consulting service on general management problems, with emphasis on resource optimization, facilities planning, physical distribution, manpower utilization, manufacturing systems, compensation costs and labor relations.

Contact: James M. Baker, pres.
Affiliates/branches: 200 Park Ave., New York, New York 10017; 67 Yonge St. Toronto, Ontario M5E 1J8 Canada
Areas Served: U.S. & Canada
Founded: 1916 *Staff:* 25-50 *Revenues:* $1-$5 million
Professional Affiliations: ACME
Services: 1.0   2.0   3.0   9.0
Industries: Most

Ransom & Casazza, Inc.
1000 Connecticut Ave., NW
Washington, D.C. 20036
(202)466-2036

Energy management consultants with broad technical, economic, financial, regulatory & management skills in oil, gas, coal & electricity for industry, utilities & government.

Contact: John A. Casazza, pres.
Affiliates/branches: 302 Passaic Ave., Hasbrouck Heights, New Jersey 07604
Areas Served: U.S., Canada & Europe
Founded: 1969 *Staff:* 3-10 *Revenues:* under $100,000

Professional Affiliations: /AGA, IGT, IEEE
Services: 3.0   4.1   11.12

Rath & Strong, Inc.
21 Worthen Rd.
Lexington, Massachusetts 02173
(617)861-1700

Emphasizing a practical approach with respect to costs and benefits to meet the long-term needs of the client. For most assignments a full-time resident acts as project leader, working closely with client personnel. Every effort is made to develop the competence of in-house personnel in the areas involved so that the transition will proceed quickly with assurance of continuing, long-term benefits.

Contact: Arnold O. Putnam, pres.
Affiliates/branches: 2020 LTV Tower, Dallas, Texas 75201; 9950 W. Lawrence Ave., Schiller Park, Illinois 60176; 647 Promontory Dr. E., Newport Beach, California 92660
Areas Served: worldwide
Founded: 1935 *Staff:* 25-50 *Revenues:* $1-$5 million
Professional Affiliations: ACME, IMC
Services: Most
Industries: Most

The Records Management Group
1 Rockefeller Plaza
New York, New York 10020
(212)247-4820

Computerized records management program, including record retention, vital records, records center layouts, microfilming, filing systems, word processing, printing, reproduction and office copying.

Contact: Jesse L. Clark, pres.
Affiliates/branches: 259 Walnut St., Newton, Massachusetts 02160
Areas Served: U.S.
Founded: 1968 *Staff:* 3-10 *Revenues:* $100-$500,000
Services: 9.1   9.5   9.6   9.7

Reel/Grobman & Associates
1052 W. Sixth St.
Los Angeles, California 90017
(213)482-8084

A facilties-consulting organization that has served more than 500 clients during the past seven years. The strength of our firm lies in our variety of professional services, our ability to perform and manage a multi-disciplinary team effort with senior personnel, and our record of maintaining consistent excellence within the time and budget parpameters established by our clients.

Contact: Roy Reel, CMC, chmn.
Affiliates/branches: 849 Mitten Rd., Burlingame, California 94010; San Francisco; Newport Beach
Areas Served: CA
Founded: 1972 *Staff:* 50-100 *Revenues:* $1-$5 million
Professional Affiliations: IMC
Services: 2.0   9.2   9.4   9.5
Industries: D.00   E.00   H.00   I.00

Reliance Consulting Group, Inc.
(division of Reliance Group, Inc.)
919 Third Ave.
New York, New York 10022
(212)750-7500

An umbrella organization that operates through its subsidiary components:
Werner Associates, Inc.; Yankelovich Skelly & White, Inc.; Fuel & Energy
Consultants, Inc.; ORU Group, Inc; etc.

Contact: Fred M. Schriever, pres.

Areas Served: worldwide

Founded: 1975 *Staff:* over 100 *Revenues:* over $10 million

Services: most

Industries: most

Research Associates & Analysts
Box 391
East Stroudsburg, Pennsylvania 18301
(717)424-6679

We serve industry and government clients in three primary areas: 1) ocean
ship/barge productivity studies; 2) petroleum transportation barge/pipeline/
trucking; 3) general background analysis of problems confronting management
prior to decision and policy making.

Contact: Lawrence A. Wills, CMC, ptnr.

Areas Served: NY,NJ, PA

Founded: 1966 *Staff:* 3-10 *Revenues:* under $100,000

Professional Affiliations: IMC

Services: 1.4   1.9   4.14   6.4   7.2

Industries: D.29   D.37   E.42   E.44   E.47

Resource Conservation Consultants
1615 NW 23rd St.
Portland, Oregon 97210
(503)227-1319

Assisting clients to develop cost-effective waste handling and waste management systems. We have specific experience in the development of solid waste
recovery programs for industrial clients.

Contact: Jerry Powell, mng. ptnr.

Areas Served: U.S.

Founded: 1977 *Staff:* 3-10 *Revenues:* $100-$500,000

Services: 1.5   1.14   2.2

Industries: D.26   E.49   I.82   J.95

Resource Planning Associates, Inc.
44 Brattle St.
Cambridge, Massachusetts 02138
(617)661-1410

An international management consulting firm specializing in strategic planning
and policy development for industry and government. Our private clients tend
to be large companies in industries significantly affected by government
regulations and policies; our public clients tend to be high-level policy-makers.

Contact: Peter Bos, off. dir.

Affiliates/branches: 1901 L. St., NW, Washington, D.C. 20006; 3 Embarcadero Ctr., San
Francisco, California 94111; Paris; London

Areas Served: North America & Western Europe
Founded: 1972 *Staff:* over 100 *Revenues:* over $10 million
Services: 1.2 1.3 1.5 1.6 1.10 4.1 10.2 10.4
Industries: D.26 D.28 D.29 D.32 D.33 E.49 J.91

Riecks Postal Consultants
7012 81st Ave. SE
Mercer Island, Washington 98040
(206)232-1404
> Our areas of competence are: cutting through postal red tape, interpreting governmentese, and obtaining dependable answers from postal officials. Analyzing company mail operations inhouse and out. Assisting company managers in implementing changes that will lower their mail costs, postage and labor. A 10-20% savings is the normal result of our work.

Contact: Henry G. Reicks, pres.
Areas Served: U.S.
Founded: 1978 *Staff:* 1-3 *Revenues:* under $100,000
Services: 1.10 1.13 9.4 11.11
Industries: E.43 J.91

Theodore Riedeburg Associates
6 Corporate Park Dr.
White Plains, New York 10604
(914)694-1223
> Solo practitioner taking complete responsibility for the conduct of studies concerning research, development, marketing research and marketing strategy related to his area of specialization - agricultural chemicals, structural pest control compounds and chemicals used on lawns and gardens. Emphasis on current primary data obtained from distributors, growers and land-grant colleges.

Contact: Theodore Riedeburg, mng. dir.
Areas Served: U.S. & Europe
Founded: 1949 *Staff:* 1-3 *Revenues:* under $100,000
Professional Affiliations: IMC, SPMC/ACS, AAA
Services: 1.0 4.0 7.0
Industries: A.01 A.07

Riffe & Associates
1013 Cleveland Ave.
Charleston, West Virginia 25302
(304)343-3347
> Productivity improvements of existing facilities, machinery, tooling, and manpower for clients in the manufacturing and distribution fields. Projects are performed solo by Jay Riffe, with assists by associates if the client consents. Engineering and projects are budgeted in advance steps of survey, design, implementation.

Contact: Jay A. Riffe
Areas Served: Eastern U.S.
Founded: 1968 *Staff:* 1-3 *Revenues:* under $100,000
Services: 1.10 2.3 2.4 2.7 2.8 2.11 2.12 2.13 6.4 6.5
Industries: D.23 D.28 D.31 D.33 D.34 D.35 F.00 I.76

Risk Planning Group, Inc.
722 Post Rd.
Darien, Connecticut 06820
(203)655-9791

> Independent risk management consulting services to corporate, institutional and governmental clients: exposure identification, risk analysis, risk & loss controls, risk financing and insurance, administration. Also conferences & seminars. Publishers of *Captive Insurance Company Reports* and *Government Risk Management Reports.*

Contact: Felix Kloman, pres.
Affiliates/branches: Paris
Areas Served: Worldwide
Founded: 1970 *Staff:* 10-25 *Revenues:* $500,000-1 million
Professional Affiliations: /IRMC
Services: 3.21   11.8   Most

RLS Consulting & Management Group, Inc.
1461 Franklin Ave.
Garden City, New York 11530
(516)747-5522

> Our firm is composed of top professionals in their fields and is dedicated to doing outstanding professional work for its clients--using senior, experienced, partner-level individuals to personally handle each assignment. While this necessarily limits the size of our practice, we believe that we can do outstanding work in this way and help our clients get the operating results expected from our engagement.

Contact: Robert L. Spohr, pres.
Affiliates/branches: 1115 Mountain Creek Tr.,NW, Atlanta, Georgia 30328
Areas Served: U.S., Canada, Europe, Central & South America
Founded: 1971 *Staff:* 3-10 *Revenues:* $100-$500,000
Professional Affiliations: IMC
Services: 1.3   1.4   1.8   1.10   3.4   9.3   9.4   9.8   11.1
Industries: D.28   D.29   E.47   G.00   H.60   H.62   H.63   I.73   I.80   I.86

R.M. Associates
151 E. Forest Ave.
Neenah, Wisconsin 54956
(414)722-8445

> Primarily serve international pulp, paper, converting and forest products industries. Each partner and associate has extensive industrial experience with many-level personal contacts. Prefer working through client personnel but capabilities for independent market studies and technology development. Multi-lingual European office. Speciality developing new products and market strategies for profit improvement.

Contact: Robert H. Mosher, mng. ptnr.
Affiliates/branches: 1925 Queen City Ave., Tuscaloosa, Alabama 35401; Amsterdam
Areas Served: worldwide
Founded: 1969 *Staff:* 3-10 *Revenues:* $100-$500,000
Professional Affiliations: AMC, IMC
Services: 1.3   1.5   1.6   1.10   4.1   4.2   4.5   4.7   7.0   10.4
Industries: D.24   D.26   D.28

Roberts Associates
140 Shore Rd.
Old Greenwich, Connecticut 06870
(203)637-3018
> Specialist in human resource management. Emphasis on improving organization effectiveness through people. Specific areas include: performance evaluation, management development, morale studies, career management, quality/work life studies, personnel assessment.

Contact: Samuel R. Connor, dir.
Areas Served: U.S.
Founded: 1975 *Staff:* 1-3 *Revenues:* under $100,000
Services: 3.1 3.4 3.5 3.8 3.9 3.10 3.11
Industries: Most

Rogers & Co.
411 W. Putnam Ave.
Greenwich, Connecticut 06830
(203)661-3800
> Work with clients on a corporate, division, and major product-line basis in the area of strategic planning. Help clients to review: where their enterprise is, where it seems to be going, where they would like it to be in 3-5 years, and the best way to get there.

Contact: Ralph W. Rogers, pres.
Areas Served: worldwide
Founded: 1975 *Staff:* 3-10 *Revenues:* $100-$500,000
Professional Affiliations: IMC
Services: 1.0 3.0 4.0
Industries: Most

Rosenau Consulting Co.
1003 Wilshire Blvd.
Santa Monica, California 90401
(213)394-0790
> Organized to assist clients with all aspects of the management of technology, including new-product development and diversification.

Contact: Milton D. Rosenau, Jr.
Areas Served: U.S.
Founded: 1978 *Staff:* 1-3 *Revenues:* under $100,000
Services: 1.6 1.12 3.1 4.2 4.5 7.1 7.2 7.3 7.4 7.5

Ross Associates, Inc.
Box 2018
Asheville, North Carolina 28802
(704)255-8778
> Our firm's goal is to provide a complete consulting service to the furniture and wood using industries. To date we have completed over 500 assignments in these industries.

Contact: Vincent R. Ross, pres.
Areas Served: U.S., Canada, Central & South America, Europe, Africa, Mid & Far East
Founded: 1963 *Staff:* 3-10 *Revenues:* $100-$500,000
Professional Affiliations: ACME, IMC
Services: 1.0 2.0 3.0 4.2 5.0 6.0 9.0 10.0
Industries: A.08 D.23 D.24 D.25 G.57

Runzheimer & Co., Inc.
Runzheimer Park
Rochester, Wisconsin 53167
(414)534-3121

Transportation division specializes in business car policies and standard costing controls for over 1,000 US/Canadian firms with employee-owned, company-owned and leased vehicles. Data source for all AAA car cost figures. Living cost division provides current, defensible living cost values keyed to any living locations and income levels/family size throughout the US and Canada; values used with relocations allowances and geographic salary differentials; site selection consulting; rental and relocation surveys.

Contact: Rufus E. Runzheimer, pres.
Areas Served: U.S. & Canada
Founded: 1933 *Staff:* 50-100 *Revenues:* $1-$5 million
Industries: Most

Ruxton Associates
Box L
Sherman, Connecticut 06784
(203)354-2007

Specialists in telecommunications, voice and data. Conduct analysis of interconnect and telephone company systems. Telephone cost reduction studies. Network design. Fixed and mobile radio studies. Plan corporate communications departments and recruit key personnel. Develop custom communications cost management control systems. Communications facilities management on retainer basis.

Contact: George H. Sutton, CMC, pres.
Areas Served: U.S.
Founded: 1973 *Staff:* 3-10 *Revenues:* $100-$500,000
Professional Affiliations: IMC
Services: 1.1 1.8 4.2 9.5 9.8 11.1 11.3 Most

Ryan Advisors, Inc.
5530 Wisconsin Ave., NW
Washington, D.C. 20015
(301)654-8822

Exclusive advisors to more than 170 hospitals and health services. Analysis of need and institutional role. Development of strategic and master program/planning recommendations. Facilities planning consultation and design. Functional and space programming. Recommendations for staffing, systems, equipment and construction. Organization, administration and management of hospitals and health related services. Health executive search.

Contact: John L. Ryan, pres.
Affiliates/branches: Rome; Singapore
Areas Served: U.S., Canada, Central America, Europe & Asia
Founded: 1969 *Staff:* 10-25 *Revenues:* $500,000-1 million
Services: 1.0 3.0 3.1 4.0 4.1 9.0 11.1
Industries: I.80

SAI
3000 Sand Hill Rd.
Menlo Park, California 94025
(415)854-2918

A production and engineering consulting firm with an extensive history of performing manufacturing and engineering services for both government and commercial clients. We are an organization of professionals who have acted as consultants to consultants, as well as to industry, in the areas of developing, evaluating, and implementing manufacturing improvement programs.

Contact: Michael F. Walters, pres.

Affiliates/branches: 659 Promontory Dr. W., Newport Beach, California 92660

Areas Served: worldwide

Founded: 1966 *Staff:* 10-25 *Revenues:* $1-$5 million

Professional Affiliations: IMC/AIIE, AEA, SME

Services: 1.0 2.0 4.1 4.2 5.3 5.4 5.9 5.10 6.0 9.0

Industries: B.00 D.00 E.48 G.54 I.73 I.89

Kurt Salmon Associates, Inc.

350 Fifth Ave.

New York, New York 10001

(212)564-3690

Specializing in manufacturers and distributors of consumer soft goods: the largest consulting practice in the apparel and textile industries, serving clients in all parts of the world. Staff of over 200 full-time consultants offering services in general management and marketing, manufacturing, management information systems, human resources development, and physical distribution.

Contact: Stig A. Kry, chmn.

Affiliates/branches: 400 Colony Sq., Atlanta, Georgia 30361; 612 Pasteur Dr., Greensboro, North Carolina 27403; 4525 Harding Rd., Nashville, Tennessee 37205; 7011 Briar Cove Dr., Dallas, Texas 75240; 21535 Hawthorn Blvd., Torrance, California 90503; Box 2058, Princeton, New Jersey 08540; 2170 Lincoln Ave. Montreal, Quebec Canada; Sao Paulo; Paris; Dusseldorf; Windsor

Areas Served: worldwide

Founded: 1935 *Staff:* over 100 *Revenues:* over $10 million

Professional Affiliations: ACME, IMC

Services: 1.0 2.0 3.0 4.0 5.0 6.0 9.0 10.0

Industries: B.00 D.00 F.51 G.00 I.00

SAM Associates, Inc.

30 W. Washington

Chicago, Illinois 60602

(312)263-1181

Strategic counseling in finance, marketing, business perpetuation, fair market valuations. Practice limited to wholesaler-distributors and their suppliers.

Contact: Richard S. Lopata, pres.

Areas Served: worldwide

Founded: 1970 *Staff:* 1-3 *Revenues:* $100-$500,000

Professional Affiliations: IMC

Services: 1.0 1.3 1.7 3.1 4.0 5.0

Industries: F.00 F.50 F.51

Samuelson & Co.

39 Cherry Hill Dr.

Waterville, Maine 04901

(207)873-4625

Solo practitioner offering generalist services with emphasis on the northeast.

Contact: Robert Samuelson

Areas Served: Northeast
Founded: 1976 *Staff:* 1-3 *Revenues:* under $100,000
Services: 1.0   2.0   4.0   5.0
Industries: A.09   D.24   D.26   D.31   I.80   J.91

Sanderhoff & Associates, Inc.
875 N. Michigan Ave.
Chicago, Illinois 60611
(312)787-2877
Our primary work is upgrading physical distribution programs . . . applied to companies with "simple" or "complex" distribution networks. That work ranges from narrow aspects of freight movements to extensive programs optimizing cost/service through strategic determination of the number/type/location of warehouses; and evolves to a total distribution system.
Contact: Erle K. Theimer, vp.
Areas Served: U.S.
Founded: 1971 *Staff:* 3-10 *Revenues:* $100-$500,000
Services: 1.0   2.2   2.10   2.12   2.13   2.16   2.17   4.0   6.4   11.1
Industries: D.00   E.00   F.00

Sanderson & Porter, Inc.
26 Broadway
New York, New York 10004
(212)344-5550
Administrative Systems: Paperwork systems and procedures; office work simplification; clerical work measurement; forms design and control; records management; electronic data processing studies; organizing and directing corporate internal management consulting groups; office layout; management and supervisory training programs in systems techniques. Industrial Engineering: Manufacturing and distribution; manpower utilization; work standards; production planning. Governmental: Postal systems; law enforcement administration; police evaluations; city and state operations; public sector training. Also international.
Contact: Arthur Ferber, dir. mgmt. svcs.
Affiliates/branches: Iran; Liberia; Brazil; Saudi Arabia; Indonesia
Founded: 1896 *Staff:* 10-25 *Revenues:* $500,000-1 million
Services: most   1.0   2.0   3.0   4.0   5.0   6.3   9.0   10.0
Industries: A.00   B.00   C.00   D.43   D.49

Wm. E. Sandman Associates Co.
715 Twining Rd.
Dresher, Pennsylvania 19025
(215)887-8755
We consult with executive management and train production managers to interact with daily solutions of the :job shop problems" (a management, not a technical problem). The problem solved, productivity typically doubles. We continue to work closely with management on an ongoing basis to "de-limit" production still further.
Contact: Wm. E. Sandman, pres.
Areas Served: U.S. & Canada
Founded: 1969 *Staff:* 3-10 *Revenues:* $1-$5 million
Services: 1.10   2.1   2.3   2.4   2.6   2.8   2.9   5.2   5.10
Industries: D.25   D.29   D.34   D.35   D.36   D.37   D.38   D.39   I.76

Robert H. Schaffer & Associates
401 Rockrimmon Rd.
Stamford, Connecticut 06903
(203)322-1604

We help large organizations to carry out major productivity and performance improvements and to establish directions for future growth. The services are designed not only to improve immediate performance but also to expand management's capacity to sustain higher levels of accomplishment. We often collaborate closely with internal staff "consultants."

Contact: Robert H. Schaffer
Affiliates/branches: Montreal
Areas Served: U.S. & Canada
Founded: 1960 *Staff:* 10-25 *Revenues:* $500,000-1 million
Professional Affiliations: IMC
Services: 1.0 1.1 1.3 1.7 1.10 1.11 3.0 3.1 3.3 3.9
Industries: Most D.00 E.00 I.80 I.83 I.86 J.91 J.95

F.R. Schwab & Associates
645 Madison Ave.
New York, New York 10022
(212)758-6800

Management organization and compensation studies; strategic planning and marketing studies; profit improvement, particularly overhead cost reduction; management training; management planning and control systems; and management recruiting. Particularly involved with the energy, natural resources and manufacturing industries.

Contact: Frank Schwab, Jr.
Areas Served: worldwide
Founded: 1965 *Staff:* 25-50 *Revenues:* $1-$5 million
Professional Affiliations: IMC
Services: 1.0 2.0 3.0 4.1 4.2 5.10 5.11
Industries: B.00 D.00 E.49

Schwarzkopf Consultants, Inc.
15285 Watertown Plank Rd.
Elm Grove, Wisconsin 53122
(414)784-4200

Enabling management to more effectively utilize human resources: general management audits; organization analysis and development; manpower planning and development; sales compensation plan development; executive recruitment; broad employee relations counsel.

Contact: E. A. Schwarzkopf, pres.
Areas Served: U.S.
Founded: 1969 *Staff:* 3-10 *Revenues:* $100-$500,000
Professional Affiliations: AMC
Services: 1.0 1.1 1.2 1.3 1.7 1.10 3.0 4.1 4.15
Industries: Most

Science Management Corporation
Fellowship Rd.
Moorestown, New Jersey 08057
(609)235-9200

A full-spectrum professional services company dedicated to providing innovative results-oriented management and engineering services to clients worldwide. Services are provided through individual operating units as well as the coordinated efforts of our total corporate capabilities. (See separate listings for Wofac and Hendrick & Co.)

Contact: James A. Skidmore, Jr., pres.

Affiliates/branches: Washington, D.C.; New York, New York; London; Paris; Frankfurt; Brussels; Sao Paulo; Algiers; Tokyo

Areas Served: North & South America, Europe, North Africa, Middle & Far East

Founded: 1946 *Staff:* over 100 *Revenues:* over $10 million

Services: 1.0   2.0   3.0   4.0   5.0   6.0   7.0   8.0   9.0   10.0

Industries: B.00   C.00   D.00   E.00   F.00   G.00   H.00   I.00   J.00

Seidman & Seidman

(Management Advisory Services)
235 Peachtree St.
Atlanta, Georgia 30303
(404)688-6841

As a specialized group within a major CPA firm, our role is to help our clients become more profitable ... and to enjoy the association while doing so.

Contact: Kenneth O. Cole, nat'l. dir. MAS

Affiliates/branches: 1120 City Nat'l. Bank Bldg., Austin, Texas 78701; 808 Fidelity Nat'l. Bank Bldg., Baton Rouge, Louisiana 70801; Capitol Bank Bldg., Boston, Massachusetts 02114; 1400 Main Place Twr., Buffalo, New York 14202; 3110 NCNB Plaza, Charlotte, North Carolina 28280; 55 E. Monroe St., Chicago, Illinois 60603; 1030 Mercantile Bank Bldg., Dallas, Texas 75201; 621 17th St., Denver, Colorado 80202; 755 W. Big Beaver, Troy, Michigan 48084; 103 Pennsylvania Ave., Dowagiac, Michigan 49047; 1202 Old Nat'l. Bank Bldg., Evansville, Indiana 47708; Worcester Co. Nat'l. Bank Bldg., Gardner, Massachusetts 01440; 206 Security First Bank Bldg., Grand Haven, Michigan 49417; 865 Old Kent Bldg., Grand Rapids, Michigan 49417; First Citizens Bank Plaza, High Point, North Carolina 27261; 700 Dresser Tower, Houston, Texas 77002; 202 Front St., Jamestown, New York 14701; 700 Ind. State Bank Bldg., Kalamazoo, Michigan 49006; 2000 Mich. Nat'l. Twr., Lansing, Michigan 48933; 1st Nat'l. Bank Bldg., Las Vegas, Nevada 89101; 9100 Wilshire Blvd., Beverly Hills, California 90212; 2500 Commerce Twr., Memphis, Tennessee 38150; 888 Brickell Ave., Miami, Florida 33131; 15 Columbus Circle, New York, New York 10023; 1970 Broadway, Oakland, California 94612; 101 Park Ave., Oklahoma City, Oklahoma 73102; 1 City Blvd. W., Orange, California 92668; Hartford Bldg., Orlando, Florida 32801; 3 Girard Plaza, Philadelphia, Pennsylvania 19102; 600 Talcott Bldg., Rockford, Illinois 61101; 1723 N. Michigan Ave., Saginaw, Michigan 48602; 1 Romana Plaza, San Antonio, Texas 78205; 110 W. A St., San Diego, California 92101; 100 Pine St., San Francisco, California 94111; 14724 Ventura Blvd., Sherman Oaks, California 91403; 818 W. Riverside Ave., Spokane, Washington 99201; 1000 N. Ashley Dr., Tampa, Florida 33601; 1227 Bay St., Traverse City, Michigan 49684; First Place-3228, Tulsa, Oklahoma 74103; 1200-18th St., NW, Washington, D.C. 20036; 1 North Broadway, White Plains, New York 10601

Areas Served: worldwide

Founded: 1910 *Staff:* 10-25 *Revenues:* $500,000-1 million

Services: Most

Industries: Most

Wilson Seney, Inc.

Box 134
Douglaston, New York 11363
(212)428-2112

Financial and accounting policies and practices. Financial and accounting aspects of marketing, production and other functions of make-and-sell and buy-and-sell companies.

Contact: Wilson Seney, pres.
Areas Served: North America
Founded: 1960 *Staff:* 1-3 *Revenues:* under $100,000
Professional Affiliations: IMC, SPMC/FEI, NAA, PEI
Services: 4.16 5.1 5.2 5.3 5.4 5.6 5.7 5.8 5.9 7.5
Industries: D.20 D.23 D.26 D.27 D.27 D.34 D.35 D.36 D.38 G.53

Senn-Delaney & Associates

400 Oceangate Blvd.
Long Beach, California 90802
(213)436-7234

We specialize in improving profits for retail operations, combining a systems/IE approach with management development and people-orientation. The result is typically significant expense reduction, improved service, better use of facilities, and improved morale.

Contact: Dr. Larry Senn, pres.
Affiliates/branches: Los Angeles; New York; Detroit; San Francisco
Areas Served: U.S.
Founded: 1968 *Staff:* 10-25 *Revenues:* $1-$5 million
Services: 1.0 2.0 3.0 4.0 5.5 9.1 9.4
Industries: D.23 D.26 D.30 D.34 F.51 G.00 H.60 H.65

Dorian Shainin Consultant, Inc.

35 Lakewood Circle S.
Manchester, Connecticut 06040
(203)646-4429

27 years assisting 550 clients solving resistant technical problems; product yield, design, reliability, testing, manufacturing costs, quality assurance-controls, federal regulation, liability prevention. Training seminars, consulting implementation. Clients range from government, GM, IBM, RCA, United Technologies, Exxon, Textron, Corning Glass, Hewlett-Packard; Philips, Lever Bros, Rolls Royce (UK), to 50-man research companies.

Contact: Dorian Shainin, pres.
Areas Served: U.S., Europe, South America
Founded: 1974 *Staff:* 1-3 *Revenues:* $100-$500,000
Professional Affiliations: IMC
Services: 1.13 2.7 2.9 2.15 6.1 7.1
Industries: Most

Shaw Communications Consultants

301 174th St.
Miami Beach, Florida 33160
(305)940-7429

Dedicated to the study and design of superior communication systems and data communication systems and data communications both through operating telephone companies and private communication companies. Specialize in auditing telephone local service bills to return errors & overbilling to our clients ...to reducing long distance costs through analysis by computer.

Contact: Howard Shaw, pres.

Areas Served: FL
Founded: 1975 *Staff:* 1-3 *Revenues:* under $100,000
Professional Affiliations: /STC
Services: 5.0   11.3
Industries: Most   E.48

Irving Shaw & Associates
16 Lyle Ave.
Wayne, New Jersey 07470
(201)942-3333
> We plan factory and warehouse space for efficient layout, efficient flow of material, and efficient storage. We've planned space for 150 client firms in widely diversified industries.

Contact: Irving Shaw, pres.
Areas Served: worldwide
Founded: 1961 *Staff:* 1-3 *Revenues:* $100-$500,000
Professional Affiliations: SPMC/APMHC, IMMS
Services: 2.3   2.4   2.11   2.12   2.13   2.16
Industries: D.23   D.26   D.27   D.28   D.30   D.31   D.34   D.36   D.39   F.50

John Sheridan Associates, Inc.
1111 Touhy Ave.
Des Plaines, Illinois 60018
(312)296-7725
> A full service consulting firm specializing in labor relations and employee relations and consisting of experts in managing union representation campaigns for employees as well as wage and salary administration, employee attitude surveys, and all phases of personnel administration. We have a prestigious client list in the following fields: academic instructions, financial, health service industry, industrial and manufacturing, insurance, retail, and service industry.

Contact: Gloria A. Morgan, assoc.
Areas Served: worldwide
Founded: 1959 *Staff:* 10-25 *Revenues:* $1-$5 million
Services: 3.1   3.3   3.4   3.5   3.6   3.7   3.8   3.9   3.10
Industries: Most

Henry Sherry Associates, Inc.
230 Peachtree St., NW
Atlanta, Georgia 30303
(404)688-9885
> Specialize solely in marketing. Our goal is to contribute to our clients' bottom-line profits. We do this by bringing creative marketing know-how to the problems we uncover through penetrating analysis. Our consistent growth attests to the success of our work.

Contact: Henry I. Sherry, pres.
Areas Served: U.S., Canada & So. America
Founded: 1971 *Staff:* 3-10 *Revenues:* $100-$500,000
Services: 4.0
Industries: Most

R. Shriver Associates
120 Littleton Rd.
Parsippany, New Jersey 07054
(201)335-7800
> We help clients define their information needs and implement computer systems to meet these needs.

Contact: Russell White, pres.
Affiliates/branches: 3155 W. Big Beaver Rd., Troy, Michigan 48084; 1530 Chestnut St., Philadelphia, Pennsylvania 19102; 1128 16th St., NW, Washington, D.C. 20036
Areas Served: U.S.
Founded: 1966 *Staff:* 10-25 *Revenues:* $500,000-1 million
Services: 2.1 2.5 4.14 5.1 5.3 6.4 9.0
Industries: D.00 E.40 E.46 H.63 I.86

Shycon Associates Inc.
1 Gateway Ctr.
Newton, Massachusetts 02158
(617)965-2410
> Development of marketing and logistics (manufacture/distribution) strategies, and operating and control techniques. Originated distribution simulation techniques (the original and principal scientific methods) for analyzing total national marketing and distribution systems - (*Harvard Business Review,* Nov-Dec 1960.) Originated customer service evaluation techniques and methods to best plan the interface between marketing and logistics - (*Harvard Business Review,* July-Aug 1955.)

Contact: Harvey N. Shycon, pres.
Areas Served: U.S., Canada, Mexico, Europe & Asia
Founded: 1974 *Staff:* 3-10 *Revenues:* $100-$500,000
Professional Affiliations: /ORSA, NCPDM, TIMS
Services: 1.0 2.0 4.0 5.3 5.6 6.0 6.4 7.3 9.0 10.0
Industries: A.00 B.00 D.00 E.00 G.00 I.70 I.78 I.82

SIAR, Inc.
22 Putnam
Cambridge, Massachusetts 02138
(617)354-2320
> An international, general management consulting group. Our work involves problems of corporate growth, and organizational change. Our methodology stresses learning by the client. We work jointly with management for one to three years on the developmental problems of the industry, business, organization, and people.

Contact: Lawrence A. Bennington, pres.
Areas Served: U.S. & Western Europe
Founded: 1979 *Staff:* 3-10 *Revenues:* $500,000-1 million
Services: 1.1 1.2 1.3 1.4 1.6 1.11 3.1 4.1 7.1 10.2
Industries: A.08 C.15 D.20 D.24 D.26 D.28 D.35 H.60 I.70

Sibson & Company, Inc.
1101 State Rd.
Princeton, New Jersey 08540
(609)924-7510
> We specialize in all areas of employee relations and personnel: from top management down. Services include compensation, manpower planning,

development, benefits. We have completed over 1000 assignments for over 500 clients in twenty years.

Contact: John A. Fischer, princ.

Affiliates/branches: 444 Madison Ave., New York, New York 10022

Areas Served: U.S.

Founded: 1959 *Staff:* 25-50 *Revenues:* $1-$5 million

Professional Affiliations: /ACA, NRMA, ASTD, ASPA, APA

Services: 1.1   1.2   1.3   1.7   3.0   3.1   3.2   3.7   3.8   3.9

Industries: Most

Silverman Consulting Services Ltd.

120 Hwy. 7

Nepean, Ottawa, Ontario K2H 5Z1, Canada

(613)820-9690

Consultants in applied policy sciences. Specialize in public policy interface and relationship between social-economic factors and technology-based activities (especially in communications and information sector). Organizational diagnostics, planning and development.

Contact: Saul N. Silverman, pres.

Areas Served: Canada

Founded: 1978 *Staff:* 1-3 *Revenues:* under $100,000

Services: 1.0   3.1   3.4   3.5   3.8   3.9   3.10   3.11   7.0   11.0

Industries: D.00   D.36   D.37   E.48   G.53   G.57   G.59   I.00   J.00

E. Ralph Sims, Jr. & Associates, Inc.

Box 646

Lancaster, Ohio 43130

(614)654-1091

Physical distribution and industrial logistics management, MRP, warehousing operations and materials handling, plant layout, transportation, facility design, system design, organization planning, and technical market research.

Contact: E. Ralph Sims, Jr., CMC, pres.

Affiliates/branches: London

Areas Served: North & South America, Europe & South Africa

Founded: 1958 *Staff:* 3-10 *Revenues:* $100-$500,000

Professional Affiliations: AMC, IMC/AIIE, ASME, NSPE

Services: 1.0   2.0   3.1   4.2   4.12   4.14   5.2   6.0   8.0   9.0

Industries: Most   B.00   D.00   E.40   E.42   E.44   E.45   E.47   F.00   G.00   K.00

Allan J. Siposs & Associates

Box 4082

Irvine, California 92716

(714)552-8494

Practical, results-oriented counsel and assistance in marketing and business developments, new ventures, expansion and diversification. We also provide active assistance and cooperation in the practical implementation of plans. Our services are particularly geared to the medium-size and smaller companies and to the needs of entrepeneurs. We are results-oriented.

Contact: Allan J. Siposs, pres.

Areas Served: U.S. & Canada

Founded: 1965 *Staff:* 10-25 *Revenues:* $100-$500,000

Services: 1.0   2.13   4.0   5.9   6.3   7.3   9.5   10.4

Industries: Most

David Sirota Associates, Inc.
11 E. 85th St.
New York, New York 10028
(212)722-8054

Industrial psychologists helping companies improve the human side of
organization effectiveness; work on issues such as turnover motivation, and
industrial conflict; heavy reliance on attitude surveys for the diagnosis of
organization problems.

Contact: David Sirota, pres.
Areas Served: U.S.
Founded: 1972 *Staff:* 1-3 *Revenues:* $100-$500,000
Services: 3.1 3.4 3.9 3.10
Industries: Most

B.R. Smith & Associates
Church St.
Spofford, New Hampshire 03462
(603)363-4475

Specialize in general consulting services to New England organizations with less
than 100 employees. Particular strengths are in business planning, marketing
research, business combinations (mergers), new venture creation, and financial
planning. Special services are provided for the entrepeneur.

Contact: Brian R. Smith, pres.
Areas Served: New England
Founded: 1968 *Staff:* 1-3 *Revenues:* under $100,000
Services: Most
Industries: Most

Sno Engineering/Resource Management Inc.
Box 65
Franconia, New Hampshire 03580
(603)823-5539

Planning, design, layout, construction supervision of major & minor resort
developments. Physical analysis, economic studies, market research. Rural
community planning and revitalization, government relations, and financial
planning environmental impact studies. Primary focus is on travel & tourism
related projects and economies.

Contact: Jim Branch
Affiliates/branches: Box 11536, Aspen, Colorado 81611
Areas Served: U.S. & Canada
Founded: 1953 *Staff:* 3-10 *Revenues:* $100-$500,000
Services: 1.0 3.4 3.10 4.1 4.8 5.0 9.5 10.4
Industries: I.70 I.73 I.79

Snyder Associates, Inc.
Box 98
Essex, Connecticut 06426
(203)767-1122

We assist large and small manufacturing firms to expand or reorganize their
businesses by providing them with studies and advice on: industrial markets,
new technology and state-of-the-art in industry, new manufacturing methods, R
& D organization and program selection, pre-investment and investment
feasibility, license search, joint venture arrangements, confidential management

studies. We specialize in manufacturing and/or service industries with high technology bases.

Contact: A.E. Snyder, pres.
Affiliates/branches: W. Germany; London
Areas Served: U.S., Europe & Japan
Founded: 1970 *Staff:* 3-10 *Revenues:* $100-$500,000
Professional Affiliations: AMC
Services: 1.3   1.4   1.5   1.6   2.3   2.10   2.13   4.2   7.2   10.0
Industries: A.09   D.34   D.35   D.36   D.37   D.38   D.39   E.00

Space/Management Programs, Inc.

230 N. Michigan Ave.
Chicago, Illinois 60601
(312)263-2995

Broad range of architectural and management consulting services involving modern approaches to administrative and office problems. Our services cover a spectrum of planning, design, vendor selection and implementation activities. We primarily serve clients in the insurance, banking, publications, broadcasting and financial industries, especially trading floor design.

Contact: Charles R. Kinsey, pres.
Areas Served: Chicago metropolitan
Founded: 1973 *Staff:* 10-25 *Revenues:* $500,000-1 million
Professional Affiliations: IMC/AIA, ASID
Services: 1.0   2.0   3.0   9.0
Industries: D.00   E.48   H.00   H.60   H.62   H.63   H.66   H.67   I.73

Sperry-Boom of Florida, Inc.

5401 W. Kennedy Blvd.
Tampa, Florida 33609
(813)879-8116

We are a full service research and consulting firm. Specializing in analytical research and systems development that help to improve access to the client's market. Areas of staff expertise include management analysis, computer systems, economic/feasibility research, market analysis, and technical writing. Clients range from large, complex multi-national companies to regional and local small businesses.

Contact: Warren A. DeBord, sr. vp.
Areas Served: U.S. & Canada
Founded: 1973 *Staff:* 10-25 *Revenues:* $1-$5 million
Services: Most
Industries: Most

SRI International

333 Ravenswood Ave.
Menlo Park, California 94025
(415)326-6200

Basic and applied research and consulting under contract for clients in business, industry, and government on a worldwide basis.

Contact: Susan E. Atkins, dir. pub. aff.
Affiliates/branches: 1611 N. Kent St., Arlington, Virginia 22209; 360 Lexington Ave., New York, New York 10017; Croydon; Paris; Madrid; Milan; Tokyo; Riyadh; Stockholm; London; Zurich
Areas Served: worldwide

Founded: 1946 *Staff:* over 100 *Revenues:* over $10 million
Services: 1.0   2.0   4.0   5.0   6.0   7.0   9.0   10.0
Industries: Most   A.00   D.00   E.00   H.00   I.00   J.00

Standard Research Consultants

345 Hudson St.
New York, New York 10014
(212)741-7300

Valuations of companies and securities for estate planning, tax matters, redemptions, reorganizations, mergers, going-private offers, and other transactions; intermediary services and structuring in mergers and acquisitions and private placements; corporate financial counseling; studies and consulting on matters of excess accumulations of earnings, excess compensation, and damage claims in commercial litigation; expert testimony.

Contact: Walter F. Forbes, pres.
Areas Served: U.S.
Founded: 1931 *Staff:* 10-25 *Revenues:* $1-$5 million
Professional Affiliations: AMC
Services: 1.6   5.9   5.10

Standards, International Inc.

8550 W. Bryn Mawr
Chicago, Illinois 60631
(312)693-7171

Work simplification: methods analyses, value analyses, job design. Work scheduling: production & inventory control systems, materials and manning requirement programs, various temporary or crash techniques such as short-interval and variable control scheduling. Work measurement: for day work programs, standard costs, merit programs/incentives, related programs of job evaluation, supervisor training, methods and work place evaluation, productivity improvement and cost control.

Contact: Clifford Sellie, pres.
Affiliates/branches: Salem, Virginia; Atlanta, Georgia; Los Angeles, California
Areas Served: worldwide
Founded: 1948 *Staff:* 10-25 *Revenues:* $1-$5 million
Professional Affiliations: /AIEE, IMS
Services: 2.1   2.3   2.4   2.6   2.11   2.14   3.8   3.10   5.2   9.4
Industries: Most

Stanley Consultants, Inc.

Stanley Bldg.
Muscatine, Iowa 52761
(319)264-6600

Services ranging from brief consultations to complete professional design and management involvement in large and complex projects: 1) investigations, evaluations, and reports on management/technical systems for contemplated projects; 2) design and preparation of plans and specifications for projects in all phases of engineering, architecture, environmental sciences, planning and management; and 3) complete construction management services.

Contact: A.G. Bardwell, sr. vp.
Affiliates/branches: 2600 Century Pkwy, NE, Atlanta, Georgia 30345; 6659 Pearl Rd., Cleveland, Ohio 44130; 1725 Eye St., NW, Washington, D.C. 20006; 208 S. LaSalle St., Chicago, Illinois 60604; 5610 Crawfordsville Rd., Indianapolis, Indiana 46224;

Dominican Republic; Bolivia; Liberia; Malaysia; Nigeria; Philippines
Areas Served: worldwide
Founded: 1913 *Staff:* over 100 *Revenues:* over $10 million
Services: Most
Industries: Most

Stanton Associates, Inc.
1821 University Ave.
St. Paul, Minnesota 55104
(612)646-7154

Services to a wide range of clients in business, industry and government: organization planning, executive compensation (current or Deferred), wage and salary administration, incentive and performance review programs. Other services: evaluation of employee policies and benefits, financial controls, merger-acquisitions and management audits. Extensive specialized experience in compensation surveys for industry and government.
Contact: Frank D. Stanton, CMC, pres.
Areas Served: U.S.
Founded: 1955 *Staff:* 3-10 *Revenues:* $100-$500,000
Professional Affiliations: AMC, IMC
Services: 1.0   2.6   3.0   5.3   5.4   5.9   9.1
Industries: Most   C.00   D.00   E.42   E.49   F.00   G.52   H.00   I.00   J.00

Edward Stark Associates
Box 265
Needham Heights, Massachusetts 02194
(617)449-1468

Creation, design, installation of management information systems; computer installation audits and feasibility studies; interactive systems design, time-sharing applications; complete accounting services, using automated methods; European experience and representation' airline and travel industry consulting, marketing services and seminars designed for profit improvement.
Contact: Ed Stark, CMC, pres.
Affiliates/branches: Munich
Areas Served: U.S. & W. Germany
Founded: 1964 *Staff:* 1-3 *Revenues:* under $100,000
Professional Affiliations: IMC
Services: 1.5   1.7   1.8   2.14   4.2   4.11   5.1   5.2   5.8   10.2
Industries: D.22   D.27   D.36   D.39   E.45   E.47   G.55   H.63   I.73   I.75

Frank A. Stasiowski
45 Van Brunt Ave.
Dedham, Massachusetts 02026
(617)723-8056

Architect/MBA provides unique management consulting services to other professionals, primarily in design related professions. Nationwide practice emphasizes highest quality of experienced professional service to the unique aspects of your professional firm.
Contact: Frank A. Stasiowski, princ.
Areas Served: U.S.
Founded: 1978 *Staff:* 1-3 *Revenues:* $100-$500,000
Professional Affiliations: /AIA, PSBMA
Services: 1.0   3.0   4.0   5.0   5.2   5.3   5.4   5.8   5.9   9.0

State Street Consultants
84 State St.
Boston, Massachusetts 02109
(617)523-4481

A professional consulting firm servicing major business organizations. Our client work draws upon a braod range of capabilities, including market analysis, product policy, strategic planning, troubleshooting, management development, management education, and policy implementation.

Contact: John P. Windle, vp.
Areas Served: U.S.
Founded: 1969 *Staff:* 3-10 *Revenues:* $500,000-1 million
Professional Affiliations: /ASTD
Services: 1.3   1.5   1.6   1.7   2.10   3.1   4.1   4.2   4.5   4.7
Industries: Most   B.00   D.26   D.27   D.36   D.38   E.48   E.49   H.00   J.94   J.95

John G. Steinle & Associates
50 E. Palisade Ave.
Englewood, New Jersey 07631
(201)568-9670

Consultants to more than 300 hospitals, health planning agencies, state agencies, municipal agencies and a wide variety of specialty health organizations and have conducted some of the most important and well known research and other projects that have had major impact on the delivery of health care in the nation.

Contact: John G. Steinle, pres.
Areas Served: U.S., Europe & Middle East
Founded: 1956 *Staff:* 10-25 *Revenues:* $500,000-1 million
Professional Affiliations: AMC/AHA, AHC
Services: 1.1   1.2   1.3   1.5   1.6   1.7   9.5
Industries: I.80

Stevens, Scheidler, Stevens, Vossler, Inc.
2600 Far Hills Avenue
Dayton, Ohio 45419
(513)299-3501

A business and industrial consulting firm specializing in employee selection and training, management and organizational development, product safety and human factors engineering.

Contact: Donna D. Shaw, mktg. coor.
Areas Served: U.S.
Founded: 1973 *Staff:* 10-25 *Revenues:* $500,000-1 million
Professional Affiliations: /HFS, AAAS, ASSE
Services: most   1.0   2.9   3.0   4.7   4.9   9.1
Industries: most   I.73

Stone Management Corporation
208 S. LaSalle St.
Chicago, Illinois 60604
(312)236-0800

Experienced, seasoned professional managers with MBA degrees from Harvard and other major universities. We bring to medium-sized businesses practical, concrete results through the implementation consulting method. The IMC code of professional ethics is carefully followed on all assignments. Key areas:

growth, cost reduction, physical distribution, turnaround.
Contact: James H. Stone, pres.
Areas Served: Chicago & Mid West
Founded: 1969 *Staff:* 3-10 *Revenues:* $100-$500,000
Professional Affiliations: IMC/APICS, NCPDM, AMA
Services: 1.3   1.6   1.10   1.11   2.17   4.2   4.5   4.14   6.1   6.4
Industries: Most

Stone & Webster Mgmt. Consultants, Inc.

90 Broad St.
New York, New York 10004
(212)269-4224

Comprehensive services to business and industry, including public utility, transportation, pipeline, land development, banking, petroleum and manufacturing companies, and to government agencies, foreign and domestic.

Contact: Robert C. Barwick, vp.
Affiliates/branches: Greenwood Plaza, Denver, Colorado 80217; 1534 Dunwoody Village, Atlanta, Georgia 30338; 1 Houston Ctr., Houston, Texas 77002
Areas Served: worldwide
Founded: 1929 *Staff:* over 100 *Revenues:* $500,000-1 million
Professional Affiliations: /AMA, AIME
Services: 1.0   2.0   3.0   4.0   5.0   6.0   9.0   10.0   11.0
Industries: B.12   B.13   D.22   D.26   D.28   D.29   D.33   E.47   E.48   E.49

Straehley Associates

1005 Roble Lane
Santa Barbara, California 93103
(805)965-2490

Specializing in providing both management and technical consulting services to organizations in electronics and related industries. Special competence and understanding in solving the problem of small to medium sized firms. Our approach integrating management and technology also applicable in solving technology-related and general management problems in other organizations.

Contact: Erwin H. Straehley, princ.
Areas Served: Primarily CA & HI
Founded: 1972 *Staff:* 1-3 *Revenues:* under $100,000
Professional Affiliations: SPMC
Services: 1.0   2.1   2.2   5.3   5.4   5.9   7.1   7.2   7.3   7.4
Industries: D.36   E.48

Sullivan & Shook, Inc.

Box 1484
East Lansing, Michigan 48823
(517)337-1547

A personnel management consulting firm specializing in: development and installation of employee compensation programs; development and installation of employee performance planning appraisal programs; administration of employee attitude surveys and attitude survey feedback programs; and development of equal employment opportunity and affirmative action programs.

Contact: John F. Sullivan, pres.
Areas Served: U.S. & Canada
Founded: 1970 *Staff:* 3-10 *Revenues:* $100-$500,000

Services: 3.0   3.2   3.7   3.8   3.10
Industries: Most

Summerour & Associates, Inc.
225 Peachtree St., NE
Atlanta, Georgia 30303
(404)577-4632

National and international consulting service to the apparel and textile industries, governments, and institutions. Flexible application of professional disciplines is achieved by the firm's specialists in diversified fields offering a total need concept. The results-oriented approach serves to keep clients in the forefront of their field.

Contact: J. William Summerour, pres.
Areas Served: worldwide
Founded: 1961 *Staff:* 25-50 *Revenues:* $1-$5 million
Professional Affiliations: /AIIE
Services: Most
Industries: D.00   D.22   D.23   I.00   I.80   J.00

R.J. Sweeney Associates
195 Wilton Rd.
Westport, Connecticut 06880
(203)226-0802

Practical, usable, and economical solutions to client problems. All assignments performed by a small group of senior consultants under close personal control. Emphasize methods improvement, customer serive, physical distribution, and personal assistance to top management.

Contact: R.J. Sweeney, mng. dir.
Areas Served: U.S., U.K., Western Europe & Far East
Founded: 1975 *Staff:* 1-3 *Revenues:* under $100,000
Professional Affiliations: IMC
Services: 1.0   2.0   4.5   4.12   4.14   6.3   6.4   8.1   10.2
Industries: Most

Synergy Corporation
6711 Bracken Court
Springfield, Virginia 22152
(703)451-5042

Marketing and business development training and counsel, consulting skills and engagement management training for consulting firms and CDP firms.

Contact: Dick Connor, pres.
Affiliates/branches: Melbourne
Areas Served: U.S., Canada, Australia & New Zealand
Founded: 1969 *Staff:* 3-10 *Revenues:* $100-$500,000
Services: 1.3   1.14   4.1   4.9   4.11
Industries: I.73

Systech & Associates
2825 Cub Hill Rd.
Baltimore, Maryland 21234
(301)665-6033

Direct consulting- helping corporate, banking and government and private clients to define and reach goals and objectives through utilization of proven techniques of planning, organization, and control. High degree of specialization in electronic funds transfer systems. Management training and development-assist management in meeting organizational objectives by increasing knowledge and skills of specific groups. Help managers improve their effectiveness and accelerate their career progression.

Contact: Walter J. Sistek, pres.

Affiliates/branches: 7518 Harford Rd., Baltimore, Maryland 21234; 640 Madison Ave., New York, New York 10022

Areas Served: worldwide

Founded: 1974 *Staff:* 3-10 *Revenues:* $100-$500,000

Professional Affiliations: AMC/AIMC

Services: Most

Industries: Most

System Planning Associates, Inc.

37 Elm St.

Westfield, New Jersey 07090

(201)232-3910

General management consulting, with specific emphasis on design, development, installation, operation and utilization of integrated computer/business systems for small to medium-size manufacturers, distributors and professional service organizations.

Contact: J. Richard Fleming, CMC, pres.

Areas Served: Mid-Atlantic & Mid-West States

Founded: 1967 *Staff:* 1-3 *Revenues:* under $100,000

Professional Affiliations: AMC, IMC

Services: 1.0   2.0   4.0   5.0   6.3   6.4   9.1   9.3   9.5   9.8

Industries: C.00   D.00   E.43   F.00   G.55   I.81   I.89

Systema Corporation

150 N. Wacker Dr.

Chicago, Illinois 60606

(312)984-5000

Consultants to marketing and sales management emphasizing predictable performance improvement of salespeople and their managers, through practical application of contemporary behavioral technology. Custom program development in sales and communication skills, interpersonal and manager skills, product knowledge and customer education. Needs and task analyses, and modifiable core programs available.

Contact: J.R. Snader, pres.

Areas Served: worldwide

Founded: 1969 *Staff:* 3-10 *Revenues:* $1-$5 million

Professional Affiliations: AMC

Services: 3.1   3.5   4.1   4.5   4.6   4.7   4.9   4.10   4.11   4.12

Industries: D.26   D.28   D.35   D.36   D.38   E.42   H.60   H.62   H.63   H.64

Systems Planning Service

663 Fifth Ave.

New York, New York 10022

(212)752-7510

We are specialists to small and medium-sized firms. We offer a broad scope of consulting services to industry, profit and non-profit organizations and

professional practices.
Contact: Lila Garber, pres.
Areas Served: NY city
Founded: 1963 *Staff:* 1-3 *Revenues:* under $100,000
Professional Affiliations: SPMC
Services: 1.0   3.0   5.4   5.8   5.9   9.0   9.1   9.5   9.6
Industries: Most

The Tanzi Organization
110 Sutter St.
San Francisco, California 94104
(415)391-9991

Marketing programs through manufacturers' representatives, marketing surveys, strategy, financial services to obtain working capital and national product
marketing plans for securing distributors/dealers. In addition we offer the
management audit and organization planning. Our specialized services include
securing venture capitalists, mergers and acquisitions.

Contact: Vito A. Tanzi, mng. dir.
Affiliates/branches: New York, New York; Beverly Hills, California
Areas Served: U.S. & Canada
Founded: 1963 *Staff:* 3-10 *Revenues:* $100-$500,000
Professional Affiliations: SPMC
Services: 1.0   3.0   4.0   5.0   9.0
Industries: B.00   C.00   D.00   F.00   G.00   H.00   I.00

The Technics Group
555 Plymouth Ave., NE
Grand Rapids, Michigan 49508
(616)451-6268

Consultants in materials handling and materials flow, serving customers who
are experiencing problems with in-process flow (manufacturing), distribution,
warehousing, inventory management, and systems management needs. We
serve a broad range of industries, offering a specialized service in a field in
which we are highly qualified.

Contact: Edwin C. Braun, dir.
Affiliates/branches: Frankfurt; Netherlands
Areas Served: worldwide
Founded: 1959 *Staff:* 10-25 *Revenues:* $500,000-1 million
Services: 1.5   1.8   2.0   Most

Technology Marketing Group Ltd.
950 Lee St.
Des Plains, Illinois 60016
(312)297-1404

A marketing resource of skilled professionals who can solve specific marketing
problems for technology-based companies, providing products and services to
medical, industrial, and consumer markets. Services range from marketing
consulting and marketing research to market development and program
implementation.

Contact: John Vanden Brink, mng. dir.
Areas Served: Midwest & East coast
Founded: 1977 *Staff:* 3-10 *Revenues:* $100-$500,000
Professional Affiliations: /AMA

Services: 1.3   1.4   1.5   1.7   4.1   4.2   4.5   4.10   4.11   4.16
Industries: D.36   D.38   E.42   I.73   I.80

Technomic Consultants

1 N. Wacker Dr.
Chicago, Illinois 60606
(312)346-5901

> A marketing-oriented research and consulting firm specializing in assisting non-consumer firms in the areas of marketing planning and research, new product planning, and acquisition selection, evaluation, and integration. Staff possesses combination backgrounds in both the technical disciplines as well as business management areas. Eighty-five percent of studies of Fortune-listed clients.

Contact: Ronald N. Paul, pres.
Areas Served: U.S.
Founded: 1966 *Staff:* 50-100 *Revenues:* $5-$10 million
Professional Affiliations: IMC
Services: 1.0   4.0   5.2   8.1   10.0
Industries: A.00   B.13   C.00   D.00   E.48   E.49   F.00   G.00   H.00   I.00

Teipel Associates Inc.

843 S. Snelling Ave.
St. Paul, Minnesota 55116
(612)227-6625

> General service to chief executive and board remanagement skills. Management training, management accountability, labor relations, compensation.

Contact: Henry N. Teipel, pres.
Areas Served: Upper midwest
Founded: 1963 *Staff:* 1-3 *Revenues:* $100-$500,000
Professional Affiliations: AMC
Services: 1.0   2.9   3.0   4.7   4.9   6.3
Industries: D.34   D.35   F.50   G.52   G.53   G.54   G.55   G.58   G.59

Temple, Barker & Sloane, Inc.

33 Hayden Ave.
Lexington, Massachusetts 02173
(617)861-7580

> Our consulting practice is concerned primarily with issues of strategy formulation, policy determination and organizational effectiveness. These services are focused chiefly in the following areas: corporate strategic development, market forecasting and analysis, financial planning, advanced management education, energy and environment, transportation and logistics, maritime studies, public policy planning, and computer-based information systems.

Contact: Carl S. Sloane, pres.
Affiliates/branches: 1629 K St., NW, Washington, D.C. 20006
Areas Served: worldwide
Founded: 1970 *Staff:* over 100 *Revenues:* $5-$10 million
Services: 1.1   1.3   1.7   1.8   2.1   2.17   3.1   4.0   5.3   5.10
Industries: B.12   E.40   E.42   E.44   E.45   E.49   G.00   H.60   H.62   H.63

Tempo
(a division of General Electric Co.)
Drawer QQ
Santa Barbara, California 93102
(805)965-0551

An objective group of consultants to perform independent studies and analyses of both immediate and lasting technological, economic, management, and social issues for domestic and international clients. The interdisciplinary approach to problems by the staff is augmented by individual consultants of note to form highly adaptable project teams.

Contact: H.E. Robson, mktg. mgr.
Affiliates/branches: Washington, D.C.; Albuquerque, New Mexico; Bel Air, Maryland
Areas Served: worldwide
Founded: 1956 *Staff:* over 100 *Revenues:* $5-$10 million
Services: 1.0 2.13 2.15 3.4 4.1 7.0 9.8 10.0
Industries: Most B.14 E.40 E.41 E.47 E.48 J.91 J.94 J.95 J.96 J.97

Ten Eyck Associates
1760 Cherryville Rd.
Littleton, Colorado 80121
(303)758-6129

Well-seasoned management insights/advise to emerging businesses ($2-50 million) on objective, no-holds-barred basis and recommend/implement remedial programs where applicable. Strengths are in all facets of industrial and financial service, sales and marketing with concentration on strategic, general business, organizational and attitudinal considerations.

Contact: Richard C. Ten Eyck, pres.
Areas Served: Rocky Mountain West
Founded: 1974 *Staff:* 1-3 *Revenues:* under $100,000
Professional Affiliations: IMC/PEI, ASTD
Services: 1.1 1.3 1.4 3.4 3.10 4.1 4.2 4.3 4.5 4.7
Industries: D.20 D.30 D.36 D.39 H.60 H.63 H.64 I.73 I.82 K.00

The THinc. Group Inc.
30 Rockefeller Plaza
New York, New York 10020
(212)397-0400

Specialize in corporate senior level executive personnel problems, including out-placement, retirement out-placement and retirement planning.

Contact: Thomas B. Hubbard, chmn. & ceo
Affiliates/branches: Chicago; Los Angeles; Washington; Houston; London
Areas Served: worldwide
Founded: 1969 *Staff:* 25-50 *Revenues:* $1-$5 million
Services: 1.1 3.4 3.8
Industries: Most

Thompson, Ferguson & Associates
2456 4th Ave.
San Diego, California 92101
(714)231-2943

We design and implement marketing programs that enable our clients to successfully enter the China market.

Contact: Mark H. Thompson, dir.

Affiliates/branches: San Francisco; Hong Kong
Areas Served: CA
Founded: 1978   *Staff:* 3-10   *Revenues:* under $100,000
Services: 4.1   4.2   4.10   10.1   10.2   10.4   10.5   10.6
Industries: Most

D.W. Thomson & Associates

Box 456, Frederiksted
St. Croix, U.S., Virgin Islands 00840
> All socioeconomic matters, with emphasis on finance and taxation in the U.S. Virgin Islands.

Contact: David W. Thomson
Founded: 1962   *Staff:* 1-3   *Revenues:* $100-$500,000
Professional Affiliations: SPMC
Services: 1.0   5.3   5.4   5.6   5.8   5.9   5.11   9.1   9.5
Industries: F.00   G.00   I.00

Time Management Center

Box 5
Grandville, Michigan 49418
(616)531-1870
> We have the answers for the time dilemma. Our answers are potent and practical. We get right to the heart of the issue. We invite you to check us out, and let us demonstrate the benefits of our service to your organization. We are confident that you will be pleased with the results.

Contact: Merrill Douglass, pres.
Founded: 1972   *Staff:* 1-3   *Revenues:* $100-$500,000
Services: 3.1   3.5
Industries: Most

TMI Systems Corp.

1 Broadway
Cambridge, Massachusetts 02142
(617)492-6520
> We solve financial management and operations problems for banks, investment institutions and corporations, providing the following services: consulting, customized system development, standardized and/or tailored software and turnkey products, and time-shared services using our standard products. We assume full responsibility for the success of the effort or will work in team with our customer's staff to produce a jointly developed solution.

Contact: C. Wade Tambor, pres.
Affiliates/branches: 80 Pine St., New York, New York 10005; 1900 M St., NW, Washington, D.C. 20036; Paris
Areas Served: U.S.
Founded: 1969   *Staff:* 50-100   *Revenues:* $5-$10 million
Services: 1.5   1.8   1.13   5.5   5.8   9.3   9.8
Industries: H.60   H.61   H.62   H.63   J.93

U. Dann Torrance

3579 W. Loma Linda St.
Fresno, California 93711
(209)431-4834

Accept assignments from industry directly or through other consulting firms. Expertise in manufacturing processes of process, foundry, electronic, and textile industries. Specialize in organization planning, performance evaluation and improvement, process control, inventory management, line balancing, and plant site selection. Also plastics, rubber, brass, carpets, bottling, insulations.

Contact: U. Dann Torrance, pres.
Areas Served: U.S.-primarily west
Founded: 1974 *Staff:* 1-3 *Revenues:* under $100,000
Professional Affiliations: /AIIE
Services: Most 1.O 2.0 3.0 4.0 6.0 8.0 9.0
Industries: Most B.14 D.00

Touche Ross & Co.

(Management Consulting Division)
1633 Broadway
New York, New York 10019
(212)489-1600

Highly trained consultants ... engineers ... mathematicians ... economists ... statisticians ... accountants ... social scientists ... and other professionals with advanced scholastic degrees and wide experience ... working for -- multinational corporations (studies on efficiency, cost control, building of new facilities, operations) ... businesses (as diverse as sophisticated European retailing establishments and rural agricultural marketing cooperatives in underdeveloped nations: devising new techniques for marketing and distribution) ... governments (helping create programs in agriculture, health services, transportation systems).

Contact: Donald Curtis, nat/l dir. con. svcs.
Affiliates/branches: Atlanta, Georgia; Boston, Massachusetts; Charlotte, North Carolina; Chicago, Illinois; Cincinnati, Ohio; Dallas, Texas; Denver, Colorado; Kansas City, Missouri; Los Angeles, California; Miami, Florida; Milwaukee, Wisconsin; Minneapolis, Minnesota; New Orleans, Louisiana; Philadelphia, Pennsylvania; Pittsburgh, Pennsylvania; Seattle, Washington; Washington, D.C.; Argentina; Australia; Austria; Bahamas; Belgium; Bermuda; Brazil; Cayman Islands; Channel Islands; Chile; Columbia; Cyprus; Denmark; France; Germany; Greece; Greenland; Guatemala; Hong Kong; Indonesia; Ireland; Jamaica; Italy; Japan; Kenya; Kuwait; Lebanon; Malaysia; Mauritus; Netherlands; New Zealand; Norway; Panama; Peru; Philippines; Puerto Rico; Rhodesia; Singapore; South Africa; Spain; Sweden; Switzerland; Trinidad & Tobago; Turkey; United Kingdom; Venezuela
Areas Served: worldwide
Founded: 1830 *Staff:* over 100 *Revenues:* over $10 million
Professional Affiliations: IMC/AICPA
Services: Most
Industries: Most

Towers, Perrin, Forster & Crosby

600 Third Ave.
New York, New York 10016
(212)661-5080

Our major goal in serving more than 2500 clients is to provide services of outstanding quality based on an understanding of an sensitivity to the individual client's needs. Our approach is to blend the ideal with the practical; to serve as doers as well as thinkers.

Contact: Quentin I. Smith, Jr., pres.

Affiliates/branches: 3400 Peachtree Rd.NE, Atlanta, Georgia 30326; 1 Boston Place, Boston, Massachusetts 02108; 233 S. Wacker Dr., Chicago, Illinois 60606; 1100 Superior Ave., Cleveland, Ohio 44114; 940 One Main Place, Dallas, Texas 75250; 1 Century Plaza, Los Angeles, California 90067; 2850 Metro Dr., Minneapolis, Minnesota 55420; 600 Third Ave., New York, New York 10016; 1500 Market St., Philadelphia, Pennsylvania 19102; 3620 One Mercantile Ctr., St. Louis, Missouri 63101; 1 Embarcadero Ctr., San Francisco, California 94111; 2010 1st Florida Twr., Tampa, Florida 33602; 2101 L St.,NW, Washington, D.C. 20037; 1111 Melville St. Vancouver, BC V6E 3V6 Canada; Box 281-TD Ctr. Toronto, Ontario M5K 1K3 Canada; Brussels; Caracas; Frankfurt; London; Paris; Sao Paulo 800 Dorchester Blvd. W. Montreal, Quebec, H3B 1X9 Canada
Areas Served: worldwide
Founded: 1934 *Staff:* over 100 *Revenues:* over $10 million
Professional Affiliations: ACME
Services: 1.0   3.0   3.2   3.6   3.7   3.9   10.0   11.8
Industries: Most

Transportation Industry Consultants, Inc.
12 Office Park Cir.
Birmingham, Alabama 35223
(205)897-8503

> Transportation industry including private and common carriers. Clients include many motor carriers and several railroads. Assignments in the railroad industry have been developing and conducting training programs for salesmen and sales managers. Trucking assignments usually in operations of sales. Will assume active short-term management of a motor carrier.

Contact: Herbert Jeff, Jr., pres.
Areas Served: U.S. & Canada
Founded: 1968 *Staff:* 3-10 *Revenues:* $100-$500,000
Services: 1.11   2.17   3.1   4.7   4.9
Industries: E.40   E.42   E.47

Trebor Health Associates
Northway 10 Exec. Park
Ballston Lake, New York 12019
(518)877-8649

> Management services to the health and hospital industry including: Productivity and organizational and corporate analysis; long range planning, education, management, engineering, personnel and labor relations, facilities management, personnel development and training and general operations analysis.

Contact: J. Robert Clement, pres.
Areas Served: U.S.-primarily East coast
Founded: 1977 *Staff:* 1-3 *Revenues:* under $100,000
Services: 1.0   3.0   4.1   4.3   7.0   9.0
Industries: I.80

TriBrook Group, Inc.
1100 Jorie Blvd.
Oak Brook, Illinois 60521
(312)654-8070

> Management consulting to hospitals, extended care facilities, clinics, planning agencies and associations. Studies include long-range role and program

planning; management services; multi-institutional ventures; certificate of preparation; project coordination; medical office building feasibility; compensation programs; educational services; and general consulting. Services performed on a fee basis.

Contact: F. Dale Whitten, exec. vp.

Affiliates/branches: 201 Office Park Dr., Birmingham, Alabama 35223; Walnut Creek, California; Vienna, Virginia

Areas Served: U.S.

Founded: 1972 *Staff:* 25-50 *Revenues:* $1-$5 million

Professional Affiliations: IMC/AAHC, ACHA

Industries: I.80

George Truell Associates

495 N. Forest Rd.
Williamsville, New York 14221
(716)643-3491

Consulting activities focus on the effective utilization of an organization's human resources. Assistance to managers is based upon practical applications of current behavioral research and includes tools, techniques and approaches to managing people which can increase their personal work satisfaction and their contribution to the operating effectiveness of an organization.

Contact: George F. Truell, pres.

Areas Served: worldwide

Founded: 1970 *Staff:* 1-3 *Revenues:* under $100,000

Professional Affiliations: IMC

Services: 3.0 3.1 3.3 3.7 3.8 3.9 3.10 3.11 11.0

Industries: Most

Trundle Consultants Inc.

5500 S. Marginal Rd.
Cleveland, Ohio 44103
(216)431-6200

Have always emphasized the practical rather than the theoretical. Staff, therefore, recruited from business and industry. A broad line personalized service. Average of seven assignments per client since inception.

Contact: Douglas P. Gould

Areas Served: U.S. & Canada

Founded: 1919 *Staff:* 3-10 *Revenues:* $100-$500,000

Professional Affiliations: IMC

Services: 1.0 2.0 3.8 4.2 4.5 4.15 4.16 5.2 5.4 5.7

Industries: C.16 D.20 D.25 D.26 D.28 D.32 D.34 D.35 D.36 F.00

K.W. Tunnell Co., Inc.

1150 First Ave.
King of Prussia, Pennsylvania 19406
(215)337-0820

Working with our clients to improve utilization of human, material, and capital resources . . . providing unlimited profit improvement through concentrated problem analysis, careful project structuring, and carrying out implementation programs to achieve desired results. Project assignments assume practical management-oriented solutions to complex problems as a result of our insistence that all staff members have successful management careers in business as well as diversified technical experience prior to joining the company.

Contact: Kenneth W. Tunnell, pres.
Affiliates/branches: 1010 Jorie Blvd., Chicago, Illinois 60521; Weybridge
Areas Served: North & South America, Europe, Mid-East
Founded: 1966 *Staff:* 25-50 *Revenues:* $1-$5 million
Professional Affiliations: ACME, IMC
Services: 1.7   2.2   2.3   2.4   3.1   4.14   6.0   6.4   9.0
Industries: D.20   D.28   D.29   D.34   D.35   D.36   D.37   E.42   E.45   E.49

University Center, Inc.
607 Boylston St.
Boston, Massachusetts 02116
(617)267-6665

> Our service exists specifically for the small and medium-sized company where every person is responsible for a larger percentage of the company's business. We're management psychologists with 20 years experience and it's our job to help you make the most of your personnel - at the least possible cost to you.

Contact: S. Sherman
Areas Served: U.S.
Founded: 1954 *Staff:* 10-25 *Revenues:* $100-$500,000
Services: 1.15   3.0   3.4   3.9   3.10   3.11
Industries: Most

Van Nuis Co., Inc.
922 Delsea Dr.
South Dennis, New Jersey 08245
(609)861-4831

> We provide individually developed programs to help clients better manage their people. These include: 1) outplacement, executive and group, for sub-managerial employees; 2) retirement outplacement and preretirement planning to help employees transition from one pattern of habits to another; 3) executive appraisal to determine the best path for continued growth and contribution; 4) client administered outplacement, retirement planning and assessment programs, including the development of manuals.

Contact: Edgar L. Van Nuis, pres.
Areas Served: U.S.
Founded: 1976 *Staff:* 1-3 *Revenues:* under $100,000
Services: 3.0
Industries: Most

H.K. von Kaas & Associates
811 E. Wisconsin Ave.
Milwaukee, Wisconsin 53202
(414)273-6935

> Manufacturing problems; industrial engineering, wage incentives, job evaluation, plant layouts, facilities planning.

Contact: H.K. Von Kaas, princ.
Areas Served: U.S.
Founded: 1960 *Staff:* 1-3 *Revenues:* under $100,000
Professional Affiliations: AMC, IMC
Services: 1.9   2.0   2.3   2.4   2.6   2.10   2.11   2.13   2.14   3.8
Industries: Most

Von Keyserling Consultants Ltd.
300 Boush St.
Norfolk, Virginia 23661
(804)623-3257
Personal involvement: organization studies, refinancing management controls, cost, company evaluations, turnarounds. Overseas: investigations, negotiations, market evaluations, financing.
Contact: Henry Von Keyserling, pres.
Areas Served: worldwide
Founded: 1974 *Staff:* 1-3 *Revenues:* under $100,000
Professional Affiliations: /FEI
Services: 1.0 2.0 3.0 4.0 5.0 6.0 7.0 9.0 10.0
Industries: D.00 F.00 G.00 H.00 I.00 J.00

Wade, McGuigan & Associates
50 Staniford St.
Boston, Massachusetts 02114
(617)742-3887
Seasoned professionals with a minimum of 15 years experience in a wide variety of industries. Our principal area of expertise is improving operational efficiency, with heavy emphasis on manufacturing. We are implementation-oriented; our projects are project controlled and geared to return the client's investment.
Contact: Michael R. Wade, ptnr.
Areas Served: worldwide
Founded: 1975 *Staff:* 3-10 *Revenues:* $100-$500,000
Services: 1.0 2.0 3.0 6.0 7.0 9.0
Industries: Most D.00 E.00 F.00 G.00 H.00 I.00 J.00

James P. Wadley & Co., Inc.
310 South St.
Morristown, New Jersey 07960
(201)540-0012
Location analysis/site selection/economic geography involves both science and art and is best handled by a small firm of competent professionals.
Contact: James P. Wadley, pres.
Affiliates/branches: 200 Park Ave., New York, New York 10017
Areas Served: U.S.
Founded: 1975 *Staff:* 1-3 *Revenues:* $100-$500,000
Services: 2.10 2.13
Industries: Most

Wagner Systems, Inc.
29 Bass Dr.
Enfield, Connecticut 06082
(203)745-3890
Our business is primarily with manufacturing and publishing clients. We provide highly competent service in the general fields of production and program management, in both data processing and manual system environments. System-related management/supervisory training and "turn-key" department operation are services also offered.
Contact: Christopher Wagner, pres.
Affiliates/branches: Indianapolis
Areas Served: East of Mississippi & St. Louis

Founded: 1975 *Staff:* 3-10 *Revenues:* $100-$500,000
Professional Affiliations: SPMC/ASM, APICS
Services: 1.8   1.12   2.0   3.1   4.12   6.3   6.4   6.5   7.2   9.0
Industries: D.23   D.27   D.31   D.34   D.35   D.36   D.37   D.38   G.00   I.80

Robert M. Wald & Associates

3540 Wilshire Blvd.
Los Angeles, California 90010
(213)385-3223

Our staff consists of senior professionals with extensive background in our service areas. Our major areas of competence encompass those aspects of human resources management of greatest concern to executive management. We serve large and small clients through in various industries and emphasize our responsibility to add value through our efforts.

Contact: R.M. Wald, pres.
Areas Served: Primarily CA & Western U.S.
Founded: 1972 *Staff:* 3-10 *Revenues:* $100-$500,000
Services: 1.1   1.7   3.1   3.2   3.7   3.9   3.10   3.11   4.5   11.1
Industries: Most

Wendell C. Walker & Associates

342 Madison Ave.
New York, New York 10017
(212)661-4985

International services to all types of commercial and industrial companies including development and implementation of recommended programs with special emphasis upon marketing management, financial management, distribution management and personnel administration.

Contact: Wendell C. Walker, pres.
Affiliates/branches: Johannesburg; Manila
Areas Served: North America, Europe, Africa & Far East
Founded: 1960 *Staff:* 10-25 *Revenues:* $500,000-1 million
Services: Most   1.0   2.0   3.0   4.0   5.0   6.0   9.0   10.0
Industries: Most   D.00   E.00   F.00   G.00   H.00   I.00   I.73

Roy W. Walters & Associates, Inc.

Whitney Industrial Park
Mahwah, New Jersey 07430
(201)891-3344

Specializing in practical applications of the behavioral sciences to achieve optimum use of human resources. Our approach is pragmatic in objectives and in methods. As consultants in many major industries and government organizations, we have demonstrated our capacity to produce significant, measurable results: high motivation, improved productivity, lower costs, and higher quality.

Contact: Roy W. Walters, pres.
Areas Served: U.S., Canada & Mexico
Founded: 1968 *Staff:* 3-10 *Revenues:* $500,000-1 million
Professional Affiliations: IMC
Services: 1.5   1.10   2.4   2.7   2.9   3.1   3.5   3.11   4.9   9.1
Industries: Most

J.F. Ward Associates
5512 Merlyn Dr.
Salt Lake City, Utah 84117
(801)942-5020

Distribution-oriented consulting firm serving wholesalers, manufacturing and retailers. Space planning, layout, distribution strategy, materials handling, data processing, and information systems. Facilities planning, site selection, size determination, and complete systems and method planning.

Contact: J.F. Ward, CMC, pres.
Affiliates/branches: London
Areas Served: North & South America, Europe & Africa
Founded: 1956 *Staff:* 3-10 *Revenues:* $100-$500,000
Professional Affiliations: AMC, IMC
Services: 2.1   2.2   2.4   2.11   2.12   4.1   4.13   4.14   9.2
Industries: D.20   D.23   D.24   D.26   D.31   D.34   D.39   F.00   G.00   I.70

Warren, McVeigh & Griffin
1420 Bristol St. N.
Newport Beach, California 92660
(714)752-1058

Risk management consulting. Conduct audits of corporate and governmental risk and insurance programs. Special studies include: 1) feasibility studies of self-insurance, captive insurance companies, etc.; 2) claims audits; 3) loss control and analysis; 4) selection of insurance brokers, claims administrators, etc.; 5) captive management audits; and 6) others.

Contact: David Warren, princ.
Affiliates/branches: 1700 Montgomery St., San Francisco, California 94111; 1154 West Chester Pike, West Chester, Pennsylvania 19380
Areas Served: U.S. & Canada
Founded: 1968 *Staff:* 3-10 *Revenues:* $500,000-1 million
Professional Affiliations: /IRMC
Services: 1.1   1.2   1.5   1.7   1.8   3.4   3.21   10.5   11.1   11.8
Industries: Most

Washington Nichibei Consultants
1000 Connecticut Ave., NW
Washington, D.C. 20036
(202)293-6958

Specialized research and consulting services to licensors or licensees for invention, R & D, high technology and technical products for international license and commercial technology transfers between U.S. and Japan. Also conducting surveys in market and product/technology utilization in U.S. and in Japan, and assisting to develop opportunities in license, joint venture and venture capital investment in high technology and new products both in U.S. and in Japan.

Contact: Claude Ryo Shirai, mng. dir.
Areas Served: U.S., Japan & East Asia
Founded: 1972 *Staff:* 1-3 *Revenues:* under $100,000
Professional Affiliations: /LES
Services: 1.3   1.5   4.1   4.2   10.0   10.2   10.3   10.4   10.5
Industries: Most

Norton Weber & Co.

320 Fairview Rd.
Pittsburgh, Pennsylvania 15238
(412)963-9522

> Helps businesses grow and become more profitable by planning and helping to implement more effective marketing and marketing communications, tailored to the company's specific needs and objectives.

Contact: Norton Weber, princ.
Areas Served: Primarily Pittsburgh tri-state area
Founded: 1961 *Staff:* 1-3 *Revenues:* under $100,000
Professional Affiliations: AMC
Services: 1.14 3.9 3.10 4.1 4.2 4.5 4.6 4.10 4.11 4.13
Industries: C.15 D.00 E.46 F.50 I.73 I.80 I.86 I.89

John P. Weil & Company

99 Brookwood Rd.
Orinda, California 94563
(415)254-1921

> General and specialized consulting, primarily for manufacturing and processing companies and for professional organizations such as attorneys, engineers and architects. Services include organization, economic studies, planning and buegeting, layout and design, production planning and control, management information systems, cost analysis and cost accounting, office systems.

Contact: John P. Weil, pres.
Areas Served: U.S.
Founded: 1966 *Staff:* 1-3 *Revenues:* under $100,000
Professional Affiliations: SPMC
Services: 1.0 2.0 3.3 3.10 9.0
Industries: A.01 D.20 F.50 F.51 I.81 I.82

Emanuel Weintraub Associates, Inc.

1633 Broadway
New York, New York 10019
(212)489-7920

> Wide range of services to reduce costs, improve efficiency and productivity. Main area of concentration: textile and sewn products and related consumer industries including apparel, home furnishings, luggage, tents and allied fields. Reviews also offered to Federal, state and educational institutions.

Contact: Emanuel Weintraub, pres.
Areas Served: U.S., Central & South America & Europe
Founded: 1952 *Staff:* 10-25 *Revenues:* $500,000-1 million
Professional Affiliations: ACME
Services: 1.0 2.0 3.0 4.0 5.0 6.0 9.0
Industries: D.22 D.23 D.25 D.28 D.30 D.31 D.34 D.39 F.50 F.51

Weiss & Associates

1624 S. Parker Rd.
Denver, Colorado 80231
(303)755-7555

> Established for the express purpose of providing data-processing expertise to corporate dp centers. Clients have come from the health, education, distribution, retail, financial, food, & manufacturing industries. Any activity that concerns itself with improving the quality of a company's dp operation:

from its hardware and software, including database, to its personnel & long range plans will be considered.

Contact: Harvey M. Weiss, pres.
Areas Served: worldwide
Founded: 1964 *Staff:* 3-10 *Revenues:* $100-$500,000
Services: 1.0   3.5   9.3   9.5   9.6   9.7   9.8
Industries: Most

Welling & Woodard
Valley Forge Plaza
King of Prussia, Pennsylvania 19406
(215)337-2900

Practice relates to corporate planning for growth; that is, market, product, organization and capital planning. Our market research is often the basis for decisions on allocation of a corporation's human and financial resources; to invest in a new product or plant; to buy a company, to sell a division, etc. Internationally we advise companies on strategies and investment requirements for effective penetration of U.S. markets.

Contact: Christopher T. Lane, exec. vp.
Affiliates/branches: Box 1037, Greenwich, Connecticut 06830; Oakbrook; London
Founded: 1947 *Staff:* 3-10 *Revenues:* $100-$500,000
Professional Affiliations: ACME, IMC
Services: 1.1   1.3   1.5   1.6   4.1   4.2   5.3   5.10   10.3   10.4
Industries: D.27   D.28   D.29   D.32   D.33   D.34   D.35   D.36   D.37   D.38

Werner Associates, Inc.
(a Reliance Group Co.)
111 W. 40th St.
New York, New York 10018
(212)730-1280

Provide measurable results-oriented services with emphasis on practical improvements and benefits rather than abstract studies. Worldwide clientele since 1951. Have conducted more than 1,000 engagements.

Contact: Jack C. Werner, pres.
Affiliates/branches: Brussels
Areas Served: worldwide
Founded: 1940 *Staff:* over 100 *Revenues:* over $10 million
Professional Affiliations: ACME
Services: 1.0   2.0   3.0   4.0   6.0   9.0   10.4
Industries: B.00   D.00   E.00   E.42   F.00   G.00   H.63   I.80

Wheeler Associates, Inc.
800 W. Hollis St.
Nashua, New Hampshire 03060
(603)883-1931

Firm serves as a generalist in office, manufacturing, and newspaper industries; specializes in profit improvement for franchised auto dealers. A pioneer in the concept of the four day workweek and variable hours.

Contact: Kenneth E. Wheeler, pres.
Areas Served: U.S. & Canada
Founded: 1967 *Staff:* 3-10 *Revenues:* $100-$500,000
Services: 1.5   1.9   1.10   2.1   2.3   2.6   6.4   9.4   9.5
Industries: Most

Thomas Wilds Associates Inc.

50 E. 41st St.
New York, New York 10017
(212)986-2515

Consulting services in office systems, records management and word processing including: administrative procedure analysis, job descriptions, equipment specification, layout planning, computerization feasibility studies, records retention programs, filing systems, microfilming, information retrieval, typing and copy/duplicating studies and machine specification. Clients include financial institutions, manufacturing companies and private foundations.

Contact: Thomas Wilds, pres.
Areas Served: worldwide
Founded: 1968 *Staff:* 1-3 *Revenues:* under $100,000
Professional Affiliations: /ARMA, IWPA
Services: 9.0   9.1   9.2   9.3   9.4   9.5   9.6   9.7   9.8
Industries: Most   H.00

Douglas Williams Associates, Inc.

230 Park Ave.
New York, New York 10017
(212)986-2321

Serve top management and board of directors in role of "corporate listener." Carry out confidential discussions with these representatives regarding corporate strategy, organizational structure, company policies, programs and practices. Report findings and recommendations back to individuals and groups involved. Also train young management comers in this approach, emphasizing the importance of listening as a management skill.

Contact: Douglas Williams
Affiliates/branches: 4350 E. Camelback Rd., Phoenix, Arizona 85018
Areas Served: U.S. & Canada
Founded: 1949 *Staff:* 1-3 *Revenues:* $100-$500,000
Professional Affiliations: IMC
Services: 1.0   1.1   1.3   1.7   1.14   3.0   4.2

W.K. Williams & Co., Inc.

140 W. 13th St.
New York, New York 10011
(212)989-2273

General consulting firm, primarily in the areas of personnel, organization, systems and procedures and productivity improvement. Variety of clients, with a heavy component of state, county and municipal government.

Contact: Wilbur K. Williams, pres.
Areas Served: U.S.
Founded: 1967 *Staff:* 3-10 *Revenues:* $100-$500,000
Professional Affiliations: IMC
Services: 1.1   1.8   3.2   3.3   3.6   3.7   3.8   9.0
Industries: Most

Harry J. Woehr & Associates

1700 Widener Bldg.
Philadelphia, Pennsylvania 19107
(215)567-0834

We serve as a catalyst for change and progress in all "people-oriented" areas --

training, organizational planning, management development, career counselling
executive recruiting and individual assessment. We are uniquely qualified to
render sensitive and sensible consultation services because of our psychological
orientation. People are people--our expertise transcends narrow, geographical,
technical and numerical boundaries.

Contact: Harry J. Woehr, pres.
Areas Served: worldwide
Founded: 1956 *Staff:* 3-10 *Revenues:* $100-$500,000
Services: 1.0   1.1   1.2   1.3   3.0

Wofac Co.
(division of Science Management Corp.)
Fellowship Rd.
Moorestown, New Jersey 08057
(609)235-9200

A full range of professional management services to improve productivity and
attain maximum effectiveness of client human and physical resources. Through
highly experienced professional staff, apply sophisticated management techniques in a practical manner, including implementation of recommendations, to
achieve meaningful and lasting results for clients.

Contact: Michael L. Sanyour, pres.
Affiliates/branches: Atlanta; Baltimore; Bloomington, Minnesota; Des Plaines, Illinois;
Ft. Wayne; Glendale; Grosse Pointe Woods; Houston; Irvine; Livonia; Los
Angeles; Memphis; Milwaukee; New York; Osterville; Palo Alto; Rexdale;
Ontario; Ridgefield; Tacoma; Westerly
Areas Served: worldwide
Founded: 1946 *Staff:* over 100 *Revenues:* over $10 million
Services: 1.0   2.0   3.0   4.0   5.0   6.0   7.2   7.4   9.0   10.2   10.3
Industries: most   A.00   B.00   C.00   D.00   E.00   F.00   G.00   H.00   I.00   J.00

Woods, Gordon & Co.
Box 253 Toronto Dom. Ctr.
Toronto, Ontario M5k 1J7, Canada
(416)864-1212

The longest-established and largest Canadian general management consultancy
firm. Competence in specific technical areas applied both in management and
development studies in Canada and internationally. Management studies
encompass systems, procedures, financial, organization and operations aspects
of small and large activities in the private or public sectors. Development
studies relate to general sector and program studies and specific assessments of
expansion potential, using economic, marketing and planning techniques.
Formal project management skills an integral part of the services provided.
Comprehensive reports assist private and government clients in reaching
decisions on future policy and action. Affiliated with Clarkson, Gordon & Co.,
chartered accountants, and Arthur Young Int'l (CPA).

Contact: J. E. Smith, chmn.
Areas Served: worldwide
Founded: 1933 *Staff:* over 100 *Revenues:* $5-$10 million
Professional Affiliations: /CAMC
Services: Most   1.0   2.0   3.0   4.0   5.0   6.4   7.4   9.0   10.0
Industries: Most   A.00   B.00   C.00   D.00   E.00   F.00   G.00   H.00   I.00   J.00

Woodward Associates

6414 Willow Lane
Shawnee Mission, Kansas 66208
(913)362-9676

Our consulting services deal primarily with people: the people who comprise the organization and those whom the organization serves through products or service. Accordingly, developing human resources, especially management and planning marketing are two major competencies we offer clients.

Contact: Harry G. Woodward, Jr.
Areas Served: U.S. & Mexico
Founded: 1972 *Staff:* 1-3 *Revenues:* under $100,000
Professional Affiliations: /ASTD
Services: 1.1 1.3 2.9 3.0 4.0 9.3 11.1
Industries: Most

Worden & Risberg, Inc.

1234 Market St. E.
Philadelphia, Pennsylvania 19107
(215)568-4400

Full range of consulting services. Provides professional counsel to management in such areas as corporate growth, acquisitions, mergers and organization structure. Conducts operational audits, feasibility studies, and salary evaluations. Designs management information systems. Develops "work out" plans for troubled companies; may serve as general managers. Provides executive recruiting service

Contact: Robert E. Fagley, pres.
Areas Served: U.S., Far East & Western Europe
Founded: 1946 *Staff:* 10-25 *Revenues:* $500,000-1 million
Services: Most
Industries: Most

Yaney Associates

65 E. Elizabeth Ave.
Bethlehem, Pennsylvania 18018
(215)867-0560

This performance improvement firm works on problems of value. We do performance analysis, advertising, market research, graphics, and management improvements. Firms hire us because we are experts in human performance technology.

Contact: John Looloian, vp.
Affiliates/branches: Columbus, Ohio; Hershey, Pennsylvania; Pittsburgh, Pennsylvania; San Francisco, California
Areas Served: U.S., Canada & Europe
Founded: 1975 *Staff:* 3-10 *Revenues:* $100-$500,000
Professional Affiliations: /ASTD
Services: Most 1.0 2.6 2.9 3.0 4.0 5.9 6.1 7.2 9.0
Industries: Most A.07 B.00 C.16 D.00 E.48 F.51 G.00 H.00 I.00 J.00

The Yankee Group

Box 43 Harvard Sq.
Cambridge, Massachusetts 02138
(617)742-2500

Market analysis, identification, strategy and implementation in technology,

more specifically communications, computing and advanced automation.
Contact: Howard Anderson, pres.
Areas Served: U.S., Europe, Japan & China
Founded: 1970 *Staff:* 10-25 *Revenues:* $1-$5 million
Services: 1.2 1.3 1.4 4.1 4.5 4.8 4.9 4.11 4.16 10.4
Industries: E.43 E.48

Arthur Young & Company
277 Park Ave.
New York, New York 10017
(212)922-3132
International CPA firm providing business advisory service to industrial,
institutional, and governmental entities.
Contact: Patterson H. Krisher, nat'l dir. MAS
Affiliates/branches: 99 Washington Ave., Albany, New York 12210; 730 I. St.,
Anchorage, Alaska 99501; 235 Peachtree St., NE, Atlanta, Georgia 30303; 807
Brazos St., Austin, Texas 78701; 10 Light St., Baltimore, Maryland 21202; 433 N.
Camden Dr., Beverly Hills, California 90210; 1900 Fifth Ave. N., Birmingham,
Alabama 35203; 1 Boston Place, Boston, Massachusetts 02102; 3700 Marine
Midland Ctr., Buffalo, New York 14203; 1800 NCNB Plaza, Charlotte, North
Carolina 28280; 1 IBM Plaza, Chicago, Illinois 60611; Central Trust Twr.,
Cincinnati, Ohio 45202; 1100 Superior Ave., Cleveland, Ohio 44114; 100 E. Broad
St., Columbus, Ohio 43215; 2900 Repub. Nat'l Bank Bldg., Dallas, Texas 75201;
2100 Security Life Bldg., Denver, Colorado 80202; 1400 Financial Ctr., Des Moines,
Iowa 50309; 100 Renaissance Ctr., Detroit, Michigan 48243; 2200 Fort Worth Nat'l
B. Bldg., Fort Worth, Texas 76102; 2030 Fresno St., Fresno, California 93721; 301
N. Main, Greenville, South Carolina 29602; 100 Chestnut St., Harrisburg,
Pennsylvania 17101; 60 Washington St., Hartford, Connecticut 06106; 700 Bishop
St., Honolulu, Hawaii 96813; 2500 Penz Oil Place, Houston, Texas 77002; 1 Indiana
Sq., Indianapolis, Indiana 46204; 1500 Independence Sq., Jacksonville, Florida
32202; 1 Jericho Plaza, Jericho, New York 11753; 1400 Ten Main Ctr., Kansas City,
Missouri 64105; 1400 MI Nat'l. Twr., Lansing, Michigan 48933; 515 S. Flower St.,
Los Angeles, California 90071; 2707 Citizens Plaza, Louisville, Kentucky 40202;
1401 Brickell Ave., Miami, Florida 33131; 777 E. Wisconsin Ave., Milwaukee,
Wisconsin 53202; 1500 First Nat'l Bldg., Minneapolis, Minnesota 55402; 1340
Pondras St., New Orleans, Louisiana 70113; 277 Park Ave., New York, New York
10017; 520 Broad St., Newark, New Jersey 07102; 1330 Broadway, Oakland,
California 94612; 1900 Liberty Twr., Oklahoma City, Oklahoma 73102; 1850 1 First
Nat'l. Ctr., Omaha, Nebraska 68102; 255 S. Orange St., Orlando, Florida 32801; 7
Penn Ctr. Plaza, Philadelphia, Pennsylvania 19103; 1700 Valley Bank Ctr., Phoenix,
Arizona 85073; 2400 Koppers Bldg., Pittsburgh, Pennsylvania 15219; 700 Maine
Savings Plaza, Portland, Maine 04111; 900 SW Fifth Ave., Portland, Oregon 97204;
111 Westminster St., Providence, Rhode Island 02903; PO Box 3-B, Richmond,
Virginia 23206; 555 Capitol Mall, Sacramento, California 95814; Park 80 Plaza W. 1,
Saddle Brook, New Jersey 07662; 515 Olive St., St. Louis, Missouri 63101; 275 E.
South Temple, Salt Lake City, Utah 84111; 1st Nat'l. Bank Bldg., San Antonio,
Texas 78201; 110 W A St., San Diego, California 92101; Crocker Plaza, San
Francisco, California 94104; 101 Park Center Plaza, San Jose, California 95113;
GPO Box G-4767, San Juan, Puerto Rico 00936; 1055 N Main St., Santa Ana,
California 92702; 2100 The Financial Ctr., Seattle, Washington 98161; 1111 Summer
St., Stamford, Connecticut 06905; 1000 Ashley Dr., Tampa, Florida 33601; 1600
Toledo Trust Bldg., Toledo, Ohio 43604; Box 1529, Tulsa, Oklahoma 74101; 1025
Conn Ave, NW, Washington, D.C. 20036; 209 E William, Wichita, Kansas 67202;
446 Main St., Worcester, Massachusetts 01608; Austria; Bahamas; Bangladesh;
Belgium; Bermuda; Bolivia; Botswana; Brazil; Canada; Cayman Islands; Chile;

Columbia; Costa Rica; Cyprus; Denmark; Dominican Republic; Ecuador; Egypt; El Salvador; Fiji; France; Gibraltar; Greece; Guam; Guatemala; Honduras; Hong Kong; India; Indonesia; Ireland; Italy; Jamaica; Japan; Kenya; Korea; Kuwait; Argentina; Australia; Malaysia; Marina Islands; Mexico; Netherlands; New Zealand; Nicaragua; Nigeria; Norway; Pakistan; Panama; Peru; Philippines; Portugal; Rhodesia; Saudi Arabia; Singapore; South Africa; South West Africa; Spain; Swaziland; Sweden; Switzerland; Taiwan; Thailand; United Arab Emirates; United Kingdom; Uraguay; Venezuela; West Germany

Areas Served: worldwide

Founded: 1894 *Staff:* over 100 *Revenues:* over $10 million

Professional Affiliations: IMC

Services: most

Industries: most

Zeyher Associates

514 Beaver Hill
Jenkintown, Pennsylvania 19046
(215)887-3685

Personalized service, with staff assistance available when required. Intellectual, practical and pragmatic guidance in the manufacturing, industrial engineering, industrial relations and training areas.

Contact: Lewis R. Zeyher, pres. & owner

Areas Served: Eastern U.S. - mostly PA & NJ

Founded: 1955 *Staff:* 1-3 *Revenues:* under $100,000

Professional Affiliations: IMC

Services: Most

Industries: Most

Basis of "Services" Classification

A few years ago, after extensive research, the Institute of Management Consultants developed a list of Principal Areas of Competence in management consulting. When Jerome H. Fuchs was writing his *Making the Most of Management Consulting Services** he modified the IMC listing slightly, and we found it the best such breakdown available. So we used it (with his permission, of course). But Fuchs did something even more helpful: he added descriptions and explanations to the bare classification titles, and the result was a 63-page Appendix that to many is the best part of his book! We recommend it highly as an adjunct to this directory.

*AMACOM, 1975, $12.95 (Available from Consultants Bookstore, Templeton Road, Fitzwilliam, NH 03447)

Principal Areas of Competence

1.0 GENERAL MANAGEMENT
1.1 Organization planning & structure
1.2 Corporate policy formation
1.3 Strategic business planning & long range objectives
1.4 General business surveys
1.5 Feasibility studies
1.6 Diversification, mergers, acquisitions, & joint ventures
1.7 Management audits
1.8 Management information systems
1.9 Management reports & controls
1.10 Profit improvement programs
1.11 Corporate turnaround
1.12 Project control methods
1.13 Operations research
1.14 Public relations
1.15 Social & minority group programs

2.0 MANUFACTURING
2.1 Production planning & control
2.2 Materials management
2.3 Industrial engineering
2.4 Manufacturing layout & workflow ping
2.5 Automation
2.6 Incentive programs
2.7 Quality control
2.8 Equipment utilization
2.9 Plant management
2.10 Plant location & site selection
2.11 Materials handling
2.12 Warehouse space ping & utilization
2.13 Facilities & capabilities studies
2.14 Standard costs
2.15 Systems engineering
2.16 Materials distribution
2.17 Transportation

3.0 PERSONNEL
3.1 Management development
3.2 Executive compensation
3.3 Labor relations
3.4 Personnel selection, placement & records
3.5 Trng programs for nonmgmt personnel
3.6 Employees services and benefits
3.7 Wage & salary administration
3.8 Job evaluation & job rating systems
3.9 Communicating with employees
3.10 Attitude surveys
3.11 Psychological & behavioral studies
3.21 Health & safety programs

4.0 MARKETING
4.1 Marketing strategy & organization
4.2 Market & product research
4.3 Consumer marketing
4.4 Direct marketing & mailing
4.5 Industrial marketing
4.6 Merchandising
4.7 Sales management
4.8 Sales forecasting
4.9 Sales training
4.10 Advertising & sales promotion
4.11 Marketing audits
4.12 Product & customer service
4.13 Dealer-operating support
4.14 Physical distribution
4.15 Salesman compensation
4.16 Pricing policy

5.0 FINANCE & ACCOUNTING
5.1 General accounting
5.2 Cost accounting
5.3 Long-range financial planning
5.4 Short term plng, budgeting & control
5.5 Credit & collection
5.6 Capital investment
5.7 Marginal income analysis
5.8 Financial information & reporting
5.9 Financial planning
5.10 Valuations & appraisals
5.11 Taxes

6.0 PROCUREMENT
6.1 Value analysis
6.2 Commodity classifications
6.3 Purchasing
6.4 Inventory management & control
6.5 Stores operation

7.0 RESEARCH & DEVELOPMENT
7.1 Basic & applied research & development
7.2 Program administration & mgmt
7.3 Project determination & evaluation
7.4 Project cost control
7.5 Financial reporting of R & D effort

8.0 PACKAGING
8.1 Packaging function
8.2 Packaging machinery
8.3 Packaging & marketing design
8.4 Structural design & testing

9.0 ADMINISTRATION
9.1 Office management
9.2 Office plng, design & space utilization
9.3 Integrated & electronic data processing
9.4 Short-interval scheduling & clerical w measurement
9.5 Systems & Procedures
9.6 Forms design
9.7 Records mgmt & information retrieval
9.8 Data Communications

10.0 INTERNATIONAL OPERATIONS
10.1 Area development
10.2 Multinational company policies, strategies
10.3 Licensing, joint ventures, & ownership
10.4 Marketing
10.5 Financing
10.6 Tariffs and quotas

11.0 SPECIALIZED SERVICES
(Not found above) Please specify: Describe

11.1 Executive Recruiting
11.2 Union Avoidance
11.3 Telecommunications
11.4 Security/Plant Protection
11.5 Consumer Affairs
11.6 Time Management
11.7 Equal Employment Opportunity
11.8 Risk Management
11.9 Anti-Trust
11.10 Process Consulting
11.11 Postal Services
11.12 Energy Management

Services Offered

Generalists: Firms Offering Most Services
(See primary listing for specific services)

Don Aux Associates, Inc.
David T. Barry Associates
Theodore Barry & Associates
N.C. Berkowitz & Co.
Boeing Computer Services, Inc.
Booz-Allen & Hamilton, Inc.
W. E. Brennan & Co., Inc.
Earl D. Brodie & Associates
Frank C. Brown & Co., Inc.
Buckley & Co.
Caribbean Consulting Services, Inc.
Case & Co., Inc.
J. P. Cavanaugh & Associates
Cicco & Associates, Inc.
Coffay, Marshall Associates, Inc.
Communication Innovation, Inc.
Consultants International Ltd.
Coopers & Lybrand
Guy Cornman
Cresap, McCormick & Paget, Inc.
Dallmeyer & Co., Inc.
Frederick C. Decker Co., Inc.
Deloitte Haskins & Sells
George D. Edwards & Co., Inc.
Ernst & Whinney
Fairbanks Associates, Inc.
Fry Consultants
GlennCo Services Inc.
Golightly & Co. International, Inc.
Hans & Associates, Inc.
Harbridge House Inc.
Henning Associates, Inc.
Hickling-Johnston Ltd.
Louis H. Howe & Associates, Inc.
Industrial Technological Associates, Inc.
Isaacs & Associates
JMG Associates Ltd.
A. T. Kearney, Inc.
Kensington Management Consultants, Inc.

Lester B. Knight & Associates, Inc.
Rex Land & Associates, Inc.
Lawrence-Leiter & Co.
Arthur D. Little, Inc.
Lund Management & Marketing Services, Inc.
Main,Jackson & Garfield
MAS International, Ltd.
McGinnis Associates
McKinsey & Co., Inc.
MWS Consultants, Inc.
Bruce Payne Consultants, Inc.
Peat, Marwick, Mitchell & Co.
Plante & Moran
Policy & Management Associates, Inc.
Harry J. Prior & Associates, Inc.
Quorum, Ltd.
Rath & Strong, Inc.
Reliance Consulting Group, Inc.
Risk Planning Group, Inc.
Ruxton Associates
Sanderson & Porter, Inc.
Seidman & Seidman
John Sheridan Associates, Inc.
B.R. Smith & Associates
Sperry-Boom of Florida, Inc.
Stanley Consultants, Inc.
Stevens, Scheidler, Stevens, Vossler, Inc.
Summerour & Associates, Inc.
Systech & Associates
The Technics Group
U. Dann Torrance
Touche Ross & Co.
Wendell C. Walker & Associates
Woods, Gordon & Co.
Worden & Risberg, Inc.
Yaney Associates
Arthur Young & Company
Zeyher Associates

Specialists: Firms Concentrating on Specfific Services

1.0 GENERAL MANAGEMENT

Louis A. Allen Associates, Inc.
Rufus Allen & Associates
Altenburg & Co., Inc.
Altman & Weil, Inc.
American Executive Management, Inc.
Arthur Andersen & Co.
Anson, Lee, Rector & Associates
Arthur Aschauer & Co., Inc.
The Austin Co.
Austin & Lindberg, Ltd.
Emory Ayers Associates
Barbrisons Management Systems, Inc.
Barry & Co.
Batten, Batten, Hudson & Swab, Inc.
Bavier, Bulger & Goodyear, Inc.
Bedford-Post Associates, Inc.
The Berwick Group, Inc.
The Billings Group
Birch & Davis Associates, Inc.
Serge A. Birn Co.
Birnberg & Associates
Donald R. Booz & Associates, Inc.

The Boston Consulting Group, Inc.
Bostrom Management Corporation
Brecker & Merryman, Inc.
A.E. Brim & Associates, Ltd.
Charles Brooks Associates, Inc.
Jack Brown & Associates, Inc.
Burgess Management Associates
Business Psychology International
Daniel J. Cantor & Co., Inc.
Caruthers Consulting Inc.
Cexec, Inc.
Joseph Shaw Chalfant
Joseph Chanko Associates
Sonia Charif Associates
Cleveland Consulting Associates
Cole & Associates
Computer-Based Business Systems, Inc.
Concepts & Systems, Inc.
The Concord Consulting Group
The Corporate Director Inc.
Cotman Consultants Inc.
Coughlin, Elkes & Senensieb, Inc.
CPS Management Co.
Craig/Cutten & Wollman, Inc.

R. Danner, Inc.
James W. Davidson Co., Inc.
Day & Zimmermann, Inc.
Decision Sciences Corporation
Decision Studies Group
John deElorza Associates
Irving A. Delloff
Delta Group, Inc.
Alfred B. DePasse & Associates
Derrick & Associates, Inc.
Dexter-Kranick & Associates
Dickson Associates
Dielman Consultants, Inc.
Donovan, Zappala & Associates, Inc.
Drake Sheahan/Stewart Dougall Inc.
Murray Dropkin & Co.
Economics Research Associates
The Emerson Consultants, Inc.
Employee Relations Consultants, Inc.
Euramco Associates, Inc.
William Exton, Jr. & Associates
Thomas A. Faulhaber
Folger & Co., Inc.
Walter Frederick Friedman & Co., Inc.
Jack Frost & Associates
Fuchs Associates
Gagnon & Associates
The Galaxy Organization
W. L. Ganong Co.
Newell Garfield & Co., Inc.
Garr Associates, Inc.
Gilbert Commonwealth
Michael R. Gingold Associates, Inc.
Global Management Services, Inc.
Goggi Associates, Inc.
Guenther Associates
Alvin R. Haerr & Co.
Hales & Associates, Inc.
H. J. Hansen Co.
Harley, Little Associates Inc.
Harris, Kerr, Forster & Co.
Hay Associates
Porter Henry & Co., Inc.
Nathaniel Hill & Associates, Inc.
William E. Hill & Co., Inc.
Hoyles Associates Ltd.
The Innovative Group
Insight Development Services
Insurance Management Group, Inc.
International Management
Interplex Management Associates, Ltd.
JDA Management Services
Robert S. Jeffries, Jr.
The Joynt Group, Inc.
Juarez & Associates, Inc.
The Kampmeier Group
The Kappa Group
William Karp Consulting Co., Inc.
Kendrick & Co.
Kennedy & Kennedy, Inc.
Kenneth Associates
Warren King & Associates, Inc.
Virginia Knauer & Associates, Inc.
Kirk Knight & Co., Inc.
Knox Consulting Services
Robert E. Koogler
Krall Management Inc.
Peter Lambros & Associates
Laventhol & Horwath
A.M. Lederer & Co., Inc.
Legge Associates, Inc.
Rensis Likert Associates, Inc.
LWFW, Inc.
MacFarlane & Co., Inc.
Macphie-James, Inc.
William J. Mager & Associates
Thomas P. Mahoney Associates
Management Analysis Center, Inc.
Management Campus, Inc.

Management Horizons, Inc.
Management & Marketing
Manley Management & Marketing Services Corp.
Marpet Consultants, Inc.
Martech Inc.
E. Gilbert Mathews, Inc.
Lawrence M. Matthews
H.B. Maynard & Co.
McClenahan Associates
McCormack & Associates
C.H. McCormack & Associates, Inc.
McCormick & Co.
McCutcheon Associates NW
McElrath & Associates
McManis Associates, Inc.
MDC Systems Corp.
Medicus Systems Corporation
Edward M. Melton Associates
Donald B. Miller
Clinton P. Mott & Associates
Paul B. Mulligan & Co., Inc.
Multinational Perspectives, Inc.
Leo Murphy Inc.
Neville & Currie Associates Inc.
Robert E. Nolan Co., Inc.
Northern Consultants Inc.
OBEX Consulting
Oppenheimer Associates
Organization Renewal, Inc.
Organization Resource Counselors, Inc.
Organizational Consultants, Inc.
Organizational Directions, Inc.
D.L. Paden & Associates
Parker, Eldridge, Sholl & Gordon
Patton Consultants, Inc.
James S. Pepitone & Associates, Inc.
Permark Management Consultants, Inc.
Planaflex Co. Inc.
Price Waterhouse & Co.
Problem Solvers for Industry
Professional Services Int'l.
Profit-Improvement, Inc.
Project Associates, Inc.
Psychological Consultants, Inc.
S. Pullano Associates
Purcell Consulting Associates, Inc.
Questor Associates
Stan Radler Associates, Inc.
Albert Ramond & Assoc., Inc.
Theodore Riedeburg Associates
Rogers & Co.
Ross Associates, Inc.
Ryan Advisors, Inc.
SAI
Kurt Salmon Associates, Inc.
SAM Associates, Inc.
Samuelson & Co.
Sanderhoff & Associates, Inc.
Robert H. Schaffer & Associates
F.R. Schwab & Associates
Schwarzkopf Consultants, Inc.
Science Management Corporation
Senn-Delaney & Associates
Shycon Associates Inc.
Silverman Consulting Services Ltd.
E. Ralph Sims, Jr. & Associates, Inc.
Allan J. Siposs & Associates
Sno Engineering/Resource Management Inc.
Space/Management Programs, Inc.
SRI International
Stanton Associates, Inc.
Frank A. Stasiowski
Stone & Webster Mgmt. Consultants, Inc.
Straehley Associates
R.J. Sweeney Associates
System Planning Associates, Inc.
Systems Planning Service
The Tanzi Organization
Technomic Consultants

Teipel Associates Inc.
Tempo
D.W. Thomson & Associates
Towers, Perrin, Forster & Crosby
Trebor Health Associates
Trundle Consultants Inc.
Von Keyserling Consultants Ltd.
Wade, McGuigan & Associates
John P. Weil & Company
Emanuel Weintraub Associates, Inc.
Weiss & Associates
Werner Associates, Inc.
Douglas Williams Associates, Inc.
Harry J. Woehr & Associates
Wofac Co.

1.1 ORGANIZATION PLANNING & STRUCTURE

Louis A. Allen Associates, Inc.
Anacapa Sciences, Inc.
Anderson/Roethle & Associates, Inc.
Applied Leadership Technologies, Inc.
Arneson & Co.
William B. Arnold Associates, Inc.
Joseph Auerbach
James S. Baker Management Consultants, Inc.
Ballew, Reinhardt & Associates, Inc.
Barron-Clayton, Inc.
Barry & Co.
Bartow Associates
Batten, Batten, Hudson & Swab, Inc.
BCMA Associates
David N. Beach Associates, Inc.
Brooks Bernhardt & Associates
D. A. Betterley Risk Consultants, Inc.
Bickert, Browne, Coddington & Associates
Wallace A. Boesch Associates
Boyle/Kirkman Associates, Inc.
A. Val Bradley Associates, Inc.
George W. Bricker
Cambridge Research Institute
C. L. Carter Jr. & Associates, Inc.
Centaur Associates, Inc.
Joseph Shaw Chalfant
Colarelli Associates, Inc.
Cole, Warren & Long Inc.
Coleman Consulting Inc.
Compass Management Group, Inc.
The Corporate Director Inc.
Coxe Associates, Inc.
Cresheim Co., Inc.
The Croner Company
Dailey Consultants & Co.
R. Danner, Inc.
Jack R. Dauner & Associates
James W. Davidson Co., Inc.
Curt Deckert Associates, Inc.
D. Dietrich Associates, Inc.
Edgar, Dunn & Conover Inc.
Fogel & Associates, Inc.
George E. Frankel & Associates
Freeman, Penrose & Kajinura, Ltd.
The Galles Resource
Gottfried Consultants Inc.
S. E. Hall & Co.
A. S. Hansen, Inc.
Paul Harthorne Associates
J. W. Haslett & Associates
Robert H. Hayes & Associates, Inc.
Health-Care Management Services
Hendrick & Co., Inc.
W. H. Higginbotham
William H. Hill Associates, Inc.
Louis A. Hradesky
J. Lloyd Johnson Associates
Jean Judge Associates, Inc.
Robert Kahn & Associates

The Kampmeier Group
Keenan, Wheeler & Bowman
Klein Behavioral Science Consultants, Inc.
James B. Kobak, Inc.
Sidney W. Koran Associates
Walter K. Levy Associates Inc.
Loer & Bradford Consultants, Inc.
Lovejoy Management Consultants
Carl F. Lutz
Macro Systems, Inc.
Mahler Associates, Inc.
Management & Marketing
Frank B. Manley & Co.
F.L. Mannix & Co., Inc.
Manplan Consultants
Manresa Management Consultants, Inc.
Bill Marcus & Associates, Inc.
George S. May International Co.
McBer & Co.
McLean Associates
Medical Management Associates
Donald R. Miller
Mitchell & Co.
Montgomery & Associates, Inc.
Leo Murphy Inc.
Rich Nelson Associates
Normandale Associates Inc.
George Odiorne Associates, Inc.
Olney Associates
Organization Consultants, Inc.
Organization Resources Inc.
Organizational Consultants, Inc.
Organizational Consulting Services
James H. Owens Associates, Inc.
Profit Planning Associates
Francis J. Przyluski
Quantum Consultants, Inc.
Quay Associates
Ruxton Associates
Robert H. Schaffer & Associates
Schwarzkopf Consultants, Inc.
SIAR, Inc.
Sibson & Company, Inc.
John G. Steinle & Associates
Temple, Barker & Sloane, Inc.
Ten Eyck Associates
The THinc. Group Inc.
Robert M. Wald & Associates
Warren, McVeigh & Griffin
Welling & Woodard
Douglas Williams Associates, Inc.
W.K. Williams & Co., Inc.
Harry J. Woehr & Associates
Woodward Associates

1.2 CORPORATE POLICY FORMATION

Ballew, Reinhardt & Associates, Inc.
Batten, Batten, Hudson & Swab, Inc.
David N. Beach Associates, Inc.
Bjorkman Associates
The Boston Consulting Group, Inc.
Cambridge Research Institute
C. L. Carter Jr. & Associates, Inc.
Joseph Shaw Chalfant
Charles River Associates Inc.
Colarelli Associates, Inc.
The Corporate Director Inc.
James W. Davidson Co., Inc.
Fensterstock & Co.
George E. Frankel & Associates
Freeman Associates
Paul Harthorne Associates
W. H. Higginbotham
William H. Hill Associates, Inc.
Institutional Strategy Associates, Inc.
Jean Judge Associates, Inc.
Robert Kahn & Associates

The Kampmeier Group
James B. Kobak, Inc.
Loer & Bradford Consultants, Inc.
Mahler Associates, Inc.
Bill Marcus & Associates, Inc.
McLean Associates
Mitchell & Co.
Moeller Associates
Montgomery & Associates, Inc.
Leo Murphy Inc.
Normandale Associates Inc.
Organization Resources Inc.
Organizational Consulting Services
The Pofcher Co.
The Product Integrity Co.
Profit Planning Associates
Quantum Consultants, Inc.
Quay Associates
Resource Planning Associates, Inc.
Schwarzkopf Consultants, Inc.
SIAR, Inc.
Sibson & Company, Inc.
John G. Steinle & Associates
Warren, McVeigh & Griffin
Harry J. Woehr & Associates
The Yankee Group

1.3 STRATEGIC BUSINESS PLANNING & LONG RANGE OBJECTIVES

Advanced Management Institute, Inc.
Louis A. Allen Associates, Inc.
Anderson/Roethle & Associates, Inc.
Arneson & Co.
Bain & Co., Inc.
James S. Baker Management Consultants, Inc.
Batten, Batten, Hudson & Swab, Inc.
David N. Beach Associates, Inc.
Brooks Bernhardt & Associates
Bjorkman Associates
The Boston Consulting Group, Inc.
A. Val Bradley Associates, Inc.
Michael Busler Group
Cambridge Research Institute
Joseph Shaw Chalfant
Colarelli Associates, Inc.
Cole, Warren & Long Inc.
Thomas Collier & Associates
The Corporate Director Inc.
Cresheim Co., Inc.
The Croner Company
Data Sciences, Inc.
James W. Davidson Co., Inc.
Curt Deckert Associates, Inc.
Edgar, Dunn & Conover Inc.
Fensterstock & Co.
Financial Concepts Inc.
Freeman Associates
Freeman, Penrose & Kajinura, Ltd.
Glendinning Associates
Gottfried Consultants Inc.
S. E. Hall & Co.
Paul Harthorne Associates
Robert H. Hayes & Associates, Inc.
Health-Care Management Services
William H. Hill Associates, Inc.
Charles L. Hoffman, Inc.
Institutional Strategy Associates, Inc.
International Commercial Services
International Resource Development, Inc.
J. Lloyd Johnson Associates
Johnson, Pratt & Stewart
Jean Judge Associates, Inc.
Robert Kahn & Associates
The Kampmeier Group
William Kather Associates, Inc.
Keenan, Wheeler & Bowman
C. H. Kline & Co., Inc.

Kirk Knight & Co., Inc.
James B. Kobak, Inc.
Walter K. Levy Associates Inc.
William T. Lorenz & Co.
MacFarlane & Co., Inc.
Mahler Associates, Inc.
Management/Marketing Associates,Inc.
McLean Associates
Medical Management Associates
Donald R. Miller
Mitchell & Co.
Moeller Associates
Montgomery & Associates, Inc.
MRP Associates
Leo Murphy Inc.
Normandale Associates Inc.
Oatman Associates, Inc.
George Odiorne Associates, Inc.
Organization Resources Inc.
Organizational Consulting Services
The Pace Consulting Group, Inc.
Paterson & Co.
Permark Management Consultants, Inc.
The Pofcher Co.
Profit Planning Associates
Projections
Quantum Consultants, Inc.
Resource Planning Associates, Inc.
RLS Consulting & Management Group, Inc.
R.M. Associates
SAM Associates, Inc.
Robert H. Schaffer & Associates
Schwarzkopf Consultants, Inc.
SIAR, Inc.
Sibson & Company, Inc.
Snyder Associates, Inc.
State Street Consultants
John G. Steinle & Associates
Stone Management Corporation
Synergy Corporation
Technology Marketing Group Ltd.
Temple, Barker & Sloane, Inc.
Ten Eyck Associates
Washington Nichibei Consultants
Welling & Woodard
Douglas Williams Associates, Inc.
Harry J. Woehr & Associates
Woodward Associates
The Yankee Group

1.4 GENERAL BUSINESS SURVEYS

Arneson & Co.
Barnett & Engel
BCMA Associates
Boyle/Kirkman Associates, Inc.
Cambridge Research Institute
C. L. Carter Jr. & Associates, Inc.
CMI Investment Corp.
The Croner Company
D. Dietrich Associates, Inc.
Fensterstock & Co.
Financial Concepts Inc.
S. E. Hall & Co.
Charles L. Hoffman, Inc.
Isaacs Associates
C. H. Kline & Co., Inc.
James B. Kobak, Inc.
Robert Kruhm
Walter K. Levy Associates Inc.
William T. Lorenz & Co.
Mahler Associates, Inc.
Marshall Institute
Donald R. Miller
Mitchell & Co.
Montgomery & Associates, Inc.
Leo Murphy Inc.
George Odiorne Associates, Inc.

Projections
Francis J. Przyluski
Quay Associates
Research Associates & Analysts
RLS Consulting & Management Group, Inc.
SIAR, Inc.
Snyder Associates, Inc.
Technology Marketing Group Ltd.
Ten Eyck Associates
The Yankee Group

1.5 FEASIBILITY STUDIES

Aquatec International, Inc.
Arneson & Co.
ASYST-Administrative Systems Consultants
Bain Management Consulting, Inc.
James S. Baker Management Consultants, Inc.
Barnett & Engel
Bjorkman Associates
Wallace A. Boesch Associates
Michael Busler Group
Cambridge Research Institute
Centaur Associates, Inc.
Compass Management Group, Inc.
Curt Deckert Associates, Inc.
Fensterstock & Co.
Financial Concepts Inc.
Foussard Associates
Elmer Fox, Westheimer & Co.
Freeman Associates
Freeman, Penrose & Kajinura, Ltd.
Gagnon & Associates
Gelb Consulting Group, Inc.
Gemar Associates
Frank N. Giampietro Associates, Inc.
Michael R. Gingold Associates, Inc.
Gladstone Associates
Group Arcon
Health-Care Management Services
Charles L. Hoffman, Inc.
William H. Hoffmann
Infotek Corporation
Institutional Strategy Associates, Inc.
Isaacs Associates
J. Lloyd Johnson Associates
Johnson, Pratt & Stewart
William Kather Associates, Inc.
C. H. Kline & Co., Inc.
Walter K. Levy Associates Inc.
Macro Systems, Inc.
Management Decision Systems, Inc.
Management/Marketing Associates,Inc.
Marshall Institute
William H. Meyer & Associates, Inc.
Mitchell & Co.
Montgomery & Associates, Inc.
Moshman Associates, Inc.
The Nielson-Wurster Group, Inc.
Normandale Associates Inc.
Profit Planning Associates
Francis J. Przyluski
Resource Conservation Consultants
Resource Planning Associates, Inc.
R.M. Associates
Snyder Associates, Inc.
Edward Stark Associates
State Street Consultants
John G. Steinle & Associates
The Technics Group
Technology Marketing Group Ltd.
TMI Systems Corp.
Roy W. Walters & Associates, Inc.
Warren, McVeigh & Griffin
Washington Nichibei Consultants
Welling & Woodard
Wheeler Associates, Inc.

1.6 DIVERSIFICATION, MERGERS, ACQUISITIONS, & JOINT VENTURES

Anderson/Roethle & Associates, Inc.
Arneson & Co.
BCMA Associates
Bickert, Browne, Coddington & Associates
Wallace A. Boesch Associates
Cambridge Research Institute
Joseph Shaw Chalfant
Sonia Charif Associates
Charles River Associates Inc.
Colarelli Associates, Inc.
Cole, Warren & Long Inc.
Coleman Consulting Inc.
Thomas Collier & Associates
Coxe Associates, Inc.
The Croner Company
Dickey Dyer Management Consultants
Edgar, Dunn & Conover Inc.
Fensterstock & Co.
Fowler, Anthony & Company
George E. Frankel & Associates
Michael R. Gingold Associates, Inc.
Glendinning Associates
Robert H. Hayes & Associates, Inc.
Duane L. Hile & Associates
William H. Hill Associates, Inc.
William H. Hoffmann
Hurdman & Cranstoun
J. Lloyd Johnson Associates
Johnson, Pratt & Stewart
Robert Kahn & Associates
William Kather Associates, Inc.
C. H. Kline & Co., Inc.
Kirk Knight & Co., Inc.
James B. Kobak, Inc.
Loer & Bradford Consultants, Inc.
William T. Lorenz & Co.
Macro Systems, Inc.
Mahler Associates, Inc.
Management Horizons, Inc.
Management/Marketing Associates,Inc.
Manley Management & Marketing Services Corp.
F.L. Mannix & Co., Inc.
Donald R. Miller
MRP Associates
Oatman Associates, Inc.
James H. Owens Associates, Inc.
Paterson & Co.
Permark Management Consultants, Inc.
The Pofcher Co.
Profit Planning Associates
Quantum Consultants, Inc.
Resource Planning Associates, Inc.
R.M. Associates
Rosenau Consulting Co.
SIAR, Inc.
Snyder Associates, Inc.
Standard Research Consultants
State Street Consultants
John G. Steinle & Associates
Stone Management Corporation
Welling & Woodard

1.7 MANAGEMENT AUDITS

James S. Baker Management Consultants, Inc.
Barnett & Engel
Batten, Batten, Hudson & Swab, Inc.
David N. Beach Associates, Inc.
Brooks Bernhardt & Associates
Betterley Consulting Group
D. A. Betterley Risk Consultants, Inc.
A. Val Bradley Associates, Inc.
Cambridge Research Institute
C. L. Carter Jr. & Associates, Inc.
Centaur Associates, Inc.

Colarelli Associates, Inc.
Cole, Warren & Long Inc.
Thomas Collier & Associates
Compass Management Group, Inc.
The Corporate Director Inc.
The Croner Company
Dailey Consultants & Co.
Datamatics Management Services, Inc.
Elmer Fox, Westheimer & Co.
Freeman, Penrose & Kajinura, Ltd.
The Galles Resource
Gemar Associates
Gottfried Consultants Inc.
J. W. Haslett & Associates
Hendrick & Co., Inc.
W. H. Higginbotham
William H. Hill Associates, Inc.
Humber, Mundie & McClary
International Commercial Services
Jean Judge Associates, Inc.
William Kather Associates, Inc.
Robert Kruhm
Walter K. Levy Associates Inc.
Lovejoy Management Consultants
MacFarlane & Co., Inc.
Mahler Associates, Inc.
Management/Marketing Associates,Inc.
Frank B. Manley & Co.
Manplan Consultants
Manresa Management Consultants, Inc.
Bill Marcus & Associates, Inc.
Marshall Institute
McLean Associates
Belden Menkus
Donald R. Miller
M & M Protection Consultants
MRP Associates
Rich Nelson Associates
Oatman Associates, Inc.
Olney Associates
Organization Resources Inc.
Organizational Consultants, Inc.
Organizational Consulting Services
Professional Practice Consultants, Inc.
Quay Associates
SAM Associates, Inc.
Robert H. Schaffer & Associates
Schwarzkopf Consultants, Inc.
Sibson & Company, Inc.
Edward Stark Associates
State Street Consultants
John G. Steinle & Associates
Technology Marketing Group Ltd.
Temple, Barker & Sloane, Inc.
K.W. Tunnell Co., Inc.
Robert M. Wald & Associates
Warren, McVeigh & Griffin
Douglas Williams Associates, Inc.

1.8 MANAGEMENT INFORMATION SYSTEMS

American Management Systems
Anacapa Sciences, Inc.
ASYST-Administrative Systems Consultants
Joseph Auerbach
Bain Management Consulting, Inc.
Bjorkman Associates
C. L. Carter Jr. & Associates, Inc.
Centaur Associates, Inc.
The Center for Applied Management, Inc.
Compass Management Group, Inc.
Dailey Consultants & Co.
Data Sciences, Inc.
Datamatics Management Services, Inc.
Curt Deckert Associates, Inc.
Distribution Projects, Inc.
Edgar, Dunn & Conover Inc.

Fenvessy Associates, Inc.
Fogel & Associates, Inc.
Fowler, Anthony & Company
Elmer Fox, Westheimer & Co.
R. L. French & Company, Inc.
Gottfried Consultants Inc.
S. E. Hall & Co.
Paul Harthorne Associates
J. W. Haslett & Associates
Health-Care Management Services
Hurdman & Cranstoun
IMS Systems Corp.
Infotek Corporation
Isaacs Associates
J. Lloyd Johnson Associates
Keenan, Wheeler & Bowman
C. H. Kline & Co., Inc.
Macro Systems, Inc.
Management Horizons, Inc.
Moshman Associates, Inc.
Naremco Services, Inc.
The Nielson-Wurster Group, Inc.
Norris Consultants Inc.
Thomas Oland & Associates, Inc.
ORU Group, Inc.
RLS Consulting & Management Group, Inc.
Ruxton Associates
Edward Stark Associates
The Technics Group
Temple, Barker & Sloane, Inc.
TMI Systems Corp.
Wagner Systems, Inc.
Warren, McVeigh & Griffin
W.K. Williams & Co., Inc.

1.9 MANAGEMENT REPORTS & CONTROLS

Advanced Management Institute, Inc.
American Management Systems
ASYST-Administrative Systems Consultants
Joseph Auerbach
David N. Beach Associates, Inc.
Bjorkman Associates
C. L. Carter Jr. & Associates, Inc.
Colarelli Associates, Inc.
Compass Management Group, Inc.
Dailey Consultants & Co.
Data Systems Consultants
James W. Davidson Co., Inc.
Fogel & Associates, Inc.
George E. Frankel & Associates
R. L. French & Company, Inc.
Paul Harthorne Associates
J. W. Haslett & Associates
Hurdman & Cranstoun
Isaacs Associates
Keenan, Wheeler & Bowman
Macro Systems, Inc.
Bill Marcus & Associates, Inc.
George S. May International Co.
McLean Associates
MRP Associates
Alan Negus Associates, Inc.
The Nielson-Wurster Group, Inc.
Normandale Associates Inc.
Norris Consultants Inc.
Oatman Associates, Inc.
Thomas Oland & Associates, Inc.
Organizational Consulting Services
ORU Group, Inc.
Profit Planning Associates
Research Associates & Analysts
H.K. von Kaas & Associates
Wheeler Associates, Inc.

1.10 PROFIT IMPROVEMENT PROGRAMS

Arneson & Co.
Peter August & Associates, Inc.

Ernest Beachley & Associates Inc.
A. Val Bradley Associates, Inc.
Michael Busler Group
Colarelli Associates, Inc.
Dailey Consultants & Co.
James W. Davidson Co., Inc.
Irving A. Delloff
Dickey Dyer Management Consultants
Edgar, Dunn & Conover Inc.
Mitchell Fein, Inc.
Fogel & Associates, Inc.
Elmer Fox, Westheimer & Co.
Bertrand Frank Associates, Inc.
R. L. French & Company, Inc.
Gagnon & Associates
Gemar Associates
S. E. Hall & Co.
Robert H. Hayes & Associates, Inc.
Hendrick & Co., Inc.
Nathaniel Hill & Associates, Inc.
Hurdman & Cranstoun
The Kampmeier Group
C. H. Kline & Co., Inc.
Kirk Knight & Co., Inc.
Walter K. Levy Associates Inc.
Management Decision Systems, Inc.
Management & Marketing
Arthur Manning Associates
Bill Marcus & Associates, Inc.
Marshall Institute
Donald R. Miller
MRP Associates
ORU Group, Inc.
The Pace Consulting Group, Inc.
Profit Planning Associates
Resource Planning Associates, Inc.
Riecks Postal Consultants
Riffe & Associates
RLS Consulting & Management Group, Inc.
R.M. Associates
Wm. E. Sandman Associates Co.
Robert H. Schaffer & Associates
Schwarzkopf Consultants, Inc.
Stone Management Corporation
Roy W. Walters & Associates, Inc.
Wheeler Associates, Inc.

1.11 CORPORATE TURNAROUND

Arneson & Co.
Ernest Beachley & Associates Inc.
Joseph Shaw Chalfant
CMI Investment Corp.
The Corporate Director Inc.
James W. Davidson Co., Inc.
Edgar, Dunn & Conover Inc.
Bertrand Frank Associates, Inc.
Freeman, Penrose & Kajinura, Ltd.
Nathaniel Hill & Associates, Inc.
Hurdman & Cranstoun
Robert Kahn & Associates
Kirk Knight & Co., Inc.
Manresa Management Consultants, Inc.
MRP Associates
Leo Murphy Inc.
Organization Resources Inc.
Organizational Consultants, Inc.
The Pace Consulting Group, Inc.
Robert H. Schaffer & Associates
SIAR, Inc.
Stone Management Corporation
Transportation Industry Consultants, Inc.

1.12 PROJECT CONTROL METHODS

Barron-Clayton, Inc.
Bartow Associates

Centaur Associates, Inc.
Compass Management Group, Inc.
Curt Deckert Associates, Inc.
Fogel & Associates, Inc.
S. E. Hall & Co.
Louis A. Hradesky
Isaacs Associates
Henry Jordan & Associates
McLean Associates
The Nielson-Wurster Group, Inc.
Norris Consultants Inc.
Rosenau Consulting Co.
Wagner Systems, Inc.

1.13 OPERATIONS RESEARCH

Advanced Management Institute, Inc.
The Center for Applied Management, Inc.
Datamatics Management Services, Inc.
Management Decision Systems, Inc.
Moshman Associates, Inc.
The Product Integrity Co.
Riecks Postal Consultants
Dorian Shainin Consultant, Inc.
TMI Systems Corp.

1.14 PUBLIC RELATIONS

Applied Leadership Technologies, Inc.
Ballew, Reinhardt & Associates, Inc.
Sonia Charif Associates
J. W. Haslett & Associates
Robert Kruhm
William T. Lorenz & Co.
Montgomery & Associates, Inc.
Resource Conservation Consultants
Synergy Corporation
Norton Weber & Co.
Douglas Williams Associates, Inc.

1.15 SOCIAL & MINORITY GROUP PROGRAMS

Applied Leadership Technologies, Inc.
Bartow Associates
Boyle/Kirkman Associates, Inc.
Sonia Charif Associates
Colarelli Associates, Inc.
Compass Management Group, Inc.
Jagerson Associates, Inc.
Loer & Bradford Consultants, Inc.
Frank B. Manley & Co.
Moeller Associates
Organizational Consultants, Inc.
University Center, Inc.

2.0 MANUFACTURING

Rufus Allen & Associates
Altenburg & Co., Inc.
Arthur Andersen & Co.
Anson, Lee, Rector & Associates
The Austin Co.
Emory Ayers Associates
Barbrisons Management Systems, Inc.
Barry & Co.
Bavier, Bulger & Goodyear, Inc.
Bedford-Post Associates, Inc.
The Berwick Group, Inc.
Serge A. Birn Co.
Donald R. Booz & Associates, Inc.
Charles Brooks Associates, Inc.
Jack Brown & Associates, Inc.
Burgess Management Associates
The Center for Applied Management, Inc.

Joseph Chanko Associates
Cleveland Consulting Associates
Computer-Based Business Systems, Inc.
Concepts & Systems, Inc.
Cotman Consultants Inc.
Day & Zimmermann, Inc.
Decision Sciences Corporation
John deElorza Associates
Irving A. Delloff
Derrick & Associates, Inc.
Dexter-Kranick & Associates
Dielman Consultants, Inc.
Donovan, Zappala & Associates, Inc.
Drake Sheahan/Stewart Dougall Inc.
Economics Research Associates
The Emerson Consultants, Inc.
William Exton, Jr. & Associates
Thomas A. Faulhaber
Mitchell Fein, Inc.
R. L. French & Company, Inc.
Walter Frederick Friedman & Co., Inc.
Jack Frost & Associates
Fuchs Associates
Gagnon & Associates
Garr Associates, Inc.
Gemar Associates
Goggi Associates, Inc.
Guenther Associates
H. J. Hansen Co.
Nathaniel Hill & Associates, Inc.
Louis A. Hradesky
Hurdman & Cranstoun
International Management
Interplex Management Associates, Ltd.
JDA Management Services
Robert S. Jeffries, Jr.
The Joynt Group, Inc.
Knox Consulting Services
Robert E. Koogler
Krall Management Inc.
Peter Lambros & Associates
Laventhol & Horwath
A.M. Lederer & Co., Inc.
Legge Associates, Inc.
Samuel F. Leigh Associates, Inc.
Rensis Likert Associates, Inc.
LWFW, Inc.
Macphie-James, Inc.
Thomas P. Mahoney Associates
E. Gilbert Mathews, Inc.
Lawrence M. Matthews
H.B. Maynard & Co.
McClenahan Associates
McCormack & Associates
McCormick & Co.
McElrath & Associates
MDC Systems Corp.
Clinton P. Mott & Associates
Multinational Perspectives, Inc.
Norris Consultants Inc.
Norris & Elliott, Inc.
Oppenheimer Associates
ORU Group, Inc.
D.L. Paden & Associates
Patton Consultants, Inc.
Price Waterhouse & Co.
Problem Solvers for Industry
Profit-Improvement, Inc.
Purcell Consulting Associates, Inc.
Albert Ramond & Assoc., Inc.
Reel/Grobman & Associates
Ross Associates, Inc.
SAI
Kurt Salmon Associates, Inc.
Samuelson & Co.
F.R. Schwab & Associates
Science Management Corporation
Senn-Delaney & Associates
Shycon Associates Inc.

E. Ralph Sims, Jr. & Associates, Inc.
Space/Management Programs, Inc.
SRI International
Stone & Webster Mgmt. Consultants, Inc.
R.J. Sweeney Associates
System Planning Associates, Inc.
The Technics Group
Trundle Consultants Inc.
H.K. von Kaas & Associates
Von Keyserling Consultants Ltd.
Wade, McGuigan & Associates
Wagner Systems, Inc.
John P. Weil & Company
Emanuel Weintraub Associates, Inc.
Werner Associates, Inc.
Wofac Co.

2.1 PRODUCTION PLANNING & CONTROL

American Executive Management, Inc.
Peter August & Associates, Inc.
Barry & Co.
Bartow Associates
Dailey Consultants & Co.
Edgar, Dunn & Conover Inc.
E & T Associates
Bertrand Frank Associates, Inc.
Paul Harthorne Associates
Isaacs Associates
Henry Jordan & Associates
Arthur Manning Associates
Manresa Management Consultants, Inc.
George S. May International Co.
Richard Muther & Associates, Inc.
Oatman Associates, Inc.
Oppenheimer Associates
Oppenheimer Associates
PA International Management Consultants, Inc.
Paterson & Co.
Wm. E. Sandman Associates Co.
R. Shriver Associates
Standards, International Inc.
Straehley Associates
Temple, Barker & Sloane, Inc.
H.K. von Kaas & Associates
J.F. Ward Associates
Wheeler Associates, Inc.

2.2 MATERIALS MANAGEMENT

Ballinger-Meserole
Barron-Clayton, Inc.
Dailey Consultants & Co.
Data Systems Consultants
Herbert W. Davis & Co.
J. George Gross & Associates
Duane L. Hile & Associates
Isaacs Associates
Henry Jordan & Associates
Richard Muther & Associates, Inc.
Thomas Oland & Associates, Inc.
PA International Management Consultants, Inc.
The Pace Consulting Group, Inc.
Resource Conservation Consultants
Sanderhoff & Associates, Inc.
Straehley Associates
K.W. Tunnell Co., Inc.
J.F. Ward Associates

2.3 INDUSTRIAL ENGINEERING

Applied Leadership Technologies, Inc.
Peter August & Associates, Inc.
Ballinger-Meserole
Ernest Beachley & Associates Inc.
Birch & Davis Associates, Inc.

Jack Brown & Associates, Inc.
Irving A. Delloff
Dickey Dyer Management Consultants
E & T Associates
Bertrand Frank Associates, Inc.
J. George Gross & Associates
Group Arcon
Manresa Management Consultants, Inc.
Marshall Institute
Richard Muther & Associates, Inc.
Oppenheimer Associates
Riffe & Associates
Wm. E. Sandman Associates Co.
Irving Shaw & Associates
Snyder Associates, Inc.
Standards, International Inc.
K.W. Tunnell Co., Inc.
H.K. von Kaas & Associates
Wheeler Associates, Inc.

2.4 MANUFACTURING LAYOUT & WORKFLOW PLNG

Peter August & Associates, Inc.
Ballinger-Meserole
Barry & Co.
E & T Associates
Euramco Associates, Inc.
J. George Gross & Associates
Group Arcon
Ingersoll Engineers Inc.
Manresa Management Consultants, Inc.
Marshall Institute
Richard Muther & Associates, Inc.
Riffe & Associates
Wm. E. Sandman Associates Co.
Irving Shaw & Associates
Standards, International Inc.
K.W. Tunnell Co., Inc.
H.K. von Kaas & Associates
Roy W. Walters & Associates, Inc.
J.F. Ward Associates

2.5 AUTOMATION

Advanced Management Institute, Inc.
Ballinger-Meserole
Coughlin, Elkes & Senensieb, Inc.
Data Sciences, Inc.
Gottfried Consultants Inc.
Ingersoll Engineers Inc.
R. Shriver Associates

2.6 INCENTIVE PROGRAMS

Peter August & Associates, Inc.
Ernest Beachley & Associates Inc.
A. Val Bradley Associates, Inc.
The Concord Consulting Group
Irving A. Delloff
Dickey Dyer Management Consultants
E & T Associates
Folger & Co., Inc.
Bertrand Frank Associates, Inc.
Frank B. Manley & Co.
Manresa Management Consultants, Inc.
George S. May International Co.
Paul B. Mulligan & Co., Inc.
Richard Muther & Associates, Inc.
Organization Renewal, Inc.
Organization Resource Counselors, Inc.
Organization Resources Inc.
Organizational Directions, Inc.
Wm. E. Sandman Associates Co.
Standards, International Inc.
Stanton Associates, Inc.

H.K. von Kaas & Associates
Wheeler Associates, Inc.

2.7 QUALITY CONTROL

Anacapa Sciences, Inc.
Barron-Clayton, Inc.
C. L. Carter Jr. & Associates, Inc.
Dawcon
Virginia Knauer & Associates, Inc.
Arthur Manning Associates
Moshman Associates, Inc.
Paul B. Mulligan & Co., Inc.
The Product Integrity Co.
Riffe & Associates
Dorian Shainin Consultant, Inc.
Roy W. Walters & Associates, Inc.

2.8 EQUIPMENT UTILIZATION

Ballinger-Meserole
Ernest Beachley & Associates Inc.
E & T Associates
J. George Gross & Associates
Group Arcon
Ingersoll Engineers Inc.
Richard Muther & Associates, Inc.
Riffe & Associates
Wm. E. Sandman Associates Co.

2.9 PLANT MANAGEMENT

American Executive Management, Inc.
Ernest Beachley & Associates Inc.
Birch & Davis Associates, Inc.
A. Val Bradley Associates, Inc.
Jack Brown & Associates, Inc.
Irving A. Delloff
E & T Associates
Folger & Co., Inc.
Loer & Bradford Consultants, Inc.
Arthur Manning Associates
Manresa Management Consultants, Inc.
Marshall Institute
Richard Muther & Associates, Inc.
Neville & Currie Associates Inc.
Robert Newsom & Associates
Organization Resource Counselors, Inc.
The Pace Consulting Group, Inc.
Wm. E. Sandman Associates Co.
Dorian Shainin Consultant, Inc.
Teipel Associates, Inc.
Roy W. Walters & Associates, Inc.
Woodward Associates

2.10 PLANT LOCATION & SITE SELECTION

Peter August & Associates, Inc.
Ernest Beachley & Associates Inc.
Jack Brown & Associates, Inc.
Joseph Shaw Chalfant
Charles River Associates Inc.
CMI Investment Corp.
Thomas Collier & Associates
Herbert W. Davis & Co.
Denmark Donovan & Oppel Inc.
E & T Associates
Euramco Associates, Inc.
Gladstone Associates
J. George Gross & Associates
C. H. Kline & Co., Inc.
Loer & Bradford Consultants, Inc.
McManis Associates, Inc.
Edward M. Melton Associates
William H. Meyer & Associates, Inc.

Moshman Associates, Inc.
Richard Muther & Associates, Inc.
OBEX Consulting
Organization Resource Counselors, Inc.
Planaflex Co. Inc.
Sanderhoff & Associates, Inc.
Snyder Associates, Inc.
State Street Consultants
James P. Wadley & Co., Inc.

2.11 MATERIALS HANDLING

Ballinger-Meserole
Ernest Beachley & Associates Inc.
Herbert W. Davis & Co.
E & T Associates
J. George Gross & Associates
Group Arcon
Ingersoll Engineers Inc.
Richard Muther & Associates, Inc.
Riffe & Associates
Irving Shaw & Associates
Standards, International Inc.
H.K. von Kaas & Associates
J.F. Ward Associates

2.12 WAREHOUSE SPACE PLNG & UTILIZATION

Ballinger-Meserole
Herbert W. Davis & Co.
Denmark Donovan & Oppel Inc.
Fenvessy Associates, Inc.
J. George Gross & Associates
Management Horizons, Inc.
Riffe & Associates
Sanderhoff & Associates, Inc.
Irving Shaw & Associates
J.F. Ward Associates

2.13 FACILITIES & CAPABILITIES STUDIES

Peter August & Associates, Inc.
Ballinger-Meserole
Barry & Co.
Herbert W. Davis & Co.
Denmark Donovan & Oppel Inc.
E & T Associates
Group Arcon
Ingersoll Engineers Inc.
Marshall Institute
Edward M. Melton Associates
Robert Newsom & Associates
Normandale Associates Inc.
Planaflex Co. Inc.
Francis J. Przyluski
Riffe & Associates
Sanderhoff & Associates, Inc.
Irving Shaw & Associates
Allan J. Siposs & Associates
Snyder Associates, Inc.
Tempo
H.K. von Kaas & Associates
James P. Wadley & Co., Inc.

2.14 STANDARD COSTS

Peter August & Associates, Inc.
Irving A. Delloff
E & T Associates
Keenan, Wheeler & Bowman
Manresa Management Consultants, Inc.
Robert Newsom & Associates
Thomas Oland & Associates, Inc.
Standards, International Inc.

Edward Stark Associates
H.K. von Kaas & Associates

2.15 SYSTEMS ENGINEERING

Joseph Auerbach
Cexec, Inc.
Datamatics Management Services, Inc.
Infotek Corporation
Ingersoll Engineers Inc.
Marshall Institute
Dorian Shainin Consultant, Inc.
Tempo

2.16 MATERIALS DISTRIBUTION

Ballinger-Meserole
Herbert W. Davis & Co.
Distribution Projects, Inc.
J. George Gross & Associates
Duane L. Hile & Associates
Henry Jordan & Associates
Sanderhoff & Associates, Inc.
Irving Shaw & Associates

2.17 TRANSPORTATION

Aviation Consultants, Inc.
Aviation Consulting Enterprises, Inc.
Ballinger-Meserole
Cexec, Inc.
Charles River Associates Inc.
Herbert W. Davis & Co.
Distribution Projects, Inc.
Sanderhoff & Associates, Inc.
Stone Management Corporation
Temple, Barker & Sloane, Inc.
Transportation Industry Consultants, Inc.

3.0 PERSONNEL

Rufus Allen & Associates
Altman & Weil, Inc.
Applied Leadership Technologies, Inc.
Arthur Aschauer & Co., Inc.
Assessment Designs, Inc.
Ballew, Reinhardt & Associates, Inc.
Barbrisons Management Systems, Inc.
Barry & Co.
Batten, Batten, Hudson & Swab, Inc.
Bavier, Bulger & Goodyear, Inc.
Bedford-Post Associates, Inc.
Birnberg & Associates
Donald R. Booz & Associates, Inc.
Bostrom Management Corporation
A. Val Bradley Associates, Inc.
Brecker & Merryman, Inc.
Charles Brooks Associates, Inc.
Daniel J. Cantor & Co., Inc.
David Caulkins Associates
The Center for Applied Management, Inc.
Sonia Charif Associates
Colarelli Associates, Inc.
Cole & Associates
Concepts & Systems, Inc.
The Concord Consulting Group
Cotman Consultants Inc.
CPS Management Co.
Craig/Cutten & Wollman, Inc.
Crickenberger Associates
Decision Studies Group
John deElorza Associates
Irving A. Delloff
Delta Group, Inc.
Derrick & Associates, Inc.

Dickson Associates
Donovan, Zappala & Associates, Inc.
Donworth, Taylor & Co.
Drake-Beam & Associates Inc.
Economics Research Associates
Employee Relations Consultants, Inc.
William Exton, Jr. & Associates
Folger & Co., Inc.
The Galaxy Organization
W. L. Ganong Co.
Garr Associates, Inc.
Gilbert Commonwealth
Global Management Services, Inc.
Goggi Associates, Inc.
H. J. Hansen Co.
Harley, Little Associates Inc.
Paul Harthorne Associates
Hay Associates
W. H. Higginbotham
Nathaniel Hill & Associates, Inc.
William E. Hill & Co., Inc.
Daniel D. Howard Associates, Inc.
Hoyles Associates Ltd.
Human Resource & Profit Associates, Inc.
Humber, Mundie & McClary
The Innovative Group
Insight Development Services
Insurance Management Group, Inc.
International Resources & Applications
The Joynt Group, Inc.
Juarez & Associates, Inc.
William Karp Consulting Co., Inc.
Kennedy & Kennedy, Inc.
Warren King & Associates, Inc.
Virginia Knauer & Associates, Inc.
Robert E. Koogler
Sidney W. Koran Associates
Krall Management Inc.
Peter Lambros & Associates
Laventhol & Horwath
Rensis Likert Associates, Inc.
Loer & Bradford Consultants, Inc.
LWFW, Inc.
MacFarlane & Co., Inc.
Macphie-James, Inc.
William J. Mager & Associates
Management Campus, Inc.
Frank B. Manley & Co.
E. Gilbert Mathews, Inc.
Lawrence M. Matthews
H.B. Maynard & Co.
McClenahan Associates
McCormack & Associates
McCutcheon Associates NW
McManis Associates, Inc.
Medicus Systems Corporation
Donald B. Miller
Paul B. Mulligan & Co., Inc.
Multinational Perspectives, Inc.
Rich Nelson Associates
Neville & Currie Associates Inc.
Robert E. Nolan Co., Inc.
Northern Consultants Inc.
Organization Renewal, Inc.
Organization Resource Counselors, Inc.
Organization Resources Inc.
Organizational Directions, Inc.
D.L. Paden & Associates
Parker, Eldridge, Sholl & Gordon
Patton Consultants, Inc.
Price Waterhouse & Co.
Profit-Improvement, Inc.
Project Associates, Inc.
Psychological Consultants, Inc.
Purcell Consulting Associates, Inc.
Quay Associates
Albert Ramond & Assoc., Inc.
Ransom & Casazza, Inc.
Rogers & Co.

Ross Associates, Inc.
Ryan Advisors, Inc.
Kurt Salmon Associates, Inc.
Robert H. Schaffer & Associates
F.R. Schwab & Associates
Schwarzkopf Consultants, Inc.
Science Management Corporation
Senn-Delaney & Associates
Sibson & Company, Inc.
Space/Management Programs, Inc.
Stanton Associates, Inc.
Frank A. Stasiowski
Stone & Webster Mgmt. Consultants, Inc.
Sullivan & Shook, Inc.
Systems Planning Service
The Tanzi Organization
Teipel Associates Inc.
Towers, Perrin, Forster & Crosby
Trebor Health Associates
George Truell Associates
University Center, Inc.
Van Nuis Co., Inc.
Von Keyserling Consultants Ltd.
Wade, McGuigan & Associates
Emanuel Weintraub Associates, Inc.
Werner Associates, Inc.
Douglas Williams Associates, Inc.
Harry J. Woehr & Associates
Wofac Co.
Woodward Associates

3.1 MANAGEMENT DEVELOPMENT

Abbott, Langer & Associates
Louis A. Allen Associates, Inc.
American Executive Management, Inc.
Anacapa Sciences, Inc.
William B. Arnold Associates, Inc.
Assessment Designs, Inc.
Barron-Clayton, Inc.
Bartow Associates
David N. Beach Associates, Inc.
Brooks Bernhardt & Associates
The Berwick Group, Inc.
Blessing/White Inc.
Boyle/Kirkman Associates, Inc.
Brecker & Merryman, Inc.
George W. Bricker
A.E. Brim & Associates, Ltd.
Burgess Management Associates
C. L. Carter Jr. & Associates, Inc.
David Caulkins Associates
The Corporate Director Inc.
Coughlin, Elkes & Senensieb, Inc.
Coxe Associates, Inc.
Cresheim Co., Inc.
Datamatics Management Services, Inc.
Jack R. Dauner & Associates
Alfred B. DePasse & Associates
D. Dietrich Associates, Inc.
Donworth, Taylor & Co.
Drake-Beam & Associates Inc.
Walter Frederick Friedman & Co., Inc.
The Galaxy Organization
The Galles Resource
Gottfried Consultants Inc.
Alvin R. Haerr & Co.
Hales & Associates, Inc.
J. W. Haslett & Associates
Porter Henry & Co., Inc.
Louis A. Hradesky
Human Resource & Profit Associates, Inc.
Humber, Mundie & McClary
International Management
International Resources & Applications
Interplex Management Associates, Ltd.
Jean Judge Associates, Inc.
The Kampmeier Group

The Kappa Group
William Karp Consulting Co., Inc.
Klein Behavioral Science Consultants, Inc.
Sidney W. Koran Associates
Michael E. Kurtz Associates
Laughlin Associates
Lee-Hecht & Associates
Lovejoy Management Consultants
Carl F. Lutz
Mahler Associates, Inc.
Management Analysis Center, Inc.
F.L. Mannix & Co., Inc.
Manplan Consultants
Martech Inc.
McBer & Co.
McElrath & Associates
McLean Associates
Mitchell & Co.
Moeller Associates
John O. Morris Associates
Rich Nelson Associates
George Odiorne Associates, Inc.
Olney Associates
Organization Consultants, Inc.
Organizational Consultants, Inc.
Organizational Consulting Services
Outlook Associates
PA International Management Consultants, Inc.
The Personnel Laboratory, Inc.
Planaflex Co. Inc.
Profit Planning Associates
Psychological Consultants, Inc.
Quay Associates
Questor Associates
Roberts Associates
Rosenau Consulting Co.
Ryan Advisors, Inc.
SAM Associates, Inc.
Robert H. Schaffer & Associates
John Sheridan Associates, Inc.
SIAR, Inc.
Sibson & Company, Inc.
Silverman Consulting Services Ltd.
E. Ralph Sims, Jr. & Associates, Inc.
David Sirota Associates, Inc.
State Street Consultants
Systema Corporation
Temple, Barker & Sloane, Inc.
Time Management Center
Transportation Industry Consultants, Inc.
George Truell Associates
K.W. Tunnell Co., Inc.
Wagner Systems, Inc.
Robert M. Wald & Associates
Roy W. Walters & Associates, Inc.

3.2 EXECUTIVE COMPENSATION

Abbott, Langer & Associates
William B. Arnold Associates, Inc.
BCMA Associates
Brooks Bernhardt & Associates
The Berwick Group, Inc.
Serge A. Birn Co.
David Caulkins Associates
Cole, Warren & Long Inc.
Coleman Consulting Inc.
Frederic W. Cook & Co., Inc.
The Corporate Director Inc.
The Croner Company
Day & Zimmermann, Inc.
D. Dietrich Associates, Inc.
Donworth, Taylor & Co.
Drake-Beam & Associates Inc.
Dickey Dyer Management Consultants
The Galles Resource
Hales & Associates, Inc.
A. S. Hansen, Inc.

Robert H. Hayes & Associates, Inc.
Porter Henry & Co., Inc.
Keenan, Wheeler & Bowman
Klein Behavioral Science Consultants, Inc.
Kwasha Lipton
Carl F. Lutz
F.L. Mannix & Co., Inc.
Manplan Consultants
Medical Management Associates
Rich Nelson Associates
Olney Associates
Organization Consultants, Inc.
Paterson & Co.
Quay Associates
Questor Associates
Sibson & Company, Inc.
Sullivan & Shook, Inc.
Towers, Perrin, Forster & Crosby
Robert M. Wald & Associates
W.K. Williams & Co., Inc.

3.3 LABOR RELATIONS

Aiken, Madden & Associates
Barry & Co.
CMI Investment Corp.
Donworth, Taylor & Co.
Human Resource & Profit Associates, Inc.
International Resources & Applications
William Karp Consulting Co., Inc.
Kwasha Lipton
Organization Consultants, Inc.
Organizational Consultants, Inc.
Robert H. Schaffer & Associates
John Sheridan Associates, Inc.
George Truell Associates
John P. Weil & Company
W.K. Williams & Co., Inc.

3.4 PERSONNEL SELECTION, PLACEMENT & RECORDS

Abbott, Langer & Associates
Anacapa Sciences, Inc.
Assessment Designs, Inc.
David N. Beach Associates, Inc.
Bess Management Services, Inc.
Boyle/Kirkman Associates, Inc.
Brecker & Merryman, Inc.
Datamatics Management Services, Inc.
James W. Davidson Co., Inc.
Alfred B. DePasse & Associates
D. Dietrich Associates, Inc.
Donworth, Taylor & Co.
Jack Frost & Associates
The Galles Resource
Human Resource & Profit Associates, Inc.
Humber, Mundie & McClary
Jagerson Associates, Inc.
The Kampmeier Group
William Karp Consulting Co., Inc.
Klein Behavioral Science Consultants, Inc.
Sidney W. Koran Associates
Laughlin Associates
Lee-Hecht & Associates
Samuel F. Leigh Associates, Inc.
Walter K. Levy Associates Inc.
Lovejoy Management Consultants
F.L. Mannix & Co., Inc.
Manplan Consultants
McBer & Co.
Edward M. Melton Associates
Rich Nelson Associates
Outlook Associates
The Pace Consulting Group, Inc.
The Personnel Laboratory, Inc.
Professional Practice Consultants, Inc.

Psychological Consultants, Inc.
RLS Consulting & Management Group, Inc.
Roberts Associates
John Sheridan Associates, Inc.
Silverman Consulting Services Ltd.
David Sirota Associates, Inc.
Sno Engineering/Resource Management Inc.
Tempo
Ten Eyck Associates
The THinc. Group Inc.
University Center, Inc.
Warren, McVeigh & Griffin

3.5 TRNG PROGRAMS FOR NONMGMT PERSONNEL

Anacapa Sciences, Inc.
Aquatec International, Inc.
Assessment Designs, Inc.
ASYST-Administrative Systems Consultants
Serge A. Birn Co.
Blessing/White Inc.
Boyle/Kirkman Associates, Inc.
Brecker & Merryman, Inc.
A.E. Brim & Associates, Ltd.
Jack Brown & Associates, Inc.
C. L. Carter Jr. & Associates, Inc.
The Corporate Director Inc.
Coughlin, Elkes & Senensieb, Inc.
Donworth, Taylor & Co.
Drake Sheahan/Stewart Dougall Inc.
Drake-Beam & Associates Inc.
Walter Frederick Friedman & Co., Inc.
The Galles Resource
J. W. Haslett & Associates
Human Resource & Profit Associates, Inc.
Humber, Mundie & McClary
International Resources & Applications
Jagerson Associates, Inc.
Jean Judge Associates, Inc.
The Kappa Group
Michael E. Kurtz Associates
Manplan Consultants
Marshall Institute
Martech Inc.
McElrath & Associates
Moeller Associates
John O. Morris Associates
Olney Associates
Organization Consultants, Inc.
Outlook Associates
PA International Management Consultants, Inc.
Professional Practice Consultants, Inc.
Psychological Consultants, Inc.
Roberts Associates
John Sheridan Associates, Inc.
Silverman Consulting Services Ltd.
Systema Corporation
Time Management Center
Roy W. Walters & Associates, Inc.
Weiss & Associates

3.6 EMPLOYEES SERVICES AND BENEFITS

Abbott, Langer & Associates
Aiken, Madden & Associates
Betterley Consulting Group
D. A. Betterley Risk Consultants, Inc.
Boyle/Kirkman Associates, Inc.
Brecker & Merryman, Inc.
D. Dietrich Associates, Inc.
The Galles Resource
Frank N. Giampietro Associates, Inc.
A. S. Hansen, Inc.
Human Resource & Profit Associates, Inc.
William Karp Consulting Co., Inc.
Laughlin Associates

Kwasha Lipton
Carl F. Lutz
Olney Associates
John Sheridan Associates, Inc.
Towers, Perrin, Forster & Crosby
W.K. Williams & Co., Inc.

3.7 WAGE & SALARY ADMINISTRATION

Abbott, Langer & Associates
Arthur Andersen & Co.
Barron-Clayton, Inc.
Ernest Beachley & Associates Inc.
Brooks Bernhardt & Associates
Serge A. Birn Co.
Cole, Warren & Long Inc.
Frederic W. Cook & Co., Inc.
The Croner Company
Day & Zimmermann, Inc.
D. Dietrich Associates, Inc.
Donworth, Taylor & Co.
Mitchell Fein, Inc.
The Galles Resource
A. S. Hansen, Inc.
Robert H. Hayes & Associates, Inc.
Human Resource & Profit Associates, Inc.
JDA Management Services
William Karp Consulting Co., Inc.
Keenan, Wheeler & Bowman
Klein Behavioral Science Consultants, Inc.
Kwasha Lipton
Carl F. Lutz
F.L. Mannix & Co., Inc.
Manplan Consultants
Clinton P. Mott & Associates
Rich Nelson Associates
Olney Associates
John Sheridan Associates, Inc.
Sibson & Company, Inc.
Sullivan & Shook, Inc.
Towers, Perrin, Forster & Crosby
George Truell Associates
Robert M. Wald & Associates
W.K. Williams & Co., Inc.

3.8 JOB EVALUATION & JOB RATING SYSTEMS

Abbott, Langer & Associates
Louis A. Allen Associates, Inc.
Arthur Andersen & Co.
Assessment Designs, Inc.
Peter August & Associates, Inc.
Ernest Beachley & Associates Inc.
Brooks Bernhardt & Associates
Serge A. Birn Co.
Brecker & Merryman, Inc.
David Caulkins Associates
CMI Investment Corp.
Frederic W. Cook & Co., Inc.
The Croner Company
D. Dietrich Associates, Inc.
Donworth, Taylor & Co.
Mitchell Fein, Inc.
The Galles Resource
Guenther Associates
A. S. Hansen, Inc.
Human Resource & Profit Associates, Inc.
Humber, Mundie & McClary
Jagerson Associates, Inc.
JDA Management Services
William Karp Consulting Co., Inc.
Klein Behavioral Science Consultants, Inc.
Lee-Hecht & Associates
Legge Associates, Inc.
Kwasha Lipton
Carl F. Lutz

Arthur Manning Associates
F.L. Mannix & Co., Inc.
Manplan Consultants
Manresa Management Consultants, Inc.
George S. May International Co.
McBer & Co.
Moeller Associates
Clinton P. Mott & Associates
Norris & Elliott, Inc.
Olney Associates
Oppenheimer Associates
Organization Consultants, Inc.
ORU Group, Inc.
Outlook Associates
Problem Solvers for Industry
Psychological Consultants, Inc.
Roberts Associates
John Sheridan Associates, Inc.
Sibson & Company, Inc.
Silverman Consulting Services Ltd.
Standards, International Inc.
Sullivan & Shook, Inc.
The THinc. Group Inc.
George Truell Associates
Trundle Consultants Inc.
H.K. von Kaas & Associates
W.K. Williams & Co., Inc.

3.9 COMMUNICATING WITH EMPLOYEES

Assessment Designs, Inc.
Boyle/Kirkman Associates, Inc.
Brecker & Merryman, Inc.
David Caulkins Associates
Donworth, Taylor & Co.
Drake-Beam & Associates Inc.
Murray Dropkin & Co.
The Galles Resource
Gelb Consulting Group, Inc.
A. S. Hansen, Inc.
Human Resource & Profit Associates, Inc.
Humber, Mundie & McClary
International Resources & Applications
Jagerson Associates, Inc.
Kendrick & Co.
Warren King & Associates, Inc.
Sidney W. Koran Associates
Robert Kruhm
Michael E. Kurtz Associates
Lee-Hecht & Associates
Kwasha Lipton
William T. Lorenz & Co.
Manuals Corporation of America
Bill Marcus & Associates, Inc.
Medical Management Associates
Moeller Associates
Multinational Perspectives, Inc.
George Odiorne Associates, Inc.
Olney Associates
Organization Consultants, Inc.
Organizational Consultants, Inc.
ORU Group, Inc.
The Personnel Laboratory, Inc.
Roberts Associates
Robert H. Schaffer & Associates
John Sheridan Associates, Inc.
Sibson & Company, Inc.
Silverman Consulting Services Ltd.
David Sirota Associates, Inc.
Towers, Perrin, Forster & Crosby
George Truell Associates
University Center, Inc.
Robert M. Wald & Associates
Norton Weber & Co.

3.10 ATTITUDE SURVEYS

Abbott, Langer & Associates
Louis A. Allen Associates, Inc.

Anacapa Sciences, Inc.
Emory Ayers Associates
David N. Beach Associates, Inc.
Boyle/Kirkman Associates, Inc.
Brecker & Merryman, Inc.
Charles River Associates Inc.
Jack R. Dauner & Associates
Alfred B. DePasse & Associates
D. Dietrich Associates, Inc.
Donworth, Taylor & Co.
Drake-Beam & Associates Inc.
Gelb Consulting Group, Inc.
Nathaniel Hill & Associates, Inc.
Nathaniel Hill & Associates, Inc.
Human Resource & Profit Associates, Inc.
Humber, Mundie & McClary
International Resources & Applications
William Karp Consulting Co., Inc.
Kendrick & Co.
Klein Behavioral Science Consultants, Inc.
Sidney W. Koran Associates
Robert Kruhm
Lee-Hecht & Associates
Kwasha Lipton
Mahler Associates, Inc.
F.L. Mannix & Co., Inc.
Manplan Consultants
Marcept Consulting & Research
Martech Inc.
McBer & Co.
Moshman Associates, Inc.
Rich Nelson Associates
George Odiorne Associates, Inc.
Olney Associates
Organization Consultants, Inc.
Organizational Consultants, Inc.
ORU Group, Inc.
The Personnel Laboratory, Inc.
Projections
Psychological Consultants, Inc.
Quay Associates
Roberts Associates
John Sheridan Associates, Inc.
Silverman Consulting Services Ltd.
David Sirota Associates, Inc.
Sno Engineering/Resource Management Inc.
Standards, International Inc.
Sullivan & Shook, Inc.
Ten Eyck Associates
George Truell Associates
University Center, Inc.
Robert M. Wald & Associates
Norton Weber & Co.
John P. Weil & Company

3.11 PSYCHOLOGICAL & BEHAVIORAL STUDIES

Abbott, Langer & Associates
Advanced Management Institute, Inc.
Anacapa Sciences, Inc.
Assessment Designs, Inc.
David N. Beach Associates, Inc.
Boyle/Kirkman Associates, Inc.
CMI Investment Corp.
Drake-Beam & Associates Inc.
Humber, Mundie & McClary
William Karp Consulting Co., Inc.
Klein Behavioral Science Consultants, Inc.
Sidney W. Koran Associates
Michael E. Kurtz Associates
Lee-Hecht & Associates
Manplan Consultants
McBer & Co.
Rich Nelson Associates
Organization Consultants, Inc.
Organizational Consultants, Inc.
ORU Group, Inc.
Outlook Associates

The Personnel Laboratory, Inc.
Psychological Consultants, Inc.
Roberts Associates
Silverman Consulting Services Ltd.
George Truell Associates
University Center, Inc.
Robert M. Wald & Associates
Roy W. Walters & Associates, Inc.

3.21 HEALTH & SAFETY PROGRAMS

Anacapa Sciences, Inc.
Betterley Consulting Group
D. A. Betterley Risk Consultants, Inc.
C. L. Carter Jr. & Associates, Inc.
Kendrick & Co.
M & M Protection Consultants
Normandale Associates Inc.
Risk Planning Group, Inc.
Warren, McVeigh & Griffin

4.0 MARKETING

Altenburg & Co., Inc.
Arthur Andersen & Co.
Arthur Aschauer & Co., Inc.
The Austin Co.
Emory Ayers Associates
Barbrisons Management Systems, Inc.
Barry & Co.
Batten, Batten, Hudson & Swab, Inc.
Bavier, Bulger & Goodyear, Inc.
David N. Beach Associates, Inc.
Bess Management Services, Inc.
The Billings Group
Birnberg & Associates
Bostrom Management Corporation
Charles Brooks Associates, Inc.
Burgess Management Associates
Caruthers Consulting Inc.
Cleveland Consulting Associates
The Concord Consulting Group
CPS Management Co.
Cresheim Co., Inc.
Day & Zimmermann, Inc.
Decision Sciences Corporation
Decision Studies Group
John deElorza Associates
Delta Group, Inc.
Alfred B. DePasse & Associates
Derrick & Associates, Inc.
Dielman Consultants, Inc.
Donovan, Zappala & Associates, Inc.
Thomas Dowdell/Associates
Drake Sheahan/Stewart Dougall Inc.
Murray Dropkin & Co.
Economics Research Associates
Euramco Associates, Inc.
William Exton, Jr. & Associates
Folger & Co., Inc.
Fowler, Anthony & Company
Jack Frost & Associates
The Galaxy Organization
Newell Garfield & Co., Inc.
Garr Associates, Inc.
Glendinning Associates
Global Management Services, Inc.
Alvin R. Haerr & Co.
Hales & Associates, Inc.
Harley, Little Associates Inc.
E. G. Harper & Company, Inc.
Harris, Kerr, Forster & Co.
William M. Hawkins
Hay Associates
Porter Henry & Co., Inc.
Duane L. Hile & Associates

William E. Hill & Co., Inc.
Hoyles Associates Ltd.
The Innovative Group
Insurance Management Group, Inc.
International Management
International Resource Development, Inc.
Interplex Management Associates, Ltd.
Robert S. Jeffries, Jr.
The Joynt Group, Inc.
The Kappa Group
Kennedy & Kennedy, Inc.
C. H. Kline & Co., Inc.
Virginia Knauer & Associates, Inc.
Kirk Knight & Co., Inc.
Robert E. Koogler
Krall Management Inc.
Peter Lambros & Associates
Laventhol & Horwath
Samuel F. Leigh Associates, Inc.
Allen Levis Organization, Inc.
Rensis Likert Associates, Inc.
LWFW, Inc.
MacFarlane & Co., Inc.
Macphie-James, Inc.
William J. Mager & Associates
Thomas P. Mahoney Associates
Management Campus, Inc.
Management & Marketing
Marcept Consulting & Research
Martech Inc.
E. Gilbert Mathews, Inc.
Lawrence M. Matthews
McClenahan Associates
McCutcheon Associates NW
Edward M. Melton Associates
Neville & Currie Associates Inc.
Organization Renewal, Inc.
Organizational Directions, Inc.
Outlook Associates
James H. Owens Associates, Inc.
D.L. Paden & Associates
Parker, Eldridge, Sholl & Gordon
James S. Pepitone & Associates, Inc.
Permark Management Consultants, Inc.
Price Waterhouse & Co.
Profit-Improvement, Inc.
S. Pullano Associates
Purcell Consulting Associates, Inc.
Stan Radler Associates, Inc.
Theodore Riedeburg Associates
Rogers & Co.
Ryan Advisors, Inc.
Kurt Salmon Associates, Inc.
SAM Associates, Inc.
Samuelson & Co.
Sanderhoff & Associates, Inc.
Science Management Corporation
Senn-Delaney & Associates
Henry Sherry Associates, Inc.
Shycon Associates Inc.
Allan J. Siposs & Associates
SRI International
Frank A. Stasiowski
Stone & Webster Mgmt. Consultants, Inc.
System Planning Associates, Inc.
The Tanzi Organization
Technomic Consultants
Temple, Barker & Sloane, Inc.
Von Keyserling Consultants Ltd.
Emanuel Weintraub Associates, Inc.
Werner Associates, Inc.
Wofac Co.
Woodward Associates

4.1 MARKETING STRATEGY & ORGANIZATION

American Executive Management, Inc.
Anderson/Roethle & Associates, Inc.

Anson, Lee, Rector & Associates
Applied Leadership Technologies, Inc.
Barnett & Engel
Bartow Associates
BCMA Associates
Bedford-Post Associates, Inc.
The Berwick Group, Inc.
Bickert, Browne, Coddington & Associates
Business Psychology International
Cambridge Research Institute
Coleman Consulting Inc.
Thomas Collier & Associates
Curt Deckert Associates, Inc.
Dickson Associates
Thomas Dowdell/Associates
Dickey Dyer Management Consultants
Edgar, Dunn & Conover Inc.
Financial Concepts Inc.
Bertrand Frank Associates, Inc.
Freeman Associates
Gelb Consulting Group, Inc.
Glendinning Associates
Alvin R. Haerr & Co.
William M. Hawkins
Robert H. Hayes & Associates, Inc.
Charles L. Hoffman, Inc.
International Commercial Services
International Resource Development, Inc.
Robert Kahn & Associates
The Kampmeier Group
William Kather Associates, Inc.
Kirk Knight & Co., Inc.
Allen Levis Organization, Inc.
Walter K. Levy Associates Inc.
Management Analysis Center, Inc.
Management Horizons, Inc.
Management/Marketing Associates,Inc.
Manley Management & Marketing Services Corp.
Marcept Consulting & Research
McLean Associates
McManis Associates, Inc.
Mitchell & Co.
Montgomery & Associates, Inc.
Northern Consultants Inc.
Oatman Associates, Inc.
OBEX Consulting
Organizational Consulting Services
PA International Management Consultants, Inc.
The Pace Consulting Group, Inc.
James S. Pepitone & Associates, Inc.
Permark Management Consultants, Inc.
Planaflex Co. Inc.
Professional Practice Consultants, Inc.
Profit Planning Associates
Projections
S. Pullano Associates
Quantum Consultants, Inc.
Questor Associates
Ransom & Casazza, Inc.
Resource Planning Associates, Inc.
R.M. Associates
Ryan Advisors, Inc.
SAI
F.R. Schwab & Associates
Schwarzkopf Consultants, Inc.
SIAR, Inc.
Sno Engineering/Resource Management Inc.
State Street Consultants
Synergy Corporation
Systema Corporation
Technology Marketing Group Ltd.
Tempo
Ten Eyck Associates
Thompson, Ferguson & Associates
Trebor Health Associates
J.F. Ward Associates
Washington Nichibei Consultants
Norton Weber & Co.
Welling & Woodard
The Yankee Group

4.2 MARKET & PRODUCT RESEARCH

American Executive Management, Inc.
Anderson/Roethle & Associates, Inc.
Anson, Lee, Rector & Associates
Aquatec International, Inc.
James S. Baker Management Consultants, Inc.
Barnett & Engel
BCMA Associates
The Berwick Group, Inc.
Bickert, Browne, Coddington & Associates
Cexec, Inc.
Sonia Charif Associates
CMI Investment Corp.
Thomas Collier & Associates
Curt Deckert Associates, Inc.
Thomas Dowdell/Associates
Freeman Associates
Gelb Consulting Group, Inc.
Glendinning Associates
Alvin R. Haerr & Co.
William M. Hawkins
Robert H. Hayes & Associates, Inc.
Charles L. Hoffman, Inc.
William H. Hoffmann
Daniel D. Howard Associates, Inc.
International Commercial Services
International Resource Development, Inc.
J. Lloyd Johnson Associates
William Kather Associates, Inc.
Kendrick & Co.
Kirk Knight & Co., Inc.
Robert Kruhm
Allen Levis Organization, Inc.
William T. Lorenz & Co.
Management Analysis Center, Inc.
Management Horizons, Inc.
Management/Marketing Associates,Inc.
Manley Management & Marketing Services Corp.
F.L. Mannix & Co., Inc.
Marcept Consulting & Research
William H. Meyer & Associates, Inc.
Montgomery & Associates, Inc.
OBEX Consulting
George Odiorne Associates, Inc.
PA International Management Consultants, Inc.
James S. Pepitone & Associates, Inc.
Planaflex Co. Inc.
Projections
Francis J. Przyluski
S. Pullano Associates
Quantum Consultants, Inc.
R.M. Associates
Rosenau Consulting Co.
Ross Associates, Inc.
Ruxton Associates
SAI
F.R. Schwab & Associates
E. Ralph Sims, Jr. & Associates, Inc.
Snyder Associates, Inc.
Edward Stark Associates
State Street Consultants
Stone Management Corporation
Technology Marketing Group Ltd.
Ten Eyck Associates
Thompson, Ferguson & Associates
Trundle Consultants Inc.
Washington Nichibei Consultants
Norton Weber & Co.
Welling & Woodard
Douglas Williams Associates, Inc.

4.3 CONSUMER MARKETING

Anderson/Roethle & Associates, Inc.
Barnett & Engel
The Berwick Group, Inc.
Jack R. Dauner & Associates
Glendinning Associates

Jean Judge Associates, Inc.
Robert Kahn & Associates
Laughlin Associates
Allen Levis Organization, Inc.
Walter K. Levy Associates Inc.
MacFarlane & Co., Inc.
Management Horizons, Inc.
Management/Marketing Associates,Inc.
Marcept Consulting & Research
OBEX Consulting
Permark Management Consultants, Inc.
Projections
Ten Eyck Associates
Trebor Health Associates

4.4 DIRECT MARKETING & MAILING

Jack R. Dauner & Associates
Thomas Dowdell/Associates
Fenvessy Associates, Inc.
William M. Hawkins
Kendrick & Co.
James B. Kobak, Inc.
Robert Kruhm
Laughlin Associates
Walter K. Levy Associates Inc.
Marcept Consulting & Research

4.5 INDUSTRIAL MARKETING

Anderson/Roethle & Associates, Inc.
Birch & Davis Associates, Inc.
Thomas Dowdell/Associates
Freeman Associates
Gelb Consulting Group, Inc.
Glendinning Associates
William M. Hawkins
Robert H. Hayes & Associates, Inc.
Charles L. Hoffman, Inc.
William H. Hoffmann
International Resource Development, Inc.
William Kather Associates, Inc.
William T. Lorenz & Co.
MacFarlane & Co., Inc.
Management/Marketing Associates,Inc.
Manley Management & Marketing Services Corp.
Marcept Consulting & Research
William H. Meyer & Associates, Inc.
OBEX Consulting
PA International Management Consultants, Inc.
James S. Pepitone & Associates, Inc.
Permark Management Consultants, Inc.
S. Pullano Associates
R.M. Associates
Rosenau Consulting Co.
State Street Consultants
Stone Management Corporation
R.J. Sweeney Associates
Systema Corporation
Technology Marketing Group Ltd.
Ten Eyck Associates
Trundle Consultants Inc.
Robert M. Wald & Associates
Norton Weber & Co.
The Yankee Group

4.6 MERCHANDISING

Bertrand Frank Associates, Inc.
Allen Levis Organization, Inc.
Management Horizons, Inc.
Donald R. Miller
Systema Corporation
Norton Weber & Co.

4.7 SALES MANAGEMENT

Birch & Davis Associates, Inc.
Jack R. Dauner & Associates
Thomas Dowdell/Associates
Employee Relations Consultants, Inc.
Gelb Consulting Group, Inc.
William M. Hawkins
Porter Henry & Co., Inc.
Charles L. Hoffman, Inc.
The Kampmeier Group
Laughlin Associates
Samuel F. Leigh Associates, Inc.
George S. May International Co.
H.B. Maynard & Co.
McBer & Co.
Northern Consultants Inc.
Oppenheimer Associates
The Pace Consulting Group, Inc.
James S. Pepitone & Associates, Inc.
S. Pullano Associates
R.M. Associates
State Street Consultants
Systema Corporation
Teipel Associates Inc.
Ten Eyck Associates
Transportation Industry Consultants, Inc.

4.8 SALES FORECASTING

Advanced Management Institute, Inc.
The Center for Applied Management, Inc.
Thomas Dowdell/Associates
Charles L. Hoffman, Inc.
Henry Jordan & Associates
Management/Marketing Associates,Inc.
Manley Management & Marketing Services Corp.
Marcept Consulting & Research
William H. Meyer & Associates, Inc.
Oppenheimer Associates
S. Pullano Associates
Sno Engineering/Resource Management Inc.
The Yankee Group

4.9 SALES TRAINING

Abbott, Langer & Associates
Applied Leadership Technologies, Inc.
Sonia Charif Associates
Cole, Warren & Long Inc.
Jack R. Dauner & Associates
Thomas Dowdell/Associates
Employee Relations Consultants, Inc.
Glendinning Associates
William M. Hawkins
Porter Henry & Co., Inc.
Charles L. Hoffman, Inc.
Daniel D. Howard Associates, Inc.
Insight Development Services
Laughlin Associates
Lee-Hecht & Associates
Allen Levis Organization, Inc.
William T. Lorenz & Co.
Frank B. Manley & Co.
George Odiorne Associates, Inc.
Organization Consultants, Inc.
PA International Management Consultants, Inc.
S. Pullano Associates
Synergy Corporation
Systema Corporation
Teipel Associates Inc.
Transportation Industry Consultants, Inc.
Roy W. Walters & Associates, Inc.
The Yankee Group

4.10 ADVERTISING & SALES PROMOTION

Barnett & Engel
Wallace A. Boesch Associates
Jack R. Dauner & Associates
Curt Deckert Associates, Inc.
Glendinning Associates
William M. Hawkins
Kendrick & Co.
Robert Kruhm
Marcept Consulting & Research
James S. Pepitone & Associates, Inc.
Professional Practice Consultants, Inc.
Projections
S. Pullano Associates
Systema Corporation
Technology Marketing Group Ltd.
Thompson, Ferguson & Associates
Norton Weber & Co.

4.11 MARKETING AUDITS

Anderson/Roethle & Associates, Inc.
Birch & Davis Associates, Inc.
Cole, Warren & Long Inc.
Coxe Associates, Inc.
Financial Concepts Inc.
Gelb Consulting Group, Inc.
Alvin R. Haerr & Co.
International Resource Development, Inc.
William Kather Associates, Inc.
Robert Kruhm
Allen Levis Organization, Inc.
William T. Lorenz & Co.
MacFarlane & Co., Inc.
Management Analysis Center, Inc.
Management Horizons, Inc.
Management/Marketing Associates,Inc.
F.L. Mannix & Co., Inc.
Marcept Consulting & Research
McManis Associates, Inc.
Mitchell & Co.
Montgomery & Associates, Inc.
James S. Pepitone & Associates, Inc.
S. Pullano Associates
Edward Stark Associates
Synergy Corporation
Systema Corporation
Technology Marketing Group Ltd.
Norton Weber & Co.
The Yankee Group

4.12 PRODUCT & CUSTOMER SERVICE

Sonia Charif Associates
Herbert W. Davis & Co.
Thomas Dowdell/Associates
Walter Frederick Friedman & Co., Inc.
Gelb Consulting Group, Inc.
William M. Hawkins
Insight Development Services
International Resource Development, Inc.
Jean Judge Associates, Inc.
McElrath & Associates
Montgomery & Associates, Inc.
James S. Pepitone & Associates, Inc.
E. Ralph Sims, Jr. & Associates, Inc.
R.J. Sweeney Associates
Systema Corporation
Wagner Systems, Inc.

4.13 DEALER-OPERATING SUPPORT

Gelb Consulting Group, Inc.
Thomas Oland & Associates, Inc.
J.F. Ward Associates
Norton Weber & Co.

4.14 PHYSICAL DISTRIBUTION

The Center for Applied Management, Inc.
Cexec, Inc.
Concepts & Systems, Inc.
Herbert W. Davis & Co.
Distribution Projects, Inc.
Bertrand Frank Associates, Inc.
Walter Frederick Friedman & Co., Inc.
Gemar Associates
H. J. Hansen Co.
Management Decision Systems, Inc.
Management Horizons, Inc.
Moshman Associates, Inc.
Permark Management Consultants, Inc.
Research Associates & Analysts
R. Shriver Associates
E. Ralph Sims, Jr. & Associates, Inc.
Stone Management Corporation
R.J. Sweeney Associates
K.W. Tunnell Co., Inc.
J.F. Ward Associates

4.15 SALESMAN COMPENSATION

Abbott, Langer & Associates
Applied Leadership Technologies, Inc.
BCMA Associates
Jack R. Dauner & Associates
Dickson Associates
Employee Relations Consultants, Inc.
A. S. Hansen, Inc.
Robert H. Hayes & Associates, Inc.
Porter Henry & Co., Inc.
Klein Behavioral Science Consultants, Inc.
Laughlin Associates
Manley Management & Marketing Services Corp.
Frank B. Manley & Co.
H.B. Maynard & Co.
Rich Nelson Associates
Quay Associates
Schwarzkopf Consultants, Inc.
Trundle Consultants Inc.

4.16 PRICING POLICY

Thomas Dowdell/Associates
Freeman Associates
Charles L. Hoffman, Inc.
J. Lloyd Johnson Associates
William Kather Associates, Inc.
William T. Lorenz & Co.
Wilson Seney, Inc.
Technology Marketing Group Ltd.
Trundle Consultants Inc.
The Yankee Group
William J. Mager & Associates

5.0 FINANCE & ACCOUNTING

Rufus Allen & Associates
Altenburg & Co., Inc.
Arthur Andersen & Co.
Anson, Lee, Rector & Associates
Austin & Lindberg, Ltd.
Emory Ayers Associates
Barbrisons Management Systems, Inc.
Barry & Co.
Bavier, Bulger & Goodyear, Inc.
Bedford-Post Associates, Inc.
Birch & Davis Associates, Inc.
Birnberg & Associates
Bostrom Management Corporation
A.E. Brim & Associates, Ltd.
Burgess Management Associates
Cambridge Research Institute
Daniel J. Cantor & Co., Inc.

Concepts & Systems, Inc.
Cotman Consultants Inc.
Craig/Cutten & Wollman, Inc.
R. Danner, Inc.
Decision Sciences Corporation
John deElorza Associates
Derrick & Associates, Inc.
Dielman Consultants, Inc.
Donovan, Zappala & Associates, Inc.
Murray Dropkin & Co.
Economics Research Associates
Thomas A. Faulhaber
Folger & Co., Inc.
George E. Frankel & Associates
Fuchs Associates
The Galaxy Organization
Gilbert Commonwealth
Michael R. Gingold Associates, Inc.
Global Management Services, Inc.
Hales & Associates, Inc.
H. J. Hansen Co.
Harris, Kerr, Forster & Co.
Nathaniel Hill & Associates, Inc.
Hoyles Associates Ltd.
Hurdman & Cranstoun
Insurance Management Group, Inc.
International Management
Interplex Management Associates, Ltd.
Juarez & Associates, Inc.
Kenneth Associates
Warren King & Associates, Inc.
Kirk Knight & Co., Inc.
Krall Management Inc.
Peter Lambros & Associates
Laventhol & Horwath
Samuel F. Leigh Associates, Inc.
Rensis Likert Associates, Inc.
LWFW, Inc.
Management Campus, Inc.
Management & Marketing
Marpet Consultants, Inc.
Lawrence M. Matthews
H.B. Maynard & Co.
McClenahan Associates
C.H. McCormack & Associates, Inc.
McCormick & Co.
McManis Associates, Inc.
MDC Systems Corp.
Medicus Systems Corporation
Edward M. Melton Associates
MRP Associates
Neville & Currie Associates Inc.
Planaflex Co. Inc.
Price Waterhouse & Co.
Profit-Improvement, Inc.
Purcell Consulting Associates, Inc.
Questor Associates
Ross Associates, Inc.
Kurt Salmon Associates, Inc.
SAM Associates, Inc.
Samuelson & Co.
Science Management Corporation
Shaw Communications Consultants
Sno Engineering/Resource Management Inc.
SRI International
Frank A. Stasiowski
Stone & Webster Mgmt. Consultants, Inc.
System Planning Associates, Inc.
The Tanzi Organization
Von Keyserling Consultants Ltd.
Emanuel Weintraub Associates, Inc.
Wofac Co.

5.1 GENERAL ACCOUNTING

A.E. Brim & Associates, Ltd.
Elmer Fox, Westheimer & Co.
Freeman, Penrose & Kajinura, Ltd.

S. E. Hall & Co.
Learned & Mahn
Macro Systems, Inc.
George S. May International Co.
Thomas Oland & Associates, Inc.
Wilson Seney, Inc.
R. Shriver Associates
Edward Stark Associates

5.2 COST ACCOUNTING

Joseph Auerbach
A.E. Brim & Associates, Ltd.
The Center for Applied Management, Inc.
Fogel & Associates, Inc.
Elmer Fox, Westheimer & Co.
Keenan, Wheeler & Bowman
Learned & Mahn
Legge Associates, Inc.
Samuel F. Leigh Associates, Inc.
Macro Systems, Inc.
George S. May International Co.
Thomas Oland & Associates, Inc.
Wm. E. Sandman Associates Co.
Wilson Seney, Inc.
E. Ralph Sims, Jr. & Associates, Inc.
Standards, International Inc.
Edward Stark Associates
Frank A. Stasiowski
Technomic Consultants
Trundle Consultants Inc.

5.3 LONG-RANGE FINANCIAL PLANNING

Advanced Management Institute, Inc.
Altman & Weil, Inc.
Arneson & Co.
James S. Baker Management Consultants, Inc.
Bjorkman Associates
Michael Busler Group
Coleman Consulting Inc.
The Corporate Director Inc.
Day & Zimmermann, Inc.
Delta Group, Inc.
Fensterstock & Co.
Elmer Fox, Westheimer & Co.
Freeman, Penrose & Kajinura, Ltd.
Health-Care Management Services
William H. Hill Associates, Inc.
William E. Hill & Co., Inc.
Institutional Strategy Associates, Inc.
Johnson, Pratt & Stewart
Kirk Knight & Co., Inc.
James B. Kobak, Inc.
Learned & Mahn
Legge Associates, Inc.
Kwasha Lipton
Management Analysis Center, Inc.
Normandale Associates Inc.
Oatman Associates, Inc.
The Pace Consulting Group, Inc.
Francis J. Przyluski
SAI
Wilson Seney, Inc.
R. Shriver Associates
Shycon Associates Inc.
Stanton Associates, Inc.
Frank A. Stasiowski
Straehley Associates
Temple, Barker & Sloane, Inc.
D.W. Thomson & Associates
Welling & Woodard

5.4 SHORT TERM PLNG, BUDGETING & CONTROL

Altman & Weil, Inc.
Bartow Associates

Bjorkman Associates
Cexec, Inc.
Coleman Consulting Inc.
The Corporate Director Inc.
Dailey Consultants & Co.
James W. Davidson Co., Inc.
Paul Harthorne Associates
Learned & Mahn
Arthur Manning Associates
McLean Associates
Mitchell & Co.
Multinational Perspectives, Inc.
Organizational Directions, Inc.
Problem Solvers for Industry
Profit Planning Associates
SAI
Wilson Seney, Inc.
Stanton Associates, Inc.
Frank A. Stasiowski
Straehley Associates
Systems Planning Service
D.W. Thomson & Associates
Trundle Consultants Inc.

5.5 CREDIT & COLLECTION

Medical Management Associates
Senn-Delaney & Associates
TMI Systems Corp.

5.6 CAPITAL INVESTMENT

Bickert, Browne, Coddington & Associates
CMI Investment Corp.
Fowler, Anthony & Company
Freeman, Penrose & Kajinura, Ltd.
Michael R. Gingold Associates, Inc.
Johnson, Pratt & Stewart
Learned & Mahn
A.M. Lederer & Co., Inc.
Martech Inc.
William H. Meyer & Associates, Inc.
Wilson Seney, Inc.
Shycon Associates Inc.
D.W. Thomson & Associates

5.7 MARGINAL INCOME ANALYSIS

Keenan, Wheeler & Bowman
Wilson Seney, Inc.
Trundle Consultants Inc.

5.8 FINANCIAL INFORMATION & REPORTING

Altman & Weil, Inc.
D. A. Betterley Risk Consultants, Inc.
Bjorkman Associates
A.E. Brim & Associates, Ltd.
Cexec, Inc.
Coughlin, Elkes & Senensieb, Inc.
Data Sciences, Inc.
William Exton, Jr. & Associates
Fensterstock & Co.
Elmer Fox, Westheimer & Co.
Health-Care Management Services
IMS Systems Corp.
Infotek Corporation
James B. Kobak, Inc.
Learned & Mahn
Kwasha Lipton
Macro Systems, Inc.
Bill Marcus & Associates, Inc.
Medical Management Associates
Multinational Perspectives, Inc.
Thomas Oland & Associates, Inc.

The Pace Consulting Group, Inc.
Wilson Seney, Inc.
Edward Stark Associates
Frank A. Stasiowski
Systems Planning Service
D.W. Thomson & Associates
TMI Systems Corp.

5.9 FINANCIAL PLANNING

Altman & Weil, Inc.
BCMA Associates
Betterley Consulting Group
D. A. Betterley Risk Consultants, Inc.
Cole & Associates
Coxe Associates, Inc.
Delta Group, Inc.
Edgar, Dunn & Conover Inc.
Fensterstock & Co.
Freeman, Penrose & Kajinura, Ltd.
Gladstone Associates
Paul Harthorne Associates
Health-Care Management Services
William H. Hill Associates, Inc.
Johnson, Pratt & Stewart
Robert Kahn & Associates
Learned & Mahn
Legge Associates, Inc.
Kwasha Lipton
Martech Inc.
Multinational Perspectives, Inc.
The Pofcher Co.
SAI
Wilson Seney, Inc.
Allan J. Siposs & Associates
Standard Research Consultants
Stanton Associates, Inc.
Frank A. Stasiowski
Straehley Associates
Systems Planning Service
D.W. Thomson & Associates

5.10 VALUATIONS & APPRAISALS

Arneson & Co.
Betterley Consulting Group
D. A. Betterley Risk Consultants, Inc.
Joseph Shaw Chalfant
Charles River Associates Inc.
Day & Zimmermann, Inc.
Fensterstock & Co.
Fowler, Anthony & Company
Gladstone Associates
William H. Hill Associates, Inc.
Johnson, Pratt & Stewart
Robert Kahn & Associates
James B. Kobak, Inc.
Thomas P. Mahoney Associates
Martech Inc.
E. Gilbert Mathews, Inc.
M & M Protection Consultants
SAI
Wm. E. Sandman Associates Co.
F.R. Schwab & Associates
Standard Research Consultants
Temple, Barker & Sloane, Inc.
Welling & Woodard

5.11 TAXES

Bickert, Browne, Coddington & Associates
Freeman, Penrose & Kajinura, Ltd.
Robert Kahn & Associates
Laughlin Associates
F.R. Schwab & Associates
D.W. Thomson & Associates

6.0 PROCUREMENT

Arthur Andersen & Co.
The Austin Co.
Emory Ayers Associates
Bavier, Bulger & Goodyear, Inc.
Bedford-Post Associates, Inc.
Serge A. Birn Co.
Jack Brown & Associates, Inc.
Burgess Management Associates
Computer-Based Business Systems, Inc.
Concepts & Systems, Inc.
Cotman Consultants Inc.
Decision Sciences Corporation
John deElorza Associates
Derrick & Associates, Inc.
Dielman Consultants, Inc.
Donovan, Zappala & Associates, Inc.
Drake Sheahan/Stewart Dougall Inc.
Economics Research Associates
Jack Frost & Associates
Fuchs Associates
Gagnon & Associates
Garr Associates, Inc.
Global Management Services, Inc.
Government Sales Consultants, Inc.
H. J. Hansen Co.
Interplex Management Associates, Ltd.
Robert S. Jeffries, Jr.
Henry Jordan & Associates
Warren King & Associates, Inc.
Knox Consulting Services
Krall Management Inc.
Peter Lambros & Associates
Laventhol & Horwath
Samuel F. Leigh Associates, Inc.
Rensis Likert Associates, Inc.
LWFW, Inc.
Lawrence M. Matthews
H.B. Maynard & Co.
McCormick & Co.
MDC Systems Corp.
Patton Consultants, Inc.
Profit-Improvement, Inc.
Ross Associates, Inc.
SAI
Kurt Salmon Associates, Inc.
Science Management Corporation
Shycon Associates Inc.
E. Ralph Sims, Jr. & Associates, Inc.
SRI International
Stone & Webster Mgmt. Consultants, Inc.
K.W. Tunnell Co., Inc.
Von Keyserling Consultants Ltd.
Wade, McGuigan & Associates
Emanuel Weintraub Associates, Inc.
Werner Associates, Inc.
Wofac Co.

6.1 VALUE ANALYSIS

Day & Zimmermann, Inc.
Financial Concepts Inc.
JDA Management Services
Henry Jordan & Associates
The Nielson-Wurster Group, Inc.
Organization Renewal, Inc.
Problem Solvers for Industry
Dorian Shainin Consultant, Inc.
Stone Management Corporation

6.2 COMMODITY CLASSIFICATIONS

Henry Jordan & Associates
D.L. Paden & Associates

6.3 PURCHASING

Anson, Lee, Rector & Associates
Cresheim Co., Inc.
Dickey Dyer Management Consultants
The Emerson Consultants, Inc.
Financial Concepts Inc.
Guenther Associates
Henry Jordan & Associates
Samuel F. Leigh Associates, Inc.
Bill Marcus & Associates, Inc.
E. Gilbert Mathews, Inc.
McElrath & Associates
Northern Consultants Inc.
Allan J. Siposs & Associates
R.J. Sweeney Associates
System Planning Associates, Inc.
Teipel Associates Inc.
Wagner Systems, Inc.

6.4 INVENTORY MANAGEMENT & CONTROL

Rufus Allen & Associates
Anson, Lee, Rector & Associates
Joseph Auerbach
Bartow Associates
The Center for Applied Management, Inc.
Joseph Chanko Associates
Cleveland Consulting Associates
Coleman Consulting Inc.
Murray Dropkin & Co.
Dickey Dyer Management Consultants
Edgar, Dunn & Conover Inc.
The Emerson Consultants, Inc.
William Exton, Jr. & Associates
Elmer Fox, Westheimer & Co.
R. L. French & Company, Inc.
Walter Frederick Friedman & Co., Inc.
Gagnon & Associates
The Galaxy Organization
Garr Associates, Inc.
Gemar Associates
Global Management Services, Inc.
Guenther Associates
Louis A. Hradesky
Hurdman & Cranstoun
Infotek Corporation
International Management
Isaacs Associates
JDA Management Services
Henry Jordan & Associates
Legge Associates, Inc.
Bill Marcus & Associates, Inc.
George S. May International Co.
Norris Consultants Inc.
Thomas Oland & Associates, Inc.
Oppenheimer Associates
ORU Group, Inc.
D.L. Paden & Associates
Problem Solvers for Industry
Purcell Consulting Associates, Inc.
Research Associates & Analysts
Riffe & Associates
Sanderhoff & Associates, Inc.
R. Shriver Associates
Shycon Associates Inc.
Stone Management Corporation
R.J. Sweeney Associates
System Planning Associates, Inc.
K.W. Tunnell Co., Inc.
Wagner Systems, Inc.
Wheeler Associates, Inc.

6.5 STORES OPERATION

The Center for Applied Management, Inc.
The Emerson Consultants, Inc.

Gemar Associates
J. George Gross & Associates
Guenther Associates
Louis A. Hradesky
Henry Jordan & Associates
Legge Associates, Inc.
Riffe & Associates
Wagner Systems, Inc.

7.0 RESEARCH & DEVELOPMENT

Altenburg & Co., Inc.
Arthur Andersen & Co.
Barbrisons Management Systems, Inc.
Burgess Management Associates
Business Psychology International
Charles River Associates Inc.
Concepts & Systems, Inc.
Curt Deckert Associates, Inc.
Dexter-Kranick & Associates
Dielman Consultants, Inc.
Economics Research Associates
Jack Frost & Associates
Garr Associates, Inc.
Glendinning Associates
H. J. Hansen Co.
William E. Hill & Co., Inc.
The Innovative Group
Insight Development Services
Interplex Management Associates, Ltd.
Robert S. Jeffries, Jr.
Juarez & Associates, Inc.
Virginia Knauer & Associates, Inc.
Krall Management Inc.
Peter Lambros & Associates
Laventhol & Horwath
Macphie-James, Inc.
Management & Marketing
Manley Management & Marketing Services Corp.
Martech Inc.
E. Gilbert Mathews, Inc.
Lawrence M. Matthews
Medicus Systems Corporation
Donald B. Miller
M & M Protection Consultants
Organization Renewal, Inc.
D.L. Paden & Associates
Planaflex Co. Inc.
Project Associates, Inc.
Theodore Riedeburg Associates
R.M. Associates
Science Management Corporation
Silverman Consulting Services Ltd.
SRI International
Tempo
Trebor Health Associates
Von Keyserling Consultants Ltd.
Wade, McGuigan & Associates

7.1 BASIC & APPLIED RESEARCH & DEVELOPMENT

Aquatec International, Inc.
BCMA Associates
Bickert, Browne, Coddington & Associates
Cexec, Inc.
Coleman Consulting Inc.
JDA Management Services
Kendrick & Co.
Macro Systems, Inc.
McBer & Co.
The Product Integrity Co.
Questor Associates
Rosenau Consulting Co.
Dorian Shainin Consultant, Inc.
SIAR, Inc.
Straehley Associates

7.2 PROGRAM ADMINISTRATION & MGMT

Bartow Associates
Cresheim Co., Inc.
James W. Davidson Co., Inc.
Decision Studies Group
Donovan, Zappala & Associates, Inc.
Murray Dropkin & Co.
Employee Relations Consultants, Inc.
The Galaxy Organization
William E. Hill & Co., Inc.
Louis A. Hradesky
Insight Development Services
Michael E. Kurtz Associates
William J. Mager & Associates
McLean Associates
McManis Associates, Inc.
Medical Management Associates
Moeller Associates
Norris Consultants Inc.
Organization Resource Counselors, Inc.
Research Associates & Analysts
Rosenau Consulting Co.
Snyder Associates, Inc.
Straehley Associates
Wagner Systems, Inc.
Wofac Co.

7.3 PROJECT DETERMINATION & EVALUATION

American Executive Management, Inc.
Aquatec International, Inc.
Centaur Associates, Inc.
Compass Management Group, Inc.
The Galaxy Organization
Gladstone Associates
Guenther Associates
William E. Hill & Co., Inc.
William Kather Associates, Inc.
Kendrick & Co.
Robert Kruhm
Moeller Associates
The Nielson-Wurster Group, Inc.
Rosenau Consulting Co.
Shycon Associates Inc.
Allan J. Siposs & Associates
Straehley Associates

7.4 PROJECT COST CONTROL

Birnberg & Associates
John deElorza Associates
Folger & Co., Inc.
The Galaxy Organization
McCormick & Co.
Problem Solvers for Industry
Profit-Improvement, Inc.
Rosenau Consulting Co.
Straehley Associates
Wofac Co.

7.5 FINANCIAL REPORTING OF R & D EFFORT

Michael Busler Group
Purcell Consulting Associates, Inc.
Rosenau Consulting Co.
Wilson Seney, Inc.

8.0 PACKAGING

J. George Gross & Associates
Samuel F. Leigh Associates, Inc.
Macphie-James, Inc.

Management & Marketing
E. Gilbert Mathews, Inc.
Science Management Corporation
E. Ralph Sims, Jr. & Associates, Inc.

8.1 PACKAGING FUNCTION

Joseph Shaw Chalfant
Donovan, Zappala & Associates, Inc.
Drake Sheahan/Stewart Dougall Inc.
Walter Frederick Friedman & Co., Inc.
Gemar Associates
Edward M. Melton Associates
D.L. Paden & Associates
R.J. Sweeney Associates
Technomic Consultants

8.2 PACKAGING MACHINERY

Northern Consultants Inc.

8.3 PACKAGING & MARKETING DESIGN

Virginia Knauer & Associates, Inc.
Edward M. Melton Associates
Projections
Stan Radler Associates, Inc.

8.4 STRUCTURAL DESIGN & TESTING

Walter Frederick Friedman & Co., Inc.

9.0 ADMINISTRATION

Altman & Weil, Inc.
Arthur Andersen & Co.
The Austin Co.
Emory Ayers Associates
Barbrisons Management Systems, Inc.
Bavier, Bulger & Goodyear, Inc.
Bedford-Post Associates, Inc.
Birch & Davis Associates, Inc.
Birnberg & Associates
Bostrom Management Corporation
Jack Brown & Associates, Inc.
Burgess Management Associates
Daniel J. Cantor & Co., Inc.
Cexec, Inc.
Computer-Based Business Systems, Inc.
Concepts & Systems, Inc.
Coughlin, Elkes & Senensieb, Inc.
Herbert W. Davis & Co.
Day & Zimmermann, Inc.
Decision Sciences Corporation
Decision Studies Group
John deElorza Associates
Dielman Consultants, Inc.
Donovan, Zappala & Associates, Inc.
Murray Dropkin & Co.
Economics Research Associates
William Exton, Jr. & Associates
Jack Frost & Associates
Fuchs Associates
Gagnon & Associates
W. L. Ganong Co.
Garr Associates, Inc.
Gilbert Commonwealth
Global Management Services, Inc.
H. J. Hansen Co.
Harris, Kerr, Forster & Co.
Nathaniel Hill & Associates, Inc.
Hoyles Associates Ltd.
Insurance Management Group, Inc.
Interplex Management Associates, Ltd.

The Joynt Group, Inc.
Kenneth Associates
Warren King & Associates, Inc.
Virginia Knauer & Associates, Inc.
Knox Consulting Services
Robert E. Koogler
Krall Management Inc.
Peter Lambros & Associates
Laventhol & Horwath
Rensis Likert Associates, Inc.
LWFW, Inc.
MacFarlane & Co., Inc.
Macro Systems, Inc.
Thomas P. Mahoney Associates
Management & Marketing
Manuals Corporation of America
E. Gilbert Mathews, Inc.
H.B. Maynard & Co.
McCormick & Co.
MDC Systems Corp.
Medicus Systems Corporation
Belden Menkus
Paul B. Mulligan & Co., Inc.
Robert E. Nolan Co., Inc.
Northern Consultants Inc.
Oppenheimer Associates
D.L. Paden & Associates
Patton Consultants, Inc.
Price Waterhouse & Co.
Profit-Improvement, Inc.
Albert Ramond & Assoc., Inc.
Ross Associates, Inc.
Ryan Advisors, Inc.
SAI
Kurt Salmon Associates, Inc.
Science Management Corporation
R. Shriver Associates
Shycon Associates Inc.
E. Ralph Sims, Jr. & Associates, Inc.
Space/Management Programs, Inc.
SRI International
Frank A. Stasiowski
Stone & Webster Mgmt. Consultants, Inc.
Systems Planning Service
The Tanzi Organization
Trebor Health Associates
K.W. Tunnell Co., Inc.
Von Keyserling Consultants Ltd.
Wade, McGuigan & Associates
Wagner Systems, Inc.
John P. Weil & Company
Emanuel Weintraub Associates, Inc.
Werner Associates, Inc.
Thomas Wilds Associates Inc.
W.K. Williams & Co., Inc.
Wofac Co.

9.1 OFFICE MANAGEMENT

Applied Leadership Technologies, Inc.
ASYST-Administrative Systems Consultants
A. Val Bradley Associates, Inc.
A.E. Brim & Associates, Ltd.
Cole & Associates
Data Systems Consultants
Dickey Dyer Management Consultants
Employee Relations Consultants, Inc.
Fenvessy Associates, Inc.
George E. Frankel & Associates
Frank K. Griesinger & Associates, Inc.
J. W. Haslett & Associates
W. H. Higginbotham
McCutcheon Associates NW
Medical Management Associates
Clinton P. Mott & Associates
Naremco Services, Inc.
Alan Negus Associates, Inc.
Organization Renewal, Inc.
Organizational Directions, Inc.

Project Associates, Inc.
Purcell Consulting Associates, Inc.
The Records Management Group
Senn-Delaney & Associates
Stanton Associates, Inc.
System Planning Associates, Inc.
Systems Planning Service
D.W. Thomson & Associates
Roy W. Walters & Associates, Inc.
Thomas Wilds Associates Inc.

9.2 OFFICE PLNG, DESIGN & SPACE UTILIZATION

ASYST-Administrative Systems Consultants
Serge A. Birn Co.
Data Systems Consultants
Euramco Associates, Inc.
Fenvessy Associates, Inc.
Financial Concepts Inc.
Frank N. Giampietro Associates, Inc.
Guenther Associates
Legge Associates, Inc.
McCutcheon Associates NW
Medical Management Associates
William H. Meyer & Associates, Inc.
Richard Muther & Associates, Inc.
Naremco Services, Inc.
Alan Negus Associates, Inc.
Normandale Associates Inc.
Reel/Grobman & Associates
J.F. Ward Associates
Thomas Wilds Associates Inc.

9.3 INTEGRATED & ELECTRONIC DATA PROCESSING

American Management Systems
Arthur Aschauer & Co., Inc.
ASYST-Administrative Systems Consultants
Joseph Auerbach
Bain Management Consulting, Inc.
Barron-Clayton, Inc.
Bjorkman Associates
Compass Management Group, Inc.
Dailey Consultants & Co.
Data Sciences, Inc.
Data Systems Consultants
Datamatics Management Services, Inc.
Derrick & Associates, Inc.
Distribution Projects, Inc.
Dickey Dyer Management Consultants
Euramco Associates, Inc.
Fenvessy Associates, Inc.
Fowler, Anthony & Company
Gottfried Consultants Inc.
Hales & Associates, Inc.
S. E. Hall & Co.
Hurdman & Cranstoun
IMS Systems Corp.
Infotek Corporation
International Resource Development, Inc.
Isaacs Associates
C.H. McCormack & Associates, Inc.
MHT Services, Inc.
Naremco Services, Inc.
The Nielson-Wurster Group, Inc.
Norris Consultants Inc.
Planaflex Co. Inc.
RLS Consulting & Management Group, Inc.
System Planning Associates, Inc.
TMI Systems Corp.
Weiss & Associates
Thomas Wilds Associates Inc.
Woodward Associates

9.4 SHORT-INTERVAL SCHEDULING & CLERICAL WORK MEASUREMENT

Barron-Clayton, Inc.
Bartow Associates
Serge A. Birn Co.
Cole, Warren & Long Inc.
Data Systems Consultants
Datamatics Management Services, Inc.
Drake Sheahan/Stewart Dougall Inc.
Bertrand Frank Associates, Inc.
R. L. French & Company, Inc.
Guenther Associates
Hales & Associates, Inc.
JDA Management Services
Peter Lambros & Associates
Naremco Services, Inc.
Norris Consultants Inc.
Norris & Elliott, Inc.
ORU Group, Inc.
Reel/Grobman & Associates
Riecks Postal Consultants
RLS Consulting & Management Group, Inc.
Senn-Delaney & Associates
Standards, International Inc.
Wheeler Associates, Inc.
Thomas Wilds Associates Inc.

9.5 SYSTEMS & PROCEDURES

American Executive Management, Inc.
Anacapa Sciences, Inc.
Anson, Lee, Rector & Associates
Applied Leadership Technologies, Inc.
ASYST-Administrative Systems Consultants
Joseph Auerbach
Peter August & Associates, Inc.
Bain Management Consulting, Inc.
Barron-Clayton, Inc.
Serge A. Birn Co.
Bjorkman Associates
A.E. Brim & Associates, Ltd.
Centaur Associates, Inc.
Joseph Chanko Associates
Compass Management Group, Inc.
Cotman Consultants Inc.
Craig/Cutten & Wollman, Inc.
Cresheim Co., Inc.
Dailey Consultants & Co.
Data Systems Consultants
Datamatics Management Services, Inc.
Derrick & Associates, Inc.
Drake Sheahan/Stewart Dougall Inc.
Employee Relations Consultants, Inc.
Fenvessy Associates, Inc.
Elmer Fox, Westheimer & Co.
George E. Frankel & Associates
Walter Frederick Friedman & Co., Inc.
Gottfried Consultants Inc.
Frank K. Griesinger & Associates, Inc.
Hales & Associates, Inc.
S. E. Hall & Co.
J. W. Haslett & Associates
Hurdman & Cranstoun
IMS Systems Corp.
Infotek Corporation
International Management
Isaacs Associates
JDA Management Services
Keenan, Wheeler & Bowman
Management & Marketing
Arthur Manning Associates
Bill Marcus & Associates, Inc.
George S. May International Co.
C.H. McCormack & Associates, Inc.
McCutcheon Associates NW
McElrath & Associates
McManis Associates, Inc.

Medical Management Associates
Edward M. Melton Associates
MHT Services, Inc.
Moshman Associates, Inc.
MRP Associates
Naremco Services, Inc.
Alan Negus Associates, Inc.
Norris Consultants Inc.
Norris & Elliott, Inc.
Thomas Oland & Associates, Inc.
Organizational Consulting Services
Problem Solvers for Industry
Professional Practice Consultants, Inc.
The Records Management Group
Reel/Grobman & Associates
Ruxton Associates
Allan J. Siposs & Associates
Sno Engineering/Resource Management Inc.
John G. Steinle & Associates
System Planning Associates, Inc.
Systems Planning Service
D.W. Thomson & Associates
Weiss & Associates
Wheeler Associates, Inc.
Thomas Wilds Associates Inc.

9.6 FORMS DESIGN

ASYST-Administrative Systems Consultants
Joseph Auerbach
A.E. Brim & Associates, Ltd.
Joseph Chanko Associates
Data Systems Consultants
Derrick & Associates, Inc.
Employee Relations Consultants, Inc.
Fenvessy Associates, Inc.
IMS Systems Corp.
Infotek Corporation
Arthur Manning Associates
McCutcheon Associates NW
MRP Associates
Naremco Services, Inc.
Alan Negus Associates, Inc.
Professional Practice Consultants, Inc.
The Records Management Group
Systems Planning Service
Weiss & Associates
Thomas Wilds Associates Inc.

9.7 RECORDS MGMT & INFORMATION RETRIEVAL

ASYST-Administrative Systems Consultants
Bain Management Consulting, Inc.
Joseph Chanko Associates
Data Sciences, Inc.
Data Systems Consultants
Fenvessy Associates, Inc.
Fogel & Associates, Inc.
S. E. Hall & Co.
Health-Care Management Services
Infotek Corporation
Naremco Services, Inc.
Alan Negus Associates, Inc.
The Nielson-Wurster Group, Inc.
Purcell Consulting Associates, Inc.
The Records Management Group
Weiss & Associates
Thomas Wilds Associates Inc.

9.8 DATA COMMUNICATIONS

Advanced Management Institute, Inc.
Data Sciences, Inc.
Datamatics Management Services, Inc.
Euramco Associates, Inc.

Gottfried Consultants Inc.
Frank K. Griesinger & Associates, Inc.
Health-Care Management Services
IMS Systems Corp.
Infotek Corporation
International Resource Development, Inc.
MHT Services, Inc.
Naremco Services, Inc.
Norris Consultants Inc.
Organization Renewal, Inc.
RLS Consulting & Management Group, Inc.
Ruxton Associates
System Planning Associates, Inc.
Tempo
TMI Systems Corp.
Weiss & Associates
Thomas Wilds Associates Inc.
Jean Judge Associates, Inc.

10.0 INTERNATIONAL OPERATIONS

Austin & Lindberg, Ltd.
Emory Ayers Associates
Donald R. Booz & Associates, Inc.
Charles Brooks Associates, Inc.
Burgess Management Associates
Thomas Collier & Associates
Decision Sciences Corporation
Dexter-Kranick & Associates
Donovan, Zappala & Associates, Inc.
Economics Research Associates
Michael R. Gingold Associates, Inc.
Global Management Services, Inc.
Hales & Associates, Inc.
H. J. Hansen Co.
A. S. Hansen, Inc.
Hay Associates
William E. Hill & Co., Inc.
Hoyles Associates Ltd.
The Innovative Group
International Management
Interplex Management Associates, Ltd.
Juarez & Associates, Inc.
C. H. Kline & Co., Inc.
Virginia Knauer & Associates, Inc.
Laventhol & Horwath
A.M. Lederer & Co., Inc.
William J. Mager & Associates
Manley Management & Marketing Services Corp.
McClenahan Associates
Edward M. Melton Associates
Multinational Perspectives, Inc.
Leo Murphy Inc.
OBEX Consulting
Planaflex Co. Inc.
Price Waterhouse & Co.
Ross Associates, Inc.
Kurt Salmon Associates, Inc.
Science Management Corporation
Shycon Associates Inc.
Snyder Associates, Inc.
SRI International
Stone & Webster Mgmt. Consultants, Inc.
Technomic Consultants
Tempo
Towers, Perrin, Forster & Crosby
Von Keyserling Consultants Ltd.
Washington Nichibei Consultants

10.1 AREA DEVELOPMENT

Barnett & Engel
Charles River Associates Inc.
Frank N. Giampietro Associates, Inc.
Michael R. Gingold Associates, Inc.
International Commercial Services
Moshman Associates, Inc.
Thompson, Ferguson & Associates

10.2 MULTINATIONAL COMPANY POLICIES, STRATEGIES

James S. Baker Management Consultants, Inc.
Cresheim Co., Inc.
Eurequip Consulting Group
Michael R. Gingold Associates, Inc.
Paul Harthorne Associates
Hay Associates
International Commercial Services
International Resources & Applications
Mitchell & Co.
Leo Murphy Inc.
Oatman Associates, Inc.
Organization Renewal, Inc.
Organization Resource Counselors, Inc.
PA International Management Consultants, Inc.
Project Associates, Inc.
Resource Planning Associates, Inc.
SIAR, Inc.
Edward Stark Associates
R.J. Sweeney Associates
Thompson, Ferguson & Associates
Washington Nichibei Consultants
Wofac Co.

10.3 LICENSING, JOINT VENTURES, & OWNERSHIP

Coleman Consulting Inc.
Thomas Collier & Associates
Michael R. Gingold Associates, Inc.
William H. Hoffmann
International Commercial Services
MacFarlane & Co., Inc.
Thomas P. Mahoney Associates
E. Gilbert Mathews, Inc.
Oatman Associates, Inc.
Stan Radler Associates, Inc.
Washington Nichibei Consultants
Welling & Woodard
Wofac Co.

10.4 MARKETING

American Executive Management, Inc.
Aquatec International, Inc.
BCMA Associates
Bickert, Browne, Coddington & Associates
The Billings Group
Bertrand Frank Associates, Inc.
Freeman Associates
Garr Associates, Inc.
William H. Hoffmann
International Commercial Services
International Resource Development, Inc.
The Kappa Group
Laughlin Associates
Martech Inc.
PA International Management Consultants, Inc.
D.L. Paden & Associates
James S. Pepitone & Associates, Inc.
Projections
Stan Radler Associates, Inc.
Resource Planning Associates, Inc.
R.M. Associates
Allan J. Siposs & Associates
Sno Engineering/Resource Management Inc.
Thompson, Ferguson & Associates
Washington Nichibei Consultants
Welling & Woodard
Werner Associates, Inc.
The Yankee Group

10.5 FINANCING

James S. Baker Management Consultants, Inc.
International Commercial Services

Johnson, Pratt & Stewart
Thompson, Ferguson & Associates
Warren, McVeigh & Griffin
Washington Nichibei Consultants

10.6 TARIFFS AND QUOTAS

Thompson, Ferguson & Associates

11.0 SPECIALIZED SERVICES

Advanced Management Institute, Inc.
Aquatec International, Inc.
Betterley Consulting Group
D. A. Betterley Risk Consultants, Inc.
Brooks/Gay & Associates, Inc.
Jack Brown & Associates, Inc.
Centaur Associates, Inc.
Cresheim Co., Inc.
Denmark Donovan & Oppel Inc.
D. Dietrich Associates, Inc.
Eurequip Consulting Group
William Exton, Jr. & Associates
First Risk Management Co.
Gottfried Consultants Inc.
Frank K. Griesinger & Associates, Inc.
A. S. Hansen, Inc.
The Innovative Group
Sidney W. Koran Associates
Lovejoy Management Consultants
William J. Mager & Associates
Manuals Corporation of America
McElrath & Associates
John O. Morris Associates
Moshman Associates, Inc.
Normandale Associates Inc.
OBEX Consulting
Psychological Consultants, Inc.
Quay Associates
Silverman Consulting Services Ltd.
Stone & Webster Mgmt. Consultants, Inc.
George Truell Associates

11.1 EXECUTIVE SEARCH

American Executive Management, Inc.
Barbrisons Management Systems, Inc.
Barron-Clayton, Inc.
Bedford-Post Associates, Inc.
Bostrom Management Corporation
Brooks/Gay & Associates, Inc.
Daniel J. Cantor & Co., Inc.
Cole, Warren & Long Inc.
The Concord Consulting Group
Cresheim Co., Inc.
John deElorza Associates
Derrick & Associates, Inc.
Dickson Associates
Eurequip Consulting Group
Fowler, Anthony & Company
Freeman Associates
Goggi Associates, Inc.
Alvin R. Haerr & Co.
Hales & Associates, Inc.
Hay Associates
Nathaniel Hill & Associates, Inc.
Kennedy & Kennedy, Inc.
Virginia Knauer & Associates, Inc.
Sidney W. Koran Associates
Lovejoy Management Consultants
Thomas P. Mahoney Associates
Manley Management & Marketing Services Corp.
McManis Associates, Inc.
Multinational Perspectives, Inc.
George Odiorne Associates, Inc.
Paterson & Co.

Price Waterhouse & Co.
RLS Consulting & Management Group, Inc.
Ruxton Associates
Ryan Advisors, Inc.
Sanderhoff & Associates, Inc.
Robert M. Wald & Associates
Warren, McVeigh & Griffin
Woodward Associates

11.2 UNION AVOIDANCE

Crickenberger Associates
Loer & Bradford Consultants, Inc.

11.3 TELECOMMUNICATIONS

Marketing & Systems Development Corporation
Ruxton Associates
Shaw Communications Consultants

11.4 SECURITY & PLANT PROTECTION

Brooks/Gay & Associates
Burns International Security Services, Inc.
Belden Menkus

11.5 CONSUMER AFFAIRS

Jean Judge Associates, Inc.
Virginia Knauer & Associates

11.6 TIME MANAGEMENT

11.7 EQUAL EMPLOYMENT OPPORTUNITY

Jagerson Associates

11.8 RISK MANAGEMENT

Betterley Consulting Group
D.A. Betterley Risk Consultants, Inc.
Blades & Macaulay
First Risk Management
Risk Planning Group, Inc.
Towers, Perrin, Forster & Crosby
Warren, McVeigh & Griffin

11.9 ANTI-TRUST

Cambridge Research Institute

11.10 PROCESS CONSULTING

Princeton Associates

11.11 POSTAL SERVICES

Riecks Postal Consultants

11.12 ENERGY MANAGEMENT

Fuel & Energy Consultants, Inc.
Ransom & Casazza, Inc.

Basis of "Industires" Classification

Rather than reinvent the wheel, we have based our classification on the U.S. Government's SIC (Standard Industrial Classification) numbers, as detailed in the 1972 Manual*.

*Stock No. 041-001-00066-6 U.S. Government Printing Office, D.C. 20402/$10.25

A.00 AGRICULTURE, FORESTRY & FISHING
A.01 Agricultural production-crops
A.02 Agricultural production-livestock
A.07 Agricultural services
A.08 Forestry
A.09 Fishing, hunting & trapping

B.00 MINING
B.10 Metal mining
B.11 Anthracite mining
B.12 Bituminous coal & lignite mining
B.13 Oil & gas extraction
B.14 Mining & quarrying of nonmetallic minerals, except fuels

C.00 CONSTRUCTION
C.15 Building construction-general contractors & operative builders
C.16 Construction other than building construction, general contractors
C.17 Construction-special trade contractors

D.00 MANUFACTURING
D.20 Food and kindred products
D.21 Tobacco manufacturers
D.22 Textile mill products
D.23 Apparel & other finished products, made from fabrics & similar materials
D.24 Lumber & wood products, except furniture
D.25 Furniture & fixtures
D.26 Paper & allied products
D.27 Printing, publishing & allied industry
D.28 Chemicals & allied products
D.29 Petroleum refining & related industry
D.30 Rubber & misc plastics products
D.31 Leather & leather products
D.32 Stone, clay, glass & concrete products
D.33 Primary metal industries
D.34 Fabricated metal products, except machinery & transportation equipment
D.35 Machinery, except electrical
D.36 Electrical & electronic machinery, equipment supplies
D.37 Transportation equipment
D.38 Measuring, analyzing & controlling instruments; photographic, medical & optical goods, watches & clocks
D.39 Misc manufacturing industries

E.00 TRANSPORTATION, COMMUNICATIONS, ELECTRIC, GAS & SANITARY SERVICES
E.40 Railroad transportation
E.41 Local & suburban transit & interurban highway passenger transportation
E.42 Motor freight transportation & warehousing
E.43 U.S. Postal Service
E.44 Water transportation
E.45 Transportation by air
E.46 Pipelines, except natural gas
E.47 Transportation services

E.48 Communication
E.49 Electric, gas & sanitary services

F.00 WHOLESALE TRADE
F.50 Wholesale trade-durable goods
F.51 Wholesale trade-nondurable goods

G.00 RETAIL
G.52 Building, materials, hardware, garden supply, mobile home dealers
G.53 General merchandise stores
G.54 Food stores
G.55 Automotive dealers, gasoline service stations
G.56 Apparel & accessory stores
G.57 Furniture, home furnishings, equipment
G.58 Eating & drinking places
G.59 Misc retail

H.00 FINANCE, INSURANCE & REAL ESTATE
H.60 Banking
H.61 Credit agencies other than banks
H.62 Security & Commodity brokers, dealers exchanges & services
H.63 Insurance
H.64 Insurance agents, brokers & service
H.65 Real estate
H.66 Combinations of real estate insurance loans, law offices
H.67 Holding & other investment offices

I.00 SERVICES
I.70 Hotels, rooming houses, camps & other lodging places
I.72 Personal services
I.73 Business services
I.75 Automotive repairs, services & garages
I.76 Misc repair services
I.78 Motion pictures
I.79 Amusement & recreation services, except motion pictures
I.80 Health services
I.81 Legal services
I.82 Educational services
I.83 Social services
I.84 Museums, art galleries, botanical & zoological gardens
I.86 Membership organizations
I.88 Private households
I.89 Misc services

J.00 PUBLIC ADMINISTRATION
J.91 Executive, legislative & general government, except finance
J.92 Justice, public order & safety
J.93 Public finance, taxation, monetary policy
J.94 Admin of human resources programs
J.95 Admin of environmental quality & housing programs
J.96 Admin of economic programs
J.97 National security & int'l affairs

K.00 NONCLASSIFIABLE ESTABLISHMENTS

Industries Served

Generalists: Firms Serving Most Industries
(See primary listing for specific industries)

Abbott, Langer & Associates
Advanced Management Institute, Inc.
Aiken, Madden & Associates
Louis A. Allen Associates, Inc.
Rufus Allen & Associates
Arthur Andersen & Co.
Anson, Lee, Rector & Associates
Applied Leadership Technologies, Inc.
Arneson & Co.
William B. Arnold Associates, Inc.
Assessment Designs, Inc.
ASYST-Administrative Systems Consultants
Peter August & Associates, Inc.
Austin & Lindberg, Ltd.
Don Aux Associates, Inc.
Aviation Consultants, Inc.
Aviation Consulting Enterprises, Inc.
Bain Management Consulting, Inc.
Bain & Co., Inc.
Ballew, Reinhardt & Associates, Inc.
Ballinger-Meserole
David T. Barry Associates
Theodore Barry & Associates
Batten, Batten, Hudson & Swab, Inc.
Brooks Bernhardt & Associates
Betterley Consulting Group
D. A. Betterley Risk Consultants, Inc.
Blades & Macaulay
Blessing/White Inc.
Booz-Allen & Hamilton, Inc.
The Boston Consulting Group, Inc.
Boyle/Kirkman Associates, Inc.
A. Val Bradley Associates, Inc.
George W. Bricker
Earl D. Brodie & Associates
Charles Brooks Associates, Inc.
Brooks/Gay & Associates, Inc.
Frank C. Brown & Co., Inc.
Buckley & Co.
Burns International Security Services, Inc.
Caribbean Consulting Services, Inc.
Case & Co., Inc.
David Caulkins Associates
J. P. Cavanaugh & Associates
Sonia Charif Associates
Cicco & Associates, Inc.
Coffay, Marshall Associates, Inc.
Colarelli Associates, Inc.
Cole, Warren & Long Inc.
Communication Innovation, Inc.
Concepts & Systems, Inc.
The Concord Consulting Group
Consultants International Ltd.
Frederic W. Cook & Co., Inc.
Coopers & Lybrand
Guy Cornman
Coughlin, Elkes & Senensieb, Inc.
Cresap, McCormick & Paget, Inc.
Dallmeyer & Co., Inc.
R. Danner, Inc.
Datamatics Management Services, Inc.
Jack R. Dauner & Associates
Herbert W. Davis & Co.
Dawcon
Deloitte Haskins & Sells
Delta Group, Inc.
Alfred B. DePasse & Associates
Distribution Projects, Inc.
Drake Sheahan/Stewart Dougall Inc.
Ernst & Whinney

Eurequip Consulting Group
William Exton, Jr. & Associates
Mitchell Fein, Inc.
Fenvessy Associates, Inc.
First Risk Management Co.
Fowler, Anthony & Company
Fry Consultants
Fuel & Energy Consultants, Inc.
Gagnon & Associates
The Galles Resource
Newell Garfield & Co., Inc.
Gemar Associates
GlennCo Services Inc.
Goggi Associates, Inc.
Golightly & Co. International, Inc.
Gottfried Consultants Inc.
Alvin R. Haerr & Co.
A. S. Hansen, Inc.
Harbridge House Inc.
Hay Associates
Robert H. Hayes & Associates, Inc.
Hendrick & Co., Inc.
Henning Associates, Inc.
Porter Henry & Co., Inc.
W. H. Higginbotham
Nathaniel Hill & Associates, Inc.
William E. Hill & Co., Inc.
Charles L. Hoffman, Inc.
William H. Hoffmann
Daniel D. Howard Associates, Inc.
Louis H. Howe & Associates, Inc.
Human Resource & Profit Associates, Inc.
Humber, Mundie & McClary
Hurdman & Cranstoun
Industrial Technological Associates, Inc.
The Innovative Group
Insight Development Services
International Commercial Services
International Resources & Applications
Isaacs Associates
Isaacs & Associates
JDA Management Services
Robert S. Jeffries, Jr.
Henry Jordan & Associates
Juarez & Associates, Inc.
William Karp Consulting Co., Inc.
A. T. Kearney, Inc.
Kensington Management Consultants, Inc.
Klein Behavioral Science Consultants, Inc.
Virginia Knauer & Associates, Inc.
Lester B. Knight & Associates, Inc.
Kirk Knight & Co., Inc.
Sidney W. Koran Associates
Krall Management Inc.
Robert Kruhm
Rex Land & Associates, Inc.
Laventhol & Horwath
Lawrence-Leiter & Co.
Learned & Mahn
Lee-Hecht & Associates
Rensis Likert Associates, Inc.
Kwasha Lipton
Arthur D. Little, Inc.
Loer & Bradford Consultants, Inc.
Lovejoy Management Consultants
Lund Management & Marketing Services, Inc.
Mahler Associates, Inc.
Main, Jackson & Garfield
Management Analysis Center, Inc.
Management Campus, Inc.

Management Decision Systems, Inc.
Frank B. Manley & Co.
Manuals Corporation of America
Marketing & Systems Development Corporation
Marshall Institute
MAS International, Ltd.
McBer & Co.
C.H. McCormack & Associates, Inc.
McCormick & Co.
McGinnis Associates
McKinsey & Co., Inc.
McLean Associates
Edward M. Melton Associates
Belden Menkus
MHT Services, Inc.
Donald B. Miller
Mitchell & Co.
M & M Protection Consultants
John O. Morris Associates
Paul B. Mulligan & Co., Inc.
Richard Muther & Associates, Inc.
MWS Consultants, Inc.
Naremco Services, Inc.
Alan Negus Associates, Inc.
Robert Newsom & Associates
Norris Consultants Inc.
Oatman Associates, Inc.
George Odiorne Associates, Inc.
Olney Associates
Organization Resource Counselors, Inc.
Organization Resources Inc.
Organizational Consultants, Inc.
Organizational Directions, Inc.
Parker, Eldridge, Sholl & Gordon
Paterson & Co.
Bruce Payne Consultants, Inc.
Peat, Marwick, Mitchell & Co.
James S. Pepitone & Associates, Inc.
Planaflex Co. Inc.
Plante & Moran
Policy & Management Associates, Inc.
Price Waterhouse & Co.
Princeton Associates, Inc.
Harry J. Prior & Associates, Inc.
The Product Integrity Co.
Projections
Psychological Consultants, Inc.
Quantum Consultants, Inc.
Quorum, Ltd.
Stan Radler Associates, Inc.
Albert Ramond & Assoc., Inc.
Rath & Strong, Inc.
Reliance Consulting Group, Inc.
Roberts Associates

Rogers & Co.
Runzheimer & Co., Inc.
Robert H. Schaffer & Associates
Schwarzkopf Consultants, Inc.
Seidman & Seidman
Dorian Shainin Consultant, Inc.
Shaw Communications Consultants
Henry Sherry Associates, Inc.
Sibson & Company, Inc.
E. Ralph Sims, Jr. & Associates, Inc.
Allan J. Siposs & Associates
David Sirota Associates, Inc.
B.R. Smith & Associates
Sperry-Boom of Florida, Inc.
SRI International
Standards, International Inc.
Stanley Consultants, Inc.
Stanton Associates, Inc.
State Street Consultants
Stevens, Scheidler, Stevens, Vossler, Inc.
Stone Management Corporation
Sullivan & Shook, Inc.
R.J. Sweeney Associates
Systech & Associates
Systems Planning Service
Tempo
The THinc. Group Inc.
Thompson, Ferguson & Associates
Time Management Center
U. Dann Torrance
Touche Ross & Co.
Towers, Perrin, Forster & Crosby
George Truell Associates
University Center, Inc.
Van Nuis Co., Inc.
H.K. von Kaas & Associates
Wade, McGuigan & Associates
James P. Wadley & Co., Inc.
Robert M. Wald & Associates
Wendell C. Walker & Associates
Roy W. Walters & Associates, Inc.
Warren, McVeigh & Griffin
Washington Nichibei Consultants
Weiss & Associates
Wheeler Associates, Inc.
Thomas Wilds Associates Inc.
W.K. Williams & Co., Inc.
Wofac Co.
Woods, Gordon & Co.
Woodward Associates
Worden & Risberg, Inc.
Yaney Associates
Arthur Young & Company
Zeyher Associates

Specialists: Firms Concentrating on Specific Industries

A.00 AGRICULTURE, FORESTRY & FISHING

Emory Ayers Associates
The Billings Group
The Corporate Director Inc.
Drake-Beam & Associates Inc.
Economics Research Associates
Employee Relations Consultants, Inc.
MacFarlane & Co., Inc.
Manley Management & Marketing Services Corp.
Sanderson & Porter, Inc.
Shycon Associates Inc.
Technomic Consultants

A.01 AGRICULTURAL PRODUCTION-CROPS

Coleman Consulting Inc.
Data Systems Consultants

Theodore Riedeburg Associates
John P. Weil & Company

A.02 AGRICULTURAL PRODUCTION-LIVESTOCK

Aquatec International, Inc.
Thomas Oland & Associates, Inc.

A.07 AGRICULTURAL SERVICES

James S. Baker Management Consultants, Inc.
Computer-Based Business Systems, Inc.
Fensterstock & Co.
Jack Frost & Associates
William J. Mager & Associates

Thomas Oland & Associates, Inc.
Theodore Riedeburg Associates

A.08 FORESTRY

Burgess Management Associates
William J. Mager & Associates
Organization Renewal, Inc.
Ross Associates, Inc.
SIAR, Inc.

A.09 FISHING, HUNTING & TRAPPING

Aquatec International, Inc.
Burgess Management Associates
Centaur Associates, Inc.
Charles River Associates Inc.
Samuelson & Co.
Snyder Associates, Inc.

B.00 MINING

Emory Ayers Associates
Barbrisons Management Systems, Inc.
Cambridge Research Institute
Cexec, Inc.
James W. Davidson Co., Inc.
Drake-Beam & Associates Inc.
Folger & Co., Inc.
Fuchs Associates
Paul Harthorne Associates
Hickling-Johnston Ltd.
C. H. Kline & Co., Inc.
McClenahan Associates
Clinton P. Mott & Associates
PA International Management Consultants, Inc.
SAI
Kurt Salmon Associates, Inc.
Sanderson & Porter, Inc.
F.R. Schwab & Associates
Science Management Corporation
Shycon Associates Inc.
The Tanzi Organization
Werner Associates, Inc.

B.10 METAL MINING

Jack Brown & Associates, Inc.
Charles River Associates Inc.
Profit Planning Associates

B.11 ANTHRACITE MINING

Charles River Associates Inc.

B.12 BITUMINOUS COAL & LIGNITE MINING

Ernest Beachley & Associates Inc.
Bickert, Browne, Coddington & Associates
Jack Brown & Associates, Inc.
Centaur Associates, Inc.
Charles River Associates Inc.
Gelb Consulting Group, Inc.
H.B. Maynard & Co.
Moshman Associates, Inc.
Stone & Webster Mgmt. Consultants, Inc.
Temple, Barker & Sloane, Inc.

B.13 OIL & GAS EXTRACTION

Charles River Associates Inc.
Derrick & Associates, Inc.

Elmer Fox, Westheimer & Co.
Gelb Consulting Group, Inc.
J. W. Haslett & Associates
Profit Planning Associates
Stone & Webster Mgmt. Consultants, Inc.
Technomic Consultants

B.14 MINING & QUARRYING OF NONMETALLIC MINERALS, EXCEPT FUELS

Birch & Davis Associates, Inc.
Jack Brown & Associates, Inc.
Interplex Management Associates, Ltd.
Manley Management & Marketing Services Corp.

C.00 CONSTRUCTION

Emory Ayers Associates
Barbrisons Management Systems, Inc.
Bedford-Post Associates, Inc.
Cambridge Research Institute
Employee Relations Consultants, Inc.
Euramco Associates, Inc.
Folger & Co., Inc.
Fuchs Associates
Michael R. Gingold Associates, Inc.
Guenther Associates
LWFW, Inc.
MacFarlane & Co., Inc.
McCormack & Associates
Organization Renewal, Inc.
ORU Group, Inc.
Project Associates, Inc.
Purcell Consulting Associates, Inc.
Sanderson & Porter, Inc.
Science Management Corporation
System Planning Associates, Inc.
The Tanzi Organization
Technomic Consultants
Manley Management & Marketing Services Corp.

C.15 BUILDING CONSTRUCTION-GENERAL CONTRACTORS AND OPERATIVE BUILDERS

American Executive Management, Inc.
Anderson/Roethle & Associates, Inc.
Burgess Management Associates
Michael Busler Group
C. L. Carter Jr. & Associates, Inc.
The Croner Company
Donovan, Zappala & Associates, Inc.
Thomas A. Faulhaber
Financial Concepts Inc.
Fogel & Associates, Inc.
Elmer Fox, Westheimer & Co.
Michael R. Gingold Associates, Inc.
Robert E. Koogler
Martech Inc.
George S. May International Co.
MDC Systems Corp.
SIAR, Inc.
Norton Weber & Co.

C.16 CONSTRUCTION OTHER THAN BUILDING CONSTRUCTION, GENERAL CONTRACTORS

American Executive Management, Inc.
Thomas A. Faulhaber
Fogel & Associates, Inc.
William T. Lorenz & Co.
H.B. Maynard & Co.
MDC Systems Corp.
Rich Nelson Associates
The Nielson-Wurster Group, Inc.

Thomas Oland & Associates, Inc.
Trundle Consultants Inc.

C.17 CONSTRUCTION-SPECIAL TRADE CONTRACTORS

American Executive Management, Inc.
Bickert, Browne, Coddington & Associates
Thomas A. Faulhaber
Fogel & Associates, Inc.
William T. Lorenz & Co.
Management & Marketing
Marpet Consultants, Inc.
Martech Inc.

D.00 MANUFACTURING

Altenburg & Co., Inc.
Anderson/Roethle & Associates, Inc.
The Austin Co.
Emory Ayers Associates
Barbrisons Management Systems, Inc.
Bavier, Bulger & Goodyear, Inc.
David N. Beach Associates, Inc.
Ernest Beachley & Associates Inc.
Bedford-Post Associates, Inc.
The Billings Group
Birch & Davis Associates, Inc.
Donald R. Booz & Associates, Inc.
Burgess Management Associates
Cambridge Research Institute
The Center for Applied Management, Inc.
Cexec, Inc.
The Corporate Director Inc.
CPS Management Co.
Data Sciences, Inc.
James W. Davidson Co., Inc.
Day & Zimmermann, Inc.
Decision Sciences Corporation
Curt Deckert Associates, Inc.
Denmark Donovan & Oppel Inc.
Derrick & Associates, Inc.
Dickson Associates
Dielman Consultants, Inc.
Donovan, Zappala & Associates, Inc.
Thomas Dowdell/Associates
Drake-Beam & Associates Inc.
Economics Research Associates
Employee Relations Consultants, Inc.
Euramco Associates, Inc.
Folger & Co., Inc.
Walter Frederick Friedman & Co., Inc.
Fuchs Associates
The Galaxy Organization
Garr Associates, Inc.
Glendinning Associates
Global Management Services, Inc.
J. George Gross & Associates
Guenther Associates
H. J. Hansen Co.
E. G. Harper & Company, Inc.
Hickling-Johnston Ltd.
Duane L. Hile & Associates
William H. Hill Associates, Inc.
IMS Systems Corp.
Interplex Management Associates, Ltd.
C. H. Kline & Co., Inc.
Knox Consulting Services
Robert E. Koogler
Legge Associates, Inc.
LWFW, Inc.
MacFarlane & Co., Inc.
Macphie-James, Inc.
Manley Management & Marketing Services Corp.
Manplan Consultants
Martech Inc.
Lawrence M. Matthews
H.B. Maynard & Co.

McClenahan Associates
McCormack & Associates
Rich Nelson Associates
Norris & Elliott, Inc.
OBEX Consulting
Oppenheimer Associates
Organization Consultants, Inc.
Organization Renewal, Inc.
Organizational Consulting Services
ORU Group, Inc.
PA International Management Consultants, Inc.
D.L. Paden & Associates
Patton Consultants, Inc.
Permark Management Consultants, Inc.
Profit-Improvement, Inc.
Project Associates, Inc.
S. Pullano Associates
Purcell Consulting Associates, Inc.
Reel/Grobman & Associates
SAI
Kurt Salmon Associates, Inc.
Sanderhoff & Associates, Inc.
F.R. Schwab & Associates
Science Management Corporation
R. Shriver Associates
Shycon Associates Inc.
Silverman Consulting Services Ltd.
Space/Management Programs, Inc.
Summerour & Associates, Inc.
System Planning Associates, Inc.
The Tanzi Organization
Technomic Consultants
Von Keyserling Consultants Ltd.
Norton Weber & Co.
Werner Associates, Inc.

D.20 FOOD AND KINDRED PRODUCTS

James S. Baker Management Consultants, Inc.
Barry & Co.
Ernest Beachley & Associates Inc.
Bess Management Services, Inc.
Joseph Shaw Chalfant
Dailey Consultants & Co.
James W. Davidson Co., Inc.
Edgar, Dunn & Conover Inc.
Thomas A. Faulhaber
Fensterstock & Co.
Jack Frost & Associates
Frank N. Giampietro Associates, Inc.
Global Management Services, Inc.
J. George Gross & Associates
Hans & Associates, Inc.
Jean Judge Associates, Inc.
A.M. Lederer & Co., Inc.
Management & Marketing
Arthur Manning Associates
F.L. Mannix & Co., Inc.
Manresa Management Consultants, Inc.
Marcept Consulting & Research
McElrath & Associates
Thomas Oland & Associates, Inc.
Oppenheimer Associates
Outlook Associates
Wilson Seney, Inc.
SIAR, Inc.
Ten Eyck Associates
Trundle Consultants Inc.
K.W. Tunnell Co., Inc.
J.F. Ward Associates
John P. Weil & Company

D.21 TOBACCO MANUFACTURERS

Fensterstock & Co.
George S. May International Co.

D.22 TEXTILE MILL PRODUCTS

John deElorza Associates
E & T Associates
Bertrand Frank Associates, Inc.
Global Management Services, Inc.
International Management
Management Horizons, Inc.
Arthur Manning Associates
Edward Stark Associates
Stone & Webster Mgmt. Consultants, Inc.
Summerour & Associates, Inc.
Emanuel Weintraub Associates, Inc.

D.23 APPAREL & OTHER FINISHED PRODUCTS, MADE FROM FABRICS & SIMILAR MATERIALS

Joseph Auerbach
Coleman Consulting Inc.
Cotman Consultants Inc.
E & T Associates
Bertrand Frank Associates, Inc.
R. L. French & Company, Inc.
Infotek Corporation
International Management
Jean Judge Associates, Inc.
Knox Consulting Services
Management Horizons, Inc.
Management & Marketing
Riffe & Associates
Ross Associates, Inc.
Wilson Seney, Inc.
Senn-Delaney & Associates
Irving Shaw & Associates
Summerour & Associates, Inc.
Wagner Systems, Inc.
J.F. Ward Associates
Emanuel Weintraub Associates, Inc.

D.24 LUMBER & WOOD PRODUCTS, EXCEPT FURNITURE

Ernest Beachley & Associates Inc.
Serge A. Birn Co.
Michael Busler Group
The Croner Company
Dexter-Kranick & Associates
R. L. French & Company, Inc.
Infotek Corporation
Peter Lambros & Associates
MacFarlane & Co., Inc.
Manresa Management Consultants, Inc.
Marcept Consulting & Research
George S. May International Co.
Leo Murphy Inc.
Thomas Oland & Associates, Inc.
Oppenheimer Associates
The Pace Consulting Group, Inc.
Profit Planning Associates
R.M. Associates
Ross Associates, Inc.
Samuelson & Co.
SIAR, Inc.
J.F. Ward Associates

D.25 FURNITURE & FIXTURES

Barry & Co.
Serge A. Birn Co.
Computer-Based Business Systems, Inc.
Cotman Consultants Inc.
Crickenberger Associates
E & T Associates
R. L. French & Company, Inc.
International Management
Keenan, Wheeler & Bowman

Knox Consulting Services
Peter Lambros & Associates
Management Horizons, Inc.
Manresa Management Consultants, Inc.
Marcept Consulting & Research
Oppenheimer Associates
Ross Associates, Inc.
Wm. E. Sandman Associates Co.
Trundle Consultants Inc.
Emanuel Weintraub Associates, Inc.

D.26 PAPER & ALLIED PRODUCTS

Jack Brown & Associates, Inc.
Joseph Shaw Chalfant
Computer-Based Business Systems, Inc.
Cotman Consultants Inc.
Cresheim Co., Inc.
Dailey Consultants & Co.
Data Sciences, Inc.
Dickey Dyer Management Consultants
E & T Associates
J. George Gross & Associates
S. E. Hall & Co.
International Resource Development, Inc.
Keenan, Wheeler & Bowman
A.M. Lederer & Co., Inc.
Samuel F. Leigh Associates, Inc.
William T. Lorenz & Co.
Macphie-James, Inc.
Thomas P. Mahoney Associates
E. Gilbert Mathews, Inc.
McElrath & Associates
Montgomery & Associates, Inc.
Neville & Currie Associates Inc.
Profit Planning Associates
Resource Conservation Consultants
Resource Planning Associates, Inc.
R.M. Associates
Samuelson & Co.
Wilson Seney, Inc.
Senn-Delaney & Associates
Irving Shaw & Associates
SIAR, Inc.
Stone & Webster Mgmt. Consultants, Inc.
Systema Corporation
Trundle Consultants Inc.
J.F. Ward Associates

D.27 PRINTING, PUBLISHING, & ALLIED INDUSTRY

Joseph Auerbach
Barry & Co.
BCMA Associates
Joseph Chanko Associates
Computer-Based Business Systems, Inc.
Dexter-Kranick & Associates
Fensterstock & Co.
International Resource Development, Inc.
Keenan, Wheeler & Bowman
A.M. Lederer & Co., Inc.
Samuel F. Leigh Associates, Inc.
Thomas P. Mahoney Associates
F.L. Mannix & Co., Inc.
E. Gilbert Mathews, Inc.
Oppenheimer Associates
The Pace Consulting Group, Inc.
The Pofcher Co.
Wilson Seney, Inc.
Wilson Seney, Inc.
Irving Shaw & Associates
Edward Stark Associates
Wagner Systems, Inc.
Welling & Woodard

D.28 CHEMICALS & ALLIED PRODUCTS

American Executive Management, Inc.
Ernest Beachley & Associates Inc.
Bjorkman Associates
Cresheim Co., Inc.
Dielman Consultants, Inc.
Fensterstock & Co.
Jack Frost & Associates
Gelb Consulting Group, Inc.
Global Management Services, Inc.
J. George Gross & Associates
International Management
The Joynt Group, Inc.
William Kather Associates, Inc.
MacFarlane & Co., Inc.
William J. Mager & Associates
Management & Marketing
Manley Management & Marketing Services Corp.
F.L. Mannix & Co., Inc.
McElrath & Associates
MDC Systems Corp.
Leo Murphy Inc.
Northern Consultants Inc.
Profit Planning Associates
Resource Planning Associates, Inc.
Riffe & Associates
RLS Consulting & Management Group, Inc.
R.M. Associates
Irving Shaw & Associates
SIAR, Inc.
Stone & Webster Mgmt. Consultants, Inc.
Systema Corporation
Trundle Consultants Inc.
K.W. Tunnell Co., Inc.
Emanuel Weintraub Associates, Inc.
Welling & Woodard

D.29 PETROLEUM REFINING & RELATED INDUSTRY

Altenburg & Co., Inc.
American Executive Management, Inc.
Ernest Beachley & Associates Inc.
Jack Brown & Associates, Inc.
Charles River Associates Inc.
Cresheim Co., Inc.
Thomas Dowdell/Associates
Gelb Consulting Group, Inc.
Paul Harthorne Associates
J. W. Haslett & Associates
William T. Lorenz & Co.
Carl F. Lutz
MDC Systems Corp.
Northern Consultants Inc.
Profit Planning Associates
Research Associates & Analysts
Resource Planning Associates, Inc.
RLS Consulting & Management Group, Inc.
Wm. E. Sandman Associates Co.
Stone & Webster Mgmt. Consultants, Inc.
K.W. Tunnell Co., Inc.
Welling & Woodard

D.30 RUBBER & MISC PLASTICS PRODUCTS

American Executive Management, Inc.
Barron-Clayton, Inc.
Barry & Co.
Serge A. Birn Co.
Cotman Consultants Inc.
Dexter-Kranick & Associates
E & T Associates
Bertrand Frank Associates, Inc.
R. L. French & Company, Inc.
Global Management Services, Inc.
JMG Associates Ltd.
William Kather Associates, Inc.

Macphie-James, Inc.
Arthur Manning Associates
F.L. Mannix & Co., Inc.
Manresa Management Consultants, Inc.
Leo Murphy Inc.
Northern Consultants Inc.
Thomas Oland & Associates, Inc.
The Pace Consulting Group, Inc.
Profit Planning Associates
Senn-Delaney & Associates
Irving Shaw & Associates
Ten Eyck Associates
Emanuel Weintraub Associates, Inc.

D.31 LEATHER & LEATHER PRODUCTS

Barron-Clayton, Inc.
Irving A. Delloff
E & T Associates
R. L. French & Company, Inc.
Management Horizons, Inc.
Manresa Management Consultants, Inc.
George S. May International Co.
Riffe & Associates
Samuelson & Co.
Irving Shaw & Associates
Wagner Systems, Inc.
J.F. Ward Associates
Emanuel Weintraub Associates, Inc.

D.32 STONE, CLAY, GLASS & CONCRETE PRODUCTS

Barron-Clayton, Inc.
Ernest Beachley & Associates Inc.
Infotek Corporation
McElrath & Associates
MDC Systems Corp.
Leo Murphy Inc.
Oppenheimer Associates
Profit Planning Associates
Resource Planning Associates, Inc.
Trundle Consultants Inc.
Welling & Woodard

D.33 PRIMARY METAL INDUSTRIES

Barron-Clayton, Inc.
Ernest Beachley & Associates Inc.
Charles River Associates Inc.
Cotman Consultants Inc.
James W. Davidson Co., Inc.
Irving A. Delloff
Thomas Dowdell/Associates
Thomas A. Faulhaber
J. George Gross & Associates
Paul Harthorne Associates
Louis A. Hradesky
Infotek Corporation
The Joynt Group, Inc.
Keenan, Wheeler & Bowman
Knox Consulting Services
Peter Lambros & Associates
Macphie-James, Inc.
F.L. Mannix & Co., Inc.
McElrath & Associates
Clinton P. Mott & Associates
Oppenheimer Associates
Quay Associates
Resource Planning Associates, Inc.
Riffe & Associates
Stone & Webster Mgmt. Consultants, Inc.
Welling & Woodard

D.34 FABRICATED METAL PRODUCTS, EXCEPT MACHINERY & TRANSPORTATION EQUIPMENT

American Executive Management, Inc.
Arthur Aschauer & Co., Inc.
Barron-Clayton, Inc.
Barry & Co.
Ernest Beachley & Associates Inc.
N.C. Berkowitz & Co.
Bess Management Services, Inc.
Serge A. Birn Co.
C. L. Carter Jr. & Associates, Inc.
Charles River Associates Inc.
Cotman Consultants Inc.
Cresheim Co., Inc.
Crickenberger Associates
Dailey Consultants & Co.
Data Sciences, Inc.
James W. Davidson Co., Inc.
John deElorza Associates
Irving A. Delloff
Thomas Dowdell/Associates
Dickey Dyer Management Consultants
Edgar, Dunn & Conover Inc.
E & T Associates
Thomas A. Faulhaber
Elmer Fox, Westheimer & Co.
R. L. French & Company, Inc.
Frank N. Giampietro Associates, Inc.
Global Management Services, Inc.
Paul Harthorne Associates
Louis A. Hradesky
Infotek Corporation
Ingersoll Engineers Inc.
International Management
The Joynt Group, Inc.
Keenan, Wheeler & Bowman
Knox Consulting Services
Peter Lambros & Associates
Macphie-James, Inc.
Management & Marketing
F.L. Mannix & Co., Inc.
Manresa Management Consultants, Inc.
Marpet Consultants, Inc.
McElrath & Associates
Clinton P. Mott & Associates
Leo Murphy Inc.
Neville & Currie Associates Inc.
Thomas Oland & Associates, Inc.
Oppenheimer Associates
The Pace Consulting Group, Inc.
Problem Solvers for Industry
Quay Associates
Riffe & Associates
Wm. E. Sandman Associates Co.
Wilson Seney, Inc.
Senn-Delaney & Associates
Irving Shaw & Associates
Snyder Associates, Inc.
Teipel Associates Inc.
Trundle Consultants Inc.
K.W. Tunnell Co., Inc.
Wagner Systems, Inc.
J.F. Ward Associates
Emanuel Weintraub Associates, Inc.
Welling & Woodard

D.35 MACHINERY, EXCEPT ELECTRICAL

American Executive Management, Inc.
Arthur Aschauer & Co., Inc.
Barron-Clayton, Inc.
Barry & Co.
Ernest Beachley & Associates Inc.
Serge A. Birn Co.
C. L. Carter Jr. & Associates, Inc.
Computer-Based Business Systems, Inc.
Cotman Consultants Inc.

Crickenberger Associates
James W. Davidson Co., Inc.
Dexter-Kranick & Associates
Dickey Dyer Management Consultants
Thomas A. Faulhaber
Elmer Fox, Westheimer & Co.
Freeman Associates
Global Management Services, Inc.
J. George Gross & Associates
Louis A. Hradesky
Infotek Corporation
Ingersoll Engineers Inc.
JMG Associates Ltd.
Knox Consulting Services
Peter Lambros & Associates
William T. Lorenz & Co.
Macphie-James, Inc.
Management & Marketing
F.L. Mannix & Co., Inc.
Manresa Management Consultants, Inc.
E. Gilbert Mathews, Inc.
McElrath & Associates
Leo Murphy Inc.
Neville & Currie Associates Inc.
Northern Consultants Inc.
Francis J. Przyluski
Riffe & Associates
Wm. E. Sandman Associates Co.
Wilson Seney, Inc.
SIAR, Inc.
Snyder Associates, Inc.
Systema Corporation
Teipel Consultants Inc.
Trundle Consultants Inc.
K.W. Tunnell Co., Inc.
Wagner Systems, Inc.
Welling & Woodard

D.36 ELECTRICAL & ELECTRONIC MACHINERY, EQUIPMENT SUPPLIES

American Executive Management, Inc.
Anacapa Sciences, Inc.
Arthur Aschauer & Co., Inc.
Barron-Clayton, Inc.
Barry & Co.
N.C. Berkowitz & Co.
Serge A. Birn Co.
C. L. Carter Jr. & Associates, Inc.
Joseph Shaw Chalfant
Thomas Collier & Associates
Computer-Based Business Systems, Inc.
Cresheim Co., Inc.
Crickenberger Associates
The Croner Company
Dailey Consultants & Co.
James W. Davidson Co., Inc.
Dexter-Kranick & Associates
Dielman Consultants, Inc.
Dickey Dyer Management Consultants
Thomas A. Faulhaber
Bertrand Frank Associates, Inc.
Freeman Associates
Global Management Services, Inc.
J. George Gross & Associates
William M. Hawkins
Health-Care Management Services
Louis A. Hradesky
Infotek Corporation
International Resource Development, Inc.
Robert Kahn & Associates
The Kappa Group
Knox Consulting Services
Peter Lambros & Associates
Manley Management & Marketing Services Corp.
F.L. Mannix & Co., Inc.
Marpet Consultants, Inc.
McElrath & Associates
Leo Murphy Inc.

Thomas Oland & Associates, Inc.
Oppenheimer Associates
The Pace Consulting Group, Inc.
Problem Solvers for Industry
Wm. E. Sandman Associates Co.
Wilson Seney, Inc.
Irving Shaw & Associates
Silverman Consulting Services Ltd.
Snyder Associates, Inc.
Edward Stark Associates
Straehley Associates
Systema Corporation
Technology Marketing Group Ltd.
Ten Eyck Associates
Trundle Consultants Inc.
K.W. Tunnell Co., Inc.
Wagner Systems, Inc.
Welling & Woodard

D.37 TRANSPORTATION EQUIPMENT

Anacapa Sciences, Inc.
Barron-Clayton, Inc.
Barry & Co.
Charles River Associates Inc.
Thomas Collier & Associates
Cotman Consultants Inc.
Crickenberger Associates
Global Management Services, Inc.
S. E. Hall & Co.
Louis A. Hradesky
Ingersoll Engineers Inc.
Jean Judge Associates, Inc.
Peter Lambros & Associates
Manresa Management Consultants, Inc.
Leo Murphy Inc.
Neville & Currie Associates Inc.
Francis J. Przyluski
Research Associates & Analysts
Wm. E. Sandman Associates Co.
Silverman Consulting Services Ltd.
Snyder Associates, Inc.
K.W. Tunnell Co., Inc.
Wagner Systems, Inc.
Welling & Woodard

D.38 MEASURING, ANALYZING, & CONTROLLING INSTRUMENTS; PHOTOGRAPHIC, MEDICAL & OPTICAL GOODS; WATCHES & CLOCKS

American Executive Management, Inc.
Barron-Clayton, Inc.
Barry & Co.
Bartow Associates
N.C. Berkowitz & Co.
C. L. Carter Jr. & Associates, Inc.
Computer-Based Business Systems, Inc.
Cotman Consultants Inc.
Crickenberger Associates
The Croner Company
Dielman Consultants, Inc.
Dickey Dyer Management Consultants
Thomas A. Faulhaber
Freeman Associates
R. L. French & Company, Inc.
Jack Frost & Associates
J. George Gross & Associates
William M. Hawkins
Infotek Corporation
International Resource Development, Inc.
Knox Consulting Services
Peter Lambros & Associates
A.M. Lederer & Co., Inc.
William T. Lorenz & Co.
Macphie-James, Inc.
William J. Mager & Associates
Management & Marketing

Manley Management & Marketing Services Corp.
F.L. Mannix & Co., Inc.
Marpet Consultants, Inc.
Leo Murphy Inc.
Problem Solvers for Industry
Wm. E. Sandman Associates Co.
Wilson Seney, Inc.
Snyder Associates, Inc.
Systema Corporation
Technology Marketing Group Ltd.
Wagner Systems, Inc.
Welling & Woodard

D.39 MISC MANUFACTURING INDUSTRIES

Joseph Auerbach
Barron-Clayton, Inc.
Bartow Associates
Serge A. Birn Co.
Bjorkman Associates
C. L. Carter Jr. & Associates, Inc.
Cole & Associates
Computer-Based Business Systems, Inc.
Cotman Consultants Inc.
Data Systems Consultants
E & T Associates
Bertrand Frank Associates, Inc.
Freeman Associates
R. L. French & Company, Inc.
S. E. Hall & Co.
Paul Harthorne Associates
Louis A. Hradesky
International Management
Jean Judge Associates, Inc.
Knox Consulting Services
Peter Lambros & Associates
A.M. Lederer & Co., Inc.
Management & Marketing
F.L. Mannix & Co., Inc.
Manresa Management Consultants, Inc.
Marcept Consulting & Research
Marpet Consultants, Inc.
George S. May International Co.
McElrath & Associates
Moshman Associates, Inc.
Leo Murphy Inc.
Northern Consultants Inc.
Problem Solvers for Industry
Francis J. Przyluski
Wm. E. Sandman Associates Co.
Irving Shaw & Associates
Snyder Associates, Inc.
Edward Stark Associates
Ten Eyck Associates
J.F. Ward Associates
Emanuel Weintraub Associates, Inc.
Sanderson & Porter, Inc.
Sanderson & Porter, Inc.

E.00 TRANSPORTATION, COMMUNICATIONS, ELECTRIC, GAS & SANITARY SERVICES

The Austin Co.
Barbrisons Management Systems, Inc.
The Billings Group
Burgess Management Associates
Cambridge Research Institute
Charles River Associates Inc.
Crickenberger Associates
Decision Sciences Corporation
Donovan, Zappala & Associates, Inc.
Drake-Beam & Associates Inc.
Economics Research Associates
Employee Relations Consultants, Inc.
Gilbert Commonwealth
Glendinning Associates
H. J. Hansen Co.

Hickling-Johnston Ltd.
IMS Systems Corp.
Interplex Management Associates, Ltd.
The Joynt Group, Inc.
Robert E. Koogler
LWFW, Inc.
MacFarlane & Co., Inc.
Manley Management & Marketing Services Corp.
H.B. Maynard & Co.
McClenahan Associates
Organization Renewal, Inc.
ORU Group, Inc.
PA International Management Consultants, Inc.
D.L. Paden & Associates
Patton Consultants, Inc.
Project Associates, Inc.
S. Pullano Associates
Reel/Grobman & Associates
Sanderhoff & Associates, Inc.
Science Management Corporation
Shycon Associates Inc.
Snyder Associates, Inc.
Werner Associates, Inc.

E.40 RAILROAD TRANSPORTATION

Bartow Associates
N.C. Berkowitz & Co.
Bjorkman Associates
Jack Brown & Associates, Inc.
Day & Zimmermann, Inc.
Gladstone Associates
J. W. Haslett & Associates
MDC Systems Corp.
Moshman Associates, Inc.
R. Shriver Associates
Temple, Barker & Sloane, Inc.
Transportation Industry Consultants, Inc.

E.41 LOCAL & SUBURBAN TRANSIT & INTERURBAN HIGHWAY PASSENGER TRANSPORTATION

Anacapa Sciences, Inc.
Bickert, Browne, Coddington & Associates
Day & Zimmermann, Inc.
Gelb Consulting Group, Inc.
Gladstone Associates
Warren King & Associates, Inc.
MDC Systems Corp.

E.42 MOTOR FREIGHT TRANSPORTATION & WAREHOUSING

Bjorkman Associates
Jack Brown & Associates, Inc.
The Croner Company
Walter Frederick Friedman & Co., Inc.
Macphie-James, Inc.
George S. May International Co.
Moshman Associates, Inc.
Rich Nelson Associates
Northern Consultants Inc.
Research Associates & Analysts
Systema Corporation
Technology Marketing Group Ltd.
Temple, Barker & Sloane, Inc.
Transportation Industry Consultants, Inc.
K.W. Tunnell Co., Inc.
Werner Associates, Inc.

E.43 U.S. POSTAL SERVICE

Dailey Consultants & Co.
Irving A. Delloff
International Resource Development, Inc.

MDC Systems Corp.
Riecks Postal Consultants
System Planning Associates, Inc.
The Yankee Group

E.44 WATER TRANSPORTATION

Edgar, Dunn & Conover Inc.
Paul Harthorne Associates
William J. Mager & Associates
Moshman Associates, Inc.
Research Associates & Analysts
Temple, Barker & Sloane, Inc.

E.45 TRANSPORTATION BY AIR

Altenburg & Co., Inc.
Bjorkman Associates
The Corporate Director Inc.
Dailey Consultants & Co.
Edgar, Dunn & Conover Inc.
Carl F. Lutz
MDC Systems Corp.
Rich Nelson Associates
Edward Stark Associates
Temple, Barker & Sloane, Inc.
K.W. Tunnell Co., Inc.

E.46 PIPE LINES, EXCEPT NATURAL GAS

Altenburg & Co., Inc.
R. Shriver Associates
Norton Weber & Co.

E.47 TRANSPORTATION SERVICES

Barnett & Engel
Cresheim Co., Inc.
Elmer Fox, Westheimer & Co.
Walter Frederick Friedman & Co., Inc.
The Pace Consulting Group, Inc.
Research Associates & Analysts
RLS Consulting & Management Group, Inc.
Edward Stark Associates
Stone & Webster Mgmt. Consultants, Inc.
Transportation Industry Consultants, Inc.

E.48 COMMUNICATION

Anacapa Sciences, Inc.
Arthur Aschauer & Co., Inc.
Emory Ayers Associates
David N. Beach Associates, Inc.
C. L. Carter Jr. & Associates, Inc.
Cresheim Co., Inc.
Crickenberger Associates
Data Sciences, Inc.
Fensterstock & Co.
Frank K. Griesinger & Associates, Inc.
International Resource Development, Inc.
Jean Judge Associates, Inc.
The Kappa Group
Organizational Consulting Services
Purcell Consulting Associates, Inc.
Quay Associates
SAI
Silverman Consulting Services Ltd.
Space/Management Programs, Inc.
Stone & Webster Mgmt. Consultants, Inc.
Straehley Associates
Technomic Consultants
The Yankee Group

E.49 ELECTRIC, GAS & SANITARY SERVICES

James S. Baker Management Consultants, Inc.
David N. Beach Associates, Inc.
Cole & Associates
Data Systems Consultants
Gelb Consulting Group, Inc.
Duane L. Hile & Associates
Clinton P. Mott & Associates
Purcell Consulting Associates, Inc.
Resource Conservation Consultants
Resource Planning Associates, Inc.
F.R. Schwab & Associates
Stone & Webster Mgmt. Consultants, Inc.
Technomic Consultants
Temple, Barker & Sloane, Inc.
K.W. Tunnell Co., Inc.

F.00 WHOLESALE TRADE

The Austin Co.
Donald R. Booz & Associates, Inc.
Cambridge Research Institute
The Corporate Director Inc.
John deElorza Associates
Denmark Donovan & Oppel Inc.
Drake-Beam & Associates Inc.
Fuchs Associates
The Galaxy Organization
Garr Associates, Inc.
Glendinning Associates
Global Management Services, Inc.
E. G. Harper & Company, Inc.
Hickling-Johnston Ltd.
Legge Associates, Inc.
LWFW, Inc.
MacFarlane & Co., Inc.
Manley Management & Marketing Services Corp.
Martech Inc.
OBEX Consulting
PA International Management Consultants, Inc.
D.L. Paden & Associates
Riffe & Associates
SAM Associates, Inc.
Sanderhoff & Associates, Inc.
Science Management Corporation
System Planning Associates, Inc.
The Tanzi Organization
Technomic Consultants
D.W. Thomson & Associates
Trundle Consultants Inc.
Von Keyserling Consultants Ltd.
J.F. Ward Associates
Werner Associates, Inc.

F.50 WHOLESALE TRADE-DURABLE GOODS

Anderson/Roethle & Associates, Inc.
Joseph Auerbach
Bavier, Bulger & Goodyear, Inc.
The Center for Applied Management, Inc.
Coleman Consulting Inc.
Cresheim Co., Inc.
Dailey Consultants & Co.
Data Sciences, Inc.
Donovan, Zappala & Associates, Inc.
Dickey Dyer Management Consultants
Euramco Associates, Inc.
Walter Frederick Friedman & Co., Inc.
J. George Gross & Associates
Guenther Associates
H. J. Hansen Co.
Duane L. Hile & Associates
Infotek Corporation
Interplex Management Associates, Ltd.
The Kampmeier Group
Legge Associates, Inc.
Walter K. Levy Associates Inc.

Lawrence M. Matthews
Rich Nelson Associates
The Pace Consulting Group, Inc.
Permark Management Consultants, Inc.
S. Pullano Associates
Purcell Consulting Associates, Inc.
SAM Associates, Inc.
Irving Shaw & Associates
Teipel Associates Inc.
Norton Weber & Co.
John P. Weil & Company
Emanuel Weintraub Associates, Inc.

F.51 WHOLESALE TRADE-NONDURABLE GOODS

Anderson/Roethle & Associates, Inc.
Joseph Auerbach
Bavier, Bulger & Goodyear, Inc.
Bjorkman Associates
Coleman Consulting Inc.
Euramco Associates, Inc.
Walter Frederick Friedman & Co., Inc.
J. George Gross & Associates
Guenther Associates
Duane L. Hile & Associates
Infotek Corporation
Walter K. Levy Associates Inc.
Thomas Oland & Associates, Inc.
Outlook Associates
Purcell Consulting Associates, Inc.
Kurt Salmon Associates, Inc.
SAM Associates, Inc.
Senn-Delaney & Associates
John P. Weil & Company
Emanuel Weintraub Associates, Inc.

G.00 RETAIL TRADE

Barbrisons Management Systems, Inc.
Bedford-Post Associates, Inc.
Bickert, Browne, Coddington & Associates
Donald R. Booz & Associates, Inc.
Cambridge Research Institute
The Corporate Director Inc.
CPS Management Co.
Day & Zimmermann, Inc.
John deElorza Associates
Derrick & Associates, Inc.
Drake-Beam & Associates Inc.
Economics Research Associates
Employee Relations Consultants, Inc.
Euramco Associates, Inc.
Walter Frederick Friedman & Co., Inc.
The Galaxy Organization
Garr Associates, Inc.
Gladstone Associates
Glendinning Associates
Guenther Associates
Hickling-Johnston Ltd.
Jean Judge Associates, Inc.
LWFW, Inc.
MacFarlane & Co., Inc.
Management Horizons, Inc.
Marcept Consulting & Research
William H. Meyer & Associates, Inc.
Donald R. Miller
Organization Renewal, Inc.
ORU Group, Inc.
Project Associates, Inc.
Purcell Consulting Associates, Inc.
RLS Consulting & Management Group, Inc.
Kurt Salmon Associates, Inc.
Science Management Corporation
Senn-Delaney & Associates
Shycon Associates Inc.
The Tanzi Organization
Technomic Consultants

Temple, Barker & Sloane, Inc.
D.W. Thomson & Associates
Von Keyserling Consultants Ltd.
Wagner Systems, Inc.
J.F. Ward Associates
Werner Associates, Inc.

G.52 BUILDING, MATERIALS, HARDWARE, GARDEN SUPPLY, MOBILE HOME DEALERS

Anderson/Roethle & Associates, Inc.
Duane L. Hile & Associates
Robert Kahn & Associates
Walter K. Levy Associates Inc.
Management Horizons, Inc.
Martech Inc.
George S. May International Co.
Rich Nelson Associates
Neville & Currie Associates Inc.
The Pace Consulting Group, Inc.
Teipel Associates Inc.

G.53 GENERAL MERCHANDISE STORES

Joseph Auerbach
Barry & Co.
Bjorkman Associates
Michael Busler Group
Coleman Consulting Inc.
Crickenberger Associates
Edgar, Dunn & Conover Inc.
Fensterstock & Co.
Glendinning Associates
S. E. Hall & Co.
H. J. Hansen Co.
The Joynt Group, Inc.
Robert Kahn & Associates
The Kampmeier Group
Walter K. Levy Associates Inc.
Management Horizons, Inc.
Martech Inc.
Donald R. Miller
Profit-Improvement, Inc.
Wilson Seney, Inc.
Silverman Consulting Services Ltd.
Teipel Associates Inc.

G.54 FOOD STORES

Bjorkman Associates
The Croner Company
Fensterstock & Co.
Jack Frost & Associates
Frank N. Giampietro Associates, Inc.
Glendinning Associates
The Joynt Group, Inc.
Robert Kahn & Associates
Donald R. Miller
Outlook Associates
James H. Owens Associates, Inc.
SAI
Teipel Associates Inc.

G.55 AUTOMOTIVE DEALERS, GASOLINE SERVICE STATIONS

Gelb Consulting Group, Inc.
Duane L. Hile & Associates
C. H. Kline & Co., Inc.
Laughlin Associates
Bill Marcus & Associates, Inc.
Marpet Consultants, Inc.
George S. May International Co.
Neville & Currie Associates Inc.
Organization Consultants, Inc.

Organizational Consulting Services
Edward Stark Associates
System Planning Associates, Inc.
Teipel Associates Inc.

G.56 APPAREL & ACCESSORY STORES

Anderson/Roethle & Associates, Inc.
Coleman Consulting Inc.
Robert Kahn & Associates
Walter K. Levy Associates Inc.
Management Horizons, Inc.

G.57 FURNITURE, HOME FURNISHINGS, EQUIPMENT

Joseph Auerbach
International Management
Robert Kahn & Associates
The Kampmeier Group
Walter K. Levy Associates Inc.
Management Horizons, Inc.
Ross Associates, Inc.
Silverman Consulting Services Ltd.

G.58 EATING & DRINKING PLACES

Emory Ayers Associates
Joseph Shaw Chalfant
Equity Services Corporation
Fensterstock & Co.
Jack Frost & Associates
Frank N. Giampietro Associates, Inc.
Glendinning Associates
Hans & Associates, Inc.
Walter K. Levy Associates Inc.
George S. May International Co.
McCutcheon Associates NW
Teipel Associates Inc.

G.59 MISC RETAIL

BCMA Associates
Bjorkman Associates
Burgess Management Associates
C. L. Carter Jr. & Associates, Inc.
Robert Kahn & Associates
The Kampmeier Group
Laughlin Associates
Walter K. Levy Associates Inc.
Marpet Consultants, Inc.
Outlook Associates
James H. Owens Associates, Inc.
Silverman Consulting Services Ltd.
Teipel Associates Inc.

H.00 FINANCE, INSURANCE & REAL ESTATE

Barbrisons Management Systems, Inc.
Cambridge Research Institute
Crickenberger Associates
Dickson Associates
Drake-Beam & Associates Inc.
Economics Research Associates
Employee Relations Consultants, Inc.
Euramco Associates, Inc.
Fuchs Associates
Gilbert Commonwealth
Michael R. Gingold Associates, Inc.
Glendinning Associates
Hickling-Johnston Ltd.
William H. Hill Associates, Inc.
IMS Systems Corp.
Interplex Management Associates, Ltd.
Robert E. Koogler

LWFW, Inc.
MacFarlane & Co., Inc.
Robert E. Nolan Co., Inc.
Organization Renewal, Inc.
PA International Management Consultants, Inc.
D.L. Paden & Associates
Project Associates, Inc.
Purcell Consulting Associates, Inc.
Reel/Grobman & Associates
Science Management Corporation
Space/Management Programs, Inc.
The Tanzi Organization
Technomic Consultants
Von Keyserling Consultants Ltd.

H.60 BANKING

Anderson/Roethle & Associates, Inc.
Arthur Aschauer & Co., Inc.
Emory Ayers Associates
James S. Baker Management Consultants, Inc.
Bavier, Bulger & Goodyear, Inc.
David N. Beach Associates, Inc.
Bedford-Post Associates, Inc.
Bickert, Browne, Coddington & Associates
Serge A. Birn Co.
Cexec, Inc.
Cole & Associates
The Croner Company
Dailey Consultants & Co.
Day & Zimmermann, Inc.
John deElorza Associates
Derrick & Associates, Inc.
Edgar, Dunn & Conover Inc.
George D. Edwards & Co., Inc.
Financial Concepts Inc.
Elmer Fox, Westheimer & Co.
Gelb Consulting Group, Inc.
Glendinning Associates
S. E. Hall & Co.
H. J. Hansen Co.
Paul Harthorne Associates
International Resource Development, Inc.
Johnson, Pratt & Stewart
The Joynt Group, Inc.
Jean Judge Associates, Inc.
Keenan, Wheeler & Bowman
Manplan Consultants
Marcept Consulting & Research
H.B. Maynard & Co.
William H. Meyer & Associates, Inc.
Montgomery & Associates, Inc.
Robert E. Nolan Co., Inc.
Northern Consultants Inc.
Organization Consultants, Inc.
ORU Group, Inc.
The Pace Consulting Group, Inc.
Profit Planning Associates
Profit-Improvement, Inc.
Questor Associates
RLS Consulting & Management Group, Inc.
Senn-Delaney & Associates
SIAR, Inc.
Space/Management Programs, Inc.
Systema Corporation
Temple, Barker & Sloane, Inc.
Ten Eyck Associates
TMI Systems Corp.

H.61 CREDIT AGENCIES OTHER THAN BANKS

Bickert, Browne, Coddington & Associates
Edgar, Dunn & Conover Inc.
Gelb Consulting Group, Inc.
S. E. Hall & Co.
Johnson, Pratt & Stewart
Keenan, Wheeler & Bowman

Neville & Currie Associates Inc.
TMI Systems Corp.

H.62 SECURITY & COMMODITY BROKERS, DEALERS, EXCHANGES & SERVICES

A.M. Lederer & Co., Inc.
William T. Lorenz & Co.
Montgomery & Associates, Inc.
Quay Associates
RLS Consulting & Management Group, Inc.
Space/Management Programs, Inc.
Systema Corporation
Temple, Barker & Sloane, Inc.
TMI Systems Corp.

H.63 INSURANCE

Bavier, Bulger & Goodyear, Inc.
David N. Beach Associates, Inc.
Serge A. Birn Co.
Birnberg & Associates
Cole & Associates
Compass Management Group, Inc.
Cresheim Co., Inc.
Data Sciences, Inc.
Day & Zimmermann, Inc.
Denmark Donovan & Oppel Inc.
Edgar, Dunn & Conover Inc.
Elmer Fox, Westheimer & Co.
Hales & Associates, Inc.
Insurance Management Group, Inc.
The Joynt Group, Inc.
Jean Judge Associates, Inc.
The Kampmeier Group
Laughlin Associates
Montgomery & Associates, Inc.
Rich Nelson Associates
Robert E. Nolan Co., Inc.
Profit-Improvement, Inc.
RLS Consulting & Management Group, Inc.
R. Shriver Associates
Space/Management Programs, Inc.
Edward Stark Associates
Systema Corporation
Temple, Barker & Sloane, Inc.
Ten Eyck Associates
TMI Systems Corp.
Werner Associates, Inc.

H.64 INSURANCE AGENTS, BROKERS & SERVICE

Joseph Auerbach
Bedford-Post Associates, Inc.
Birnberg & Associates
Hales & Associates, Inc.
Hans & Associates, Inc.
Insurance Management Group, Inc.
Laughlin Associates
Montgomery & Associates, Inc.
Profit-Improvement, Inc.
Systema Corporation
Ten Eyck Associates

H.65 REAL ESTATE

Anderson/Roethle & Associates, Inc.
Emory Ayers Associates
Birnberg & Associates
Michael Busler Group
Joseph Shaw Chalfant
Coleman Consulting Inc.
The Croner Company
John deElorza Associates
Donovan, Zappala & Associates, Inc.

Equity Services Corporation
The Galaxy Organization
Michael R. Gingold Associates, Inc.
Gladstone Associates
Hans & Associates, Inc.
Laughlin Associates
Normandale Associates Inc.
Outlook Associates
Questor Associates
Senn-Delaney & Associates

H.66 COMBINATIONS OF REAL ESTATE, INSURANCE, LOANS, LAW OFFICES

Donovan, Zappala & Associates, Inc.
Gladstone Associates
The Kampmeier Group
Laughlin Associates
Thomas Oland & Associates, Inc.
Space/Management Programs, Inc.

H.67 HOLDING & OTHER INVESTMENT OFFICES

James S. Baker Management Consultants, Inc.
N.C. Berkowitz & Co.
Bickert, Browne, Coddington & Associates
Cole & Associates
The Croner Company
Denmark Donovan & Oppel Inc.
Thomas A. Faulhaber
The Galaxy Organization
Michael R. Gingold Associates, Inc.
Gladstone Associates
Profit Planning Associates
Quay Associates
Space/Management Programs, Inc.

I.00 SERVICES

Emory Ayers Associates
Bedford-Post Associates, Inc.
Donald R. Booz & Associates, Inc.
Cexec, Inc.
The Corporate Director Inc.
CPS Management Co.
James W. Davidson Co., Inc.
John deElorza Associates
Dickson Associates
Dielman Consultants, Inc.
Drake-Beam & Associates Inc.
Economics Research Associates
Employee Relations Consultants, Inc.
Euramco Associates, Inc.
Fuchs Associates
Michael R. Gingold Associates, Inc.
Glendinning Associates
Guenther Associates
Hans & Associates, Inc.
Hickling-Johnston Ltd.
William H. Hill Associates, Inc.
IMS Systems Corp.
Interplex Management Associates, Ltd.
The Joynt Group, Inc.
Robert E. Koogler
LWFW, Inc.
MacFarlane & Co., Inc.
Manley Management & Marketing Services Corp.
Marpet Consultants, Inc.
McCormack & Associates
Robert E. Nolan Co., Inc.
Organization Renewal, Inc.
D.L. Paden & Associates
Project Associates, Inc.
Purcell Consulting Associates, Inc.
Reel/Grobman & Associates
Kurt Salmon Associates, Inc.

Science Management Corporation
Silverman Consulting Services Ltd.
The Tanzi Organization
Technomic Consultants
D.W. Thomson & Associates
Von Keyserling Consultants Ltd.

I.70 HOTELS, ROOMING HOUSES, CAMPS & OTHER LODGING PLACES

David N. Beach Associates, Inc.
Derrick & Associates, Inc.
Edgar, Dunn & Conover Inc.
Equity Services Corporation
Freeman, Penrose & Kajinura, Ltd.
Frank N. Giampietro Associates, Inc.
Gladstone Associates
Hans & Associates, Inc.
Harley, Little Associates Inc.
Harris, Kerr, Forster & Co.
William T. Lorenz & Co.
McCutcheon Associates NW
Montgomery & Associates, Inc.
Clinton P. Mott & Associates
ORU Group, Inc.
Shycon Associates Inc.
SIAR, Inc.
Sno Engineering/Resource Management Inc.
J.F. Ward Associates

I.72 PERSONAL SERVICES

Murray Dropkin & Co.
The Galaxy Organization
Hans & Associates, Inc.
The Kampmeier Group
Montgomery & Associates, Inc.
James H. Owens Associates, Inc.

I.73 BUSINESS SERVICES

Altman & Weil, Inc.
The Billings Group
Birnberg & Associates
Burgess Management Associates
CMI Investment Corp.
Coxe Associates, Inc.
James W. Davidson Co., Inc.
Donovan, Zappala & Associates, Inc.
Murray Dropkin & Co.
Fogel & Associates, Inc.
Michael R. Gingold Associates, Inc.
Hales & Associates, Inc.
S. E. Hall & Co.
Hans & Associates, Inc.
H. J. Hansen Co.
Health-Care Management Services
International Resource Development, Inc.
The Kampmeier Group
The Kappa Group
Kennedy & Kennedy, Inc.
Laughlin Associates
William T. Lorenz & Co.
William J. Mager & Associates
Marcept Consulting & Research
Martech Inc.
E. Gilbert Mathews, Inc.
McCutcheon Associates NW
Moeller Associates
Montgomery & Associates, Inc.
Organizational Consulting Services
Professional Practice Consultants, Inc.
Professional Services Int'l.
RLS Consulting & Management Group, Inc.
SAI
Sno Engineering/Resource Management Inc.
Space/Management Programs, Inc.

Edward Stark Associates
Synergy Corporation
Technology Marketing Group Ltd.
Ten Eyck Associates
Norton Weber & Co.

I.75 AUTOMOTIVE REPAIRS, SERVICES & GARAGES

Burgess Management Associates
Duane L. Hile & Associates
Legge Associates, Inc.
Bill Marcus & Associates, Inc.
Clinton P. Mott & Associates
Neville & Currie Associates Inc.
Edward Stark Associates

I.76 MISC REPAIR SERVICES

Donovan, Zappala & Associates, Inc.
Thomas Dowdell/Associates
E. G. Harper & Company, Inc.
Riffe & Associates
Wm. E. Sandman Associates Co.

I.78 MOTION PICTURES

Dailey Consultants & Co.
Shycon Associates Inc.

I.79 AMUSEMENT & RECREATION SERVICES, EXCEPT MOTION PICTURES

Bartow Associates
James W. Davidson Co., Inc.
Equity Services Corporation
Frank N. Giampietro Associates, Inc.
Hans & Associates, Inc.
Harley, Little Associates Inc.
Questor Associates
Sno Engineering/Resource Management Inc.

I.80 HEALTH SERVICES

Bartow Associates
Birch & Davis Associates, Inc.
Jack Brown & Associates, Inc.
Cambridge Research Institute
Centaur Associates, Inc.
Data Sciences, Inc.
Day & Zimmermann, Inc.
Dielman Consultants, Inc.
Donovan, Zappala & Associates, Inc.
Murray Dropkin & Co.
Dickey Dyer Management Consultants
Foussard Associates
Elmer Fox, Westheimer & Co.
Walter Frederick Friedman & Co., Inc.
Fuchs Associates
W. L. Ganong Co.
Gelb Consulting Group, Inc.
Gladstone Associates
S. E. Hall & Co.
Harley, Little Associates Inc.
Health-Care Management Services
Institutional Strategy Associates, Inc.
J. Lloyd Johnson Associates
Kendrick & Co.
Kenneth Associates
Warren King & Associates, Inc.
Michael E. Kurtz Associates
Legge Associates, Inc.
Carl F. Lutz
Macro Systems, Inc.
Management & Marketing

Manplan Consultants
Marcept Consulting & Research
Martech Inc.
MDC Systems Corp.
Medical Management Associates
Medicus Systems Corporation
Moshman Associates, Inc.
Clinton P. Mott & Associates
Robert E. Nolan Co., Inc.
Normandale Associates Inc.
Oppenheimer Associates
James H. Owens Associates, Inc.
RLS Consulting & Management Group, Inc.
Ryan Advisors, Inc.
Samuelson & Co.
John G. Steinle & Associates
Summerour & Associates, Inc.
Technology Marketing Group Ltd.
Trebor Health Associates
TriBrook Group, Inc.
Wagner Systems, Inc.
Norton Weber & Co.
Werner Associates, Inc.

I.81 LEGAL SERVICES

Altman & Weil, Inc.
Cambridge Research Institute
Daniel J. Cantor & Co., Inc.
Irving A. Delloff
Murray Dropkin & Co.
Elmer Fox, Westheimer & Co.
The Kampmeier Group
Kendrick & Co.
Moshman Associates, Inc.
System Planning Associates, Inc.
John P. Weil & Company

I.82 EDUCATIONAL SERVICES

Anacapa Sciences, Inc.
Anderson/Roethle & Associates, Inc.
Associated Consultants in Education
Bartow Associates
BCMA Associates
David N. Beach Associates, Inc.
Jack Brown & Associates, Inc.
C. L. Carter Jr. & Associates, Inc.
Compass Management Group, Inc.
Irving A. Delloff
Murray Dropkin & Co.
W. L. Ganong Co.
Harley, Little Associates Inc.
Institutional Strategy Associates, Inc.
The Kappa Group
Kendrick & Co.
Warren King & Associates, Inc.
Michael E. Kurtz Associates
Laughlin Associates
A.M. Lederer & Co., Inc.
Legge Associates, Inc.
Carl F. Lutz
Macro Systems, Inc.
Management Horizons, Inc.
Martech Inc.
McElrath & Associates
McManis Associates, Inc.
Clinton P. Mott & Associates
Robert E. Nolan Co., Inc.
Outlook Associates
The Pace Consulting Group, Inc.
Resource Conservation Consultants
Shycon Associates Inc.
Ten Eyck Associates
John P. Weil & Company

I.83 SOCIAL SERVICES

Anacapa Sciences, Inc.
Bartow Associates
Compass Management Group, Inc.
Murray Dropkin & Co.
Dickey Dyer Management Consultants
Health-Care Management Services
Institutional Strategy Associates, Inc.
Kendrick & Co.
Warren King & Associates, Inc.
Macro Systems, Inc.
Norris & Elliott, Inc.

I.84 MUSEUMS, ART GALLERIES, BOTANICAL & ZOOLOGICAL GARDENS

Institutional Strategy Associates, Inc.
Quay Associates

I.86 MEMBERSHIP ORGANIZATIONS

James S. Baker Management Consultants, Inc.
David N. Beach Associates, Inc.
Bess Management Services, Inc.
Cambridge Research Institute
Data Sciences, Inc.
Day & Zimmermann, Inc.
Murray Dropkin & Co.
Equity Services Corporation
Fairbanks Associates, Inc.
Institutional Strategy Associates, Inc.
Kendrick & Co.
Laughlin Associates
Macro Systems, Inc.
Martech Inc.
McManis Associates, Inc.
Donald R. Miller
Moeller Associates
Montgomery & Associates, Inc.
Outlook Associates
Professional Practice Consultants, Inc.
RLS Consulting & Management Group, Inc.
R. Shriver Associates
Norton Weber & Co.

I.89 MISC SERVICES

Joseph Auerbach
S. E. Hall & Co.
Hoyles Associates Ltd.
The Kampmeier Group
The Kappa Group
Montgomery & Associates, Inc.
SAI
System Planning Associates, Inc.
Norton Weber & Co.
CMI Investment Corp.
Summerour & Associates, Inc.

J.00 PUBLIC ADMINISTRATION

American Management Systems
Barbrisons Management Systems, Inc.
Bedford-Post Associates, Inc.
Cexec, Inc.
Compass Management Group, Inc.
The Corporate Director Inc.
Decision Sciences Corporation
John deElorza Associates
Drake-Beam & Associates Inc.
Economics Research Associates
Employee Relations Consultants, Inc.
Gilbert Commonwealth
Gladstone Associates
Government Sales Consultants, Inc.
Hickling-Johnston Ltd.

IMS Systems Corp.
Interplex Management Associates, Ltd.
The Joynt Group, Inc.
Robert E. Koogler
LWFW, Inc.
Organization Renewal, Inc.
PA International Management Consultants, Inc.
Project Associates, Inc.
Purcell Consulting Associates, Inc.
Science Management Corporation
Silverman Consulting Services Ltd.
Summerour & Associates, Inc.
Von Keyserling Consultants Ltd.
McCutcheon Associates NW
McCutcheon Associates NW

J.91 EXECUTIVE, LEGISLATIVE, & GENERAL GOVERNMENT, EXCEPT FINANCE

Altman & Weil, Inc.
Anacapa Sciences, Inc.
Arthur Aschauer & Co., Inc.
James S. Baker Management Consultants, Inc.
Barnett & Engel
Birch & Davis Associates, Inc.
C. L. Carter Jr. & Associates, Inc.
Centaur Associates, Inc.
Compass Management Group, Inc.
Data Sciences, Inc.
Day & Zimmermann, Inc.
Decision Studies Group
Dickson Associates
Murray Dropkin & Co.
Edgar, Dunn & Conover Inc.
Guenther Associates
J. W. Haslett & Associates
Health-Care Management Services
Kendrick & Co.
Warren King & Associates, Inc.
Michael E. Kurtz Associates
Legge Associates, Inc.
Carl F. Lutz
Macro Systems, Inc.
McManis Associates, Inc.
Moeller Associates
OBEX Consulting
Organizational Consulting Services
D.L. Paden & Associates
Resource Planning Associates, Inc.
Riecks Postal Consultants
Samuelson & Co.

J.92 JUSTICE, PUBLIC ORDER, & SAFETY

Altman & Weil, Inc.
Anacapa Sciences, Inc.
Compass Management Group, Inc.
Dailey Consultants & Co.
Data Sciences, Inc.
S. E. Hall & Co.
Kendrick & Co.
Warren King & Associates, Inc.
Legge Associates, Inc.
Macro Systems, Inc.
McManis Associates, Inc.
Moshman Associates, Inc.

J.93 PUBLIC FINANCE, TAXATION, MONETARY POLICY

Derrick & Associates, Inc.
Murray Dropkin & Co.
Elmer Fox, Westheimer & Co.
J. W. Haslett & Associates
Health-Care Management Services
Warren King & Associates, Inc.
McManis Associates, Inc.

Questor Associates
TMI Systems Corp.

J.94 ADMIN OF HUMAN RESOURCES PROGRAMS

Anacapa Sciences, Inc.
Bartow Associates
Birch & Davis Associates, Inc.
Jack Brown & Associates, Inc.
Cole & Associates
Compass Management Group, Inc.
Decision Studies Group
Derrick & Associates, Inc.
Murray Dropkin & Co.
Dickey Dyer Management Consultants
The Galaxy Organization
W. L. Ganong Co.
Kendrick & Co.
Warren King & Associates, Inc.
Michael E. Kurtz Associates
Legge Associates, Inc.
Carl F. Lutz
Macro Systems, Inc.
Arthur Manning Associates
H.B. Maynard & Co.
McManis Associates, Inc.
Moeller Associates
Moshman Associates, Inc.
Organizational Consulting Services
Problem Solvers for Industry

J.95 ADMIN OF ENVIRONMENTAL QUALITY & HOUSING PROGRAMS

James S. Baker Management Consultants, Inc.
Cole & Associates
Compass Management Group, Inc.
Dickey Dyer Management Consultants
Warren King & Associates, Inc.

William T. Lorenz & Co.
McManis Associates, Inc.
William H. Meyer & Associates, Inc.
Resource Conservation Consultants

J.96 ADMIN OF ECONOMIC PROGRAMS

Barnett & Engel
Burgess Management Associates
Centaur Associates, Inc.
Cresheim Co., Inc.
Day & Zimmermann, Inc.
Denmark Donovan & Oppel Inc.
Kendrick & Co.
Warren King & Associates, Inc.
Legge Associates, Inc.
Macro Systems, Inc.
H.B. Maynard & Co.
McManis Associates, Inc.
Moshman Associates, Inc.
OBEX Consulting

J.97 NATIONAL SECURITY & INT'L AFFAIRS

Anacapa Sciences, Inc.
Birch & Davis Associates, Inc.
Business Psychology International
Guenther Associates
OBEX Consulting

K.00 NONCLASSIFIABLE ESTABLISHMENTS

Barbrisons Management Systems, Inc.
Bjorkman Associates
D. Dietrich Associates, Inc.
Laughlin Associates
A.M. Lederer & Co., Inc.
Ten Eyck Associates

Geographical Index

A. T. Kearney, Inc.
Klein Behavioral Science Consultants, Inc.
Rex Land & Associates, Inc.
Laventhol & Horwath
Marketing & Systems Development Corporation
H.B. Maynard & Co.
McKinsey & Co., Inc.
Paterson & Co.
Peat, Marwick, Mitchell & Co.
Price Waterhouse & Co.
Professional Services Int'l.
Profit-Improvement, Inc.
Reel/Grobman & Associates
Senn-Delaney & Associates
Standards, International Inc.
The THinc. Group Inc.
Touche Ross & Co.
Towers, Perrin, Forster & Crosby
Robert M. Wald & Associates
Wofac Co.
Arthur Young & Company

Marina Del Rey
Case & Co., Inc.

Menlo Park
The Boston Consulting Group, Inc.
Kirk Knight & Co., Inc.
SAI
SRI International

Monterey
Bostrom Management Corporation

Newport Beach
Delta Group, Inc.
Fogel & Associates, Inc.
Laventhol & Horwath
Rath & Strong, Inc.
Reel/Grobman & Associates
SAI
Warren, McVeigh & Griffin

Northridge
Dailey Consultants & Co.

Oakland
Arthur Andersen & Co.
Coleman Consulting Inc.
Craig/Cutten & Wollman, Inc.
Elmer Fox, Westheimer & Co.
Seidman & Seidman
Arthur Young & Company

Orange
Seidman & Seidman

Orinda
John P. Weil & Company

Palo Alto
Louis A. Allen Associates, Inc.
Kensington Management Consultants, Inc.
Wofac Co.

Pasadena
Elmer Fox, Westheimer & Co.

Rancho Palos Verdes
Thomas Dowdell/Associates

Rolling Hills Estates
E & T Associates

Sacramento
Hurdman & Cranstoun
Arthur Young & Company

San Diego
Arthur Andersen & Co.

Michael R. Gingold Associates, Inc.
Laventhol & Horwath
Seidman & Seidman
Thompson, Ferguson & Associates
Arthur Young & Company

San Francisco
Altman & Weil, Inc.
American Management Systems
Arthur Andersen & Co.
BCMA Associates
N.C. Berkowitz & Co.
Birnberg & Associates
Booz-Allen & Hamilton, Inc.
Earl D. Brodie & Associates
Daniel J. Cantor & Co., Inc.
Case & Co., Inc.
Coopers & Lybrand
Cresap, McCormick & Paget, Inc.
Deloitte Haskins & Sells
Economics Research Associates
Edgar, Dunn & Conover Inc.
The Emerson Consultants, Inc.
W. L. Ganong Co.
Gottfried Consultants Inc.
A. S. Hansen, Inc.
Hay Associates
Hurdman & Cranstoun
A. T. Kearney, Inc.
Kenneth Associates
Lester B. Knight & Associates, Inc.
Rex Land & Associates, Inc.
Laventhol & Horwath
Arthur D. Little, Inc.
Management Analysis Center, Inc.
Management Decision Systems, Inc.
Management Horizons, Inc.
George S. May International Co.
McKinsey & Co., Inc.
M & M Protection Consultants
Rich Nelson Associates
Oatman Associates, Inc.
Price Waterhouse & Co.
Questor Associates
Reel/Grobman & Associates
Resource Planning Associates, Inc.
Seidman & Seidman
Senn-Delaney & Associates
The Tanzi Organization
Thompson, Ferguson & Associates
Towers, Perrin, Forster & Crosby
Warren, McVeigh & Griffin
Yaney Associates
Arthur Young & Company

San Jose
Arthur Andersen & Co.
Arthur Young & Company

San Marino
Aiken, Madden & Associates

Santa Ana
Arthur Andersen & Co.
Curt Deckert Associates, Inc.
Arthur Young & Company

Santa Barbara
Anacapa Sciences, Inc.
Freeman Associates
Straehley Associates
Tempo

Santa Clara
Donald B. Miller

Santa Monica
Rosenau Consulting Co.
Organization Resource Counselors, Inc.

Sherman Oaks
Seidman & Seidman

Stockton
Elmer Fox, Westheimer & Co.

Sunset Beach
Michael E. Kurtz Associates

Torrance
Organizational Directions, Inc.
Kurt Salmon Associates, Inc.

Walnut Creek
TriBrook Group, Inc.

COLORADO

Aspen
Sno Engineering/Resource Management Inc.

Colorado Springs
Elmer Fox, Westheimer & Co.

Denver
William B. Arnold Associates, Inc.
Bickert, Browne, Coddington & Associates
Coopers & Lybrand
R. Danner, Inc.
Deloitte Haskins & Sells
Ernst & Whinney
Elmer Fox, Westheimer & Co.
Government Sales Consultants, Inc.
A. S. Hansen, Inc.
Harbridge House Inc.
Lovejoy Management Consultants
Peat, Marwick, Mitchell & Co.
Price Waterhouse & Co.
Seidman & Seidman
Stone & Webster Mgmt. Consultants, Inc.
Touche Ross & Co.
Weiss & Associates
Arthur Young & Company

Grand Junction
Elmer Fox, Westheimer & Co.

Littleton
Ten Eyck Associates

CONNECTICUT

Bristol
JMG Associates Ltd.

Brookfield
Frederick C. Decker Co., Inc.

Darien
J. W. Haslett & Associates
James B. Kobak, Inc.
Samuel F. Leigh Associates, Inc.
Risk Planning Group, Inc.

East Haddam
Quay Associates

Enfield
The Product Integrity Co.
Wagner Systems, Inc.

Essex
Snyder Associates, Inc.

Fairfield
MRP Associates

Greenwich
Gemar Associates
Manley Management & Marketing Services Corp.
Frank B. Manley & Co.
Norris & Elliott, Inc.
Rogers & Co.
Welling & Woodard

Guilford
Aquatec International, Inc.
E. Gilbert Mathews, Inc.

Hartford
Arthur Andersen & Co.
Ernst & Whinney
Marketing & Systems Development Corporation
H.B. Maynard & Co.
The Pace Consulting Group, Inc.
Price Waterhouse & Co.
Arthur Young & Company

Manchester
Dorian Shainin Consultant, Inc.

New Canaan
Birch & Davis Associates, Inc.
International Resource Development, Inc.
Robert S. Jeffries, Jr.
Montgomery & Associates, Inc.

New Haven
Bavier, Bulger & Goodyear, Inc.

Old Greenwich
David Caulkins Associates
Roberts Associates

Sherman
Ruxton Associates

Simsbury
McLean Associates
Robert E. Nolan Co., Inc.

Stamford
Arthur Andersen & Co.
Case & Co., Inc.
Insurance Management Group, Inc.
Kensington Management Consultants, Inc.
McKinsey & Co., Inc.
The Personnel Laboratory, Inc.
Robert H. Schaffer & Associates
Arthur Young & Company

Weatogue
Charles L. Hoffman, Inc.

West Hartford
John O. Morris Associates

Westport
Barnett & Engel
Glendinning Associates
R.J. Sweeney Associates

Wilton
Permark Management Consultants, Inc.

D.C.

Washington
Arthur Andersen & Co.
Applied Leadership Technologies, Inc.
BCMA Associates
Blessing/White Inc.
Booz-Allen & Hamilton, Inc.
Bostrom Management Corporation

Business Psychology International
Centaur Associates, Inc.
Coopers & Lybrand
Cresap, McCormick & Paget, Inc.
Datamatics Management Services, Inc.
Day & Zimmermann, Inc.
Decision Studies Group
Deloitte Haskins & Sells
Drake-Beam & Associates Inc.
Economics Research Associates
Elmer Fox, Westheimer & Co.
Gladstone Associates
A. S. Hansen, Inc.
Harbridge House Inc.
Hay Associates
William E. Hill & Co., Inc.
A. T. Kearney, Inc.
Kendrick & Co.
Virginia Knauer & Associates, Inc.
Lester B. Knight & Associates, Inc.
Arthur D. Little, Inc.
William J. Mager & Associates
Management Analysis Center, Inc.
McKinsey & Co., Inc.
McManis Associates, Inc.
Moshman Associates, Inc.
MWS Consultants, Inc.
Organization Resource Counselors, Inc.
James S. Pepitone & Associates, Inc.
Price Waterhouse & Co.
Project Associates, Inc.
Ransom & Casazza, Inc.
Resource Planning Associates, Inc.
Ryan Advisors, Inc.
Science Management Corporation
Seidman & Seidman
R. Shriver Associates
Stanley Consultants, Inc.
Temple, Barker & Sloane, Inc.
Tempo
The THinc. Group Inc.
TMI Systems Corp.
Touche Ross & Co.
Towers, Perrin, Forster & Crosby
Washington Nichibei Consultants

DELAWARE

Frankford
MAS International, Ltd.

FLORIDA

Ernst & Whinney

Cocoa Beach
McGinnis Associates

Coral Gables
Laventhol & Horwath

Coral Springs
The Kappa Group

Fort Lauderdale
Arthur Andersen & Co.
Serge A. Birn Co.
Joseph Chanko Associates
GlennCo Services Inc.
Louis A. Hradesky

Ft. Lauderdale
Ernst & Whinney

Jacksonville
Communication Innovation, Inc.

Ernst & Whinney
William H. Hill Associates, Inc.
Arthur Young & Company

Miami
Arthur Andersen & Co.
Coopers & Lybrand
Deloitte Haskins & Sells
Elmer Fox, Westheimer & Co.
Gladstone Associates
Peat, Marwick, Mitchell & Co.
Price Waterhouse & Co.
Seidman & Seidman
Touche Ross & Co.
Arthur Young & Company

Miami Beach
Shaw Communications Consultants

Orlando
Arthur Andersen & Co.
Economics Research Associates
Seidman & Seidman
Arthur Young & Company

Sarasota
Alan Negus Associates, Inc.

Tallahassee
Associated Consultants in Education

Tampa
Arthur Andersen & Co.
Barbrisons Management Systems, Inc.
A. S. Hansen, Inc.
Laventhol & Horwath
Seidman & Seidman
Sperry-Boom of Florida, Inc.
Towers, Perrin, Forster & Crosby
Arthur Young & Company

Tarpon Springs
Anson, Lee, Rector & Associates

Winter Park
Assessment Designs, Inc.

GEORGIA

Atlanta
Arthur Andersen & Co.
Theodore Barry & Associates
A. Val Bradley Associates, Inc.
Charles Brooks Associates, Inc.
Coopers & Lybrand
Dawcon
Deloitte Haskins & Sells
Equity Services Corporation
Ernst & Whinney
Elmer Fox, Westheimer & Co.
Garr Associates, Inc.
A. S. Hansen, Inc.
Hay Associates
Peter Lambros & Associates
Laventhol & Horwath
MacFarlane & Co., Inc.
Management Campus, Inc.
McKinsey & Co., Inc.
MWS Consultants, Inc.
Peat, Marwick, Mitchell & Co.
James S. Pepitone & Associates, Inc.
Price Waterhouse & Co.
RLS Consulting & Management Group, Inc.
Kurt Salmon Associates, Inc.
Seidman & Seidman
Henry Sherry Associates, Inc.
Standards, International Inc.
Stanley Consultants, Inc.

Stone & Webster Mgmt. Consultants, Inc.
Summerour & Associates, Inc.
Touche Ross & Co.
Towers, Perrin, Forster & Crosby
Wofac Co.
Arthur Young & Company

Columbus
Ernst & Whinney
A. S. Hansen, Inc.

Decatur
Purcell Consulting Associates, Inc.

Gainesville
International Management

Stone Mountain
Henry Jordan & Associates

HAWAII

Honolulu
CMI Investment Corp.
Deloitte Haskins & Sells
Ernst & Whinney
Freeman, Penrose & Kajinura, Ltd.
Arthur Young & Company

IDAHO

Boise
Arthur Andersen & Co.
Ernst & Whinney
Elmer Fox, Westheimer & Co.
Learned & Mahn
Marcept Consulting & Research

ILLINOIS

Carbondale
Laventhol & Horwath

Chicago
Louis A. Allen Associates, Inc.
American Management Systems
Arthur Andersen & Co.
Theodore Barry & Associates
BCMA Associates
Bess Management Services, Inc.
Birnberg & Associates
Blessing/White Inc.
Donald R. Booz & Associates, Inc.
The Boston Consulting Group, Inc.
Bostrom Management Corporation
Jack Brown & Associates, Inc.
Case & Co., Inc.
Coopers & Lybrand
Cresap, McCormick & Paget, Inc.
Dallmeyer & Co., Inc.
Day & Zimmermann, Inc.
Deloitte Haskins & Sells
Distribution Projects, Inc.
Drake Sheahan/Stewart Dougall Inc.
Economics Research Associates
Ernst & Whinney
Fensterstock & Co.
Fenvessy Associates, Inc.
Elmer Fox, Westheimer & Co.
George E. Frankel & Associates
Hales & Associates, Inc.
A. S. Hansen, Inc.
Harbridge House Inc.
Hay Associates
Robert H. Hayes & Associates, Inc.
Daniel D. Howard Associates, Inc.
Hurdman & Cranstoun

Interplex Management Associates, Ltd.
Isaacs Associates
William Karp Consulting Co., Inc.
William Kather Associates, Inc.
A. T. Kearney, Inc.
Warren King & Associates, Inc.
Lester B. Knight & Associates, Inc.
Peter Lambros & Associates
Laventhol & Horwath
Management Analysis Center, Inc.
Manplan Consultants
Marketing & Systems Development Corporation
McKinsey & Co., Inc.
M & M Protection Consultants
MWS Consultants, Inc.
Peat, Marwick, Mitchell & Co.
Price Waterhouse & Co.
Albert Ramond & Assoc., Inc.
SAM Associates, Inc.
Sanderhoff & Associates, Inc.
Seidman & Seidman
Space/Management Programs, Inc.
Standards, International Inc.
Stanley Consultants, Inc.
Stone Management Corporation
Systema Corporation
Technomic Consultants
The THinc. Group Inc.
Touche Ross & Co.
Towers, Perrin, Forster & Crosby
K.W. Tunnell Co., Inc.
Arthur Young & Company

Cleveland
Hales & Associates, Inc.

Des Plaines
Drake-Beam & Associates Inc.
Patton Consultants, Inc.
John Sheridan Associates, Inc.
Technology Marketing Group Ltd.
Wofac Co.

Elgin
Elmer Fox, Westheimer & Co.

Evanston
The Austin Co.
W. E. Brennan & Co., Inc.
Humber, Mundie & McClary
Medicus Systems Corporation
OBEX Consulting

Lake Bluff
A. S. Hansen, Inc.

Lake Forest
E. G. Harper & Company, Inc.

Marquette
Ernst & Whinney

Northbrook
Harbridge House Inc.

Northfield
J. Lloyd Johnson Associates
Allen Levis Organization, Inc.

Oak Brook
H.B. Maynard & Co.
TriBrook Group, Inc.

Oakbrook
Welling & Woodard

Palos Heights
Dielman Consultants, Inc.

Park Forest
Abbott, Langer & Associates

Park Ridge
H. J. Hansen Co.
George S. May International Co.

Peoria
Alvin R. Haerr & Co.

Rockford
Ingersoll Engineers Inc.
Thomas P. Mahoney Associates
Seidman & Seidman

Roselle
Laughlin Associates

Schiller Park
Rath & Strong, Inc.

Winnetka
Organization Renewal, Inc.

INDIANA

Evansville
Seidman & Seidman

Fort Wayne
J. P. Cavanaugh & Associates
Ernst & Whinney

Ft. Wayne
Wofac Co.

Indianapolis
Arthur Andersen & Co.
Data Sciences, Inc.
Ernst & Whinney
Loer & Bradford Consultants, Inc.
Price Waterhouse & Co.
Stanley Consultants, Inc.
Wagner Systems, Inc.
Arthur Young & Company

New Albany
Joseph Shaw Chalfant

South Bend
R. L. French & Company, Inc.

West LaFayette
Organizational Consultants, Inc.

IOWA

Des Moines
Batten, Batten, Hudson & Swab, Inc.
Ernst & Whinney
Arthur Young & Company

Fort Dodge
Aviation Consulting Enterprises, Inc.

Muscatine
Stanley Consultants, Inc.

KANSAS

Dodge City
Elmer Fox, Westheimer & Co.

El Dorado
Elmer Fox, Westheimer & Co.

Fairway
Quorum, Ltd.

Hays
Elmer Fox, Westheimer & Co.

Leawood
Arneson & Co.

Russell
Elmer Fox, Westheimer & Co.

Shawnee Mission
Woodward Associates

Topeka
Elmer Fox, Westheimer & Co.

Wichita
Elmer Fox, Westheimer & Co.
A. S. Hansen, Inc.

KENTUCKY

Lexington
Ernst & Whinney

Louisville
Serge A. Birn Co.
Coopers & Lybrand
Ernst & Whinney
Arthur Young & Company

LOUISIANA

Baton Rouge
Ernst & Whinney
Seidman & Seidman

New Orleans
Arthur Andersen & Co.
A. S. Hansen, Inc.
Peat, Marwick, Mitchell & Co.
Price Waterhouse & Co.
Touche Ross & Co.
Arthur Young & Company

MAINE

Bangor
Northern Consultants Inc.

Cape Elizabeth-Portland
Martech Inc.

Falmouth
Paul Harthorne Associates

Portland
Arthur Young & Company

Waterville
Samuelson & Co.

Westbrook
Altenburg & Co., Inc.

MARYLAND

Annapolis
Louis H. Howe & Associates, Inc.

Baltimore
Arthur Andersen & Co.
Coffay, Marshall Associates, Inc.
Ernst & Whinney

NEW HAMPSHIRE

Fitzwilliam
Kennedy & Kennedy, Inc.

Franconia
Sno Engineering/Resource Management Inc.

Keene
Projections

Manchester
Ernst & Whinney

Nashua
Wheeler Associates, Inc.

New London
Professional Practice Consultants, Inc.

Spofford
B.R. Smith & Associates

NEW JERSEY

Bloomfield
Applied Leadership Technologies, Inc.

Brant Beach
McGinnis Associates

E. Brunswick
Laventhol & Horwath

Edison
Goggi Associates, Inc.

Englewood
John G. Steinle & Associates

Englewood Cliffs
Datamatics Management Services, Inc.
Herbert W. Davis & Co.
Kwasha Lipton
MHT Services, Inc.

Fairfield
C. H. Kline & Co., Inc.

Fair Lawn
Irving A. Delloff

Green Brook
ASYST-Administrative Systems Consultants

Hackensack
Ernst & Whinney
Jean Judge Associates, Inc.

Hasbrouck Heights
Ransom & Casazza, Inc.

Hillsdale
Advanced Management Institute, Inc.
Mitchell Fein, Inc.

Lawrenceville
Jack Frost & Associates

Long Island Beach
McGinnis Associates

Lyndhurst
Marketing & Systems Development Corporation

Mahwah
Roy W. Walters & Associates, Inc.

Middleville
Belden Menkus

Midland Park
Mahler Associates, Inc.

Montclair
Profit Planning Associates

Moorestown
Decision Studies Group
Science Management Corporation
Wofac Co.

Morristown
James P. Wadley & Co., Inc.

Newark
Arthur Andersen & Co.
Deloitte Haskins & Sells
Arthur Young & Company

New Brunswick
Murray Dropkin & Co.

Paramus
Arthur Andersen & Co.

Parsippany
R. Shriver Associates

Paterson
Elmer Fox, Westheimer & Co.

Princeton
Blessing/White Inc.
Dickey Dyer Management Consultants
Kurt Salmon Associates, Inc.
Sibson & Company, Inc.

Princeton Junction
Robert E. Koogler

Rahway
Michael R. Gingold Associates, Inc.

Ridgefield
Wofac Co.

Saddle Brook
Arthur Young & Company

Somerville
Marpet Consultants, Inc.

South Dennis
Van Nuis Co., Inc.

Trenton
Marshall Institute

Union
Blades & Macaulay
John deElorza Associates

Upper Montclair
Burgess Management Associates
Arthur Manning Associates

Wayne
Irving Shaw & Associates

Westfield
System Planning Associates, Inc.

West Orange
Walter Frederick Friedman & Co., Inc.
Insight Development Services

R. Shriver Associates
Touche Ross & Co.
Towers, Perrin, Forster & Crosby
Harry J. Woehr & Associates
Worden & Risberg, Inc.
Arthur Young & Company

Phoenixville
D. Dietrich Associates, Inc.

Pittsburgh
Arthur Andersen & Co.
Hay Associates
Henning Associates, Inc.
Marketing & Systems Development Corporation
H.B. Maynard & Co.
Touche Ross & Co.
Norton Weber & Co.
Yaney Associates
Arthur Young & Company

Radnor
Krall Management Inc.

Reading
Gilbert Commonwealth

Swarthmore
Bartow Associates

Towanda
Moeller Associates

West Chester
Warren, McVeigh & Griffin

Wilkes-Barre
Laventhol & Horwath

Wyncote
First Risk Management Co.

PUERTO RICO

Hato Rey
Arthur Andersen & Co.
A. S. Hansen, Inc.
Laventhol & Horwath

San Juan
Deloitte Haskins & Sells
First Risk Management Co.
Arthur Young & Company

Santurce
Bjorkman Associates

RHODE ISLAND

Newport
Gladstone Associates

Providence
Laventhol & Horwath
Arthur Young & Company

Rumford
Guenther Associates

Westerly
Wofac Co.

SOUTH CAROLINA

Charleston
Ernst & Whinney

Columbia
Arthur Andersen & Co.
Ernst & Whinney

Greenville
Case & Co., Inc.
MWS Consultants, Inc.
James S. Pepitone & Associates, Inc.
Arthur Young & Company

Summerville
MAS International, Ltd.

TENNESSEE

Chattanooga
Arthur Andersen & Co.
Ernst & Whinney

Knoxville
Ernst & Whinney

Memphis
Arthur Andersen & Co.
Ballew, Reinhardt & Associates, Inc.
Ernst & Whinney
A. S. Hansen, Inc.
Price Waterhouse & Co.
Seidman & Seidman
Wofac Co.

Nashville
Arthur Andersen & Co.
Kurt Salmon Associates, Inc.

TEXAS

Austin
Arthur Andersen & Co.
Ernst & Whinney
Carl F. Lutz
LWFW, Inc.
Seidman & Seidman
Arthur Young & Company

Corpus Christi
Ernst & Whinney

Dallas
Arthur Andersen & Co.
Cexec, Inc.
Coopers & Lybrand
Deloitte Haskins & Sells
Ernst & Whinney
Elmer Fox, Westheimer & Co.
A. S. Hansen, Inc.
Hay Associates
Robert H. Hayes & Associates, Inc.
International Resources & Applications
Laventhol & Horwath
LWFW, Inc.
Marketing & Systems Development Corporation
McKinsey & Co., Inc.
MWS Consultants, Inc.
Peat, Marwick, Mitchell & Co.
Price Waterhouse & Co.
Rath & Strong, Inc.
Kurt Salmon Associates, Inc.
Seidman & Seidman
Touche Ross & Co.
Towers, Perrin, Forster & Crosby
Arthur Young & Company

El Paso
Ernst & Whinney
Elmer Fox, Westheimer & Co.
Kenneth Associates

Fort Worth
Arthur Andersen & Co.
Bain Management Consulting, Inc.
Ernst & Whinney
A. S. Hansen, Inc.
Manresa Management Consultants, Inc.
Arthur Young & Company

Houston
Louis A. Allen Associates, Inc.
Arthur Andersen & Co.
Coopers & Lybrand
Deloitte Haskins & Sells
Drake-Beam & Associates Inc.
Ernst & Whinney
Eurequip Consulting Group
Elmer Fox, Westheimer & Co.
Gelb Consulting Group, Inc.
Golightly & Co. International, Inc.
A. S. Hansen, Inc.
Harbridge House Inc.
Laventhol & Horwath
LWFW, Inc.
C.H. McCormack & Associates, Inc.
McKinsey & Co., Inc.
Peat, Marwick, Mitchell & Co.
Price Waterhouse & Co.
Seidman & Seidman
Stone & Webster Mgmt. Consultants, Inc.
The THinc. Group Inc.
Wofac Co.
Arthur Young & Company

Kingwood
Batten, Batten, Hudson & Swab, Inc.

Laredo
Ernst & Whinney

Midland
Elmer Fox, Westheimer & Co.

Richardson
C. L. Carter Jr. & Associates, Inc.

San Antonio
Peter Lambros & Associates
Seidman & Seidman
Arthur Young & Company

UTAH

Ogden
Elmer Fox, Westheimer & Co.

Provo
Elmer Fox, Westheimer & Co.

Salt Lake City
Arthur Andersen & Co.
Austin & Lindberg, Ltd.
Deloitte Haskins & Sells
Elmer Fox, Westheimer & Co.
Johnson, Pratt & Stewart
Clinton P. Mott & Associates
J.F. Ward Associates
Arthur Young & Company

VIRGINIA

Alexandria
Outlook Associates

Annadale
Government Sales Consultants, Inc.

Arlington
American Management Systems

Cexec, Inc.
SRI International

McLean
MWS Consultants, Inc.

Midlothian
Human Resource & Profit Associates, Inc.

Norfolk
Von Keyserling Consultants Ltd.

Richmond
Psychological Consultants, Inc.
Arthur Young & Company

Roanoke
Crickenberger Associates

Salem
Standards, International Inc.

Springfield
Synergy Corporation

Sterling
MAS International, Ltd.

Vienna
TriBrook Group, Inc.

VIRGIN ISLANDS

Christiansted, St. Croix
Caribbean Consulting Services, Inc.

St. Croix, U.S.
D.W. Thomson & Associates

WASHINGTON

Bellevue
Compass Management Group, Inc.
Hay Associates

Issaquah
Bartow Associates

Mercer Island
Riecks Postal Consultants

Portland
Management/Marketing Associates,Inc.

Seattle
Arthur Andersen & Co.
Boeing Computer Services, Inc.
Coopers & Lybrand
Deloitte Haskins & Sells
Donworth, Taylor & Co.
Laventhol & Horwath
Price Waterhouse & Co.
Harry J. Prior & Associates, Inc.
Touche Ross & Co.
Arthur Young & Company

Spokane
Data Systems Consultants
Seidman & Seidman

Tacoma
Wofac Co.

WEST VIRGINIA

Charleston
Ernst & Whinney
Riffe & Associates

WISCONSIN

Brookfield
Infotek Corporation

Elm Grove
Schwarzkopf Consultants, Inc.

Greenfield
The Center for Applied Management, Inc.

Menomonie
Computer-Based Business Systems, Inc.

Milwaukee
Arthur Andersen & Co.
Anderson/Roethle & Associates, Inc.
Consultants International Ltd.
Dexter-Kranick & Associates
A. S. Hansen, Inc.
Humber, Mundie & McClary
Laventhol & Horwath
Peat, Marwick, Mitchell & Co.
Price Waterhouse & Co.
Touche Ross & Co.
H.K. von Kaas & Associates
Wofac Co.
Arthur Young & Company

Neenah
Dickson Associates
Infotek Corporation
R.M. Associates

Rochester
Runzheimer & Co., Inc.

WYOMING

Casper
Elmer Fox, Westheimer & Co.

CANADA

Calgary
Arthur Andersen & Co.
Ernst & Whinney
Hay Associates

Edmonton
Coopers & Lybrand
Ernst & Whinney
Harley, Little Associates

Islington
A. S. Hansen

Kitchener
Ernst & Whinney

Montreal
Arthur Andersen & Co.
Coopers & Lybrand

Ernst & Whinney
Hay Associates
Hickling-Johnston Ltd.
George S. May International
Kurt Salmon Associates
Robert Schaeffer & Associates
Towers, Perrin, Forster & Crosby

Ottawa
Arthur Andersen & Co.
Coopers & Lybrand
Ernst & Whinney
Hickling-Johnston Ltd.
Silverman Consulting Services

Quebec City
Coopers & Lybrand

Rexdale
Wofac Company

Toronto
Arthur Andersen & Co.
Ernst & Whinney
Harley, Little Associates
Hay Associates
Hickling-Johnston Ltd.
International Commercial Associates
Kappa Group
Arthur D. Little
MacFarlane & Co.
McKinsey & Company
M & M Protection Consultants
Albert Ramond Associates
Towers, Perrin, Forster & Crosby
Woods, Gordon & Associates

Vancouver
Arthur Andersen & Co.
Coopers & Lybrand
Ernst & Whinney
Hay Associates
Hoyles Associates Ltd.
Towers, Perrin, Forster & Crosby

Victoria
Ernst & Whinney

Willowdale
Coopers & Lybrand

Winnipeg
Arthur Andersen & Co.
Ernst & Whinney

MEXICO

Mexico City
Arthur Andersen & Co.
Coopers & Lybrand
Hay Associates
MacFarlane & Co.
McKinsey & Co.

Notes and Additions